SOURCES
Notable Selections
in Education

FRED SCHULTZ

SOURCES

Notable Selections in *Education*

About the Editor

FRED SCHULTZ has been a professor of education at the University of Akron in Akron, Ohio, since 1969. He received his B.S. in social science education in 1962, his M.S. in history and philosophy of education in 1966, and his Ph.D. in history and philosophy of education and American studies in 1969, all from Indiana University in Bloomington, Indiana. His B.A. degree in Spanish was conferred from the University of Akron in 1985. He also likes to study modern languages. Professor Schultz has been the editor of *Annual Editions: Education* (The Dushkin Publishing Group) since the 1978/79 edition of that volume, and he also edits *Annual Editions: Multicultural Education,* currently available in its 1995/96 edition. He is the coauthor, with James Monroe Hughes, of *Education in America* (Harper & Row, 1976). He is a fellow of the Philosophy of Education Society in the United States and a member of the Philosophy of Education Society of Great Britain. His other professional memberships include the American Educational Research Association and the American Sociological Association. Professor Schultz was also president of the Ohio Valley Philosophy of Education Society in 1976. His articles and papers have appeared in numerous journals, including *Educational Theory, The Journal of Thought, Educational Considerations, Proceedings of the Philosophy of Education Society,* and *Proceedings of the Ohio Valley Philosophy of Education Society* (now *Philosophical Studies in Education*). In the 1970s Professor Schultz did freelance book manuscript editing for New York publishers, in addition to his primary work as a professor. He has also been a visiting professor at Kent State University in Kent, Ohio, and at Oberlin College.

SOURCES

Notable Selections
in *Education*

Edited by

FRED SCHULTZ
University of Akron

DPG

The Dushkin Publishing Group, Inc.

Manufactured in the United States of America

First Edition

10 9 8 7 6 5 4 3 2 1

Library of Congress Cataloging-in-Publication Data
  Main entry under title:
    Sources: notable selections in education/edited by Fred Schultz.
      Includes bibliographical references and index.
      1. Education—United States—Philosophy—History. 2. Education—United
    States—Aims and objectives—History. I. Schultz, Frederick
    Marshall, *comp.*
      LA209.S59   370'.973—dc20
      1–56134–332–3   94–48861

 Printed on Recycled Paper

ACKNOWLEDGMENTS

1.1   From Robert M. Hutchins, *The Conflict in Education in a Democratic Society* (Harper
      & Brothers, 1953). Copyright © 1953 by Harper & Row Publishers, Inc. Copyright
      renewed 1981 by Vesta S. Hutchins. Reprinted by permission of HarperCollins
      Publishers, Inc.

1.2   From Mortimer Adler, "The Paideia Proposal: Rediscovering the Essence of Edu-
      cation," *The American School Board Journal* (July 1982). Copyright © 1982 by The
      National School Boards Association. Reprinted by permission. All rights reserved.

Acknowledgments and copyrights are continued at the back of the book on pages
392–394, which constitute an extension of the copyright page.

Preface

*T*he study of education has been approached from several conflicting, and competing, perspectives. This has always been true, although the conflict has become even more pronounced in the past 100 years. The Greek philosopher Aristotle noted in his *Politics* that people in Athens in his time (about 2,350 years ago) could not come to a consensus over what the purposes and content of education should be. This is just as true in industrialized countries today. There are currently several competing ideological perspectives regarding the social and academic purposes of schooling. *Sources: Notable Selections in Education* explores and samples some important perspectives and debates on the roles of schools, of teachers, and on the content of school curricula that have emerged over the past several decades. The book also samples important sources regarding the struggle of both cultural minorities and women to attain equality of opportunity in the field of education.

The study of education has a rich and compelling legacy, and the 41 selections in this volume are from primary sources, both older and contemporary sources, that have greatly influenced American education since the 1890s. As we come to the end of the twentieth century, we can see that the literature on American education encompasses the classical humanist tradition in education, the revolutionary ideas concerning what education ought to be about that developed in the United States in the early and middle decades of the twentieth century, and the most current viewpoints and ideas on the psychology of learning that are emerging in the 1990s, and which have already achieved the status of contemporary classics. I have attempted to bring together in one volume a collection of notable selections that uniquely summarizes the conflicting ideological and cultural perspectives that make up the literature in the field of education.

The reader will quickly be able to see the incredible magnitude of the differences between the competing perspectives placed side by side in this volume. For instance, the selections in Part 1 clearly demonstrate the differences in the points of view of the classical humanist tradition (of which Robert M. Hutchins and Mortimer Adler are two of the foremost twentieth-century champions), the liberal-progressive tradition (represented by John Dewey and William Heard Kilpatrick), and the critical pedagogical perspective (evident in the writing of Henry A. Giroux) with regard to the ultimate aims of education. So it is throughout this volume, as competing perspectives on each of the areas of education examined are presented to the reader for his or her own judgment and evaluation.

i

There were several conceptual parameters that I tried to remain alert to as I went through the process of developing this book of readings. First, I wanted it to sample some highly important sources on education that either have, are, or are going to affect how people respond to the great debates now going on over how to improve the quality of what students learn in school as well as over proposals for new and different sorts of opportunities in the field of education. Second, I wanted the book to reflect the enormous struggle for human dignity and freedom of opportunity in the field of education in American society—in particular, the struggle of racial and ethnic minorities and the struggle of women to attain equal rights in the field of education. Third, I wanted the selections in this volume to accurately and fairly represent the conflicting ideological perspectives now competing for public acceptance in the recent literature on education. Fourth, I sought to sample some of the documentary sources on testing and assessment in American education in recent years. Finally, I wanted to include selections that reflect the great vein of literature that has developed on the inescapable interrelationships between formal educational institutions and the cultures that produce them, as well as the universe of discourse that governs differing conceptions of freedom and culture in the education of persons. I believe that this collection of notable selections does address all of these concerns.

Organization of the book The selections are organized topically around the major areas of study within education. Part 1 includes selections on the Foundations of Education; Part 2, Curriculum and Instruction; Part 3, Schools in a Multicultural Society; Part 4, The American Constitutional Tradition and Education; Part 5, Testing and Assessment of Learning; and Part 6, Society, Culture, and Education. Each selection is preceded by a short introductory headnote that places the selection in the context of its relevance to the literature in the field of education and that provides biographical information on the author.

Suggestions for reading the selections Student readers of this book are encouraged to read the introductory headnotes prior to reading the selections to which they refer. The headnotes will get you started in the right direction for reading the selection. It is also a good idea to keep in mind—and this is especially true in several of the older selections—that how language is used can and does change over time. The language used in some of the older selections is frequently sexist or nonstandard as compared to current usage. Until the middle of the twentieth century, writers commonly used the terms *he, him,* and *man,* among others, to make generic references to both males and females. Today we are much more sensitive to potentially sexist and racist language. Try to take into account the social contexts in which these older essays were written. Finally, keep in mind that all of the selections in this volume either had or are having notable impact on education and what takes place in the classroom.

Supplements An *Instructor's Manual With Test Questions* (multiple-choice and essay) is available through the publisher for instructors using *Sources: Notable Selections in Education* in the classroom.

Acknowledgments I was very pleased when Mimi Egan, publisher for the Sources series at The Dushkin Publishing Group, contacted me about developing this volume. It has been a unique opportunity to place in the hands of readers notable sources that have had great impact on the directions of debate over the social purposes of education in American society. Mimi provided enthusiastic, effective support and encouragement to me at each step of the publication process. I would also like to thank Mrs. Roberta Reese, word processing operator at the University of Akron, for her fast, accurate, and insightful work in the development of the support material for this volume. My thanks as well to David Dean, administrative editor at the DPG, for his advice and support, and to David Brackley, copy editor, as well. There were many other selections by other famous authors that I wanted to include in this volume. Space limitations prevented inclusion of many equally important selections in this first edition of *Sources: Notable Selections in Education*. I would welcome any comments or suggestions you may have about selections for the book. Please write to me in care of SOURCES, The Dushkin Publishing Group.

Fred Schultz
University of Akron

SOURCES

Contents

"Here is a race transplanted through the criminal foolishness of your fathers. Whether you like it or not the millions are here, and here they will remain. If you do not lift them up, they will pull you down. Education and work are the levers to uplift a people. Work alone will not do it unless inspired by the right ideals and guided by intelligence. Education must not simply teach work—it must teach life."

"The purpose of education, finally, is to create in a person the ability to look at the world for himself, to make his own decisions, to say to himself this is black or this is white, to decide for himself whether there is a God in heaven or not. To ask questions of the universe, and then learn to live with those questions, is the way he achieves his own identity. But no society is really anxious to have that kind of person around."

"Midcentury marked a turning point in the history of black America. The movement for equality came under black leadership, embraced unprecedented numbers of Negroes, and became national in scope. A persistent black initiative forced a reformulation of public policies in education."

"The students' voice should never be sacrificed, since it is the only means through which they make sense of their own experience in the world."

"Powerlessness is a justification for rebellion, but it is not a license for mindlessness. The reality of being without a voice can become part of a good argument, but it is not the same thing as a good argument; it certainly does not exempt the powerless and the voiceless from the obligation to offer good reasons. Indeed, this is precisely why there is both a need and a right to be heard—a right secured only through an education in liberty."

"From the academy the boys of my class went to Union College at Schenectady. When those with whom I had studied and contended for prizes for five years came to bid me good-by, and I learned of the barrier that prevented me from following in their footsteps—'no girls admitted here'—my vexation and mortification knew no bounds. . . . I felt more keenly than ever the humiliation of the distinctions made on the ground of sex."

"At the end of the 1960s, a great deal of work was conducted on children's
learning; during the 1970s, the main emphasis shifted to memory research.
We will argue that, at the end of the 1970s and into the 1980s, the focus will
again be on learning mechanisms, but this time guided by a cognitive theory of learning that draws its theoretical insights and empirical support
from much wider domains than was previously the case."

"Our goal in this article is to discuss some of the relevant research and to
consider its implications for the issue of teaching thinking and problem
solving."

"Cognitive scientists study how our minds work—how we think, remember, and learn. Their studies have profound implications for restructuring
schools and improving learning environments."

PART SIX   *Society, Culture, and Education   349*

"I shall do what I can, then, to indicate the factors that seem to me to enter
into the problem, together with some of the reasons that prove that the
schools do have a role—and an important one—in *production* of social
change."

"Education does not proceed in a vacuum; its character is determined by
the group culture, and schools are institutions created by society to attain
certain specific ends."

PART ONE

Foundations of
Education

CHAPTER 1 The Classical Humanist Agenda

1.1 ROBERT M. HUTCHINS

The Conflict in Education in a Democratic Society

Robert M. Hutchins (1899–1977) was one of the foremost champions of traditional Western ideals as the basis of a liberal education. He advocated the educational values of the Greek philosophers Socrates, Plato, and Aristotle, as well as their later European interpreters who were associated with the classical humanist tradition in the arts and sciences.

Hutchins attended Oberlin College in Ohio and Yale University, and he received a B.A. in 1921 and a law degree in 1925, both from Yale. He stayed on to teach at the Yale University School of Law—serving as dean of the school in his last year—until 1929, when he was called to be president of the University of Chicago (when he was only 30 years old). From 1945 to 1951 Hutchins was chancellor of the University of Chicago. Although a traditionalist in his educational views, he was considered very innovative during his years at the university. Hutchins held the position of associate director of the Ford Foundation from 1951 to 1954, when he became president of the Fund for the Republic. In the last years of his life he was director of the Center for the Study of Democratic Institutions in California.

Hutchins's 1936 book *The Higher Learning in America* was severely criticized by the then-pragmatic, progressive establishment in teacher edu-

3

cation programs because it promoted the teaching of the traditional ideas of the Western cultural heritage. The following selection is from *The Conflict in Education in a Democratic Society* (Harper & Brothers, 1953), in which Hutchins discusses what he feels education should and should not be about.

Key Concept: the aim of education

THE BASIS OF EDUCATION

The obvious failures of the doctrines of adaptation, immediate needs, social reform, and of the doctrine that we need no doctrine at all may suggest to us that we require a better definition of education. Let us concede that every society must have some system that attempts to adapt the young to their social and political environment. If the society is bad, in the sense, for example, in which the Nazi state was bad, the system will aim at the same bad ends. To the extent that it makes men bad in order that they may be tractable subjects of a bad state, the system may help to achieve the social ideals of the society. It may be what the society wants; it may even be what the society needs, if it is to perpetuate its form and accomplish its aims. In pragmatic terms, in terms of success in the society, it may be a "good" system.

But it seems to me clearer to say that, though it may be a system of training, or instruction, or adaptation, or meeting immediate needs, it is not a system of education. It seems clearer to say that the purpose of education is to improve men. Any system that tries to make them bad is not education, but something else. If, for example, democracy is the best form of society, a system that adapts the young to it will be an educational system. If despotism is a bad form of society, a system that adapts the young to it will not be an educational system, and the better it succeeds in adapting them the less educational it will be.

Every man has a function as a man. The function of a citizen or a subject may vary from society to society, and the system of training, or adaptation, or instruction, or meeting immediate needs may vary with it. But the function of a man as man is the same in every age and in every society, since it results from his nature as a man. The aim of an educational system is the same in every age and in every society where such a system can exist: it is to improve man as man.

If we are going to talk about improving men and societies, we have to believe that there is some difference between good and bad. This difference must not be, as the positivists think it is, merely conventional. We cannot tell this difference by any examination of the effectiveness of a given program as the pragmatists propose; the time required to estimate these effects is usually too long and the complexity of society is always too great for us to say that the consequences of a given program are altogether clear. We cannot discover the difference between good and bad by going to the laboratory, for men and societies are not laboratory animals. If we believe that there is no truth, there is no knowledge, and there are no values except those which are validated by laboratory experiment, we cannot talk about the improvement of men and societies, for we can have no standard of judging anything that takes place among men or in societies.

Society is to be improved, not by forcing a program of social reform down its throat, through the schools or otherwise, but by the improvement of the individuals who compose it. As Plato said, "Governments reflect human nature. States are not made out of stone or wood, but out of the characters of their citizens: these turn the scale and draw everything after them." The individual is the heart of society.

To talk about making men better we must have some idea of what men are, because if we have none, we can have no idea of what is good or bad for them. If men are brutes like other animals, then there is no reason why they should not be treated like brutes by anybody who can gain power over them. And there is no reason why they should not be trained as brutes are trained. A sound philosophy in general suggests that men are rational, moral, and spiritual beings and that the improvement of men means the fullest development of their rational, moral, and spiritual powers. All men have these powers, and all men should develop them to the fullest extent.

Man is by nature free, and he is by nature social. To use his freedom rightly he needs discipline. To live in society he needs the moral virtues. Good moral and intellectual habits are required for the fullest development of the nature of man.

To develop fully as a social, political animal man needs participation in his own government. A benevolent despotism will not do. You cannot expect the slave to show the virtues of the free man unless you first set him free. Only democracy, in which all men rule and are ruled in turn for the good life of the whole community, can be an absolutely good form of government.

The community rests on the social nature of men. It requires communication among its members. They do not have to agree with one another; but they must be able to understand one another. And their philosophy in general must supply them with a common purpose and a common concept of man and society adequate to hold the community together. Civilization is the deliberate pursuit of a common ideal. The good society is not just a society we happen to like or to be used to. It is a community of good men.

Education deals with the development of the intellectual powers of men. Their moral and spiritual powers are the sphere of the family and the church. All three agencies must work in harmony; for, though a man has three aspects, he is still one man. But the schools cannot take over the role of the family and the church without promoting the atrophy of those institutions and failing in the task that is proper to the schools.

We cannot talk about the intellectual powers of men, though we can talk about training them, or amusing them, or adapting them, and meeting their immediate needs, unless our philosophy in general tells us that there is knowledge and that there is a difference between true and false. We must believe, too, that there are other means of obtaining knowledge than scientific experimentation. If knowledge can be sought only in the laboratory, many fields in which we thought we had knowledge will offer us nothing but opinion or superstition, and we shall be forced to conclude that we cannot know anything about the most important aspects of man and society. If we are to set about developing the intellectual powers of men through having them acquire knowledge of the most important subjects, we have to begin with the proposition that experimentation and empirical data will be of only limited use to us, contrary to the convictions of many American social scientists, and that philosophy, history, literature, and art give us knowledge, and significant knowledge, on the most significant issues.

If the object of education is the improvement of men, then any system of education that is without values is a contradiction in terms. A system that seeks bad values is bad. A system that denies the existence of values denies the possibility of education. Relativism, scientism, skepticism, and anti-intellectualism, the four horsemen of the philosophical apocalypse, have produced that chaos in education which will end in the disintegration of the West.

The prime object of education is to know what is good for man. It is to know the goods in their order. There is a hierarchy of values. The task of education is to help us understand it, establish it, and live by it. This Aristotle had in mind when he said: "It is not the possessions but the desires of men that must be equalized, and this is impossible unless they have a sufficient education according to the nature of things."

Such an education is far removed from the triviality of that produced by the doctrines of adaptation, of immediate needs, of social reform, or of the doctrine of no doctrine at all. Such an education will not adapt the young to a bad environment, but it will encourage them to make it good. It will not overlook immediate needs, but it will place these needs in their proper relationship to more distant, less tangible, and more important goods. It will be the only effective means of reforming society.

This is the education appropriate to free men. It is liberal education. If all men are to be free, all men must have this education. It makes no difference how they are to earn their living or what their special interests or aptitudes may be. They can learn to make a living, and they can develop their special interests and aptitudes, after they have laid the foundation of free and responsible manhood through liberal education. It will not do to say that they are incapable of such education. This claim is made by those who are too indolent or unconvinced to make the effort to give such education to the masses.

Nor will it do to say that there is not enough time to give everybody a liberal education before he becomes a specialist. In America, at least, the waste and frivolity of the educational system are so great that it would be possible through getting rid of them to give every citizen a liberal education and make him a qualified specialist, too, in less time than is now consumed in turning out uneducated specialists.

A liberal education aims to develop the powers of understanding and judgment. It is impossible that too many people can be educated in this sense, because there cannot be too many people with understanding and judgment. We hear a great deal today about the dangers that will come upon us through the frustration of educated people who have got educated in the expectation that education will get them a better job, and who then fail to get it. But surely this depends on the representations that are made to the young about what education is. If we allow them to believe that education will get them better jobs and encourage them to get educated with this end in view, they are entitled to a sense of frustration if, when they have got the education, they do not get the jobs. But, if we say that they should be educated in order to be men, and that everybody, whether he is a ditch-digger or a bank president, should have this education because he is a man, then the ditch-digger may still feel frustrated, but not because of his education.

Nor is it possible for a person to have too much liberal education, because it is impossible to have too much understanding and judgment. But it is possible to undertake too much in the name of liberal education in youth. The object of liberal education in youth is not to teach the young all they will ever need to know. It is to give them the habits, ideas, and techniques that they need to continue to educate themselves. Thus the object of formal institutional liberal education in youth is to prepare the young to educate themselves throughout their lives.

I would remind you of the impossibility of learning to understand and judge many of the most important things in youth. The judgment and understanding of practical affairs can amount to little in the absence of experience with practical affairs. Subjects that cannot be understood without experience should not be taught to those who are without experience. Or, if these subjects are taught to those who are without experience, it should be clear that these subjects can be taught only by way of introduction and that their value to the student depends on his continuing to study them as he acquires experience. The tragedy in America is that economics, ethics, politics, history, and literature are studied in youth, and seldom studied again. Therefore the graduates of American universities seldom understand them.

This pedagogical principle, that subjects requiring experience can be learned only by the experienced, leads to the conclusion that the most important branch of education is the education of adults. We sometimes seem to think of education as something like the mumps, measles, whooping-cough, or chicken-pox. If a person has had education in childhood, he need not, in fact he cannot, have it again. But the pedagogical principle that the most important things can be learned only in mature life is supported by a sound philosophy in general. Men are rational animals. They achieve their terrestrial felicity by the use of reason. And this means that they have to use it for their entire lives. To say that they should learn only in childhood would mean that they were human only in childhood.

And it would mean that they were unfit to be citizens of a republic.[1] A republic, a true *res publica*, can maintain justice, peace, freedom, and order only by the exercise of intelligence. When we speak of the consent of the governed, we mean, since men are not angels who seek the truth intuitively and do not have to learn it, that every act of assent on the part of the governed is a product of learning. A republic is really a common educational life in process. So Montesquieu said that, whereas the principle of a monarchy was honor, and the principle of a tyranny was fear, the principle of a republic was education.

Hence the ideal republic is the republic of learning. It is the utopia by which all actual political republics are measured. The goal toward which we started with the Athenians twenty-five centuries ago is an unlimited republic of learning and a world-wide political republic mutually supporting each other.

All men are capable of learning. Learning does not stop as long as a man lives, unless his learning power atrophies because he does not use it. Political freedom cannot endure unless it is accompanied by provision for the unlimited acquisition of knowledge. Truth is not long retained in human affairs without continual learning and relearning. Peace is unlikely unless there are continuous, unlimited opportunities for learning and unless men continuously avail themselves of them. The world of law and justice for which we yearn, the world-wide political republic, cannot be realized without the world-wide republic of learning. The civilization we seek will be achieved when all men are citizens of the world republic of law and justice and of the republic of learning all their lives long.

LIBERAL EDUCATION

As Aristotle remarked, politics is the architectonic science. This is one way of saying that the political philosophy accepted by a state will determine the kind of education it has. It is also a way of saying that the practical political situation in which a state finds itself has an overwhelming effect on its educational system. Plato arrived at his curriculum by asking what made a good man and a good soldier. A discipline was included only if it met both requirements. If, as it is sometimes argued, it is the destiny of the West to go to war with the East, then the educational system of the West will have to be designed with this end in view. Education is a secondary subject.

One difficulty is that we cannot answer any educational question of importance by appealing to the test of experience. The countries of the West appear determined to become industrial, scientific, and democratic. There have never been countries that were industrial, democratic, and scientific before. Entirely apart, therefore, from the usual difficulty of proving anything from history, and entirely apart from the difficulty of showing that any social experiment has succeeded or failed, which results from the inordinate number of variables that is always present, the experience of earlier societies would be of little use to us in solving the present problems of education. Even if we knew what their experience showed, it would be almost irrelevant now.

And yet there has always been an education that has been regarded as the best for the best. It has been regarded as the education for those who were to rule the state and for those who had leisure. Unless experimental science has made all the difference, it would seem that some light might be obtained by asking whether and to what degree the education that has always been regarded as the best for the best is still good for them or for anybody else.

... What is a good life? What is a good society? What is the nature and destiny of man? These questions and others like them are not susceptible of scientific investigation. On some aspects of them science can shed some light, and such light should be welcomed. But these questions do not yield to scientific inquiry. Nor do they become nonsense, as the logical positivists would have us believe, because they are not scientific.

Here we see again that education is a secondary subject, depending in this case upon philosophy. If there is no knowledge except scientific knowledge, if one object of education is to communicate knowledge, then the object cannot be achieved except through education in science. Unfortunately, the question whether there is knowledge other than scientific knowledge is one that science can never answer. It is a philosophical question.

If the rise of experimental science does not change the educational situation beyond adding new and most important branches of knowledge, does the rise of industry and democracy change it? It certainly does change it in very significant respects. But does it change it in the respect in which we are now interested, in respect to content? Let us look at the education that has been regarded as the best for the best and ask ourselves whether this is still the education that states the ideal, to what extent it is the best today, and to what extent it may be usefully offered to those who were not regarded as the best when this education was developed.

In the West this education has gone by the name of liberal education. It has consisted of the liberal arts, the arts of reading, writing, listening, speaking, and figuring, and of the intellectual and artistic tradition that we inherit. It was designed for those who were to rule the commonwealth, and for those who had leisure. It has always been thought that those who could profit by it were a small fraction of the population. It has never been denied, as far as I know, that it was the best education for the best. The question I wish to raise is first, whether it actually was the best education, and second whether it is so today, and for whom.

For reasons I have already given, I cannot prove that this education was the best. I cannot prove it in any scientific way. It is dangerous to try to prove it by the quality of the men it produced. Who knows that it produced the men? So it is dangerous for a university president to boast about his distinguished alumni. If he is entitled to credit for them, he must also take the responsibility for those who go to the penitentiary. I can appeal to the common opinion of mankind; but mankind could have been wrong. I think it enough to show that this education was characteristically human and that it was characteristically western. When I say that it was characteristially human, I am saying once more that education is a dependent subject; for what I mean is, of course, that liberal education conformed to an idea of man that I regard as sound. This is the conception of man as a rational animal, an animal who seeks and attains his highest felicity through the exercise and perfection of his reason. It is impossible to avoid being a liberal artist; for a man cannot choose whether he will be human or not. He can make the choice only between being a good liberal artist or a poor one.

Liberal education was characteristically western, because it assumed that everything was to be discussed. Liberal education aimed at the continuation of the dialogue that was the heart of western civilization. Western civilization is the civilization of the dialogue. It is the civilization of the Logos. Liberal education made the student a participant in the Great Conversation that began with the dawn of history and continues at the present day. Great as other civilizations have been in other respects, no other civilization has been as great as this one in this respect.

Such an education can be called a good education, relative to the conditions under which it developed and flourished. But can it be called nothing more than that? Must we say that industrialism and democracy mean that some other education should now supplant it? We know that this education has already been supplanted in the United States.

By the end of the nineteenth century liberal education in the United States was largely in the hands of the teachers of Greek and Latin. A liberal education was a classical education. The teachers of the classics devoted themselves for the most part to instruction in the languages. It was possible to spend years in the study of the Greek and Latin writers without discovering that they had any ideas. The teachers of Greek and Latin were not interested in ideas. They were drillmasters. The languages in which they gave instruction were required for graduation from all respectable colleges, from all preparatory schools, and even from some public high schools.

In the first twenty-five years of this century the flood overwhelmed the high schools and colleges of the United States. Neither the students nor their parents were prepared to believe that what the classical drillmasters were doing was of any importance. And it must be admitted that the students and their parents were largely right. The classical drillmasters did not reform. They did not insist upon the importance of the classical heritage to modern western man. They were, as I have said, not much interested in that. Instead they insisted that their courses continue to be required. By 1925 the flood swept them away. It was characteristic that in the final battle at Yale, at which I was present, the issue was not about liberal education, or about the importance of the classical heritage, but only about whether one year of Latin should be required for the degree of Bachelor of Arts.

The Twentieth Century was right about the classical drillmasters. It was wrong about liberal education. And it was certainly wrong about what it substituted for liberal education. It substituted for it an infinite, incoherent proliferation of courses largely vocational in aim.

Liberal education consists of training in the liberal arts and of understanding the leading ideas that have animated mankind. It aims to help the human being learn to think for himself, to develop his highest human powers. As I have said, it has never been denied that this education was the best for the best. It must still be the best for the best unless modern times, industry, science, and democracy have made it irrelevant. The social, political, and economic changes that have occurred have not required that liberal education be abandoned. How could they? It is still necessary to try to be human; in fact it is more necessary, as well as more difficult, than ever.

. . . Aristotle remarked that learning is accompanied by pain. One reason why the philosophy of John Dewey as distorted by his followers remade American education in forty years is that the education it was thought to propose was relatively painless, both for the pupils and the teachers. The principal reason for the popularity in the United States of what is called Progressive Education, in which Mr. Dewey also had a hand, is that the children have a good time in school. In a child-centered society, like that of the United States, any effort to insist on painful work in school naturally encounters resistance.

. . . Since the content of liberal education is the greatest ideas that the greatest men have had, regardless of the time at which they lived or the kind of society they lived in, and since the methods of liberal education include the methods of history, philosophy, and language as well as of science, liberal education can hardly arise in the face of pragmatism, positivism, or Marxism. Education is a secondary, dependent subject. . . .

Since education in the West is built very largely on the doctrine of individual differences, so that the study of the individual child and his individual interests is supposed to be the principal preoccupation of his teachers from his earliest days, and premature and excessive specialization is a common characteristic of both the American college and the British public school, it will be argued that a program of liberal education for all ignores the most important thing about men, and that is that they are different. I do not ignore it; I deny it. I do not deny the fact of individual differences; I deny that it is the most important fact about men or the one on which an educational system should be erected.

Men are different. They are also the same. And at least in the present state of civilization the respects in which they are the same are more important than those in which they are different. Politics, the architectonic science, teaches us that we are remorselessly headed toward the unification of the world. The only question is whether that unification will be achieved by conquest or consent. The most pressing task of men everywhere is to see to it that this consummation is achieved by consent. And this can be done only by the unremitting effort to move toward world community and world organization. The liberal arts are the arts of communication. The great productions of the human mind are the common heritage of all mankind. They supply the framework through which we understand one another and without which all factual data and area studies and exchanges of persons among countries are trivial and futile. They are the voices in the Great Conversation that constitutes the civilization of the dialogue.

Now, if ever, we need an education that is designed to bring out our common humanity rather than to indulge our individuality. Our individual differences mean that our individual development must vary. If we all struggle to make the most of our individual human powers, the results will be different, because our powers differ. But the difference is one of degree, and not of kind. In a modern, industrial, scientific democracy every man has the responsibility of a ruler and every man has the leisure to make the most of himself. What the modern, industrial, scientific democracy requires is wisdom. The aim of liberal education is wisdom. Every man has the duty and every man must have the chance to become as wise as he can. . . .

The strand in the civilization of the West that has saved it from materialism and its consequences is the tradition of free inquiry. It is this that has made it possible to say that western civilization is the civilization of the Logos. Liberal education, up to the end of the twentieth century, carried forward the Great Conversation. The collapse of liberal education in the United States has taken us into the doctrines of immediate needs and adjustment to the environment, and has ended in the concept of the educational system as a gigantic play-pen in which the young are to amuse themselves until we are ready to have them do something serious. This concept deprives free inquiry of its justification, threatens academic freedom, and puts the educational system at the mercy of any individual or organization that confuses patriotism with conformity. A year or so ago I talked with a distinguished doctor from Los Angeles about the attempt of the Board of Regents of the University of California to extort an illegal and unconstitutional oath of loyalty from the faculty of that great institution. "Yes, but," he said, "if we are going to hire these people to look after our children we are entitled to know what their opinions are." I think it is clear that the collapse of liberal education in the United States is related as cause or effect or both to the notion that professors are people who are hired to look after children.

Our task in North America, where we are the proud and prosperous inheritors of the great tradition of the West, is not performed by making this continent the arsenal, or the granary, or the powerhouse of the world. Our task is to preserve and develop the civilization of the Logos for all mankind.

NOTE

1. I owe this discussion to the suggestions of Scott Buchanan.

The Paideia Proposal: Rediscovering the Essence of Education

Mortimer Adler (b. 1902) is an advocate of freedom and individual responsibility who champions classical humanist educational ideals. An American philosopher and educator, Adler developed the "great books" seminars and curricula with Robert M. Hutchins. Rooted in the belief that education should be universal, the great books curricula were based on more than 400 works of major Western authors (classical and modern). Adler and Hutchins identified many of these great works in a 54-volume set of books entitled *Great Books of the Western World Between 1945 and 1952.*

Adler has many other publications to his credit, including *The American Testament* (Praeger, 1975); *Aristotle for Everybody* (Macmillan, 1978); *The Conditions of Philosophy* (Atheneum, 1965); and *The Great Ideas: A Lexicon of Western Thought* (Maxwell Macmillan International, 1992).

In the selection that follows, from "The Paideia Proposal: Rediscovering the Essence of Education," *The American School Board Journal* (July 1982), Adler sets down what he believes are the basic aims of education. He argues that there should be a common school curriculum that everyone should follow at some level. Adler then explores some of the basic essential characteristics upon which a common curriculum would focus.

Key Concept: the Paideia Proposal

*I*n the first 80 years of this century, we have met the obligation imposed on us by the principle of equal educational opportunity, but only in a quantitative sense. Now, as we approach the end of the century, we must achieve equality in qualitative terms.

This means a completely one-track system of schooling. It means, at the basic level, giving all the young the same kind of schooling, whether or not they are college bound.

We are aware that children, although equal in their common humanity and fundamental human rights, are unequal as individuals, differing in their capacity to learn. In addition, the homes and environments from which they come to school are unequal—either predisposing the child for schooling or doing the opposite.

Consequently, the Paideia Proposal, faithful to the principle of equal educational opportunity, includes the suggestion that inequalities due to environmental factors must be overcome by some form of preschool preparation—at least one year for all and two or even three for some. We know that to make such preschool tutelage compulsory at the public expense would be tantamount to increasing the duration of compulsory schooling from 12 years to 13, 14, or 15 years. Nevertheless, we think that this preschool adjunct to the 12 years of compulsory basic schooling is so important that some way must be found to make it available for all and to see that all use it to advantage.

THE ESSENTIALS OF BASIC SCHOOLING

The objectives of basic schooling should be the same for the whole school population. In our current two-track or multitrack system, the learning objectives are not the same for all. And even when the objectives aimed at those on the upper track are correct, the course of study now provided does not adequately realize these correct objectives. On all tracks in our current system, we fail to cultivate proficiency in the common tasks of learning, and we especially fail to develop sufficiently the indispensable skills of learning.

The uniform objectives of basic schooling should be threefold. They should correspond to three aspects of the common future to which all the children are destined: (1) Our society provides all children ample opportunity for personal development. Given such opportunity, each individual is under a moral obligation to make the most of himself and his life. Basic schooling must facilitate this accomplishment. (2) All the children will become, when of age, full-fledged citizens with suffrage and other political responsibilities. Basic schooling must do everything it can to make them good citizens, able to perform the duties of citizenship with all the trained intelligence that each is able to achieve. (3) When they are grown, all (or certainly most) of the children will engage in some form of work to earn a living. Basic schooling must prepare them for earning a living, but not by training them for this or that specific job while they are still in school.

To achieve these three objectives, the character of basic schooling must be general and liberal. It should have a single, required, 12-year course of study for all, with no electives except one—an elective choice with regard to a second language, to be selected from such modern languages as French, German, Italian, Spanish, Russian, and Chinese. The elimination of all electives, with this one exception, excludes what *should* be excluded—all forms of specialization, including particularized job training.

In its final form, the Paideia Proposal will detail this required course of study, but I will summarize the curriculum here in its bare outline. It consists of three main columns of teaching and learning, running through the 12 years and progressing, of course, from the simple to the more complex, from the less difficult to the more difficult, as the students grow older. Understand: The three columns represent three distinct modes of teaching and learning. They do not represent a series of courses. A specific course or class may employ more than one mode of teaching and learning, but all three modes are essential to the overall course of study.

The first column is devoted to acquiring knowledge in three subject areas: (A) language, literature, and the fine arts; (B) mathematics and natural science; (C) history, geography, and social studies.

The second column is devoted to developing the intellectual skills of learning. These include all the language skills necessary for thought and communication—the skills of reading, writing, speaking, listening. They also include mathematical and scientific skills; the skills of observing, measuring, estimating, and calculating; and skills in the use of the computer and of other scientific instruments. Together, these skills make it possible to think clearly and critically. They once were called the liberal arts—the intellectual skills indispensable to being competent as a learner.

The third column is devoted to enlarging the understanding of ideas and values. The materials of the third column are books (*not* textbooks), and other products of human artistry. These materials include books of every variety—historical, scientific, and philosophical as well as poems, stories, and essays—and also individual pieces of music, visual art, dramatic productions, dance productions, film or television productions. Music and works of visual art can be used in seminars in which ideas are discussed; but as with poetry and fiction, they also are to be experienced aesthetically, to be enjoyed and admired for their excellence. In this connection, exercises in the composition of poetry, music, and visual works and in the production of dramatic works should be used to develop the appreciation of excellence.

The three columns represent three different kinds of learning on the part of the student and three different kinds of instruction on the part of teachers.

In the first column, the students are engaged in acquiring information and organized knowledge about nature, man, and human society. The method of instruction here, using textbooks and manuals, is didactic. The teacher lectures, invites responses from the students, monitors the acquisition of knowledge, and tests that acquisition in various ways.

In the second column, the students are engaged in developing habits of performance, which is all that is involved in the development of an art of skill. Art, skill, or technique is nothing more than a cultivated, habitual ability to do a certain kind of thing well, whether that is swimming and dancing or reading and writing. Here, students are acquiring linguistic, mathematical, scientific, and historical *know-how* in contrast to what they acquire in the first column, which is *know-that* with respect to language, literature, and the fine arts, mathematics and science, history, geography, and social studies. Here, the method of instruction cannot be didactic or monitorial; it cannot be dependent on textbooks. It must be coaching, the same kind used in the gym to develop bodily skills; only here it is used by a different kind of coach in the classroom to develop intellectual skills.

In the third column, students are engaged in a process of enlightenment, the process whereby they develop their understanding of the basic and controlling ideas in all fields of subject matter and come to appreciate better all the human values embodied in works of art. Here, students move progressively from understanding less to understanding more—understanding better what they already know and appreciating more what they already have experienced. Here, the method of instruction cannot be either didactic or coaching. It must be the Socratic, or maieutic, method of questioning and discussing. It should not occur in an ordinary classroom with the students sitting in rows and the teacher in front of the class, but in a seminar room, with the students sitting around a table and the teacher sitting with them as an equal, even though a little older and wiser.

Of these three main elements in the required curriculum, the third column is completely innovative. Nothing like this is done in our schools, and because it is completely absent from the ordinary curriculum of basic schooling, the students never have the experience of having their minds addressed in a challenging way or of being asked to think about important ideas, to express their thoughts, to defend their opinions in a reasonable fashion.

The only thing that is innovative about the second column is the insistence that the method of instruction here must be coaching carried on either with one student at a time or with very small groups of students. Nothing else can be effective in the development of a skill, be it bodily or intellectual. The absence of such individualized coaching in our schools explains why most of the students cannot read well, write well, speak well, listen well, or perform well any of the other basic intellectual operations.

The three columns are closely interconnected and integrated, but the middle column—the one concerned with linguistic, mathematical, and scientific skills—is central. It both supports and is supported by the other two columns. All the intellectual skills with which it is concerned must be exercised in the study of the three basic subject-matters and in acquiring knowledge about them, and these intellectual skills must be exercised in the seminars devoted to the discussion of books and other things.

In addition to the three main columns in the curriculum, ascending through the 12 years of basic schooling, there are three adjuncts: One is 12 years of physical training, accompanied by instruction in bodily care and hygiene. The second, running through something less than 12 years, is the development of basic manual skills, such as cooking, sewing, carpentry, and the operation of all kinds of machines. The third, reserved for the last year or two, is an introduction to the whole world of work—the range of occupations in which human beings earn their livings. This is not particularized job training. It is the very opposite. It aims at a broad understanding of what is involved in working for a living and of the various ways in which that can be done. If, at the end of 12 years, students wish training for specific jobs, they should get that in two-year community or junior colleges, or on the job itself, or in technical institutes of one sort or another.

Everything that has not been specifically mentioned as occupying the time of the school day should be reserved for after-hours and have the status of extracurricular activities.

Please, note: The required course of study just described is as important for what it *displaces* as for what it introduces. It displaces a multitude of elective courses, especially those offered in our secondary schools, most of which make little or no contribution to general, liberal education. It eliminates all narrowly specialized job training, which now abounds in our schools. It throws out of the curriculum and into the category of optional extracurricular activities a variety of things that have little or no educational value.

If it did not call for all these displacements, there would not be enough time in the school day or year to accomplish everything that is essential to the general, liberal learning that must be the content of basic schooling.

THE QUINTESSENTIAL ELEMENT

So far, I have set forth the bare essentials of the Paideia Proposal with regard to basic schooling. I have not yet mentioned the quintessential element—the *sine qua non*—without which nothing else can possibly come to fruition, no matter how sound it might be in principle. The heart of the matter is the quality of learning and the quality of teaching that occupies the school day, not to mention the quality of the homework after school.

First, the learning must be active. It must use the whole mind, not just the memory. It must be learning by discovery, in which the student, never the teacher, is the primary agent. Learning by discovery, which is the only genuine learning, may be either unaided or aided. It is unaided only for geniuses. For most students, discovery must be aided.

Here is where teachers come in—as aids in the process of learning by discovery, not as knowers who attempt to put the knowledge they have into the minds of their students. The quality of the teaching, in short, depends crucially upon how the teacher conceives his role in the process of learning, and that must be as an aid to the student's process of discovery.

I am prepared for the questions that must be agitating you by now: How and where will we get the teachers who can perform as teachers should? How will we be able to staff the program with teachers so trained that they will be competent to provide the quality of instruction required for the quality of learning desired?

The first part of our answer to these questions is negative: We *cannot* get the teachers we need for the Paideia program from schools of education *as they are now constituted.* As teachers are now trained for teaching, they simply will not do. The ideal—an impracticable ideal—would be to ask for teachers who are, themselves, truly educated human beings. But truly educated human beings are too rare. Even if we could draft all who are now alive, there still would be far too few to staff our schools.

Well, then, what can we look for? Look for teachers who are actively engaged in the process of *becoming* educated human beings, who are themselves deeply motivated to develop their own minds. Assuming this is not too much to ask for the present, how should teachers be schooled and trained in the future? First, they should have the same kind of basic schooling that is recommended in the Paideia Proposal. Second, they should have additional schooling, at the college and even the university level, in which the same kind of general, liberal learning is carried on at advanced levels—more deeply, broadly, and intensively than it can be done in the first 12 years of schooling. Third, they must be given something analogous to the clinical experience in the training of physicians. They must engage in practice-teaching under supervision, which is another way of saying that they must be *coached* in the arts of teaching, not just given didactic instruction in educational psychology and in pedagogy. Finally, and most important of all, they must learn how to teach well by being exposed to the performances of those who are masters of the arts involved in teaching.

It is by watching a good teacher at work that they will be able to perceive what is involved in the process of assisting others to learn by discovery. Perceiving it, they must then try to emulate what they observe, and through this process, they slowly will become good teachers themselves.

The Paideia Proposal recognizes the need for three different kinds of institutions at the collegiate level: The two-year community or junior college should offer a wide choice of electives that give students some training in one or another specialized field, mainly those fields of study that have something to do with earning a living. The four-year college also should offer a wide variety of electives, to be chosen by students who aim at the various professional or technical occupations that require advanced study. Those elective majors chosen by students should be accompanied, for all students, by one required minor, in which the kind of general and liberal learning that was begun at the level of basic schooling is continued at a higher level in the four years of college. And we should have still a third type of collegiate institution—a four-year college in which general, liberal learning at a higher level constitutes a required course of study that is to be taken by all students. *It is this third type of college, by the way, that should be attended by all who plan to become teachers in our basic schools.*

At the university level, there should be a continuation of general, liberal learning at a still higher level to accompany intensive specialization in this or that field of science or scholarship, this or that learned profession. Our insistence on the continuation of general, liberal learning at all the higher levels of schooling stems from our concern with the worst cultural disease that is rampant in our society—*the barbarism of specialization.*

There is no question that our technologically advanced industrial society needs specialists of all sorts. There is no question that the advancement of knowledge in all fields of science and scholarship, and in all the learned professions, needs intense specialization. But for the sake of preserving and enhancing our cultural traditions, as well as for the health of science and scholarship, we need specialists who also are generalists—generally cultivated human beings, not just good plumbers. We need truly educated human beings who can

perform their special tasks better precisely because they have general cultivation as well as intensely specialized training.

Changes indeed are needed in higher education, but those improvements
cannot reasonably be expected unless improvement in basic schooling makes
that possible.

THE FUTURE OF OUR FREE INSTITUTIONS

I already have declared as emphatically as I know how that the quality of
human life in our society depends on the quality of the schooling we give our
young people, both basic and advanced. But a marked elevation in the quality
of human life is not the only reason improving the quality of schooling is so
necessary—not the only reason we must move heaven and earth to stop the
deterioration of our schools and turn them in the opposite direction. The other
reason is to safeguard the future of our free institutions.

They cannot prosper, they may not even survive, unless we do something
to rescue our schools from their current deplorable deterioration. Democracy,
in the full sense of that term, came into existence only in this century and only
in a few countries on earth, among which the United States is an outstanding
example. But democracy came into existence in this century only in its initial
conditions, all of which hold out promises for the future that remain to be
fulfilled. Unless we do something about improving the quality of basic schooling for all and the quality of advanced schooling for some, there is little chance
that those promises ever will be fulfilled. And if they are not, our free institutions are doomed to decay and wither away.

We face many insistently urgent problems. Our prosperity and even our
survival depend on the solution of those problems—the threat of nuclear war,
the exhaustion of essential resources and of supplies of energy, the pollution or
spoilage of the environment, the spiraling of inflation accompanied by the
spread of unemployment.

To solve these problems, we need resourceful and innovative leadership.
For that to arise and be effective, an educated populace is needed. Trained
intelligence—not only on the part of leaders, but also on the part of followers—
holds the key to the solution of the problems our society faces. Achieving
peace, prosperity, and plenty could put us on the threshold of an early paradise. But a much better educational system than now exists also is needed, for
that alone can carry us across the threshold. Without it, a poorly schooled
population will not be able to put to good use the opportunities afforded by
the achievement of the general welfare. Those who are not schooled to enjoy
society can only despoil its institutions and corrupt themselves.

The
Progressive-Liberal Agenda

2.1 JOHN DEWEY

Democracy and Education: An Introduction to the Philosophy of Education

In 1916 John Dewey published what was to become one of the most influential and debated works on the philosophy of education. *Democracy and Education: An Introduction to the Philosophy of Education* (Macmillan, 1916), from which the following selection has been excerpted, is a comprehensive textbook on the philosophy of education and a sharp, progressive-liberal pedagogical response to the rhetoric of classical humanist scholars. The book became a major focus of controversy because there was a spirited classical humanist opposition to Dewey's pragmatic-progressive theory of education.

At the time that *Democracy and Education* was published, Dewey (1859–1952) was in his 12th year as a professor of philosophy at Columbia University and his 32d year as a university professor. Dewey taught a total of 33 years at Columbia before retiring from teaching in 1937. He then became a world traveler and a highly acclaimed commentator on the challenges facing democratic societies in the 1930s. He continued to write and publish right up to his death at almost 93 years of age. In addition to *Democracy and Education,* Dewey is also the author of *Essays in Experimental Logic* and *Reconstruction in Philosophy,* both of which were published in 1916.

Key Concept: education as a reconstruction or reorganization of experience

Education as Reconstruction

In its contrast with the ideas both of unfolding of latent powers from within, and of formation from without, whether by physical nature or by the cultural products of the past, the ideal of growth results in the conception that education is a constant reorganizing or reconstructing of experience. It has all the time an immediate end, and so far as activity is educative, it reaches that end—the direct transformation of the quality of experience. Infancy, youth, adult life—all stand on the same educative level in the sense that what is really *learned* at any and every stage of experience constitutes the value of that experience, and in the sense that it is the chief business of life at every point to make living thus contribute to an enrichment of its own perceptible meaning.

We thus reach a technical definition of education: It is that reconstruction or reorganization of experience which adds to the meaning of experience, and which increases ability to direct the course of subsequent experience. (1) The increment of meaning corresponds to the increased perception of the connections and continuities of the activities in which we are engaged. The activity begins in an impulsive form; that is, it is blind. It does not know what it is about; that is to say, what are its interactions with other activities. An activity which brings education or instruction with it makes one aware of some of the connections which had been imperceptible. . . . [A] child who reaches for a bright light gets burned. Henceforth he *knows* that a certain act of touching in connection with a certain act of vision (and *vice-versa*) means heat and pain; or, a certain light means a source of heat. The acts by which a scientific man in his laboratory learns more about flame differ no whit in principle. By doing certain things, he makes perceptible certain connections of heat with other things, which had been previously ignored. Thus his acts in relation to these things get more meaning; he knows better what he is doing or 'is about' when he has to do with them; he can *intend* consequences instead of just letting them happen—all synonymous ways of saying the same thing. At the same stroke, the flame has gained in meaning; all that is known about combustion, oxidation, about light and temperature, may become an intrinsic part of its intellectual content.

(2) The other side of an educative experience is an added power of subsequent direction or control. To say that one knows what he is about, or can intend certain consequences, is to say, of course, that he can better anticipate

what is going to happen; that he can, therefore, get ready or prepare in advance so as to secure beneficial consequences and avert undesirable ones. A genuinely educative experience, then, one in which instruction is conveyed and ability increased, is contradistinguished from a routine activity on one hand, and a capricious activity on the other. (*a*) In the latter one 'does not care what happens'; one just lets himself go and avoids connecting the consequences of one's act (the evidences of its connections with other things) with the act. It is customary to frown upon such aimless random activity, treating it as willful mischief or carelessness or lawlessness. But there is a tendency to seek the cause of such aimless activities in the youth's own disposition, isolated from everything else. But in fact such activity is explosive, and due to maladjustment with surroundings. Individuals act capriciously whenever they act under external dictation, or from being told, without having a purpose of their own or perceiving the bearing of the deed upon other acts. One may learn by doing something which he does not understand; even in the most intelligent action, we do much which we do not mean, because the largest portion of the connections of the act we consciously intend are not perceived or anticipated. But we learn only because after the act is performed we note results which we had not noted before. But much work in school consists in setting up rules by which pupils are to act of such a sort that even after pupils have acted, they are not led to see the connection between the result—say the answer—and the method pursued. So far as they are concerned, the whole thing is a trick and a kind of miracle. Such action is essentially capricious, and leads to capricious habits. (*b*) Routine, action, action which is automatic, may increase skill to do a *particular* thing. In so far, it might be said to have an educative effect. But it does not lead to new perceptions of bearings and connections; it limits rather than widens the meaning-horizon. And since the environment changes and our way of acting has to be modified in order successfully to keep a balanced connection with things, an isolated uniform way of acting becomes disastrous at some critical moment. The vaunted 'skill' turns out gross ineptitude.

The essential contrast of the idea of education as continuous reconstruction with . . . other one-sided conceptions . . . is that it identifies the end (the result) and the process. This is verbally self-contradictory, but only verbally. It means that experience as an active process occupies time and that its later period completes its earlier portion; it brings to light connections involved, but hitherto unperceived. The later outcome thus reveals the meaning of the earlier, while the experience as a whole establishes a bent or disposition toward the things possessing this meaning. Every such continuous experience or activity is educative, and all education resides in having such experiences.

It remains only to point out (what will receive more ample attention later) that the reconstruction of experience may be social as well as personal. For purposes of simplification we have spoken . . . somewhat as if the education of the immature which fills them with the spirit of the social group to which they belong, were a sort of catching up of the child with the aptitudes and resources of the adult group. In static societies, societies which make the maintenance of established custom their measure of value, this conception applies in the main. But not in progressive communities. They endeavor to shape the experiences of the young so that instead of reproducing current habits, better habits shall be formed, and thus the future adult society be an improvement on their own. Men have long had some intimation of the extent to which education may be consciously used to eliminate obvious social evils through starting the young on paths which shall not produce these ills, and some idea of the extent in which education may be made an instrument of realizing the better hopes of men. But we are doubtless far from realizing the potential efficacy of education as a constructive agency of improving society, from realizing that it represents not only a development of children and youth but also of the future society of which they will be the constituents. . . .

THE DEMOCRATIC CONCEPTION IN EDUCATION

For the most part, save incidentally, we have hitherto been concerned with education as it may exist in any social group. We have now to make explicit the differences in the spirit, material, and method of education as it operates in different types of community life. To say that education is a social function, securing direction and development in the immature through their participation in the life of the group to which they belong, is to say in effect that education will vary with the quality of life which prevails in a group. Particularly is it true that a society which not only changes but which has the ideal of such change as will improve it, will have different standards and methods of education from one which aims simply at the perpetuation of its own customs. To make the general ideas set forth applicable to our own educational practice, it is, therefore, necessary to come to closer quarters with the nature of present social life.

The Implications of Human Association

Society is one word, but many things. Men associate together in all kinds of ways and for all kinds of purposes. One man is concerned in a multitude of diverse groups, in which his associates may be quite different. It often seems as if they had nothing in common except that they are modes of associated life. Within every larger social organization there are numerous minor groups: not only political subdivisions, but industrial, scientific, religious, associations. There are political parties with differing aims, social sets, cliques, gangs, corporations, partnerships, groups bound closely together by ties of blood, and so in endless variety. In many modern states, and in some ancient, there is great diversity of populations, of varying languages, religions, moral codes, and traditions. From this standpoint, many a minor political unit, one of our large cities, for example, is a congeries of loosely associated societies, rather than an inclusive and permeating community of action and thought.

The terms society, community, are thus ambiguous. They have both a eulogistic or normative sense, and a descriptive sense; a meaning *de jure* and a meaning *de facto*. In social philosophy, the former connotation is almost always uppermost. Society is conceived as one by its very nature. The qualities which accompany this unity, praiseworthy community of purpose and welfare, loyalty to public ends, mutuality of sympathy, are emphasized. But when we look at the facts which the term *denotes* instead of confining our attention to its intrinsic *connotation,* we find not unity, but a plurality of societies, good and bad. Men banded together in a criminal conspiracy, business aggregations that prey upon the public while serving it, political machines held together by the interest of plunder, are included. If it is said that such organizations are not societies because they do not meet the ideal requirements of the notion of society, the answer, in part, is that the conception of society is then made so "ideal" as to be of no use, having no reference to facts; and in part, that each of these organizations, no matter how opposed to the interests of other groups, has something of the praiseworthy qualities of "Society" which hold it together. There is honor among thieves, and a band of robbers has a common interest as respects its members. Gangs are marked by fraternal feeling, and narrow cliques by intense loyalty to their own codes. Family life may be marked by exclusiveness, suspicion, and jealousy as to those without, and yet be a model of amity and mutual aid within. Any education given by a group tends to socialize its members, but the quality and value of the socialization depends upon the habits and aims of the group.

Hence, once more, the need of a measure for the worth of any given mode of social life. In seeking this measure, we have to avoid two extremes. We cannot set up, out of our heads, something we regard as an ideal society. We must base our conception upon societies which actually exist, in order to have any assurance that our ideal is a practicable one. But, as we have just seen, the ideal cannot simply repeat the traits which are actually found. The problem is to extract the desirable traits of forms of community life which actually exist, and employ them to criticize undesirable features and suggest improvement. Now in any social group whatever, even in a gang of thieves, we find some interest held in common, and we find a certain amount of interaction and coöperative intercourse with other groups. From these two traits we derive our standard. How numerous and varied are the interests which are consciously shared? How full and free is the interplay with other forms of association? If we apply these considerations to, say, a criminal band, we find that the ties which consciously hold the members together are few in number, reducible almost to a common interest in plunder; and that they are of such a nature as to isolate the group from other groups with respect to give and take of the values of life. Hence, the education such a society gives is partial and distorted. If we take, on the other hand, the kind of family life which illustrates the standard, we find that there are material, intellectual, aesthetic interests in which all participate and that the progress of one member has worth for the experience of other members—it is readily communicable—and that the family is not an isolated whole, but enters intimately into relationships with business groups, with schools, with all the agencies of culture, as well as with other similar groups, and that it plays a due part in the political organization and in return receives support from it. In short, there are many interests consciously communicated and shared; and there are varied and free points of contact with other modes of association.

. . . The two elements in our criterion both point to democracy. The first signifies not only more numerous and more varied points of shared common interest, but greater reliance upon the recognition of mutual interests as a factor in social control. The second means not only freer interaction between social groups (once isolated so far as intention could keep up a separation) but change in social habit—its continuous readjustment through meeting the new situations produced by varied intercourse. And these two traits are precisely what characterize the democratically constituted society.

Upon the educational side, we note first that the realization of a form of social life in which interests are mutually interpenetrating, and where progress, or readjustment, is an important consideration, makes a democratic community more interested than other communities have cause to be in deliberate and systematic education. The devotion of democracy to education is a familiar fact. The superficial explanation is that a government resting upon popular suffrage cannot be successful unless those who elect and who obey their governors are educated. Since a democratic society repudiates the principle of external authority, it must find a substitute in voluntary disposition and interest; these can be created only by education. But there is a deeper explanation. A democracy is more than a form of government; it is primarily a mode of associated living, of conjoint communicated experience. The extension in space of the number of individuals who participate in an interest so that each has to refer his own action to that of others, and to consider the action of others to give point and direction to his own, is equivalent to the breaking down of those barriers of class, race, and national territory which kept men from perceiving the full import of their activity. These more numerous and more varied points of contact denote a greater diversity of stimuli to which an individual has to respond; they consequently put a premium on variation in his action. They secure a liberation of powers which remain suppressed as long as the incitations to action are partial, as they must be in a group which in its exclusiveness shuts out many interests.

The widening of the area of shared concerns, and the liberation of a greater diversity of personal capacities which characterize a democracy, are not of course the product of deliberation and conscious effort. On the contrary, they were caused by the development of modes of manufacture and commerce, travel, migration, and intercommunication which flowed from the command of science over natural energy. But after greater individualization on one hand, and a broader community of interest on the other have come into existence, it is a matter of deliberate effort to sustain and extend them. Obviously a society to which stratification into separate classes would be fatal, must see to it that intellectual opportunities are accessible to all on equable and easy terms. A society marked off into classes need be specially attentive only to the education of its ruling elements. A society which is mobile, which is full of channels for the distribution of a change occurring anywhere, must see to it that its members are educated to personal initiative and adaptability. Otherwise, they will be overwhelmed by the changes in which they are caught and whose significance or connections they do not perceive. The result will be a confusion in which a few will appropriate to themselves the results of the blind and externally directed activities of others.

The Project Method

William Heard Kilpatrick (1871–1965) is regarded as one of the principal founders of progressive, experience-based education. He attended Mercer University in Macon, Georgia, and did his graduate studies at Johns Hopkins University in Baltimore, Maryland. He was a teacher in the Mercer public schools and at Mercer University, and he was appointed to the faculty of Teachers College, Columbia University, as a professor of the philosophy of education in 1909. This appointment allowed Kilpatrick to develop a close working relationship with fellow progressive educator John Dewey, a faculty member in the Department of Philosophy at Columbia. Kilpatrick became one of the leading exponents of child-centered, experience-based schooling in the early decades of the twentieth century, and his long, active career at Teachers College continued until 1938. Kilpatrick was a major interpreter of the early writings of John Dewey, and he had many works published, including *Education for a Changing Civilization* (1926). The following selection is from "The Project Method," which was published in Columbia University's *Teachers College Record* in September 1918. In it, Kilpatrick describes his "project method" of teaching, emphasizing the use of purposeful activity as the basis of education.

Key Concept: the project method

My whole philosophic outlook had made me suspicious of so-called 'fundamental principles'. Was there yet another way of attaining unity? I do not mean to say that I asked these questions, either in these words or in this order. Rather is this a retrospective ordering of the more important outcomes. As the desired unification lay specifically in the field of method, might not some typical unit of concrete procedure supply the need—some unit of conduct that should be, as it were, a sample of life, a fair sample of the worthy life and consequently of education? As these questionings rose more definitely to mind, there came increasingly a belief—corroborated on many sides—that the unifying idea I sought was to be found in the conception of wholehearted purposeful activity proceeding in a social environment, or more briefly, in the unit element of such activity, the hearty purposeful act.

It is to this purposeful act with the emphasis on the word purpose that I myself apply the term 'project'. I did not invent the term nor did I start it on its educational career. Indeed, I do not know how long it had already been in use. I did, however, consciously appropriate the word to designate to myself and for my classes the typical unit of the worthy life described above. Others who were using the term seemed to me either to use it in a mechanical and partial sense or to be intending in a general way what I tried to define more exactly. The purpose of this article is to attempt to clarify the concept underlying the term as much as it is to defend the claim of the concept to a place in our educational thinking. The actual terminology with which to designate the concept is, as was said before, to my mind a matter of relatively small moment. If, however, we think of a project as a pro-ject, something pro-jected, the reason for adopting the term may better appear.

Postponing yet a little further the more systematic presentation of the matter, let us from some typical instances see more concretely what is contemplated under the term project or hearty purposeful act. Suppose a girl has made a dress. If she did in hearty fashion purpose to make the dress, if she planned it, if she made it herself, then I should say the instance is that of a typical project. We have in it a wholehearted purposeful act carried on amid social surroundings. That the dressmaking was purposeful is clear; and the purpose once formed dominated each succeeding step in the process and gave unity to the whole. That the girl was wholehearted in the work was assured in the illustration. That the activity proceeded in a social environment is clear; other girls at least are to see the dress. As another instance, suppose a boy undertakes to get out a school newspaper. If he is in earnest about it, we again have an effective purpose as the essence of a project. So we may instance a pupil writing a letter (if the hearty purpose is present), a child listening absorbedly to a story, Newton explaining the motion of the moon on the principles of terrestrial dynamics, Demosthenes trying to arouse the Greeks against Philip, Da Vinci painting the *Last Supper*, my writing this article, a boy solving with felt purpose an 'original' in geometry. All of the foregoing have been acts of individual purposing, but there are just as truly group projects: a class presents a play, a group of boys organize a baseball nine, three pupils prepare to read a story to their comrades. It is clear then that projects may present every variety that purposes present in life. It is also clear that a mere description of outwardly observable facts might not disclose the essential factor, namely the presence of a dominating purpose. It is equally true that there can be every degree of approximation to full projects according as the animating purpose varies in clearness and strength. If we conceive activities as ranging on a scale from those performed under dire compulsion up to those into which one puts his 'whole heart', the argument herein made restricts the term 'project' or purposeful act to the upper portions of the scale. An exact dividing line is hard to draw, and yields indeed in importance to the notion that psychological value increases with the degree of approximation to 'wholeheartedness'. As to the social environment element, some may feel that, however important this is to the fullest educative experience, it is still not essential to the conception of the purposeful act as here presented. These might, therefore, wish to leave this element out of the defining discussion.

Chapter 2
The
Progressive-
Liberal Agenda

To this I should not object if it were clearly understood that the resulting concept—now essentially psychological in character—demands, generally speaking, the social situation both for its practical working and for the comparative valuation of proffered projects.

With this general introduction, we may, in the first place, say that the purposeful act is the typical unit of the worthy life. Not that all purposes are good, but that the worthy life consists of purposive activity and not mere drifting. We scorn the man who passively accepts what 'fate' or mere chance brings to him. We admire the man who is master of his fate, who with deliberate regard for a total situation forms clear and far-reaching purposes, who plans and executes with nice care the purposes so formed. A man who habitually so regulates his life with reference to worthy social aims meets at once the demands for practical efficiency and of moral responsibility. Such a one presents the ideal of democratic citizenship. It is equally true that the purposeful act is not the unit of life for the serf or the slave. . . .

As the purposeful act is thus the typical unit of the worthy life in a democratic society, so also should it be made the typical unit of school procedure. We of America have for years increasingly desired that education be considered as life itself and not as a mere preparation for later living. The conception before us promises a definite step toward the attainment of this end. If the purposeful act be in reality the typical unit of the worthy life, then it follows that to base education on purposeful acts is exactly to identify the process of education with worthy living itself. The two become then the same. All the arguments for placing education on a life basis seem, to me at any rate, to concur in support of this thesis. On this basis education has become life. And if the purposeful act thus makes of education life itself, could we reasoning in advance expect to find a better preparation for later life than practice in living now? We have heard of old that "we learn to do by doing," and much wisdom resides in the saying. If the worthy life of the coming day is to consist of well-chosen purposeful acts, what preparation for that time could promise more than practice now, under discriminating guidance, in forming and executing worthy purposes? To this end must the child have within rather large limits the opportunity to purpose. For the issues of his act he must—in like limits—be held accountable. That the child may properly progress, the total situation—all the factors of life, including comrades—speaking, if need be through the teacher, must make clear its selective judgment upon what is done, approving the better, rejecting the worse. In a true sense the whole remaining discussion is but to support the contention here argued in advance that education based on the purposeful act prepares best for life while at the same time it constitutes the present worthy life itself. . . .

How then does the purposeful act utilize the laws of learning? A boy is intent upon making a kite that will fly. Hitherto he has not succeeded. His purpose is clear. This purpose is but the 'set' consciously and volitionally bent on its end. As set the purpose is the inner urge that carries the boy on in the face of hindrance and difficulty. It brings 'readiness' to pertinent inner resources of knowledge and thought. Eye and hand are made alert. The purpose acting as aim guides the boy's thinking, directs his examination of plan and material, elicits from within appropriate suggestions, and tests these several suggestions by their pertinency to the end in view. The purpose in that it contemplates a specific end defines success: the kite must fly or he has failed. The progressive attaining of success with reference to subordinate aims brings satisfaction at the successive stages of completion.... The purpose thus supplies the motive power, makes available inner resources, guides the process to its preconceived end, and by this satisfying success fixes in the boy's mind and character the successful steps as part and parcel of one whole. The purposeful act does utilize the laws of learning.

But this account does not yet exhaust the influence of the purpose on the resulting learning. Suppose as extreme cases two boys making kites, the one with wholeheartedness of purpose, as we have just described, the other under direct compulsion as a most unwelcome task. For simplicity's sake suppose the latter under enforced directions makes a kite identical with the other. The steps that in either case actually produced the kite let us call the *primary* responses for that case. Evidently these will, in the two cases, in part agree, and in part differ. The respects in which they agree furnish the kind of responses that we can and customarily do assign as tasks—the external irreducible minimum for the matter at hand. Upon such we can feasibly insist, even to the point of punishment if we do so decide. Additional to the primary responses which produced the respective kites, there will be yet other responses that accompany the kitemaking, not so much by way of outward doing as of inward thought and feeling. These additional responses may be divided into *associate* and *concomitant* responses. By associate responses we refer to those thoughts which are suggested in rather close connection with the primary responses and with the materials used and the ends sought.[1] By the term concomitant reference is made to certain responses yet a little further off from the immediate operation of kitemaking, which result ultimately in attitudes and generalizations. It is in this way that such attitudes are produced as self-respect or the contrary, and such relatively abstract ideals as accuracy or neatness. These words, primary, associate, and concomitant, will be used as well of the resulting learning as of the responses that bring the learning. The terminology is not entirely happy, and exact lines of division are not easy to draw; but the distinctions may perhaps help us to see a further function of purpose.

... The factor of 'set' conditions the learning process. A strong set acting through the satisfaction which attends success fixes quickly and strongly the bonds which brought success. In the case of coercion, however, a different state of affairs holds. There are in effect two sets operating: one set, kept in existence solely through coercion, is concerned to make a kite that will pass muster; the other set has a different end and would pursue a different course were the coercion removed. Each set in so far as it actually exists means a possible satisfaction and in that degree a possible learning. But the two sets, being opposed, mean at times a confusion as to the object of success; and in every case each set destroys a part of the other's satisfaction and so hampers the primary learning. Moreover, for the wholehearted act the several steps of the primary responses are welded together, as it were, at the forge of conscious purpose, and so have not only a stronger connection of part with part but greater flexibility of the whole to thought. So far then as concerns even the barest mechanics of kitemaking, the boy of wholehearted purpose will emerge with a higher degree of skill and knowledge and his learning will longer abide with him.

In the case of the associate responses, the difference is equally noticeable. The unified set of wholeheartedness will render available all the pertinent connected inner resources. A wealth of marginal responses will be ready to come forward at every opportunity. Thoughts will be turned over and over, and each step will be connected in may ways with other experiences. Alluring leads in various allied directions will open before the boy, which only the dominant present purpose could suffice to postpone. The element of satisfaction will attend connections seen, so that the complex of allied thinking will the longer remain as a mental possession. All of this is exactly not so with the other boy. The forbidden 'set', so long as it persists, will pretty effectually quench the glow of thought. Unreadiness will rather characterize his attitude. Responses accessory to the work at hand will be few in number, and the few that come will lack the element of satisfaction to fix them. Where the one boy has a wealth of associated ideas, the other has poverty. What abides with the one, is fleeting with the other. Even more pronounced is the difference in the by-products or concomitants from these contrasted activities. The one boy looks upon his school activity with joy and confidence and plans yet other projects; the other counts his school a bore and begins to look elsewhere for the expression there denied. To the one the teacher is a friend and comrade; to the other, a taskmaster and enemy. The one easily feels himself on the side of the school and other social agencies, the other with equal ease considers them all instruments of suppression. Furthermore, under the allied readiness which follows purpose, attention is more easily led to helpful generalizations of method and to such ideals as exactness or fairness. Desirable concomitants are more likely with the hearty purposeful act.

The contrasts here made are consciously of extremes. Most children live between the two. The question is whether we shall not consciously put before us as an ideal the one type of activity and approximate it as closely as we can rather than supinely rest content to live as close to the other type as do the general run of our American schools. Does not the ordinary school among us put its almost exclusive attention on the primary responses and the learning of these in the second fashion here described? Do we not too often reduce the subject matter of instruction to the level of this type alone? Does not our examination system—even our scientific tests at times—tend to carry us in the same direction? How many children at the close of a course decisively shut the book and say, "Thank gracious, I am through with that!" How many people 'get an education' and yet hate books and hate to think?

The thought suggested at the close of the preceding paragraph may be generalized into a criterion more widely applicable. The richness of life is seen upon reflection to depend, in large measure at least, upon the tendency of what one does to suggest and prepare for succeeding activities. Any activity—beyond the barest physical want—which does not thus 'lead on' becomes in time stale and flat. Such 'leading on' means that the individual has been modified so that he sees what before did not see or does what before he could not do. But this is exactly to say that the activity has had an educative effect. Not to elaborate the argument, we may assert that the richness of life depends exactly on its tendency to lead one on to other like fruitful activity; that the degree of this tendency consists exactly in the educative effect of the activity involved; and that we may therefore take as the criterion of the value of any activity— whether intentionally educative or not—its tendency directly or indirectly to lead the individual and others whom he touches on to other like fruitful activity. If we apply this criterion to the common run of American schools we find exactly the discouraging results indicated above. It is the thesis of this paper that these evil results must inevitably follow the effort to found our educational procedure on an unending round of set tasks in conscious disregard of the element of dominant purpose in those who perform the tasks. This again is not to say that every purpose is good nor that the child is a suitable judge as between purposes nor that he is never to be forced to act against a purpose which he entertains. We contemplate no scheme of subordination of teacher or school to childish whim; but we do mean that any plan of educational procedure which does not aim consciously and insistently at securing and utilizing vigorous purposing on the part of the pupils is founded essentially on an ineffective and unfruitful basis. Nor is the quest for desirable purposes hopeless. There is no necessary conflict in kind between the social demands and the child's interests. . . . It is the special duty and opportunity of the teacher to guide the pupil through his present interests and achievement into the wider interests and achievement demanded by the wider social life of the older world.

The question of moral education was implicitly raised in the preceding paragraph. What is the effect on morals of the plan herein advocated? A full discussion is unfortunately impossible. Speaking for myself, however, I consider the possibilities for building moral character in a régime of purposeful activity one of the strongest points in its favor; and contrariwise the tendency toward a selfish individualism one of the strongest counts against our customary set-task sit-alone-at-your-own-desk procedure. Moral character is primarily an affair of shared social relationships, the disposition to determine one's conduct and attitudes with reference to the welfare of the group. This means, psychologically, building stimulus-response bonds such that when certain ideas are present as stimuli certain approved responses will follow. We are then concerned that children get a goodly stock of ideas to serve as stimuli for conduct, that they develop good judgment for selecting the idea appropriate in a given case, and that they have firmly built such response bonds as will bring—as inevitably as possible—the appropriate conduct once the proper idea has been chosen. In terms of this (necessarily simplified) analysis we wish such school procedure as will most probably result in the requisite body of ideas, in the needed skill in judging a moral situation, and in unfailing appropriate response bonds. To get these three can we conceive of a better way than by living in a social *milieu* which provides, under competent supervision, for shared coping with a variety of social situations? In the school procedure here advocated children are living together in the pursuit of a rich variety of purposes, some individually sought, many conjointly. As must happen in social commingling, occasions of moral stress will arise, but here—fortunately—under conditions that exclude extreme and especially harmful cases. Under the eye of the skillful teacher the children as an embryonic society will make increasingly finer discriminations as to what is right and proper. Ideas and judgment come thus. Motive and occasion arise together; the teacher has but to steer the process of evaluating the situation. The teacher's success—if we believe in democracy—will consist in gradually eliminating himself or herself from the success of the procedure. . . .

The question of the growth or building of interests is important in the theory of the plan here discussed. Many points still prove difficult, but some things can be said. Most obvious is the fact of 'maturing' (itself a difficult topic). At first an infant responds automatically to his environment. Only later, after many experiences have been organized, can he, properly speaking, entertain purposes; and in this there are many gradations. Similarly, the earliest steps involved in working out a 'set' are those that have been instinctively joined with the process. Later on, steps may be taken by 'suggestion' (the relatively automatic working of acquired associations). Only comparatively late do we find true adaptation of means to end, the conscious choice of steps to the attainment of deliberately formed purposes. These considerations must qualify any statements made regarding child purposes. One result of the growth here discussed is the 'leading on' it affords. A skill acquired as end can be applied as means to new purposes. Skill or idea arising first in connection with means may be singled out for special consideration and so form new ends. This last is one of the most fruitful sources of new interests, particularly of the intellectual kind.

In connection with this 'maturing' goes a general increase in the 'interest span', the length of time during which a set will remain active, the time within which a child will—if allowed—work at any given project. What part of this increase is due to nature and physical maturing, what part to nurture, why the span is long for some activities and short for others, how we can increase the span in any given cases, are questions of the greatest moment for the educator. It is a matter of common knowledge that within limits 'interests' may be built up, the correlative interest spans appreciably increased. . . .

It may be well to come closer to the customary subject matter of the school. Let us consider the classification of the different types of projects: Type I, where the purpose is to embody some idea or plan in external form, as building a boat, writing a letter, presenting a play; type 2, where the purpose is to enjoy some (esthetic) experience, as listening to a story, hearing a symphony, appreciating a picture; type 3, where the purpose is to straighten out some intellectual difficulty, to solve some problem, as to find out whether or not dew falls, to ascertain how New York outgrew Philadelphia; type 4, where the purpose is to obtain some item or degree of skill or knowledge, as learning to write grade 14 on the Thorndike Scale, learning the irregular verbs in French. It is at once evident that these groupings more or less overlap and that one type may be used as means to another as end. It may be of interest to note that with these definitions the project method logically includes the problem method as a special case. The value of such a classification as that here given seems to me to lie in the light it should throw on the kind of projects teachers may expect and on the procedure that normally prevails in the several types. For type I the following steps have been suggested: purposing, planning, executing, and judging. It is in accord with the general theory here advocated that the child as far as possible take each step himself. Total failure, however, may hurt more than assistance. The opposed dangers seem to be on the one hand that the child may not come out master of the process, on the other, that he may waste time. The teacher must steer the child through these narrows, taking care meanwhile to avoid the other dangers previously discussed. The function of the purpose and the place of thinking in the process need but be mentioned. Attention may be called to the fourth step, that the child as he grows older may increasingly judge the result in terms of the aim and with increasing care and success draw from the process its lessons for the future.

Type 2, enjoying an esthetic experience, may seem to some hardly to belong in the list of projects. But the factor of purpose undoubtedly guides the process and—I must think—influences the growth of appreciation. I have, however, as yet no definite procedure steps to point out.

Type 3, that of the problem, is of all the best known, owing to the work of Professors Dewey and McMurry. The steps that have been used are those of the Dewey analysis of thought.[2] The type lends itself, next to type 4, best of all to our ordinary schoolroom work. For this reason I have myself feared its over-emphasis. Our schools—at least in my judgment—do emphatically need a great increase in the social activity possible in type I. Type 4, where the purpose has to do with specific items of knowledge or skill, would seem to call for the same steps as type I—purposing, planning, executing, and judging. Only here, the planning had perhaps best come from the psychologist. In this type also there is danger of over-emphasis. Some teachers indeed may not closely discriminate between drill as a project and a drill as a set task, although the results will be markedly different. . . .

In conclusion, then, we may say that the child is naturally active, especially along social lines. Heretofore a régime of coercion has only too often reduced our schools to aimless dawdling and our pupils to selfish individualists. Some in reaction have resorted to foolish humoring of childish whims. The contention of this paper is that wholehearted purposeful activity in a social situation as the typical unit of school procedure is the best guarantee of the utilization of the child's native capacities now too frequently wasted. Under proper guidance purpose means efficiency, not only in reaching the projected end of the activity immediately at hand, but even more in securing from the activity the learning which it potentially contains. Learning of all kinds and in its all desirable ramifications best proceeds in proportion as wholeheartedness of purpose is present. With the child naturally social and with the skillful teacher to stimulate and guide his purposing, we can especially expect that kind of learning we call character building. The necessary reconstruction consequent upon these considerations offers a most alluring 'project' to the teacher who but dares to purpose.

NOTES

1. The term accessory was used in the original article where the word associate is now used with a slight difference of meaning, however.
2. Dewey, *How We Think,* Chap. VI.

CHAPTER 3

The Critical
Pedagogical
Perspective

3.1 HENRY A. GIROUX

Culture, Power and Transformation in the Work of Paulo Freire: Toward a Politics of Education

Henry A. Giroux, a scholar in critical theory of education, is considered one of the most important writers on critical pedagogy. A former professor at Miami University in Oxford, Ohio, he presently holds an endowed professorial chair at the Pennsylvania State University at University Park, Pennsylvania. His many publications, including *Theory and Resistance: A Pedagogy for the Opposition* (1983), have been widely read and cited. Among his most recent books are *Border Crossings* (Routledge, 1992) and *Living Dangerously* (Peter Lang, 1993). He is also the coeditor, with Paulo Freire, of the Critical Studies in Education Series (Bergin & Garvey).

In the selection that follows, which is from *Teachers as Intellectuals: Toward a Critical Pedagogy of Learning* (Bergin & Garvey, 1988), Professor Giroux discusses the ideas of culture, power, and transformation in the work of educator Paulo Freire. He points out that Freire sees education as an empowering force for people, that education necessarily addresses a kind of cultural politics. Giroux agrees with Freire that cultural politics is a broader concept than any particular political doctrine. Giroux concludes that the liberation of persons through education must necessarily involve critical engagement with and evaluation of the dominant cultural and political forces in any society.

Key Concept: education and cultural politics

Paulo Freire's work continues to represent a theoretically refreshing and politically viable alternative to the current impasse in educational theory and practice in North America. Freire has appropriated the unclaimed heritage of emancipatory ideas in those versions of secular and religious philosophy located within the corpus of bourgeois thought. He has also critically integrated into his work a heritage of radical thought without assimilating many of the problems that have plagued it historically. In effect, Freire combines what I have called the "language of critique" with the "language of possibility."

Utilizing the language of critique, Freire has fashioned a theory of education that takes seriously the relationship between radical critical theory and the imperatives of radical commitment and struggle. Drawing upon his experiences in Latin America, Africa, and North America, he has generated a discourse that deepens our understanding of the dynamics and complexity of domination. In this instance, Freire rightly argues that domination cannot be reduced exclusively to a form of class domination. With the notion of difference as a guiding theoretical thread, Freire rejects the idea that there is a universalized form of oppression. Instead, he acknowledges and locates within different social fields forms of suffering that speak to particular modes of domination and, consequently, diverse forms of collective struggle and resistance. By recognizing that certain forms of oppression are not reducible to class oppression, Freire steps outside standard Marxist Analyses; he argues that society contains a multiplicity of contradictory social relations, over which social groups can struggle and organize themselves. This is manifest in those social relations in which the ideological and material conditions of gender, racial, and age discrimination are at work.

Equally important is the insight that domination is more than the simple imposition of arbitrary power by one group over another. Instead, for Freire, the logic of domination represents a combination of historical and contemporary ideological and material practices that are never completely successful, always embody contradictions, and are constantly being fought over within asymmetrical relations of power. Underlying Freire's language of critique, in this case, is the insight that history is never foreclosed. Just as the actions of men and women are limited by the specific constraints in which they find themselves, they also make those constraints and the possibilities that may follow from challenging them.

Within this theoretical juncture Freire introduces a new dimension to radical educational theory and practice. I say new because he links the process of struggle to the particularities of people's lives while simultaneously arguing for a faith in the power of the oppressed to struggle in the interests of their own liberation. This is a notion of education fashioned in more than critique and Orwellian pessimism; it is a discourse that creates a new starting point by trying to make hope realizable and despair unconvincing.

Education in Freire's view becomes both an ideal and a referent for change in the service of a new kind of society. As an ideal, education "speaks" to a form of cultural politics that transcends the theoretical boundaries of any one specific political doctrine, while simultaneously linking social theory and practice to the deepest aspects of emancipation. Thus, as an expression of radical social theory, Freire's cultural politics is broader and more fundamental than any one specific political discourse such as classical Marxist theory, a point that often confuses his critics. In fact, his represents a theoretical discourse whose underlying interests are fashioned around a struggle against all forms of subjective and objective domination as well as a struggle for forms of knowledge, skills, and social relations that provide the conditions for social and, hence, self-emancipation.

As a referent for change, eduction represents both a site and a particular type of engagement with the dominant society. For Freire, education includes and moves beyond the notion of schooling. Schools are only one important site where education takes place, where men and women both produce and are the product of specific social and pedagogical relations. Education represents, in Freire's view, both a struggle for meaning and a struggle over power relations. Its dynamic springs from the dialectical relation between individuals and groups who live out their lives within specific historical conditions and structural constraints, on the one hand, and those cultural forms and ideologies that give rise to the contradictions and struggles that define the lived realities of various societies on the other. Education is that terrain where power and politics are given a fundamental expression, where the production of meaning, desire, language, and values engage and respond to the deeper beliefs about what it means to be human, to dream, and to name and struggle for a particular future and form of social life. Education becomes a form of action that joins the languages of critique and possibility. It represents, finally, the need for a passionate commitment by educators to make the political more pedagogical, that is, to make critical reflection and action fundamental parts of a social project that not only engages forms of oppression but develops a deep and abiding faith in the struggle to humanize life itself. It is the particular nature of this social project that gives Freire's work its theoretical distinctiveness.

The theoretical distinctiveness of Freire's work can best be understood by examining briefly how his discourse stands between two radical traditions. On the one hand, the language of critique as it is expressed in Freire's work embodies many of the analyses that characterize what has been called the new sociology of education. On the other hand, Freire's philosophy of hope and struggle is rooted in a language of possibility that draws extensively from the tradition of liberation theology. It is from the merging of these two traditions that Freire has produced a discourse that not only gives meaning and theoretical coherence to his work, but also provides the basis for a more comprehensive and critical theory of pedagogical struggle.

The new sociology of education emerged in full strength in England and the United States over a decade ago as a critical response to what can be loosely termed the discourse of traditional educational theory and practice. The central question, against which it developed its criticism of traditional schooling as well as its own theoretical discourse, is typically Freirean: How does one make education meaningful so as to make it critical and, one hopes, emancipatory.

Radical critics, for the most part, agree that educational traditionalists generally ignore the question. They elude the issue through the paradoxical depoliticizing [of] the language of schooling while reproducing and legitimating capitalist ideologies. The most obvious expression of this approach can be seen in the positivist discourse used by traditional educational theorists. A positivist discourse, in this case, takes as its most important concerns the mastery of pedagogical techniques and the transmission of knowledge instrumental to the existing society. In the traditional world view, schools are merely instructional sites.

Critical educational theorists argue that traditional educational theory suppresses important questions regarding knowledge, power, and domination. Furthermore, schools do not provide opportunities in the broad western humanist tradition for self- and social empowerment in the society at large. In contrast, critical educators provide theoretical arguments and enormous amounts of empirical evidence to suggest that schools are in fact, agencies of social, economic and cultural reproduction. At best, public schooling offers limited individual mobility to members of the working class and other oppressed groups, but, in the final analysis, public schools are powerful instruments for the reproduction of capitalist relations of production and the legitimating ideologies of everyday life.

For the new sociology of education, schools are analyzed primarily within the language of critique and domination. Yet, since schools are viewed primarily as reproductive in nature, left critics fail to provide a programmatic discourse through which the opportunity for counterhegemonic practices could be established. The agony of the left in this case is that its language of critique offered no hope for teachers, parents, or students to wage a political struggle within the schools themselves. Consequently, the language of critique is subsumed within the discourse of despair.

Freire's earlier work shares a remarkable similarity with some of the major theoretical tenets found in the new sociology of education. By redefining and politicizing the notion of literacy, Freire develops a similar type of critical analysis in which he claims that traditional forms of education function primarily to objectify and alienate oppressed groups. Moreover, Freire explores in great depth the reproductive nature of dominant culture and systematically analyzed how it functions through specific social practices and texts to produce and maintain a "culture of silence" among the Brazilian peasants with whom he worked. Though Freire does not use the term "hidden curriculum" as part of his discourse, he demonstrates pedagogical approaches through which groups of learners can decode ideological and material practices whose form, content, and selective omissions contain the logic of domination and oppression. In addition, Freire links the selection, discussion, and evaluation of knowledge to the pedagogical processes that provide a context for such activity. In his view, it is impossible to separate one from the other, and any viable pedagogical practice has to link radical forms of knowledge with corresponding radical social practices.

The major difference between Freire's work and the new sociology of education is that the latter appears to start and end with the logic of political, economic, and cultural reproduction, whereas Freire's analysis begins with the process of production, that is, the various ways human beings construct their own voices and validate their contradictory experiences within specific historical settings and constraints. The reproduction of capitalist rationality and other forms of oppression is only one political and theoretical moment in the process of domination, rather than an all-encompassing aspect of human existence. It is something to be decoded, challenged, and transformed but only within the ongoing discourse, experiences, and histories of the oppressed themselves. It is in this shift from the discourse of reproduction and critique to the language of possibility and engagement that Freire draws from other traditions and fashions a more comprehensive and radical pedagogy.

LIBERATION THEOLOGY AND THE LANGUAGE OF POSSIBILITY

Central to Freire's politics and pedagogy is a philosophical vision of a liberated humanity. The nature of this vision is rooted in a respect for life. The hope and vision of the future that it inspires are not meant to provide consolation for the oppressed as much as to promote ongoing forms of critique and a struggle against objective forces of oppression. By combining the dynamics of critique and collective struggle with a philosophy of hope, Freire has created a language of possibility, what he calls a permanent prophetic vision. Underlying this prophetic vision is a faith, which Dorothée Soelle argues in *Choosing Life*, "makes life present to us and so makes it possible. . . . It is a great 'Yes' to life . . . [one that] presupposes our power to struggle."

Freire's opposition to all forms of oppression, his call to link ideology critique with collective action, and the prophetic vision central to his politics are heavily indebted to the spirit and ideological dynamics that have both informed and characterized the Liberation Theology Movement that has emerged primarily out of Latin America in the last decade. In truly dialectical fashion, Freire has both criticized and rescued the radical underside of revolutionary Christianity. As the reader will discover, Freire is a harsh critic of the reactionary church. At the same time, he situates his faith and sense of hope in the God of history and the oppressed whose teachings make it impossible, in Freire's words, to "reconcile Christian love with the exploitation of human beings."

Within the discourse of liberation theology, Freire fashions a powerful antidote to the cynicism and despair of many left radical critics. Though utopian, his analysis is concrete in its nature and appeal, taking as its starting point collective actors in their various historical settings and the particularity of their problems and forms of oppression. It is utopian only in its refusal to surrender to the risks and dangers that face all challenges to dominant power structures. It is prophetic in that it views the Kingdom of God as something to be created on earth but only through a faith in both other human beings and the necessity of permanent struggle. The notion of faith that emerges in Freire's work is informed by the memory of the oppressed, the suffering that must not be allowed to continue, and the need never to forget that the prophetic vision is an ongoing process, a vital aspect of the very nature of human life. By combining the discourses of critique and possibility Freire joins history and theology so as to provide the theoretical basis for a radical pedagogy that expresses hope, critical reflection, and collective struggle.

It is at this juncture that the work of Paulo Freire becomes crucial to the development of a radical pedagogy. For in Freire we find the dialectician of contradictions and emancipation. His discourse bridges the relationship between agency and structure, situates human action in constraints forged in historical and contemporary practices, while simultaneously pointing to the spaces, contradictions, and forms of resistance that raise the possibility for social struggle. I will conclude by turning briefly to those theoretical elements in Freire's work that seem vital to developing a new language and theoretical foundation for a radical theory of pedagogy, particularly in a North American context.

Two qualifications must be made before I begin. First, Freire's mode of analysis cannot be dismissed as irrelevant to a North American context. Although critics have argued that his experiences with Brazilian peasants do not translate adequately for educators in the advanced industrial countries of the West, Freire makes it clear through the force of his examples and the variety of pedagogical experiences he provides that the context for his work is international in scope. Not only does he capitalize on his experiences in Brazil, he also draws on his work in Chile, Africa, and the United States. Furthermore, he not only takes as the object of his criticism adult education, but also the pedagogical practices of the Catholic Church, social workers, and public education. As he has pointed out repeatedly, the object of his analysis and the language he uses is for the oppressed everywhere; his concept of the Third World is ideological and political rather than merely geographic.

This leads to the second qualification. In order to be true to the spirit of Freire's most profound pedagogical beliefs, it must be stated that he would never argue that his work is meant to be adopted unproblematically to any site or pedagogical context. What Freire does provide is a metalanguage that generates a set of categories and social practices. Freire's work is not meant to offer radical recipes for instant forms of critical pedagogy, it is a series of theoretical signposts that need to be decoded and critically appropriated within the specific contexts in which they might be useful.

THE DISCOURSE OF POWER

Power, for Freire, both a negative and a positive force, its character is dialectical, and its mode of operation is always more than simply repressive. Power works on and through people. Domination is never so complete that power is experienced exclusively as a negative force, yet power is at the basis of all forms of behavior in which people resist, struggle, and fight for a better world. In a general sense, Freire's theory of power and his demonstration of its dialectical character serve the important function of broadening the spheres and terrains on which power operates. Power, in this instance, is not exhausted in those public and private spheres by governments, ruling classes, and other dominant groups. It is more ubiquitous and is expressed in a range of oppositional public spaces and spheres that traditionally have been characterized by the *absence* of power and thus any form of resistance.

Freire's view of power suggests not only an alternative perspective to those radical theorists trapped in the straitjacket of despair and cynicism, it also stresses that there are always cracks, tensions, and contradictions in various social spheres such as schools where power can be exercised as a positive force in the name of resistance. Furthermore, Freire understands that power—domination—is not simply imposed by the state through agencies such as the police, the army, and the courts. Domination is also expressed in the way in which power, technology, and ideology come together to produce knowledge, social relations, and other concrete cultural forms that indirectly silence people. It is also found in the way in which the oppressed internalize and thus participate in their own oppression. This is an important point in Freire's work and directs us to the ways in which domination is subjectively experienced through its internalization and sedimentation in the very needs of the personality. What is at work here is an important attempt to examine the psychically repressive aspects of domination and the internal obstacles to self-knowledge and, thus, to forms of social and self emancipation.

Freire broadens the notion of learning to include how the body learns tacitly, how habit translates into sedimented history, and, most importantly, how knowledge itself may block the development of certain subjectivities and ways of experiencing the world. Ironically, emancipatory forms of knowledge may be refused by those who could most benefit from such knowledge. In this case, accommodation to the logic domination by the oppressed may take the form of actively resisting forms of knowledge that pose a challenge to their world view. Rather than a passive acceptance of domination, knowledge becomes instead an active dynamic of negation, an active refusal to listen, to hear, or to affirm one's own possibilities. The pedagogical questions that emerge from this view of domination are: How do radical educators assess and address the elements of repression and forgetting at the heart of this domination? What accounts for the conditions that sustain an active refusal to know or to learn in the face of knowledge that may challenge the nature of domination itself?

The message that emerges from Freire's pedagogy is relatively clear. If radical educators are to understand the meaning of liberation, they must first be aware of the form that domination takes, the nature of its location, and the problems it poses to those who experience it as both a subjective and objective force. But such a project would be impossible unless one took the historical and cultural particularities, the forms of social life, of subordinate and oppressed groups as a starting point for such an analysis. It is to this issue in Freire's work that I now turn.

One of the most important theoretical elements for a radical pedagogy that Freire provides is his view of experience and cultural production. Freire's notion of culture is at odds with both conservative and progressive positions. In the first instance, he rejects the notion that culture can be divided easily into high, popular, and low forms, with high culture representing the most advanced heritage of a nation. Culture, in this view, hides the ideologies that legitimate and distribute specific forms of culture as if they were unrelated to ruling class interests and existing configurations of power. In the second instance, he rejects the notion that the moment of cultural creation rests solely with ruling groups and that dominant cultural forms harbor merely the seeds of domination. Related to this position, and also rejected by Freire, is the assumption that oppressed groups possess by their very location in the apparatus of domination a progressive and revolutionary culture waiting only to be released from the fetters of ruling class domination.

For Freire, culture is the representation of lived experiences, material artifacts, and practices forged within the unequal and dialectical relations that different groups establish in a given society at a particular historical point. Culture is a form of production whose processes are intimately connected with the structuring of different social formations, particularly those that are gender, age, racial, and class related. It is also a form of production that helps human agents, through their use of language and other material resources, to transform society. In this case, culture is closely related to the dynamics of power and produces asymmetries in the ability of individuals and groups to define and achieve their goals. Furthermore, culture is also an arena of struggle and contradiction, and there is no one culture in the homogeneous sense. On the contrary, there are dominant and subordinate cultures that express different interests and operate from different and unequal terrains of power.

Freire argues for a notion of cultural power that takes as its staring point the social and historical particularities that constitute the problems, sufferings, visions, and acts of resistance that comprise the cultural forms of subordinate groups. Cultural power then has a dual focus as part of his strategy to make the political more pedagogical. First, educators will have to work with the experiences that students bring to schools and other educational sites. This means making these experiences, public and private, the object of debate and confirmation; it means legitimating such experiences in order to give those who live and move within them a sense of affirmation and to provide the conditions for students and others to display an active voice and presence. The pedagogical experience here becomes an invitation to make visible the languages, dreams, values, and encounters that constitute the lives of those whose histories are often actively silenced. But Freire does more than argue for the legitimation of the culture of the oppressed. He also recognizes that such experiences are contradictory in nature and harbor not only radical potentialities but also the sedimentations of domination. Cultural power takes a twist in this instance and refers to the need to *work on* the experiences that make up the lives of the oppressed. Such experiences in their varied cultural forms have to be recovered critically so as to reveal both their strengths and weaknesses. Moreover, self-critique is complimented in the name of a radical pedagogy designed to unearth and critically appropriate those unclaimed emancipatory moments in bourgeois knowledge and experience that further provide the skills the oppressed will need to exercise leadership in the dominant society.

What is striking in this presentation is that Freire has fashioned a theory of cultural power and production that begins with popular education. Instead of offering abstract generalities about human nature, he rightly argues for pedagogical principles that arise from the concrete practices—the terrains on which people live out their everyday experiences. All of this suggests taking seriously the cultural capital of the oppressed, developing critical and analytical tools to interrogate it, and staying in touch with dominant definitions of knowledge so we can analyze them for their usefulness and for the ways in which they bear the logic of domination.

FREIRE, TRANSFORMATIVE INTELLECTUALS, AND THE THEORY-PRACTICE RELATIONSHIP

Radical social theory has been plagued historically by the development of the relationship between intellectuals and the masses, on the one hand, and the relationship between theory and practice. Under the call for the unity of theory and practice, the possibility for emancipatory practice has often been negated through forms of vanguardism in which intellectuals effectively removed from the popular forces the ability to define for themselves the limits of their aims and practice. By assuming a virtual monopoly in the exercise of theoretical leadership, intellectuals unknowingly reproduced the division of mental and manual labor that was at the core of most forms of domination. Instead of developing theories of practice, which were rooted in the concrete experience of listening and learning with the oppressed, Marxist intellectuals developed theories for practice or technical instruments for change that ignored the necessity for a dialectical reflection on the everyday dynamics and problems of the oppressed within the context of radical social transformation.

Freire refutes this approach to the theory-practice relationship and redefines the very idea of the intellectual. Like the Italian social theorist, Antonio Gramsci, Freire redefines the category of intellectual and argues that all men and women are intellectuals. That is, regardless of social and economic function all human beings perform as intellectuals by constantly interpreting and giving meaning to the world and by participating in a particular conception of the world. Moreover, the oppressed need to develop their own organic and transformative intellectuals who can learn with such groups while simultaneously helping to foster modes of self-education and struggle against various forms of oppression. In this case, intellectuals are organic in that they are *not* outsiders bringing theory to the masses. On the contrary, they are theorists fused organically with the culture and practical activities of the oppressed.

Rather than casually dispense knowledge to the grateful masses, intellectuals fuse with the oppressed in order to make and remake the conditions necessary for a radical social project.

This position is crucial in highlighting the political function and importance of intellectuals. Equally significant is the way it redefines the notion of political struggle by emphasizing its pedagogical nature and the centrality of the popular and democratic nature of such a struggle. This raises the important question of how Freire defines the relation between theory and practice.

For Freire, "there is no theoretic context if it is not in a dialectical unity with the concrete context." Rather than call for the collapse of theory into practice, Freire argues for a certain distance between theory and practice. He views theory as anticipatory in its nature and posits that it must take the concepts of understanding and possibility as its central moments. Theory is informed by an oppositional discourse that preserves its critical distance from the "facts" and experiences of the given society. The tension, indeed, the conflict with practice belongs to the essence of theory and is grounded in its very structure. Theory does not dictate practice; rather, it serves to hold practice at arm's length so as to mediate and critically comprehend the type of praxis needed within a specific setting at a particular time. There is no appeal to universal laws or historical necessity here; theory emerges within specific contexts and forms of experience in order to examine such contexts critically and then to intervene on the basis of an informed praxis.

But Freire's contribution to the nature of theory and practice and the role of the intellectual in the process of social transformation contains another important dimension. Theory must be seen as the production of forms of discourse that arise from various specific social sites. Such a discourse may arise from the universities, from peasant communities, from workers councils, or from within various social movements. The issue here is that radical educators recognize that these different sites give rise to various forms of theoretical production and practice. Each of these sites provides diverse and critical insights into the nature of domination and the possibilities for social and self-emancipation, and they do so from the historical and social particularities that give them meaning. What brings them together is a mutual respect forged in criticism and the need to struggle against all forms of domination.

PART TWO

Curriculum and Instruction

**4.1 KATHERINE CAMP MAYHEW
AND ANNA CAMP EDWARDS**

The Dewey School: The Laboratory School of the University of Chicago, 1896–1903

Katherine Camp Mayhew and Anna Camp Edwards were teachers in the Laboratory School of the University of Chicago, which was founded by John Dewey in 1896. This school was an educational laboratory for exploring the ideas on curriculum and instruction being developed by Dewey. The school, which later became the School of Education, was created to involve parents, teachers, and professors in dialogue regarding the 10 ideas about experience-based pedagogy being developed by Dewey and other progressive educators. Mayhew and Edwards published a now-classic book on the early years of this experimental school entitled *The Dewey School: The Laboratory School of the University of Chicago: 1896–1903* (D. Appleton-Century, 1936). The selection that follows is from that book.

The students of the Dewey school were broken into groups by relative age. Each group was designated by a Roman numeral. To give the reader a flavor for how the school was conducted, this selection includes the authors' descriptions of the experiments in specialized activities by "Group XI" (ages 14 to 15) for the 1901–1902 school year. Also included are brief comments by Mayhew and Edwards regarding the school's philosophy of student growth.

Key Concept: the Dewey school

EXPERIMENTS IN SPECIALIZED ACTIVITIES

Group XI (Age Fourteen to Fifteen)

In a developing experiment such as that of the school, the work of the oldest children is of necessity highly exploratory and tentative in character. Because of the school's early demise also, many of the courses for this age were repeated but once, or at the most twice. An account of them is, therefore, only suggestive of a way in which the interests and activities of the elementary stage may be guided into the deviating paths of the more specialized interests and subject-matter of the secondary period.

Careful study of the school's brief and very condensed records during the year 1901–1902 seems to indicate that in this year the two older groups were united into one. This was true for at least certain of their studies. The oldest members of this united group (who normally would have been classified as Group XII) were given special tutoring and review courses in preparation for their college board examinations, which were complicating the program. Had the group consisted solely of those who had followed the consecutively developing program of the school, and had it not been hampered by the demands of college entrance examinations, the various courses for the oldest children doubtless would have followed a far different and more logical plan, hints of which appear in the records. Roman history would have been studied from the point of view of the political state; the history of industry and of social groupings would have been developed; and more of the specialized sciences gradually would have found their places in the curriculum. As it was, the theoretical plan for the oldest children was greatly altered by circumstances. There was also lack of space and of proper laboratories and equipment for older children. Many of these difficulties were swept away in the following year when the Laboratory School, for one year, became a part of the School of Education, and moved into its beautiful new building. Records of the work of that year (1902–1903), however, were not available; hence the history of the school ends with the records of Group XI.

The Work of the Fall Quarter

For two years the course in general science for these children had been separated into its physiographical and biological aspects. The year before the children had continued the study of the various forms of energy with special emphasis on light. This course had included a fundamental consideration of various theories of energy and had been in the nature of an introduction to the technical study of physics, which would soon enter the program of those preparing for college entrance examinations. The science course planned for Group XI was a continued and more detailed consideration of their earlier study of existing types of animal life. This was constantly related to the evolutionary processes touched upon in the geological study of North America the preceding year. It was characterized by more laboratory work and outdoor excursions than usually mark a study of biology in the secondary period. The aim was to preserve the spirit of individual investigation and rediscovery that had characterized the children's scientific work from the beginning.

The study of mathematics also became more highly specialized. The work in algebra included involution, evolution, the theory of exponents, and operations involving radical quantities. In geometry, each member of the group worked out, for the most part independently, from twenty to thirty propositions and exercises and wrote up his demonstrations with a varying degree of care. In addition to that of clarifying the children's fundamental mathematical ideas, three ulterior purposes were kept in view by the teacher of this course: to train each individual into the highest degree of independence and perseverance in attacking new and difficult work, to aid him in developing a clear concept of what constitutes a geometrical demonstration, to attain clear, definite, and concise expression.

The Work of the Winter Quarter

In the second quarter the pupils used Will's *Essentials of Geometry* as the basis of their work and were able to work more rapidly than when they had had to make constructions as well as work out demonstrations from dictated exercises. The propositions of Book I and many other related exercises were covered—in all about one hundred. In order to have time to finish the desired work in algebra, geometry was discontinued in May without reviewing the work done. The remainder of the quarter was spent in the study of radical equations, quadratic equations, the theory of quadratics, and problems involving quadratics. Although all the work usually prescribed for college entrance was taken up, only a few of the group completed the course in a satisfactory way. Some of them were hampered by lack of a ready command of fundamental principles and processes. Others did not put sufficient time on study to acquire familiarity with and ready application of the principles. The work of three was highly satisfactory, but even these needed a month of review before taking college examinations. It was felt that other members of the group would require at least another quarter's work on the important and more technical parts of the subject.

The work in history was also more specialized than in previous years. Six years' study of social living the world over, as well as that of their own present, had more or less adequately prepared these children to appreciate a study of certain thoroughly differentiated and, so to speak, peculiar types of social life.

It was hoped that on the basis of their rather thorough knowledge of both the principles and facts of social life they would be able to discover for themselves the special significance of each civilization and the particular contribution it had made to the world's history. The plan, therefore, was to change from the psychological approach to a study of history to the chronological, to begin with the ancient world around the Mediterranean and come down again through the European story to the peculiar and differentiating factors of American history. The plan, however, was tried for two years only, and the records of the work of the last year are too meagre for inferences of any value to be drawn as to its ultimate success. In history, much time was also given to making up the lacks in the consecutive study of history required by college entrance examinations.

The shop-work of this group for the quarter was not up to the standard of that of Groups VIII or IX. The pupils chose their own work, and the results were unsatisfactory. Some showed a lack of ambition to undertake any worthy object; some were ambitious beyond their skill; and some lacked decision and perseverance. When careful work was required, most of the group worked very slowly. The boys took some time to complete the tool drawers in their benches, did some repair work about the school and finished a tripod for a camera and a bread board. The girls completed tool boxes, a mail box, two or three book racks, a window seat, an oak table, an oak music rack, and other smaller articles. The whole-hearted effort and genuine interest of other years seems to have been lacking. The cooking as a course had been discontinued with Group IX, but on occasions when distinguished guests were present at luncheon, the older groups were called in to plan, prepare, and serve the meal.

The work in languages, French, Latin, and English, took on a specialized character. In Latin, before beginning Caesar's Commentaries, the class read his biography from *Viri Romae*. In translation, emphasis was laid on syntax. In composition, the aim was to help the children to gain a free use of Latin idioms in their translation of English into Latin and in their condensed historical reports. Sight reading was also part of the program, and in connection with work on the Gallic wars a detailed study of the life of Caesar's times was made, of its outstanding men and the social, intellectual, and political events of the period. In this year the children also started their first formal study of the English language, and English was chosen as the subject for special emphasis during the year. Some intensive work was done on Latin derivatives. The points emphasized were: (1) consonant and vowel changes; (2) suffixes and prefixes, their value and changes; (3) growth and change in the meaning of derivatives. Coöperation with the French teacher was necessary as the Latin element in the English language, while partly derived directly from Latin, has, in the main, come through French, and has been largely modified in the process.

The first piece of work in composition was a theme relating to summer experience. The children's style was clear and fluent, but inclined to be loose and inaccurate in sentence structure. Careful criticism brought out some difficult grammatical points which were analyzed and discussed; considerable logical power was evidenced in attacking these grammatical problems. After this preliminary work, the reading of one of Shakespeare's plays was undertaken. As these children had not the habit of reading aloud, they were very awkward. They had never read a play, with the exception of two pupils. They knew nothing of Shakespeare, nor of dramatic history, so a brief sketch of Shakespeare's life and the prominent social features of his time was made from books which the children read themselves. They had no way of expressing their ideas of meter and in the beginning found it difficult to tell when they omitted a syllable or inserted one which did not belong in the phrase. As their attention had to be continually interrupted to discover errors in reading, the work went very slowly at first. They had had Roman History so that they understood the story of the play. They committed to memory some couplets and short passages, and as soon as the study of the first act was completed, they prepared an abstract. By this time they had enough command of method to understand the character of work expected of them, and their interest in the story and the dramatic setting was thoroughly aroused. The play was completed by Christmas time; abstracts of each act were written; and an outline of the entire play given by every pupil in the class. In a general way they understood the difference between the Shakespearean drama and preceding English drama. They were familiar with the versification so far as its use went, although no technical terms were given to them. The class showed particular interest in the character study. Two members carried on a two-day debate over the comparative virtues of Brutus and Cassius. Each member of the class had weighed all the main characters and could give an opinion on their virtues or vices and the relative importance of the part each had in the drama.

Katherine Camp Mayhew and Anna Camp Edwards

This study cleared the way for a return to a study of the village life and history of Shakespeare's time. Notes were made of the many incidental allusions to the commercial changes which were taking place in England. To explain these allusions a study of the Tudor family's position and importance in history was made in the winter quarter. The religious attitude of France, Spain, Italy, and the Netherlands was also discussed. Since the pupils had no idea of the reasons why this period was called the Renaissance of Learning, biographies of the great discoverers in science were read. The discovery of the New World and its commercial importance they already understood. They studied the lives of Copernicus, of Sir Thomas More, Martin Luther, the inventors of printing, and the story of the rise of Protestantism and the settlement of Ireland. Working back in history from Shakespeare and Queen Elizabeth to the Wars of the Roses, they studied Shakespeare's *King Richard III*, following the same method used in *Julius Caesar*. About five or six weeks were spent on the play. The class was much shocked by the evil portrayed, and interest was somewhat depressed by the shock to their feelings. The outlines and abstracts of the acts were prepared, and a very good idea of the historical setting was gained. The class was somewhat critical of the play and inclined to compare it with *Julius Caesar*, which they considered much superior. However, in the end they were all impressed by the intellect of King Richard, as well as horrified by his wickedness.

The Work of the Spring Quarter

In the spring quarter work followed quite different lines. It consisted of a critical analysis of the class papers prepared in science. The subjects of these papers were volcanoes, glaciers, and other physiographical features. The first task was to prepare an outline of what they themselves were to write. They had no idea how to attack this and in the first attempt were quite as likely to put descriptions into their outlines as to separate the headings or main topics. However, as the subject-matter had been given them in logical order in the science class, they soon grasped the idea that the order of composition was simply the logic of thought or subject-matter, and rapidly gained power to prepare clear and accurate outlines. The only details taken up were those of grammar and sentence structure. The differentiation between English and Latin caused them some difficulty. In the former, they had to learn to depend upon their own analysis to determine the relation of a word to the sentence. They were inclined at first to define such terms as subject and object in too restricted a way. They came to see that where no endings existed to place the word, the difficulty of defining its use was increased. The main points in sentence analysis, they soon grasped. Certain forms of diagramming sentences were given, but these were not used for more than two days, although the class showed an inclination to come back to them. As time went on, they improved greatly in definiteness of statement and in ability to criticize their own forms of expression. Considerable time was spent throughout the entire year in studying the derivations of words and the historical development of their meanings. At the beginning of the year the whole class was satisfied with a very loose explanation of the meaning of a word, but after the year's study not one was satisfied until he had looked it up in the Century Dictionary. They often followed a word to its roots in other languages.

Group XI also carried on the printing of a daily newspaper for a short time, as did other groups. This did much to interest the children in language expression. On account of the pressure of time, inconvenient quarters, and type of press, the work was more limited than it might have been under more flexible conditions. At one time the press was of great service in printing the reading lessons for the younger children. Developments in later progressive schools have shown that carried out in the same way in which other occupations in the school were pursued, printing might have been an absorbing interest and of great educational value.

The group was active in school clubs and in the club-house project. The Educational Club was under the special guidance of these children. It started out with fine spirit the last year of the school. The constitution of the club allowed any member of the school to become a member, and several new names were voted on. A committee was appointed to attend to the finances of the club-house and to confer with an adviser to consider the best method of raising the money for it. A new president, secretary, and treasurer were elected. The club then voted to take charge of the Friday afternoon exercises of the school. A committee of three members was appointed for this purpose. The children voted to have a general adviser, and a teacher was appointed. At a special meeting the Monday before Thanksgiving, the club decided to raise the dues of club members to twenty-five cents a month until the house was paid for. They also formed an athletic department, and the president appointed a committee of three to decide definitely on the work of this department.

*Katherine
Camp Mayhew
and Anna
Camp Edwards*

The weekly general assembly of the older children on Friday afternoon of each week was always a social occasion and was usually directed by the older groups. In the beginning, one of the girls read a story of her own composition. The children were then asked to bring in suggestions for programs. One offered to have a friend come and play the piano. A girl offered the play that she had been writing, volunteering to select the actors and actresses and drill them in it. They all voted to ask Professor Judson of the University to come to talk about the trouble in China, requesting that they be allowed to ask all the questions they wished. Extracts from the records of some of these assemblies follow:

At the general exercises held on the Wednesday afternoon before Thanksgiving, the children sang their songs of last year. Professor MacClintock read a Thanksgiving story—Whittier's *The Pumpkin*. On another occasion, papers written by the children of the various groups on their class work were read. One read a long account of the conquest of Peru, another, an account of a series of experiments carried on in science during the fall.

One week Mr. F— gave a very informal talk to the children about his experiences in Cuba during the late war. The children were so much interested that they stayed half an hour afterwards asking questions. In February Mr. Jenkin Lloyd Jones was invited to talk on the subject of Lincoln. He accepted the invitation and entertained them for half an hour with stories illustrating Lincoln's characteristics.

At the next meeting the children celebrated Washington's birthday, Group IX prepared the program, in which each child had a part. One played the boyhood of Washington; another, his school-days; another, his part in the French and Indian War; Washington in the Revolution; Washington as president; and Washington at home. One girl said that she knew several stories of Washington which did not come under any of these heads, so she wrote and read a paper on "Incidents in the life of Washington." On this occasion they worked together as a class better than ever before. Another afternoon Miss Harmer talked to the children on the Horace Mann School, and they asked many questions and seemed interested in the subject. At the next assembly Dr. Coulter gave a description of his trip to the Yellowstone Park in 1870 when he went out with an expedition appointed by the government to explore the Wyoming geysers. On one occasion when a speaker failed to come, the children had an old-fashioned spelling contest, Groups IX and X doing themselves credit. On another, to which friends were invited, the program consisted of a German play, the composition of which had formed the basis of Group VIII-*b's* work for the winter quarter; in addition there were songs and English and French recitations.

In the later years of the school the debating society became very active and frequently took charge of the assembly program. It was noticeable that a child speaking to children always got rapt attention, and judgment of points in a debate grew to be very discerning. All these weekly assemblies were productive of good results, but a great handicap was the lack of an auditorium and any stage facilities.

The boys and girls of Group XI were divided for their music periods. The latter sang well and with much enthusiasm. Sight singing was emphasized, and they learned Schumann's "The Wanderer," Schubert's "Haiden Roslein" (in German) by note and spent a large portion of their time in writing a long two-part song which they notated on the board and copied. The boys of the group, having completed the work on key and time signatures, were told that unless they wished to sing, there was nothing further to do, for them, in music. They responded to this by suggesting that they write a song and chose as a topic "La Journée" such as they had seen described in their recent study of *Ivanhoe* in a literature course. The words finished, they were at a loss for the music, and finally decided that the teacher had better write it. Accordingly, she put a phrase of music on the board which they proceeded to change by telling on what line or space each note should be placed. They then listened to and criticized the result. In this manner the song was completed. The three older groups were allowed to learn it. They were then to invite the composers to chorus practice and sing it for them. The latter, however, were not pleased with the result, saying the voices were too high to do justice to the song, and finally decided to learn to sing it themselves. This they did and, finding they could, continued to sing for the rest of the quarter.

The work in the art studio centered around the furnishing and decorating of the now completed club-house. All the groups of the school had been drawn into interested participation in the final touches on the cherished project, but the older groups designed and made most of the furniture, hangings, and rugs. At various times the center of activity shifted from the studio to the science laboratory for experimentation on vegetable dyes (aniline dyes were viewed with scorn) or for the right mixture of stain for the woodwork; again the carpentry shop was sought out for some necessary construction of wood or metal; or it was back to the textile studio for sewing and embroidery of the curtains, or weaving the rugs already planned and designed. Through all these activities ran the artistic motive—a genuine longing that the house and all that was to be put therein should be beautiful and appropriate. Interest and effort harnessed as a team, driven by genuine desire that sprang from genuine need, accomplished results of real quality. Although skilled guidance was at hand and irremediable errors were not permitted, the children had great freedom in directing their project. Naturally many mistakes were made, some of which took much time and hard labor to correct, but which taught much otherwise never learned. The groups primarily responsible for the project had organized themselves into various executive committees. The committee on house decoration decided in favor of a dark stain (then in vogue) for the woodwork of the house and, in spite of the advice of those guiding the work, carried their idea through. They were much criticized by the rest for the gloomy effect of their choice, a criticism some of them recall to this day.

Summary

The little house when finished represented the best thought and genuine interest as well as labor of many children, and it grew out of genuine need. Its construction and decoration had been guided by skilled persons, interested in helping the children to conceive and achieve their ideals, and in the process to learn to judge and critically evaluate their own results. With these older children, as with all the groups in the school, the motives for art expressions sprang out of other activities and thus held vital relations for the children. The ideal of the school was that skill in the technique of artistic expression should keep pace with the children's intellectual concepts of the way they wished to refine, adorn, or represent in line, color, or clay the thing they were making. This was an ideal difficult to attain and more often than not failed of achievement. That it was achieved, in a measure, in art, in music, and to a still more limited degree in drama was a real achievement for those in charge. These were pioneer days, and previous attempts to cultivate artistic quality of expression from the kindergarten to the studio were quite unknown. Since these early days great progress has been made in the teaching of the musical and those representative activities usually called the fine arts. There is great value in this type of activity for securing freedom of expression and joyous creative effort. For the child this is what might be called consummatory experience.

In justice it should be said that at all times the experiment was much hampered by its limited quarters and equipment. Because of the lack of library and laboratory facilities especially, many of the things done with the three older groups were second choices as to subject-matter. The very nature of the school also made it necessary for the children to concentrate under difficult conditions of noise and interruption. This was not conducive to the development of the habit of consecutive study necessary to the best expression of individual thought in language or in any other medium. Lack of a library, lack of quiet, lack of beauty, lack of adequate space for club meetings, all made it impossible to carry out many individual and group plans. As was stated at the time, "It was never practically possible to act adequately upon the best ideas obtained, because of administrative difficulties, due to lack of funds, difficulties centering in the lack of a proper building and appliances and in inability to pay the amounts necessary to secure the complete time of teachers in some important lines. Indeed, with the growth of the school in numbers and in the age and maturity of the pupils, it was always a grave question how long it was fair to the experiment to carry it on without more adequate facilities."

Although the school had a number of children who were finishing the third stage of growth of the elementary period, it was not in existence long enough so that many typical inferences as to results for this period could be safely drawn. There did seem reason to hope, however, that with the consciousness of difficulties, needs, and resources gained in the experience of five years, children can be brought to and through this period not only without sacrifice of thoroughness, mental discipline, and command of the technical tools of learning, but also with a positive enlargement of life, and a wider, freer, and more open outlook upon it.

At least it can be said that at fourteen these children had the background of an unusually wide first-hand experience upon which to base their more technical study, not only of artistic forms and appreciations, but of all forms of knowledge, whether scientific or practical, that had come within the range of their activities. Where these experiences had taken root in the good soil of native aptitudes, tendrils of intellectual and spiritual appreciations of beauty of color, line, and form, of harmony and rhythm, of ethical, social, and moral values and responsibilities were reaching out, searching for the light of broader opportunities. They represented permanently rooted motives and vocational interests which, given a chance, would grow into continuing purposes and well-planned social action. This was by no means true of all the children who had come through the processes of the school. It possibly was true only of a very few, but it is not too much to hold that what was accomplished gave those who had eyes to see and ears to hear faith to believe that here lay the way of an education that was also the way of developing life.

PRINCIPLES OF GROWTH GUIDING SELECTION OF ACTIVITIES

In the school, education was recognized as a maturing process, in which the young child grows in body and mind and in ability to handle himself in his physical environment and in his social relationships. The conditions for healthy bodily growth had long been recognized, but the idea that power to think depends upon the healthy growth and proper functioning of the mechanism of thought and its expression was, at that time, quite new. The bearing upon education of psychological science as a study of this mechanism, and of the conditions that minister to and promote its normal development in mental power and intelligent action was still for the most part unrecognized.

Two psychological assumptions of the school's hypothesis, basic to its theory and controlling its practices, were radically different from those that underlay the prevalent educational theory and practice. The first of these recognized a psychological and biological distinction between the child and the adult, as a result of which it is neither physiologically nor mentally possible to describe children as "little men and women." The adult is a person with a calling and position in life. These place upon him specific responsibilities which he must meet. They call into play formed habits. The child's primary calling is growth. He is forming habits as well as using those already formed. He is, therefore, absorbed in making contacts with persons and things and in getting that range of acquaintance with the physical and ideal factors of life which should be the background and afford the material for the specialized activities of later life. Recognition of this difference, therefore, conditioned the selection and arrangement of all school materials and methods in order to facilitate full normal growth. It also required faith in the results of growth to provide the power and ability for later specialization.

The second assumption was that the conditions which make for mental and moral progress are the same for the child as for the adult. For one, as for the other, power and control are obtained through realizing personal ends and problems, through personal choosing of suitable ways and means, and through adapting, applying and thereby testing what is selected in experimental and socially acceptable action.

The Child-Centered School: An Appraisal of the New Education

Harold Rugg and Ann Shumaker published *The Child-Centered School: An Appraisal of the New Education* (World Book) in 1928. This important book described and synthesized the basic underlying principles of the rapidly growing progressive, child-centered school movement in America. Rugg (1886–1960) went on to publish 57 more books on education. Through his works, he interpreted the socially conscious ideas on education that developed in the first six decades of the twentieth century. Shumaker (1899–1936) was a teacher at the Lincoln School, the experimental elementary school at Teachers College, Columbia University, where she did her graduate studies. Her enthusiasm for the ideas of John Dewey and William Heard Kilpatrick shines through in the following excerpt from *The Child-Centered School.* Shumaker is considered by many to be America's first published woman philosopher of education.

In the first part of Rugg and Shumaker's book, the authors explore how the early writings of Dewey and Kilpatrick on child-centered ideas about teaching have influenced education, and they note several of the experimental schools that developed in the United States in the first 25 years of the twentieth century. In the excerpt that follows, the authors describe the "new articles of faith"—the bases of the child-centered school—in what they consider to be the revolution in educational thought.

Key Concept: child-centered schooling

*I*t was John Dewey, . . . Professor of Philosophy and Head of the Department of Education at the University of Chicago from 1894 to 1904, who ignited the first flame of the current educational revolution. Dewey, curious combination of the arid New England Puritanism and Middle West democratic practi-

57

cality, first phrased the educational philosophy of the developing American culture. Thoroughgoing Darwinian and firm believer in democracy, he, more than all others, rationalized the rapidly evolving industrial civilization. He was third in the line of the pragmatic succession. Two other original thinkers preceded him in phrasing the hypotheses of the new Americanism: Charles Sanders Peirce, engineer, statistician, professor of logic, inventor of pragmaticism; and William James, organizer of the first psychological laboratory in America, true experimental scientist, phraser of the philosophy of radical empiricism, for whom "there was no conclusion."

It is to Dewey's everlasting credit that his mind was able to stay above the maelstrom of economic exploitation, rapid urbanization, mass education, and to frame critical hypotheses for the intellectual base of the new national school system.

It was in 1896 that John and Alice Dewey, in company with colleagues and neighbors, started their little laboratory school. A thoroughly radical institution it was, with neither school subjects nor conventional furniture, the first important overt expression of the growing protest against the formal school. Of course, in this, their first escape from the conventional order, they swung far with the experimental pendulum. Many thought that their experiment exemplified only scholastic chaos. For several years it grew slowly, a true innovation, throwing overboard most of the established principles of order. Leading "educators" of the country visiting it went away determined not to practice that form of educational anarchy in their own institutions.

Nevertheless, it was in these formative years and through the trial and error of radical experimentation that John Dewey succeeded in phrasing the new doctrines of educational reconstruction. Under the impetus of round-table staff meetings, lectures to the parents and teachers of the laboratory school, there emerged the essays, "School and Society" and "The Child and the Curriculum." Papers were contributed to the proceedings of the Herbart Society and of the National Education Association on the practical reconstruction of the elementary and secondary schools. Dewey displayed a catholicity of interests. Hence his "Interest as Related to Will,"[1] and also "Ethical Principles Underlying Education,"[2] the essay in which he developed the basic theses of his orienting theory.

In striving to cut through the crust of the disciplinary conception he seized upon the doctrine of growth and activity. This leader of the first real protest school of our times was guided, therefore, by children's "full spontaneous interests and intentions." Hence, school subjects—reading, writing, arithmetic—were to develop out of children's "life activities," out of methods of living and learning, not out of the memorization of "distinct studies."

According to Dewey's theory, therefore, the life of the school was to be active, not passive; the children were to work, not merely to listen. The curriculum was to be organized around four chief impulses: the social instinct of the children, the instinct of making—the constructive impulse, the expressive instinct—the art instinct, and the impulse toward inquiry or finding out things.[3]

The preparatory work was going on, however, and then appeared William H. Kilpatrick and his monograph, *The Project Method*.

Professor Kilpatrick,[4] strategically located in the first and most influential of the new teachers' colleges, has succeeded not only in making the philosophy of the child-centered school intelligible to thousands of teachers in service, but also in inciting widespread experimentation with the new point of view. In 1910 the movement needed analysis and concrete illustration. Vigorous preachment was required in order to provide the impulse for the next step—widespread experimentation.

NEW ARTICLES OF FAITH

The pageant historical of the new schools has passed in review, a procession of novel educational tableaux. The parade convinces the spectator that at last rebellious preachment is producing action in the school.

The new school is different—different in practice, different in theory. Dynamic articles of faith have been precipitated from the reaction of the new culture of industrialism on the Puritan scene.

Semi-phrased; relatively unformulated; beyond such catch slogans as freedom, initiative, activity, interest, self-expression, was the theoretical basis of most of the radical innovations. For years little advance was made in theory. Until 1920 Dewey's philosophic writings, supplemented by Kilpatrick's pamphlets, constituted the bulk of frontier thinking. Then suddenly emerged an accumulating wealth of description—yearbooks, records, bulletins, reprinted addresses, what not. And in 1919 the need of the rebels for mutual support, for discussion, for comparison of practices produced the Progressive Education Association[5] and in 1924, its magazine, *Progressive Education.* In Europe the corresponding New Education Fellowship and its tri-language magazine[6] perform a similar service.

The meetings of the American as well as the European organization have brought out encouraging reiterations and confirmations of faith, and thrilling exhibits of the productivity of the creative environment. Slowly this fellowship has helped to focus and clarify the vocabulary (and correspondingly the thinking) of the new educationists. Haltingly the new philosophy is being evolved; bit by bit a mosaic of theory is being constructed, mostly of excerpts culled from the educational writings of Dewey and his followers. Gradually basic articles of faith are emerging, to which all these new schools subscribe. For back of the varying, overt manifestations of the new spirit stand a few fundamental beliefs, a few distinctly new conceptions of growth, experience, the course of learning and of education.

Freedom vs. Control

And the first of these articles of faith is freedom. "Free the legs, the arms, the larynx of a child," say these advocates of the new education, "and you have taken the first step towards freeing his mind and spirit."

Hence the revolution in school furniture, schedules of work, all the paraphernalia of administration. Fixed seats nailed to the floor, lock-step precision, rigidity, conformity, are disappearing. In their places are coming the informal, intimate atmosphere—the air of happy, cheerful living. Light, movable tables and chairs that may be shoved aside at any time to make room for work or play; children moving freely about, talking with one another, leaving the room to go to other parts of the building relatively at their own discretion. The fixed, elaborate machinery of mass education is being abandoned: large classes; emphasis upon grades; housing in stereotyped, barrack-like buildings; adherence to strict time schedules; the oppressive silence of restraint; the labored compulsion—all the stringent coercion of the old order is passing.

The new freedom reveals itself, therefore, in an easier, more natural group life. At great expense to itself it maintains mere corporal's guards of classes—ten, twelve, fifteen, rarely over twenty pupils—in sharp contrast to the huge regiments of the formal, graded school. Thus the formal question-and-answer recitation is giving way to the free interchange of thought in group conferences and progress through individual work.

Freedom to develop naturally, to be spontaneous, unaffected, and unselfconscious, is, therefore, the first article of faith.

Child Initiative vs. Teacher Initiative

What is this new freedom based upon? Nothing less than the reorientation of the entire school around the child. These schools are child-centered institutions in contrast to the teacher-centered and principal-centered schools of the conventional order. They believe that the ability to govern one's self grows only through the practice of self-government. They have learned wisely the lesson of democracy in the western world; namely, that no people, however potentially able, will learn how to carry on its collective affairs except under freedom to practice self-government. Wherever adult societies have imposed democratic forms of government on a people uneducated in democracy, chaos has resulted. Throughout a century of national history in America our schools have adopted the form and the catch slogans of democracy, but never its true technique.

In this respect, however, another day has come in the new schools. These schools believe that boys and girls should share in their own government, in the planning of the program, in the administering of the curriculum, in conducting the life of the school. In the elementary division of some of these schools, during an informal morning discussion period, children, with the teacher as a wise but inconspicuous adult member of the group, consider together what they are to undertake during the day. The routine needs of the school, as well as the lesson assignments, the planning of excursions and exhibits, and the criticism of reports are taken over by the pupils. This is, indeed, a revolution in educational procedure and stands in sharp contrast to the conventional mode of conducting a school.

The difference in amount of work done by teachers and pupils respectively under these two plans of work—the pupil-initiating plan *vs.* the teacher-initiating plan—is conspicuous. In the formal school of today the teacher still does the thinking, planning, and initiating. Pupils are passive, quiescent, generally uninterested if not actively antagonistic. Learning is at a low ebb, if not at a standstill. In the child-centered school, however, pupils are alive, active, working hard, inventing, organizing, contributing original ideas, assembling materials, carrying out enterprises. As individuals and as social groups pupils grow, and they grow in the capacity to govern themselves, to organize machinery for handling their collective affairs, as well as in individual capacity for creative self-expression. So it is that the true theory of democracy is being put into practice in these new schools.

This centering of responsibility and initiative in the pupil brings into the forefront the child's own needs. His immediate interests are to furnish the starting point of education, according to the new schools. But, even of the most rebellious reformers, few advocate that the entire work of the school be based solely upon these naïve and spontaneous interests of children. However, the last twenty-five years of experimentation have undoubtedly contributed no more revolutionary articles of faith than that involved in this reorientation of the school about the child.

The Active School

Freedom, pupil initiative—therefore, the active school.

Naturally, from the free atmosphere in which pupil initiative plays the chief role it is but a next step to pupil activity. In these free, child-centered schools, therefore, pupils are active—physically active, mentally active, artistically active. There is a large amount of actual physical exertion, of overt bodily movement, of a wide variety of sensory contacts, of the type of energy-release which is ordinarily designated as play. Hence the terms, "activity schools," "play schools," and so on.

Education is to be based on child experience—experience not only in the physical sense but in the intellectual and emotional sense too. Thus do these child-centered schools want experience to be real. They depend as little as possible upon described experience. The wiser among their leaders know, of course, that in the adult world much real experience is abstract, described, vicarious, verbal. Therefore the child who is growing toward adulthood will appropriate to his uses an increasingly larger amount of described experience. In the higher reaches of the school, indeed, many described experiences must be made the very center of educational development. However, as far as possible, and predominantly in the lower years of the child-centered schools, real life is reproduced in physical miniature. Excursions are made into the neighborhood, the community. The scholastic environment is extended outward to include *realia* of a variegated sort, and within the school itself plants, animals, tools, materials, machines, are provided to stimulate activity and to give rise to interests which will require activity in their development. Much free play is permitted for the experiences in self-direction it affords.

Now the most deep-seated tendency in human life is movement, impulse, activity. The new schools, therefore, are experimenting vigorously with this fundamental psychological law—that the basis of all learning is reaction. That they are making a contribution is unquestioned.

In the formal schools the conditions of true growth were exactly reversed. One found outward quiet, orderliness, apparent concentration, little physical movement. Actually, however, this condition was one of restlessness, of much inner activity—a continual mutiny against the aims of the school. The iron rule of the school succeeded only in inhibiting the outward symptoms of inattention. There was fidgeting, uneducative scattering of interest and attention, and little conscious reflection on the matters in hand.

The new schools, with freedom of activity and movement, with apparent lack of concentration, produce nevertheless a much more truly educative absorption. The newer education regards the active child as the truly growing child. Not activity for activity's sake—energy exploding in random movements—but activity which is a growing toward something more mature, a changing for the better. The true criterion of educative activity is prolonged attention and concentrated effort. Such then is the activity which the new education writes into its articles of faith.

Child Interest as the Basis of the New Educational Program

Freedom, not restraint.
Pupil initiative, not teacher initiative.
The active, not the passive, school.
There is a fourth new article of faith—child interest as the orienting center of the school program.

In the formal schools, even in those of today, the program of the child's education is organized about school subjects. Not so in the new schools. We find a new educational vocabulary exponential of a unique educative program. Compare the schedules of the new and the old schools. What a difference! The logically arranged subjects of the past—reading, writing, arithmetic, spelling, geography, history—are replaced by projects, units of work, creative work periods, industrial arts, creative music, story hour, informal group conferences, and other vastly intriguing enterprises.

This curriculum does not look well on paper. It is a chaos of irregular time allotments. School principals might have a difficult time trying to fit the orderly movement of a large school into it. But it does give promise of active learning.

The new school is setting up a program of work which has a personal connection with the immediate life of the child. It starts from his needs and interests. The units of the new program approximate as nearly as possible what to the children are real-life situations. Hence the new school organizes its program around the centers of interest rather than around academic subjects. Wherever school subjects, however, coincide with life needs, then the new centers of interest coincide with the old school subjects; for example, the subjects of reading and creative music, the story hour. But because the formal school subjects were the product of academic research interests, most of them do not coincide with life interests, either of children or of adults. Hence in the new educational order they must go. This new plan of organizing the curriculum around units of pupil activity gives greater promise of wide-spreading, educational achievement for the pupil than does the dry, intellectualized, logical arrangement of subjects-to-be-learned of the old school. It is vitalized by interesting and purposeful activity that has an intimate connection with the child's personal life.

That the new schools are evolving an educational program in which school subjects are rejected in favor of broader and more integrative centers of work is illustrated also in the tendency to organize materials in a few broad departments of knowledge. The old school organized knowledge into many minute, disparate, academic departments. In the upper grades of some of the new schools the initiating center of organization is the interest of the child in some contemporary institution or problem. In the lower grades the focus is the immediate school scene. In the higher grades the emphasis shifts to adult society; in the foreground always stand the fundamental movements or trends, the crucial institutions or problems of contemporary life.

All this does not mean that the new school entirely avoids school subjects, but the subjects in these schools differ materially from those of the formal school. The new-school subjects represent new departmentalizations of knowledge which include a broad view of race experience rather than mere devitalized definitions and long lists of factual enumerations. They are concerned at bottom with big concepts, themes, movements, that explain broad, fundamental phases of human life.

The old school spent its time and energy in drilling pupils into a state of passable efficiency in minimal essentials. The new school treats these minimal essentials, which are largely skills, as by-products of the educative situation. Usually it has succeeded in teaching them much more adequately than the old school, and in less time.

Creative Self-Expression

"I would have a child say not, 'I know,' but, 'I have experienced.' "

Education as conformity *vs.* education as creative self-expression, adaptation and adjustment *vs.* creative experience—these are some of the phrases which are recurring with accumulating momentum in the discussions of the new education.

We find as sharp a contrast in theory between the old and the new at this point in our analysis as in our consideration of other aspects. The spirit of the old school was centered about social adjustment, adaptation to the existing order. The aim of conventional education was social efficiency. Growth was seen as increasing power to conform, to acquiesce to a schooled discipline; maturity was viewed from the standpoint of successful compliance with social demands.

In the new school, however, it is the creative spirit from within that is encouraged, rather than conformity to a pattern imposed from without. The success of the new school has been startling in eliciting self-expression in all of the arts, in discovering a marvelously creative youth. The child as artist, poet, composer, is coming into his own.

This success is due not so much to the changed viewpoint concerning the place of art in education as to the whole new theory of self-expression, the emphasis on the place of creative originality in life. Art in the new school is permitted; in the old it was imposed. The new school assumes that every child is endowed with the capacity to express himself, and that this innate capacity is immensely worth cultivating. The pupil is placed in an atmosphere conducive to self-expression in every aspect. Some will create with words, others with light. Some will express themselves through the body in the dance; others will model, carve, shape their ideas in plastic materials. Still others will find expression through oral language, and some through an integrated physical, emotional, and dramatic gesture. But whatever the route, the medium, the materials—each one has some capacity for expression.

The artist in Everyman's child is being discovered, not only in the unusual, the gifted, the genius; the lid of restraint is being lifted from the child of the common man in order that he may come to his own best self-fulfillment. The new schools are providing "drawing-out" environments in sharp contrast to the "pouring-in" environments of the old.

Art in the new schools is naïve, neo-primitive. The child is permitted to set his own standards as he works. The "masters" are not set out to be worshiped respectfully—they are admired in the frank and critical spirit of intimate companionship. Appreciation of the finished works of genius is best built up, say the new schools, by first encouraging the creative products of the child's own pen, voice, brush. The emphasis is not upon finished work, skill, and technical perfection, but upon the release of the child's creative capacities, upon growth in his power to express his own unique ideas naturally and freely, whatever the medium.

Personality and Social Adjustment

The leaders of our schools are confronted by no more important and overwhelming problem than that of providing an environment by which each child can learn to live with others and yet retain his personal identity. To live with others, learn how to adjust himself to them, and yet grow in the confident knowledge that he, like each of them, is a unique individuality, a rare personality; to live with others and yet grow in the assurance that he too is superior, that he, and he alone, is distinctive in some trait or traits and that he has something unique to contribute to the groups in which he lives. How are the new and the old schools trying to solve this problem?

The old school, with its mass-education machinery, seemed to treat children in social groups, to develop social attitudes, but in reality it sacrificed the individual to mythical group needs. Social contacts during school hours were dominated by an arbitrary authority—the teacher—and had to conform to a rigid formality in order that discipline might be maintained. The old school, therefore, left the child entirely unaided in coping with social situations. Under mass education—hyper-intellectual, hyper-individualistic—with pupils isolated in seats, no opportunity was offered to practice cooperative living except in the undirected out-of-school contacts. The child was not assisted in learning to work effectively with a group at a common interest. A false notion of individuality was erected; namely, that superiority could be asserted only through personal competition. The old school over-emphasized competition because it was a convenient, effective, and inexpensive device for attaining greater effort from pupils. However, it was often used at the cost of successful social living.

The new school, on the other hand, encourages the child to be a distinct personality, an individualist, to believe in his ability—but of course not to an unjustifiable degree. It sets up situations which provide constant practice in cooperative living. It encourages activities in which he can make a personal contribution to group enterprises; in which he has social experiences, graded to fit his level of social development; in which he feels himself an accepted and respected member of a society of which he himself approves.

The new school bridges the gap, therefore, between the development of individuality on the one hand and successful social participation on the other by insisting that the true development of the individual and the fulfillment of personality are best attained as one expresses himself most successfully and adequately *with* others and *toward* others.

How does the new school propose to secure this cooperative endeavor?

It does so by means of a wide variety of group activities. Dramatics which require concerted effort toward a common goal; assemblies through which frequent interchange of mutually interesting ideas takes place; student committees and clubs managing student affairs; miniature social organizations and group games—these are some of the social situations which the new school deliberately encourages. The group dance also is coming into its own as a vehicle for more than rhythmic physical development. Indeed, rhythmics gives promise of usurping the place in the lower school that has formerly been given to competitive athletics. Active experience in grace and physical poise, as an agency for the education of personality of each and every individual, is the aim, rather than development of a few stellar performers with the mass remaining mere passive, untransformed observers.

The new school has no extracurricular activities. These group activities are a regular and important part of school life—they are not a side issue indulged in at the end of the day or week as unrelated recreation or relief from the real business of the school.

Again, where the old school maintained a noisy silence as the ideal schoolroom atmosphere, the new removes the ban from speech, encourages communication as a vehicle for social understanding and personal development. Indeed the new school has gone so far in this respect as to be accused at times of being garrulous. However, it is well known that practice in the free use of language, with guidance, helps to develop qualities desirable for successful social living. Fluent, natural speech is the basis for effective self-expression and mutual understanding.

In ways like these the new school is evolving its informal real-life organization, encouraging common aims and purposes, the interpenetration of minds, producing in the school a life of happy intimacy—creating a "wholesome medium for the most complete living."[7]

NOTES

1. First Yearbook of the Herbart Society for the Scientific Study of Teaching. University of Chicago Press; 1894.
2. Third Yearbook of the National Herbart Society. University of Chicago Press; 1897.
3. Dewey, John. *School and Society*, page 11. University of Chicago Press; 1899.
4. William Heard Kilpatrick (1871–), teacher and principal of public schools of Georgia until 1907; Professor of Mathematics, 1897–1906, Acting President 1903–1905 at Mercer University; Lecturer in Education, 1909–1911, Assistant Professor, 1911–1915, Associate Professor, 1915–1918, Professor Philosophy of Education, from 1918, at Teachers College, Columbia University. Author: *The Dutch Schools of New Netherland and Colonial New York*, 1912; *The Montessori System Examined*, 1914; *Froebel's Kindergarten Principles Critically Examined*, 1916; *Source Book in the Philosophy of Education*, 1923; *Foundations of Method*, 1925; *Education for a Changing Civilization*, 1926; and numerous articles on educational topics.
5. Headquarters, 10 Jackson Place, Washington, D.C.
6. The *New Era*, edited by Beatrice Ensor. 11, Tavistock Square, London, W.C. 1. *Das Werdende Zeitalter*, edited by Dr. Elizabeth Rotten. Kohlgraben, bei Vacha (Rhön), Berlin. *Pour L'ère Nouvelle*, edited by Dr. Adolph Ferrière. Chemin Psechier 10, Geneva.

   There are also Bulgarian, Hungarian, Italian, Spanish, and other editions. The various editions are not translations of each other, each editor being free to fill the special needs of his own readers.
7. Tippett, James S., and Others. *Curriculum Making in an Elementary School*, page 8. Ginn & Co., Boston; 1927.

4.3 BOYD HENRY BODE

Education from a Pragmatic Point of View

Boyd Henry Bode (1873–1953) was a professor of education at Ohio State University. He became highly respected for his accurate interpretations of the educational philosophies of John Dewey, William Heard Kilpatrick, and other "experimentalist" educators of Bode's time. In his important book *How We Learn* (D. C. Heath, 1940), from which the following selection is excerpted, Bode discusses how the education of persons should proceed from a pragmatic philosophical perspective. Bode contrasts the biological-social interpretations of the development of intelligence (or "mind") with the mechanistic theories of human learning (and the measurement thereof) of early behaviorist psychologists and others. He concludes that thought occurs in episodes of communicative experience with other persons living together in the world. "Mind" emerges from these communicative episodes, which suggests that how we learn should be in harmony with how we think. This finding has several implications for how teachers ought to teach.

Key Concept: the "mind" as a function and a result of interactive experience

*I*n approaching the problem of learning, our clue must come from the idea that mind is such a process of "progressively shaping up the environment." This process was illustrated earlier by the example of the pedestrian making his way along a difficult path. He picks and chooses, as we say; which means that a whole field, consisting of environmental relationships and bodily reactions, is in continuous reorganization. This process of reorganization is not, indeed, the same as learning, since no new elements may be involved. The case is different if our pedestrian discovers, as a result of his experience, that clay is slippery, whereas sod or gravel affords a firm footing. He learns about clay, for example, provided that he notes the connection between the appearance of clay and what the clay does to him when he tries to walk on it. To note the connection is to learn something, and the learning takes the form of changing the experience. The clay now *looks* slippery; it has acquired meaning. Such change in an experience whereby it becomes more serviceable for the guidance of behavior is what is meant by learning.

In this illustration learning is an intellectual affair, since it is identified with the perception of significant relationships. This kind of learning naturally occupies a prominent place in formal education. Instruction in golf, for example, is possible because the reason why a beginner "hooks" his drives or fails to get distance can be analyzed out. The significant relationships can be brought to the attention of the learner. Where such analysis is difficult, instruction is correspondingly difficult, as, for example, in teaching a boy how to balance himself on a bicycle, or to wag his ears, or to be at ease in a social gathering. Such accomplishments are also classed as learning, but they are generally acquired by trial and error, and perhaps without any perception of significant relationships. The result may be achieved without any knowledge of how it was done. But, even so, the learning is a process of getting the "feel" of the thing; which is to say that the experience is changed so as to provide better control for behavior.

To what extent relationships are clearly perceived in learning is sometimes open to doubt. If a baby touches a hot stove and thereafter avoids the stove, we are tempted to assume that the baby sees the relationship between "stove" and "hot." It is evident that the experience of being burned changes the infant's response to the stove, and the inference is warranted that there has been a change in his experience of the stove. The precise nature of this change, however, is not so clear. Psychologically there is a vast difference between seeing the stove as "stove-meaning-burn" and seeing it merely as "bad" or "hot." In the former case there is a clear distinction between the object and the thing meant or pointed to; in the latter case the meaning is so completely incorporated that there is no clear distinction. This complete assimilation of the meaning to the thing is exemplified in all cases of simple recognition. Persons seeing a lemon will sometimes "make a face"; they react to the object as sour, but they may not make the distinction which we ordinarily make when we infer that a person broken out with rash has measles or smallpox. That is, we do not distinguish between "thing" and "meaning"; we "recognize" the thing without this internal distinction. Recognition, however, implies a change in the perceived object; a lemon *looks* different after we have had experience with it. Moreover, the lemon thus seen controls behavior in terms of future consequences; we decline, for example, to bite into it. Hence the lemon exercises the function which we have identified with mind. But this is mind in its lowest terms, so to speak; the "sour" is not definitely marked off as something symbolized, or indicated, or pointed to. The function is performed but it is not definitely intellectualized.

In the case of the lemon it is easy enough for the average person to distinguish between "lemon" and its meaning, "sour," if there is occasion to do so. There are many situations, however, where we are unable to draw a satisfactory contrast between "thing" and "meaning." An experienced physician, for example, may "sense" that a patient stands no chance, before he has even started to make a diagnosis; a lawyer may "sense" that there is something crooked about the case that is brought to him, even if it baffles him to find anything wrong. The expert has learned to "size up" situations in advance of tangible evidence. Cases of this kind are not wholly devoid of the contrast between thing and meaning; but they suggest how thing and meaning can run together and blend, and they suggest why we speak of being guided by "intuition." They also suggest the possibility that there are experiences where the *contrast* between "thing" and "meaning" is not present at all. Sometimes the contrast is lacking because it has gradually faded out. The child learns at one stage that the man in uniform *means* letters; later on he simply recognizes the man as the mailman. But there may be other instances when the experience may undergo an adaptive change without the clear intervention of this contrast at any point. This case of the baby and the stove may perhaps be explained either way. . . .

Learning, then, is a term that covers a variety of meanings. Sometimes the emphasis is on the co-ordination that is acquired, as in the case of the batsman who learns to hit the ball safely, or the golfer who learns to correct a fault, without, in either case, knowing how it has been done. All we can say is that there is an improvement in skill, together with a difference in the "feel" of the thing. Then there is the kind of learning in which the emphasis falls on this change in the "feel" or the quality of the experience; as when we learn to judge the speed of an automobile or to distrust certain persons, without being able to specify the clues on which we rely. Lastly, there is the kind of learning which is based on some trait or fact or relationship that can be analyzed out and offered as evidence, as when we infer from the appearance of a lawn that it needs sprinkling or when we abstain from coffee because it keeps us awake at night. The clear perception of relationships is what is sometimes designated as insight.

These differences in kinds of learning derive whatever significance they may have from the fact that they are connected with corresponding differences in the procedure by which they are acquired. They are primarily differences of emphasis. It seems safe to assume, on the one hand, that all learning involves some perception of relationship, however dim, and, on the other hand, that analysis, or insight into relationship, however extensive, never keeps abreast with the adaptive changes in our experience. Mind, as Dewey has told us, is "the power to understand things in terms of the use made of them." Understanding has to do with relationships. This understanding, however, may take various forms. It seems fair to describe the experience of the benighted pike in the tank as an obscure comprehension that the little fish were "to-be-let-alone." Some such quality of "futurity," therefore, inheres in all learning. It is worth noting that the expert who devotes himself to the business of analysis or the picking out of relationships does not thereby diminish the area of his unanalyzed experience. On the contrary, he increases it; he develops a kind of sixth sense or "instinct" or "intuition" which constantly outruns his ability to make clean-cut analyses and which guides him in situations that he cannot handle adequately by analysis. In other words, the expert never gets away from a certain resemblance to the pike. All this is reminiscent of the familiar advice given by an old judge to a young colleague, to the effect that a judge should make his decisions without giving the reasons therefor, because "the decisions are likely to be right, but the reasons are bound to be wrong."

All forms of learning, then, have a common element. They all involve a change in the experiential situation which gives greater control in relation to subsequent behavior. To the boy who has learned to swim, water has become a different medium, to which he responds differently. To the veteran salesman the reactions of his "prospects" when he approaches them take on the same kind of difference. The experiential situation has changed for them as truly as for the automobile mechanic who discovers that the trouble with an automobile is due to a defective carburetor. This change finds expression in the control of behavior, whether or not there is a *specific* reference to the future, in much the same way that the visual perception of a flame as "hot" controls behavior, without any such specific relationship as "flame *means* burn." All learning, then, is a change in experience such as to provide for increased control of behavior.[1]

We can now plot the curve of learning as it ordinarily goes on. It starts on the level of everyday living and it has to do with the changes made in things by our responses. These changes are speeded up and made more extensive by the process of analysis, or insight into relationships—a process in which the relationship of meaning or "pointing" is prominent and which aims to bring new elements into the picture. With familiarity this relationship of pointing drops out; the new elements become increasingly absorbed into the original experiences; recognition takes the place of inference. The experiences as thus modified become the basis for a repetition of the process; and thus experience continues to grow or to become enriched without any assignable limit.

This process of inference giving way to recognition is exemplified rather strikingly by language. When we first start to learn a foreign language, we rely extensively on the relationship, "this means that," (e.g., *cheval* means *horse*). If we reach a point, however, where we can speak and think in terms of the new language, this relationship disappears. The words begin to *look* different and to *sound* different. This change in the quality or *feel* of words takes place in much the same way in the case of our mother tongue. As William James remarks:

> Our own language would sound very different to us if we heard it without understanding, as we hear a foreign tongue. Rises and falls of voice, odd sibilants and other consonants, would fall on our ear in a way of which we can now form no notion. Frenchmen say that English sounds to them like the *gazouillement des oiseaux*—an impression which it certainly make on no native ear. Many of us English would describe the sound of Russian in similar terms. All of us are conscious of the strong inflections of voice and explosives and gutturals of German speech in a way in which no German can be conscious of them.[2]

The inference to be drawn is that the term "meaning" has different applications. In one sense the term denotes the function of pointing or symbolizing. To make a clear contrast between the thing and whatever is pointed to is to "intellectualize" the experience of the thing. When this contrast drops out, the thing is still considered to retain the meaning, but the term meaning is now used in a different sense. It is now a name for a certain quality of the total experience. To use an illustration, we avoid an onrushing automobile, and we ordinarily do so without the help of a specific relationship, such as "automobile means danger." The quality of danger has become a part of the automobile, in the same way as its shape or color; it remains, indeed, just as effective in the control of behavior, but meaning is now better described as "appreciation" rather than "pointing." In the language of Dewey:

> Definiteness, depth, and variety of meaning attach to the objects of an experience just in the degree in which they have been previously thought about, even when present in an experience in which they do not evoke inferential procedures at all. Such terms as "meaning," "significance," "value" have a double sense. Sometimes they mean a function: the office of one thing representing another, or pointing to it as implied; the operation, in short, of serving as a sign. In the word "symbol" this meaning is practically exhaustive. But the terms also sometimes mean an inherent quality, a quality intrinsically characterizing the thing experienced and making it worth while. . . . In the situation which follows upon reflection, meanings are intrinsic; they have no instrumental or subservient office—because they have no office at all. They are as much qualities of the objects in the situation as are red and black, hard and soft, square and round.[3]

If we turn now to the consideration of the implications contained in this general point of view for school procedures, we are at once confronted with what Dewey calls the principle of the continuity of experience. All learning, whether in school or out of school, has to do with the transformation of experience in the interests of better control. In order to bring about this transformation, it is necessary to do something that will produce the desired change. This contradicts the familiar assumption that pupils should go to school in order to draw upon a storehouse of knowledge, in somewhat the same way that a railroad car goes to the mine in order to take on a load of coal. The school, from the present point of view, is simply a place which is especially designed to facilitate the business of securing the desired transformation of experience. It is a place where new experiences are provided in such a form as to best promote that reconstruction or reorganization of experience which is identified with education.

All this is but another way of saying that the school, ideally, is a place where pupils go in order to carry on certain activities, from which certain reconstructions or reorganizations of experience are expected to result. This emphasis on activities explains why *interest* occupies so prominent a place in the picture. It also explains the prominence given to "activity" programs, especially on the lower levels. For city children in particular the necessity of enabling them to get their hands on things is obvious, if we proceed on the theory that the character or quality of our experiences is determined by our responses. The principle involved here is not limited to the dealings of pupils with material objects. In this modern age the environment that is inescapably with us all the time is the social environment, and this environment, like the material environment, is all of one piece with our responses. We learn to recognize rights and duties, we learn to admire and to disapprove, we learn to recognize some things as complimentary and others as insulting, we learn to give support or co-operation in some situations and to withhold it in others. We learn, in brief, to act like social beings, according to our lights; and this learning, like all learning, relates to behavior. Social behavior must be so fashioned as to result in desirable insights and appreciations and habits. In other words, the school must provide for experiences in social relationships as well as for experiences with material things. The school should be the living embodiment of our highest ideal of social relationships.

School experiences, in brief, should be of such a kind as to widen and enrich and give greater meaning to life as it goes on in the out-of-school environment. To some degree this enrichment of experience goes on anyhow, whether a person goes to school or not. Learning does not normally come to a dead stop under any circumstances. Some circumstances, however, are more favorable than others, and even the most favorable circumstances in the out-of-school environment do not forward the business of learning as much as the conditions of modern life make necessary or desirable. A person who does not go to school, for example, is likely to pick up some of the elements of arithmetic and he may even acquire a certain acquaintance with a few printed words, but ordinarily such a person is listed in the census as illiterate. Hence the school is designed as a special made-to-order environment, so devised or organized that the activities which are carried on in it will do what the life outside does not do. The same applies to social relationships. The life of the school is designed to promote such attitudes as consideration for others, a sense of responsibility for the common good, respect for personal property, co-operation involving discussion and free give and take—in a word, the basic attitudes which in the outside world are all too frequently neglected or at best cultivated in a haphazard fashion.

The general idea back of all this is that the school, in making itself a special environment, must avoid the danger of separating itself from the life outside. An outstanding weakness of the traditional school has been that it devoted itself to matters which, from the standpoint of the pupil, bore no discernible relation to anything outside the school. This tendency was due, in large measure, to a misconception of the nature of learning. When schooling is regarded as a process of absorbing the funded knowledge of the past, or, in poetic phrase, "drinking at the fountain of learning," the connection of learning with living is left to chance. On the other hand, the theory that learning is a matter of reconstructing experience in the interests of better adaptation creates an insistence that the principle of the continuity of experience must be respected at all times. The application of this principle has led to a certain emphasis on incidental learning, to reliance on the project method, to studies of community life, and the like, so as to protect the organic continuity between the school and the larger life surrounding the school.

The difference in point of view regarding the nature of learning traces back, of course, to differences in the conception of mind. Dualism has tended to separate intellectual insight from both skill and appreciations, and to separate these latter from each other. The result has been a tendency to cultivate each of them in isolation from the others. Mathematics, for example, has to do with thinking; reading, spelling, etc., have to do with skills; poetry has to do with appreciation, and so on.[4] On the other hand, if we stress reconstruction of experience, in accordance with the conception of the "field" theory, it becomes apparent at once that such separation is essentially artificial. Thinking, appreciation, skill, and information are intimately interrelated. Thinking has to do with the removal of obstacles, and this involves an element of concern or value; else why take the trouble to think at all? The successful culmination of thinking has an attendant esthetic quality, as when we speak in mathematics of a "beautiful demonstration." Thinking, moreover, involves the gathering of data for the testing of hypotheses, which in turn is related both to the acquisition of information and to the development of skills or techniques in observation, in analysis, and in the organization of material. The point is that learning is neither a matter of developing faculties nor of forming apperceptive masses according to a fixed procedure. If we keep our eye on the fact that learning is a reconstruction of experience, which is a distinctive thing in the case of each individual pupil, we avoid the danger of mechanizing the learning process. Learning as reconstruction combines thinking, skill, information, and appreciation in a single unitary process, and it is characterized by flexibility, since it must constantly adapt itself to the circumstances of the situation.

This flexibility is exemplified in the newer conception of habit formation. In the past habits were commonly supposed to have a certain rigidity, as is required by the reflex-arc concept and the notion of the "stamping in" of S–R [stimulus–response] bonds. If the "field" theory is to be trusted, the reflex-arc concept is an oversimplification of the facts of behavior. The evidence indicates that even the simplest behavior involves a reorganization of some range, i.e., that there is no such thing as exact repetition. If so, it follows that the ordinary notion of habit-formation must be revised. The essence of habit-formation is not repetition but smoothness of co-ordination. Learning to play golf, for example, is pretty much a matter of acquiring such co-ordination. The feet must be placed in a certain way, there must be a certain grip on the club, the body must move with a certain rhythm, the swing must follow through, and the eye must be kept on the ball. Taken separately the elements that enter into the total response are, for the most part, simple enough; it is the co-ordination of them that requires laborious practice. This co-ordination is a flexible thing, which can be adapted to various exigencies as they occur. In a similar way experience gives to the salesman, the teacher, the diner-out, a certain facility or resourcefulness in dealing with situations which is wholly mysterious if we think of habits as consisting of fixed connections, but which may be described as ease and flexibility of co-ordination. But if we describe habit in such terms, then habit is significant only in connection with the ends or purposes by which the co-ordinations are directed or controlled. Habit-formation must be linked up with learning as a process of reorganizing or reconstructing experience in a certain way, which means that the relation to ends must be constantly kept in view.

The central fact is that all normal behavior is controlled by ends, in some sense and to some extent. Our experiences change willy-nilly, and they change in ways that make for better adaptation. The infant that has been scratched by the cat is bound to see the cat differently from that moment on; a new relationship of "scratching" has been introduced; the infant's experience of the cat has been "reorganized." Frequently, however, the process of reorganization is more complicated. It may not be evident what the thing or the situation *means* or points to; and so it is necessary to have recourse to guessing or hypothesizing; after which prudence suggests that the guess should be verified or tested before we proceed to act on it. This whole process is called thinking, which may be defined most simply as the finding and testing of meanings. The great difference between the world of the civilized man and the world of the savage is the difference that is made by thinking. To the astronomer the comet in the sky is composed of certain materials; it travels at a certain rate and in accordance with the law of gravitation; to the savage it is an embodiment of fantastic superstitions and fears. The same kind of difference exists in other fields. It is clear, therefore, that the cultivation of effective thinking is a major responsibility of the schools. In terms of pragmatic theory, this thinking must relate itself at all times to the reconstruction of experience; the problems dealt with must be "real" problems in the sense that they present difficulties in the experience of the pupil which are of concern to him in the interests of better adaptation. "The sole direct path to enduring improvement in the methods of instruction and learning consists in centering upon the conditions which exact, promote, and test thinking. Thinking *is* the method of intelligent learning, of learning that employs and rewards mind."[5]

To summarize, the distinctive features of this theory of learning all flow from what Dewey calls the continuity of experience. According to this principle of continuity school experiences are educative only in so far as they serve to modify or "reconstruct" the background of experience which the pupil brings with him when he comes to school. This reconstruction goes on in any case, but our chief reliance in this connection is on thinking. A school operating on the basis of this theory will protect the continuity of the school with the life outside of the school and it will provide various kinds of experiences, both with things and with social relations, so as to serve the overarching purpose of reconstruction. On the negative side it will avoid the fallacies of faculty psychology and rote learning and mechanistic conceptions of habit-formation; on the positive side it will stress insight and the practice of thinking which is required if these insights are to serve the purpose of giving our experience a new quality and a deeper meaning.

NOTES

1. "We thus reach a technical definition of education: It is that reconstruction or reorganization of experience which adds to the meaning of experience, and which increases the ability to direct the course of subsequent experience." J. Dewey, *Democracy and Education*, p. 89.
2. W. James, *Principles of Psychology*, Vol. II, p. 80.
3. J. Dewey, *Essays in Experimental Logic*, pp. 16, 17.
4. J. Dewey, *Democracy and Education*, Chap. XII.
5. J. Dewey, *Democracy and Education*, p. 179.

CHAPTER 5 Curriculum Theory and Practice

5.1 HILDA TABA

Current Conceptions of the Function of the School

Hilda Taba (1902–1967) was a major influence on curriculum theory and practice during her career in teacher education. Strongly grounded in educational theory and philosophy, Taba committed herself to working in schools and observing relations among students and teachers. She conducted pioneering longitudinal research studies on human relations in school settings, and she wrote books and guides on improving intergroup understanding in schools. Her work laid a solid foundation in curriculum theory and development for what would later be called multicultural education.

The selection that follows is from Taba's *Curriculum Development: Theory and Practice* (Harcourt, Brace & World, 1962), which was heavily cited by the United States Commission on Civil Rights in its 1975 report *A Better Chance to Learn*. Taba believed that it is important to understand the social context of education and the cultural forces that impact those who create school curricula. Here she provides a synthesis of the leading theories of her time on the roles that schools play in human cultures.

Key Concept: schools and society

*S*ociety's concept of the function of the public school determines to a great extent what kind of curriculum schools will have. Yet, in a complex culture with a pluralistic value system, it is difficult to establish a single central function for any agency. In a democratic society these formulations are further complicated by the fact that different layers of society participate in the process of determining what education in general and public schools specifically should be and do. It is, therefore, more difficult to determine the central function of schools in a democracy than in a totalitarian society where a small power group decides both what society should be and what role schools shall play in it.

Our society today has by no means agreed about what the central function of the school should be. One could even say that "the great debate about schools and their function" is in effect a debate about many of the issues our society faces: the balance between freedom and control and between change and tradition, whether the elite should be of power or of intellect, who should participate in shaping the public policy, and many others. It is generally agreed that the main outlines of the "crisis in education" are shaped and complicated by the convergence of two phenomena: the transformative effects of science and technology on society and the emergence of Communist totalitarianism as an expanding imperialist power. In the light of this setting the examination of the functions of the public school is highly pertinent, but extremely difficult, because the issues tend to be confused and the viewpoints somewhat less than objective.

Whatever the specific viewpoints regarding the functions of the public schools, there seems to be little disagreement about the importance of the role of education. American society has always expected a great deal of education and, in Walter Lippmann's phrase, has expressed great faith in it as the "life-giving principle of national power." Historically the American people have assumed that education has the power to reduce poverty and distress, to prevent child delinquency and crime, and to promote the well-being of the individual, the intelligent use of suffrage, and the welfare and stability of the state. Indeed, even today education, if not the public school, is considered an antidote against evils in the minds of men and an ally in achieving all good causes. The very attacks on the schools express the faith of the American public that the schools matter because of their influence not only on individuals, but on society as well. Some critics, for example, seem to reason that the strength of our current enemies is the *result* of *their* education and, correspondingly, that the weakness in our position is the *fault* of *our* education.

These high expectations and the naive faith in the power of education are at once a curse and a blessing. No doubt they have given American education a certain vigor by insisting that it respond to social ideologies and needs. They have also made it more subject to passing hysterias and changing moods of the public than may have been good for a healthy development. Anyone tracing the various "trends" in curriculum development in the United States will note a zigzag movement in which one "trend" swallows and annihilates the preceding one with an almost unbelievable discontinuity in theoretical thought. When education is overly sensitive to public opinion, changes are bound to be made thoughtlessly. Continuity in capitalizing on past achievements is jeopardized in the heat of hastily formulated reforms and changes. It is no wonder, then, that in periods of crisis the question of the central function of schools in society becomes a subject of heated controversy, with the nature of the relationships of education to society at the very core of that controversy. It is no wonder also that there are many variations in the conceptions of what the essential function of the public school is.

There is relatively little disagreement also about the idea that schools function on behalf of the culture in which they exist. The school is created by a society for the purpose of reproducing in the learner the knowledge, attitudes, values, and techniques that have cultural relevancy or currency. There is generally also no quarrel with the idea that of the many educative agencies of society, the school is the one which specializes in inducting youth into the culture and is thus responsible for the continuity of that culture.

However, opinion is divided about the precise nature of this function. The differences range from conceptions which assume a strong cultural determination of everything schools do and should do to postulations about ideals of individual development which are quite independent of cultural norms. This division of opinion extends also to views on the extent to which the program of the school is or should be subject to the values and norms of the culture, and in what measure the materials it uses and the ideologies that control its shaping should be drawn from the life of the culture. While in all concepts it is accepted that schools must transmit culture, there are sharp differences about what should be transmitted and the manner in which it is to be done. Some conceptions emphasize education as an agent of change, while others stress its preserving functions.

Sometimes, especially in theoretical discussions, these divisions of views appear as rather stark and even unrealistic alternatives. Speaking of the function of general education, Conant states one such alternative neatly:

> Roughly speaking, the basic argument about general education turns on the degree to which the literary and philosophical traditions of the western world, as interpreted by scholars and connoisseurs before World War I, should be the basis of the education of *all* American youth. The watershed between two fundamentally opposed positions can be located by raising the question: For what purpose do we have a system of public education? If the answer is to develop effective citizens of a free democratic country, then we seem to be facing in one direction. If the answer is to develop the student's rational powers and immerse him in the stream of our cultural heritage, then we appear to be facing in the opposite direction. By and large, the first position represents the modern approach to education; the latter the more conventional view. Those who look down one valley regard conventional "book learning" as only one element in the landscape; those who look down the other believe that developing the "life of the mind" is the primary aim of civilization and this can be accomplished only by steeping youth in our literary and philosophical heritage.

All the same, the overlappings in these conceptions are too great to make possible a refined classification of concepts of the function of education. . . .

EDUCATION AS PRESERVER AND TRANSMITTER
OF THE CULTURAL HERITAGE

One group of theorists stresses the preserving function of education: the preserving of the cultural heritage, especially that of the Western culture. This group argues that since all cultural traditions have roots, cultural continuity is possible only if education preserves this heritage by passing on the truths worked out in the past to the new generation, thus developing a common cultural background and loyalties. The specific ideas regarding what this heritage consists of are not always clear. In the main the transmission of the accumulated wisdom of the race and of basic truths and values is emphasized.

The Harvard Report on General Education is one example of an emphasis on the importance of preserving tradition and maintaining roots from the past. This report argues that education can develop a unifying purpose and idea only as it develops this sense of heritage, which in turn requires a common ground in training and outlook. This heritage is basic to education because it uses the past to clarify or even to determine what is important in the present. The report points out that it is the function of education to pass on the *inherited* (italics mine) view of man and society, and that its main task is to perpetuate such ideas as the dignity of man and common beliefs in what is good. "Classical antiquity handed on a working system of truths which relied on both reason and experience and was designed to provide a norm for civilized life." It is the business of education to instill a commitment to these truths.

This assertion of the necessity for imparting the common heritage is, however, modified by a certain recognition of the role of new experience and change. The report attempts to reconcile the necessity for common belief with the equally obvious necessity for new and independent insight by pointing out that a certain tough-mindedness in reaching conclusions by scientific methods of thought, a curiosity, and a readiness for change are also necessary; that education cannot be wholly devoted to the commitment to tradition or to the view that means are valuable apart from ideals; that it upholds at the same time the tradition and the experiment, the ideal and the means, and, like our culture itself, change within the commitment. While the report makes a bow to experiment and change, it seems to say that the basic ideals of what constitutes a good man in our society come from tradition. In other words, since the modern society is only an extension of the traditional one, changes will come from applying the ancient truths to the modern scene. Because the common heritage is a way of building unity in culture, and since the classical tradition has handed down a norm for civilized life, the task of education is to "shape the student" to "receive" this ideal.

This preserving or conserving function of education is still more strongly accentuated by a group of theorists philosophically classified as rational humanists and classicists. Their conception of the function of education is intimately bound up with and derived from their conception of human nature, which has as its major premise that the essence of human nature is its rational character. Rationality is a common characteristic of all men, apart and independent of the culture in which they exist. The world can be understood by the exercise of this faculty of rationality. Therefore, the chief function of education is to develop this rationality, and the understanding of the eternal truths revealed by these rational faculties. "Education, if it is rightly understood, is the cultivation of the intellect. Only this is what belongs to man as man, and his individuality is only his caprice, self-will, and unique propensities."

Being preoccupied with the essence of things, this viewpoint also insists that learning should be concerned with *essentials,* that is, the first principles articulated in the great books and the classical tradition. Since rationality is essential, the subjects of greatest rational content should also have priority in the curriculum. These subjects are the liberal arts and, among the liberal arts, the humanities.

This viewpoint does not deny that societies differ, that education must train citizens for its own society, or that problems of societies vary. However, it insists that these differences are ephemeral and idiosyncratic and that these problems must be understood and interpreted in the light of the universal eternal truths embodied in the classical literature of great books. Such truths are our main cultural heritage, which education must transmit. They constitute the liberalizing education. Further, liberalizing education is the same everywhere, because "truth" is the same everywhere. Thus is set the case not only for the preserving function of education, but also for the requirements for "essentials" and for the uniformity of curriculum.

A rejection of technical subjects and of vocational education of any sort as a narrowing influence is the logical consequence of this viewpoint. That type of "education" is considered to be not education, but training. It is an uncalled-for "encroachment" on the essential task of liberal education.

While this view of the function of education was originally put forth in reference to college education, recently the same orientation has been applied to criticism of and proposals for the public-school curriculum by a group organized around the concept of basic education. This group insists also that the transmission of cultural heritage is the chief function of public schools. This heritage is defined by stress on three points, each of which has consequences on what may be proposed for the curriculum.

First, a strong case is made for intellectual development as the distinctive function of public schools. As defined by Bestor this intellectual development must stress the understanding of principles and the ability to handle and to apply complex ideas, to make use of a wide range of accurate knowledge, and to command the means of effective communication. No one would quarrel with this definition. But there is reason to quarrel with another assumption Bestor makes—namely, that because education has been extended to classes and groups which have hitherto been deprived of it, any "weakness" in intellectual training creates a void into which steps anti-intellectualism. In order to prevent this from happening, the case for this intellectual purpose of the school must be made so clear that the anti-intellectual masses cannot distort it.

Second, this type of intellectual training is possible only by centering the educational effort on basic skills and disciplines: reading, writing, and arithmetic on the lower level, and logic, history, philosophy, mathematics, science, art, and philosophy on the higher levels. These lead the hierarchy of subjects, or the "basics" of education. The assumption that there is a hierarchy of subjects according to "their power to enhance intellectual development" and that the traditional liberal arts subjects are at the top of that hierarchy runs through most of the writings of the basic educators.

This belief that certain subjects are superior to others as means for intellectual training is made perfectly clear by Clifton Fadiman, who argues that since the cultural tradition includes many more things than can be handled in schools "without running into chaos," men in the past have imposed on cultural tradition a form and a hierarchy which is constituted into the disciplines of liberal arts, as encompassed in a New York City public school he attended. . . .

The third characteristic of "basic education" is a complete rejection of certain current functions of the schools, among them education for democratic citizenship, for moral values, and for ability to deal with social problems, and the concern for the "whole child" or any form of "life adjustment," including education for vocations. These functions put basic educators in an especially aggressive and combative mood. According to Bestor, modern education suffers from an enormous extension of functions which schools have no business in assuming: In this extension there is peril to basic education and to the development of intelligence. This extension also unnecessarily pre-empts the functions of other agencies. Thus, job training is the problem of industry. Training in cultural traits, mores, and the ethical systems belongs to the family and the church. Neither should the school be concerned about "social conditioning," partly because it works against tremendous odds and therefore is ineffectual, partly because the socialization of the individual is the very means of squelching the creativity and independence of the intellect. A thoughtless transfer of functions from one agency to another only creates problems; this transfer should be resisted, even though pressures exist for it.

In other words, basic education is a case against any goals for schools beyond those for intellectual development, for a return to the pure form of disciplines as defined by classical tradition, and for limiting general education to those who show a certain level of intellectual promise.

There are, of course, many criticisms of and questions about this definition of the function of the public school. One criticism pertains to the validity of the assumption that, since men are rational and truth is everywhere the same, education everywhere must be uniformly addressed to these truths and to the exclusive task of developing the rational powers. The recent explosion of knowledge seems to have disestablished many truths that were considered perennial. Rational powers seems to be interlocked with cultural conditions and personal factors in a way that forces reinterpretation of ancient truths. "Ancient truths" are not always applicable to the realities and the needs of modern society except in a sense so general as to be unachievable short of a lifetime of study. Further, modern social analysis seems to indicate a greater break with tradition than any of the basic educators are willing to admit, and therefore the transmission of outdated wisdom might even be dangerous. It seems more likely that society today needs to create its own image of the true, the beautiful, and the just.

It is questionable also whether intellectual development can take place effectively in such a grand isolation from the cultural milieu as the advocates of this viewpoint seem to assume. This assumption contradicts the tenor of many studies which point to the relationship between the development of an individual and his cultural milieu. Further, while there is a general agreement about the central importance of intellectual development, the weight of recent knowledge about learning points to the fact that intellectuality cannot be neatly separated from other aspects of personality development without the danger of cultivating an academic intellectuality instead of a functioning intelligence.

Finally, the argument for the purified liberal arts disciplines as a sole way to wisdom is strongly contradicted by the very developments in these disciplines. Often so-called practical application of what is known becomes the very mainspring of theory, or "pure" thought.

EDUCATION AS AN INSTRUMENT FOR TRANSFORMING CULTURE

An opposing view is held by many educators and social analysts who maintain, in effect, that education can and does play a creative role in modifying and even reshaping the culture in which it functions, that education and public policy are intimately related, and that progress in one is limited without progress in the other. They maintain that education must deal with the needs of current culture and even help to shape the future.

The idea that education has a constructive role to play in shaping the society has deep roots in American tradition. It is implicitly expressed in the general public faith in the power of education to deal with problems of culture. It is also articulated in much of educational writing over a long period of time. Horace Mann underscored the integral relationship between popular education and social problems, such as freedom and the republican government. This theme resounds through his twelve reports: "A nation cannot long remain ignorant and free. No political structure, however artfully devised, can inherently guarantee the rights and liberties of citizens, for freedom can be secure only as knowledge is widely distributed among the populace." Facing the social reality of the times, the public discord of a nation not yet unified, and "Fearing the destructive possibilities of religious, political and class discord," he sought a common value system which might undergird American republicanism and within which a healthy diversity might thrive. His quest was for *public philosophy,* a sense of community which might be shared by Americans of every variety and persuasion. His effort was to use education to fashion a new American character out of a maze of conflicting cultural traditions. And his tool was the *Common School.* The common school for him was the instrument for his limitless faith in the perfectibility of human life and institutions. In this sense, then, Horace Mann regarded education as an arm of public policy and an instrument for dealing with the problems facing the nation at that time.

A flowering of the idea that education is a social process, the primary and most effective instrument of social reconstruction, came with the work and writings of Dewey and his followers. The main thesis of this group was that the school is not merely a residual institution to maintain things as they are: education has a creative function to play in the shaping of individuals and through them in the shaping of the culture. Dewey consistently saw the function of the school in both psychological and social terms. As early as 1897 he wrote:

> I believe that: all education proceeds by the participation of the individuals in the social consciousness of the race. This process ... is continually shaping the individual's powers, saturating his consciousness, forming his habits, training his ideas, and arousing his feelings and emotions. ... The most formal and technical education in the world cannot safely depart from this general process. ... This educational process has two sides—one psychological, and one sociological and ... neither can be subordinated to the other, or neglected, without evil consequences ... knowledge of social conditions of the present state of civilization is necessary in order to properly interpret the child's powers ... and that the school is primarily a social institution.

In subsequent development one fork of this dual orientation of Dewey on the function of education matured into an elaboration of the social responsibilities of the school, while the other centered more emphatically on individual development.

Dewey's concept of democracy was that of an intentionally progressive society, committed to change, organized as intelligently and as scientifically as possible. The role of education in such a society is to inculcate the habits that would make it possible for individuals to control their surroundings rather than merely to submit to them. A progressive society would "endeavor to shape the experience of the young so that instead of reproducing current habits, better habits shall be formed, and thus the future adult society be an improvement on their own. ... We are doubtless far from realizing the potential efficacy of education as a constructive agency of improving society, from realizing that it represents not only a development of children and youth but also of the future society of which they will be the constituents."

This viewpoint dictated priorities for curriculum. Dewey was concerned that essentials be placed first and refinements second, but he defined as essentials the things which are most fundamental socially, which have to do with experience shared by the widest groups. He was also deeply critical of the dualism between culture and vocation and concerned with the effects on democracy of a scheme of education in which there is a narrow utilitarian education for one class of people and a broad liberal education for another. In addition to insisting on the cultivation of the "method of intelligence" and of scientific inquiry as the first tasks of the curriculum, he also stressed the necessity of introducing vocational subjects not merely to build utilitarian skills but as "points of departure" for increasingly intellectualized ventures into the life and meaning of industrial society.

The subsequent elaborations of the social function of the school took on several different shadings, which ranged from emphasis on changing society by changing individuals to stress on planned reconstruction of the social system.

Some of the elaborations stress primarily the responsibility of the school to meet current social needs. The deeper interpretation of this responsibility involves shaping the school program according to a long-term perspective on the realities of the changing society, and an adequate study of a whole range of social needs. A shallower interpretation makes demands on the school on behalf of immediate difficulties and problems. The current insistence on redoubled study of mathematics and physical science, growing in part out of the "somewhat adolescent feeling of national humiliation" at Soviet advances in missile technology and in part out of temporary anxieties regarding manpower needs in these fields, illustrates the shallow perspective.

Others see the social function of education as one of promoting a critical orientation toward the current scene. This interpretation has led to an emphasis on problem solving in the social sciences and to the introduction of problem courses. An emphasis on an understanding of the social forces that generate cultural lag and dislocation is part of this orientation. Some educators interpret the social function of education chiefly as an instrument for social change, either through gradual reform by reshaping the outlook of the oncoming generation or through planned effort at reconstruction.

But whatever the variations in concepts of the social functions of education, certain fundamental ideas tend to run through all. One is the understanding that education must, and usually does, work in the cultural setting of a given society, at a given time, in a given place, shaping the individual in some measure to participate in that society. All decisions about education, including those about curriculum, are made within the context of a society. The values and forces of that society determine not only what manner of man exists but also to some extent what manner of man is needed. The decision-makers themselves are immersed in the culture and therefore subject to the culturally conditioned conceptions of how education is to serve that society. As Childs puts it, the schools are doubly social in nature. They are the arm instituted by society for the education of the young. But the very materials which constitute the program of the school are also drawn from the life of that society.

This concept means that not only is intellectual training to be directed to understanding the forces of the culture and to mastering the intellectual tools necessary for that understanding, but also that there is a fundamental responsibility for training in the culture's essential values and loyalties. In this view, then, social cohesion depends not so much on transmission of the common knowledge as the sharing of common values and concerns.

A second important element in these concepts is the profound appreciation of the fact of change in modern culture and of the meaning of social change. If the society and the culture are changing, then it is the task of schools to play a constructive role in that change. Education must adjust its aims and program to changing conditions, and, if possible, foreshadow them, especially under the conditions of rapid change introduced by modern technology. Without a continual reorientation to changing conditions, education becomes unreal and in a sense useless because it does not prepare youth for life's problems and responsibilities. To meet changing conditions means, of course, that both the aims of education and the programs devised to implement these aims, including the orientation brought to bear on materials used, must be changed also. It is of central importance to use critical intelligence (not intellectuality as described in the preceding section) and scientific attitudes in understanding and solving human and social problems. These qualities of mind can be cultivated to the extent that the "subject matter" of education is significant to the ongoing experience and concerns of the culture, and that experience is used as the key for giving meaning to knowledge and for translating subject matter into behavior and action.

The third important element of this concept is the idea that education is a moral undertaking. It begins and ends with value decisions. Educational decisions, whether regarding aims or curricular selections, always involve value judgments. For this reason education always will involve an element of prescription. Although scientific inquiry will determine what is, it will not prescribe what should be. Education is a moral enterprise also in that it selects which parts of the culture, what wisdom, which values, what ideals to transmit. No school in any society can be completely neutral; the difference lies in whether the basis for selection is made clear and whether the selection is made with some degree of rational method and scientific inquiry.

The concept of education as a reconstruction of society goes further than any of the above. The proponents of this view speak of education as management and control of social change and as social engineering, and of educators as statesmen. The idea that education should not only foster changes in society but should change the very social order was first expressed by Counts. It was later reiterated in *The Educational Frontier*, the thesis of which was that the task of education is "to prepare individuals to take part intelligently in the management of conditions under which they live, to bring them to an understanding of the forces which are moving, to equip them with the intellectual tools by which they can themselves enter into the direction of these forces." To implement such an education it would be necessary to launch a massive adult program that would build political and educational support for a radically different school curriculum, to develop a public which is education conscious and wise in the realities of industrial civilization, to reorient professional education, and to alert teachers to the pressing social issues of the day.

More recently a group of educators who call themselves the "reconstructionists" have argued in a similar vein and with the same sense of urgency about the social mission of education. In analyzing the orientation needed for developing a curriculum theory, B. Othanel Smith concludes by observing: "It is clear that the time for building a comprehensive social perspective is here. We are now living in a time when we can no longer depend upon custom and unconscious control to regulate our social existence. There is no longer any substitute for human management of the vast social machine. As a people we have much knowledge of and techniques for social engineering. The question is: can we learn to use it rapidly enough to control the social machine before it either enslaves us or destroys us?"

The main theses of the reconstructionist position are somewhat as follows: the transformation of society by technological and scientific revolution is so radical as to require a new moral and intellectual consensus capable of molding and directing this transformation. It is the task of educators to analyze the social trends, to discern the problems society is facing, to speculate on the consequences of the current social dynamics, and to project the values and the goals which need to be sought to maintain a democratic way of life. Because social changes today are rapid and radical, and because there are blind consequences to the technological revolution which seem to endanger the democratic way of life, tradition is a poor guide. A continuous critical reexamination of the meaning of the democratic way of life under the altered social conditions is needed. Critical examination and reconstruction of the cultural heritage—or social ideas, beliefs, and institutions—in the light of current problems and conditions, rather than inculcation of traditional ideas, must constitute the core of the educational program of today. In addition, educators must be statesmen, and in cooperation with other agencies must study and discuss the implication of the new "intellectual and moral order" for the "institutional structure of society."

In this scheme a rather exalted role is allotted to education and the schools. Educators must take close account of social forces, of the social institutions, and of their educative effects. They must translate this knowledge of culture and society into "educational policy," that is, a curriculum which will aid students in understanding these forces and in developing the techniques and attitudes necessary for participation in democratic reconstruction. The total educative impact of the school must encompass and coordinate changes in beliefs, personality structures, and social arrangements. Educators must carry the rest of the community to an agreement with their proposals. Curriculum planning needs to focus on building "social goals" and a "common social orientation." Individual goals and diverse group goals must be integrated into a system of social ends. Curriculum development in this sense becomes a way of making public policy.

The capacity of education in general and of public schools in particular to assume a leading role in changing the society and particularly the social structure has been seriously questioned. To sociologists concerned with the relationship of school and society it seems altogether unrealistic for schools to be animated by goals which differ radically from those of the culture in which they work. They point out that usually the aims of education are conservative—that is, they are consonant with the conceptions of the ideal adult which society wishes to produce—and educational institutions can pursue only those aims that society considers desirable. Historically, the aims of education have shifted, but these shifts have followed, not preceded, the changes in society's ideals of a desirable adult. It is therefore somewhat utopian to think of education as a means for a radical reconstruction of society, such as a new social order.

Other critics suggest, in addition, that it is easy to exaggerate both the actual and the potential ability of any formal institution, including the schools, to contribute to consensus in society, whether the means to achieve this consensus be the formation of basic personality or inculcation of a common set of values. This is especially so in industrial societies with their mass patterns of educational service, in which instruction looms larger than education, and in school settings in which it is impossible except under extreme conditions either to isolate or to exclude from its personnel those groups who do not share the dominant goals of the institution. It is possible, of course, that the sociologists and other critics may because of their own limited insight into the dynamics of the educational process underestimate what schools can do. The conditions under which creative educational aims can be conceived and implemented might well form the subject of further serious study and research.

5.2 HARRY S. BROUDY, B. OTHANEL SMITH, AND JOE R. BURNETT

Reassessment of the Uses of Schooling

Harry S. Broudy, B. Othanel Smith, and Joe R. Burnett all taught at the University of Illinois, and they were all prominent philosophers of education and curriculum theorists. The selection that follows is from chapter 3, "Reassessment of the Uses of Schooling," of Broudy, Smith, and Burnett's *Democracy and Excellence in American Secondary Education: A Study in Curriculum Theory* (Rand McNally, 1964). In it, the authors take a close look at what the functions of schooling really are as part of their effort to develop a national curriculum for American secondary education that would "connect life outcomes with schooling." In reassessing the uses of schooling, the authors identify and discuss four typical uses of knowledge gained in schools: associative, replicative, applicative, and interpretive. They then relate this discussion to the goal of developing critical thinking skills as an important objective for American secondary schools.

The scholars of the mid-1960s witnessed and reflected on the fierce national debate over the quality of American public school education, which had been raging since the late 1950s. Broudy, Smith, and Burnett developed a proposal for reforming American secondary education that was intended to counter more conservative proposals. The controversy continued; educators in the 1980s experienced another decade of fierce national debate over the level of excellence in American education, partly sparked by the publication of the June 1983 report *A Nation at Risk* by President Ronald Reagan's Commission on Excellence in Education. This debate is not yet resolved; competing alternative conceptions of excellence in education recommend contradictory agendas for American education today.

Key Concept: connecting life outcomes with schooling

Characteristic of educational literature is a dutiful listing of goals, objectives, and outcomes. Common sense tells us that a purposive enterprise such as education ought to map out its destination before undertaking its journey. What common sense sometimes overlooks is that maps can be of varying degrees of detail and size. Life maps are large, covering a long span of years. The destination of a lifetime is not a single location, but rather a whole area of experience to be traversed by a number of routes. It is to this broad area or region that one refers when speaking of the aim of life as growth, self-realization, and the like.

A school, on the other hand, can be compared to a small segment of the life map with fairly definite routes over relatively short distances. To be sure, these segments *should* lead to more remote destinations, and one designs them so that they will feed into many life goals. Nevertheless, the school must in the first instance be judged by how well it achieves the outcomes that make it a distinctive social institution. That a man ends his career as a forger in the penitentiary does not disqualify handwriting as a proper school outcome.

In trying to devise a curriculum that will connect life outcomes with schooling, several different approaches are possible. For example, it was fashionable in the twenties to make the connection by noting the skills, knowledge, and attitudes a person would need to hold a certain type of job. Later, one heard a good deal about a curriculum that would prepare the individual to carry out certain developmental tasks such as family membership, emotional maturity, vocational competence, and so on.

Such analyses tended to result in long lists of specific informational items, skills, principles, and attitudes. Does an auto mechanic, for example, need the same cluster of attitudes, skills, and knowledge as a dairy farmer? If not, then different lists must be made for auto mechanics and dairy farmers. And should they be the same for mechanics A and B? If this approach were to be followed to its logical end, all hope for common education would have to be abandoned, and, in practice, the schools, especially those which could afford a rich variety of course offerings, did abandon it.

The terms "general" and "common," when used to qualify education, are related but not synonymous. Whatever the total population of a school studies is common in the sense that it is shared by all pupils. In this sense, our elementary school curriculum is regarded as common, and the school has been known as the common school. "General," on the other hand, refers or could profitably refer to a characteristic of the subject being studied. The general is the opposite of the specific or of the particular and is therefore more likely to be abstract than concrete. In this sense, mathematics is more general than geography, and geography more general than corn agriculture.

This book sets forth a theory of the curriculum that is general, that is, made up of general studies, but it also urges that it be common as well. The writers believe that in the scientifically based mass society, vocational training increasingly presupposes thorough grounding in general studies. One can expect that with automation reducing the number of unskilled jobs, the cognitive component of job training will rise in amount and level. Even now, careers at the technician level in mechanics and electronics require a secondary schooling comparable to that needed for college entrance.

To be sure, not even automation will remove from the occupational market all low-skilled jobs, but the case for *common, general* education does not rest entirely, or perhaps even primarily, on vocational considerations. If the analysis of the new emergent mass society is correct, the needs of citizenship and self-development for general studies are even more urgent than the vocational needs. For, if the analysis is right, to exploit the possibilities of the technological civilization for a society that can in any genuine sense be called democratic will call upon a very large proportion of our people, not an elite handful, to think and feel as educated men and women think and feel. The enlargement of vision that this entails makes mandatory a common curriculum emphasizing the general studies.

Accordingly, cues as to the nature of the curriculum will be sought, not in the particular jobs that youth are likely to hold, nor in the diverse roles they will play in life, but rather in the ways that schooling or school learnings are used in modern life. In this domain, as in so many others, specialization and differentiation have created new educational problems.

The writers have distinguished four typical uses of knowledge or school learnings and have called them replicative, associative, applicative, and interpretive. The point of making such distinctions is not to multiply terms or to make the obvious seem esoteric and learned. The justification for distinctions among concepts and terms is that they denote processes that are more or less independent of each other or that cannot be substituted for each other. If such differences exist, the curriculum designer should be alerted, lest his efforts produce effects he did not anticipate and fail to produce those he had a right to expect.

We use school learnings in nonschool situations in ways that range from the apparently unconscious to the most deliberatively explicit use. There is the report of an experiment concerning the effect of reading Greek poetry to an infant on the child's ability to learn Greek poetry many years later. In the same vein, subliminal advertising on television has been banned, presumably because it effectively uses stimuli of which the viewer is not conscious. One can only speculate on the potency of "forgotten" learnings to affect adult behavior. Who knows how much of what we call "individuality," "creativeness," and "charm" is caused by learnings that operate at the unconscious or preconscious level? Various schools of psychiatric thought have capitalized on "forgotten" learnings and their role in neurotic behavior. The schools have not capitalized on them, partly because students of schooling have not taken the trouble to perfect methods for studying their effects.

ASSOCIATIVE USE OF SCHOOLING

Many learnings, while not subliminal or unconscious, have an air of the accidental about them, as when something we have learned comes to mind because it has something in common with what is before us. For example, we read the word "Greek" in the newspaper, and the thought of Achilles or Homer occurs to us, to be followed, perhaps, by the thought of rubber heels.

This is an example of the associative use of learning. When we are asked to respond to a question, we resurrect from memory something or other that the cue suggests. The laws of association—resemblance, contiguity, and satisfaction—purport to tell us what learnings the given cue is most likely to elicit.

Resemblance, contiguity, satisfaction, and vividness can determine what is associated with what, but these are not logical relations. "Red Square" and "redhead" are not related logically, although they have the word "red" in common. We cannot say logically that, given the stimulus "Red Square," the subject must respond with "redhead" or red-anything-else, but psychologically one might have expected something like this on the basis of what is known about people's speech patterns and the law of resemblance in association of ideas.

Nevertheless, the subliminal and associative modes of using what is learned in school are important, partly because many students and perhaps even some teachers mistake an associative response for a logical one. For example, if the teacher asks, "Why is the sun hot?" the pupil may reply, "Because it is round and bright." This is not a logical answer, although it is understandable as an associative use of learning, because the sun *is* round and it *is* bright.

Unfortunately, neither students nor teachers display adequate sensitivity to this distinction. . . . Here, it may be remarked that many a conscientious student has passed high school courses by using learnings associatively in answering questions on essay examinations. In other words, students learn to respond with everything they can recall that is in any way related to some word or phrase in the examination question. Such an answer may contain nothing that is false and nothing that was not in the textbook and yet be completely irrelevant to the point of the question. If this answer is written in legible hand and with due respect for grammar and spelling, chances are better than even that the student will get a passing grade. Indeed, if there is anything that might qualify as a universal learning pattern in American schooling, it is precisely the method of using the instructor's questions as cues for the recall and statement of any and all associated materials. The valiant attempts of the Progressive critics to change this pattern unfortunately were in vain. The discovery that such responses will not earn passing grades for the student in college—although in many colleges they will—must be traumatic. Every time, therefore, an instructor accepts a psychologically relevant answer in place of a logically relevant one, he is an accessory after a pedagogical crime, and if in his teaching he ignores this distinction, he is an accessory to the crime.

Another reason for the importance of the associative use of school learnings is that it constitutes an important matrix of meaning for the appreciation of the arts. Much of the imagery in the reading of poetry, fiction, and drama depends on learned materials that cannot be recalled exactly as learned. Much of the effectiveness of figures of speech rests on comparisons once noted, now forgotten, yet still amenable to partial recall.[1] We perhaps have overlooked the importance of this use of school learnings because, as has been pointed out, we cannot trace their origins to particular school experiences.

Much of what has been called concomitant learnings by William H. Kilpatrick and others illustrates what is here meant by the associative use of schooling. The stress on this type of learning is justified both by the fact that it probably does occur and by its important effects. The difficulty in using it as a basis for curriculum theory arises because it makes too much depend on what, in the nature of the case, is highly idiosyncratic and uncontrollable. It should also be noted that associative uses of schooling do not all originate in the interpersonal relationships of pupils and teachers. Content, if rightly chosen, also teaches more than meets the eye or the test.

REPLICATIVE USE OF SCHOOLING

At almost the opposite pole of the unconscious and randomly associative use of learnings is the replicative use. When we read a newspaper, compute a sum, look up a word in the dictionary, read a map, or recite a poem, we repeat an operation performed many times in our school days and pretty much as we performed it in those days. The replicative use of schooling is most noticeable in the practice of the skills. Ordinarily we do not say that we "apply" our skills of reading and writing in nonschool situations; rather we repeat the school performance in writing and reading situations, and such situations are virtually self-announcing in school and out. When does one write? When paper and pen are before him and when the situation says, "Write it down."

Attitudes presumably are instances of the same use, except that the triggering situations vary over a wider range. That neatness in school will transfer to tasks outside of the classroom is not so certain as that writing will take place in writing situations. Yet when the neatness attitude is instated in an unpracticed task, it is a repetition of much the same sort of experience that the learner underwent at the times when the attitude was formed.

We rely on the replicative use of schooling for those operations and contents that are used very much as learned in a wide range of frequently occurring situations. They are the most reliable type of school learnings precisely because life affords opportunities to overlearn them to the point of virtually faultless performance. Because the school can anticipate only a small portion of the behavior that is demanded by life, the replicative use of schooling is limited less in importance than in range.

The traditional emphasis on reading, writing, and arithmetic placed great reliance on the replicative use of schooling. Life was to make repeated demands on the individual to use these symbolic skills; hence, to overlearn them was the primary task of elementary schooling, whatever else might be added to garnish the education menu.

There is another ingredient of schooling that is sometimes used replicatively, the use of "facts" or, more precisely, statements of fact. If one is asked, "When did Columbus discover America?" the replicative response is "1492," a repetition of an oft-repeated response made in similar situations.

How many of the facts learned in school are used in this way is impossible to estimate. A repertory of facts is assuredly indispensable to life and thought. The building of such a repertory has been belittled first, because compared to the total stock of knowledge, any individual's stock is bound to be minuscule and second, because fact-storing is generally regarded as being of a lower order of mentation than thinking and reasoning. Yet all thinking requires facts as well as meanings and relations. Even in purely formal logical thinking one cannot wholly dispense with facts, for example, that certain symbols stand for certain logical meanings and operations, that there are logical rules, and the like. So in every thinking situation some elements are regarded as fact and when so taken they are used replicatively, that is, as given or as learned.

Thus, while it is admittedly futile to attempt to store all the facts one will need, the replicative use of facts is such that schooling should give attention to the strategy of fact-storage and retrieval, to use the language of the computer. Such strategy concerns itself, on the one hand, with selection of key facts to be stored, and, on the other, with conceptual nets or maps that facilitate both the storage of facts and their recall. These are the direct objective of general studies.

APPLICATIVE USE OF SCHOOLING

The most serious limitation on the replicative use of any learning is its lack of flexibility. It works best when the new situation is almost a replica of those in which the learning was acquired. We are told that whenever new materials or new designs are introduced in house-building, even master craftsmen are disturbed. This is so because well-established habits and skills can no longer function replicatively.

Our technological civilization depends on the application of knowledge to particular problems of practice rather than on its replicative use. Mathematics and physics *applied* to problems of mechanics give us the profession of engineering, that in turn solves problems of transportation, construction, mechanical toasters, and space probes. Hence the enormous importance of applying school learning, or the *applicative* use of learning. Here a learning—usually in the form of some principle, generalization, or statement of fact—is used to solve a problem or to analyze a situation. The cues for what knowledge is needed and how it is to be used are limited and often hidden. Sometimes the situation is so unstructured and open that the bulk of the cues must come from the problem-solver himself. Accordingly, we rightly prize the applicative use of knowledge, for it greatly enhances our powers of understanding and control. The applicative use of knowledge is, however, more complicated than might first appear; otherwise we would not be so often chagrined that we had not applied knowledge that was in our possession all the time. If application of knowledge were a simple matter, would we not ourselves make those discoveries and inventions which seem so obvious after they have been made by others?

Knowledge is applied, of course, whenever one recognizes an object or an event as a member of a class or an instance of a generalization or a law. This is application by subsumption, and there is some justice in believing that it is a basic way of applying knowledge. In the more complex case one does not, as a rule, deal with one object or event. Rather, one deals with problems or problem situations, and to solve them one seeks some resemblance to a familiar problem or situation. This type of application may be thought of as filling in the missing terms of a proportional equation.

We have

$$\frac{Familiar\ problem}{New\ problem} = \frac{Familiar\ solution}{?}$$

As an example, we might consider the familiar situation of boys in slum neighborhoods resisting delinquency when an extensive recreational program is introduced. If another neighborhood is afflicted by a high rate of juvenile delinquency, it occurs to us to apply a familiar solution, namely, instituting recreational facilities.

This is, of course, an argument by analogy. Whoever first applied his knowledge of the power of an electric current to magnetize a bar of iron within a coil of wire, and thus to operate a bell, completed the analogy

$$\frac{hand}{clapper} = \frac{?}{clapper}$$

and hit on the notion of using the magnetized iron bar to activate the clapper as the hand ordinarily does. Someone had to note the resemblance between the power of steam in a kettle and in an engine; between the phenomenon of parallax and the possibility of measuring the distance to inaccessible yet visible objects by sightings from differing positions.

Another example of applying knowledge is furnished when we work backwards and ask, "What will tell us how cold or warm it is?" In measuring other properties of objects such as weight or size, we often rely on pointers that move over a numerical scale. What in the temperature situation would move a pointer? If we know (or can use replicatively) the fact that heat and cold affect the volume of metals or liquids, we are on the road to completing an analogy and devising some kind of thermometer. One could illustrate the same sort of thinking process by raising a question such as, "What will turn salt water into fresh?" Here, knowledge about evaporation might furnish the clues to the solution, or knowledge about the chemical reactions that produce precipitates might be the starting point.

Applying knowledge is, therefore, not simply to recall it or to recite it. It is to use it for problem-solving, and, if we are not to use "application" trivially, we mean dealing with problems whose solutions are neither easy nor easily available from an expert or a handbook.

It is noteworthy that after we have solved the same type of problem many times, another problem of the same sort elicits a response that *replicates* at least part of the previous response. When this happens, one no longer applies knowledge, but rather uses a *skill*, much as one uses the skills of reading, writing, and spelling. In other words, even when we observe someone solving a problem, perhaps a difficult problem, we cannot be sure that he is applying knowledge; he may be merely replicating a skill. The human race has inherited the earth not because it can have knowledge or apply it, but primarily because it makes a habit of doing so.

For the curriculum designer, the important point is that in ordinary life the applicative use of knowledge is relatively rare. We do not solve many of our problems by thinking our way through them. On the contrary, we consult someone who has the solution for sale, or we look up the answer in some manual. Our behavior follows the law of least cognitive strain; we think no more than we have to.

. . . The highest applicative use of knowledge is to expand knowledge itself, as in the work of the scholar and researcher. The generalist is satisfying the requirements of thinking and intelligence when he uses knowledge interpretively.

Why do we stress the relative rarity of the applicative use of knowledge? Because in educational thinking it has generally been taken for granted that it is the applicative use of knowledge that justifies schooling in general and the teaching of any subject in particular. At times the schools have operated on the assumption that a large repertory of facts, rules, and principles learned for replication on cue would automatically be used applicatively when the life situation became problematic. At other times, disappointed that automatic application of school learnings did not occur, the schools urged that the pupil be given practice in application, so that applying a piece of knowledge became a standard part of a lesson. These Herbartian applications, usually practiced on problems within a given subject, served as an admirable test of the pupil's understanding, but they did not guarantee that the learning would be used to solve nonschool problems.

This was due partly to the fact that life problems are "molar," that is, more complex and massive than problems in a single discipline like mathematics or physics or chemistry. It was also due to the technological complexity of our culture. In such a culture, one depends more and more on specialized problem-solvers who have the knowledge, tools, and skills required. In such a state of affairs, to justify a curriculum on applicative uses is neither practically nor theoretically defensible, unless it is the curriculum for the training of specialists.

INTERPRETIVE USE OF SCHOOLING

Much of what in ordinary language we call application of knowledge is better regarded as interpretation, a process related to application but far less specific and detailed.

Experience becomes intelligible only as we categorize it, conceptualize it, or classify it. In other words, experience becomes intelligible and intelligently manageable insofar as we impose form upon it. But which forms, and from whence do they come?

The ultimate answer to this question is still a profound philosophical mystery, but for our purpose it is safe to say that every intellectual discipline, every science, every poem, and every picture is a source of forms or molds into which experience must flow and be shaped if we are to understand it at all. Our language is the great prefigurer or premolder of ordinary everyday experience; the sciences use molds or categories that allow us to understand our world in terms of atoms and electrons, galaxies and solar systems, acids and bases, causes and effects; our works of art enable us to feel the world as pervaded by human values.

Whenever we use our school learnings in these areas to perceive, understand, or feel life situations, we say that we are using our learnings primarily
for interpretation, and not replicatively, associatively, or applicatively, although, strictly speaking, these uses do not necessarily exclude each other.
There is a sense, however, in which the interpretive use of knowledge is the
most fundamental of all, for without a prior interpretation of the situation we
are not sure what we shall replicate, associate, or apply.

The interpretive use of schooling, accordingly, is primarily for orientation
and perspective rather than for action and problem-solving. Although interpretation is a necessary preliminary to all the other uses of knowledge, there are
many situations in which orientation toward a problem is as far as we can go, that
is, in virtually all of the situations in which we cannot function as specialists.

CRITICAL THINKING

What about critical thinking? Is critical thinking an interpretive or an applicative use of schooling? Is it confined to the specialist, or must we all make use of
it? There is little doubt that all citizens are expected to think critically and to be
good at it in all domains of life. By critical thinking, we mean the scrutiny of
discourse for truth and validity. We think critically when we attend closely to
such questions as, "Is this statement true?" "Does this statement follow from
the evidence presented in its behalf?" "Is this statement more or less probable
on the evidence than alternative statements?"

Good thinking has both form and content. The form is provided and
regulated by logic, or the rules for correct definition, classification, and inference. Good thinking or critical thinking also involves knowledge *about* the field
in which the thinking is being done. It is this content that enables us to judge
the truth and relevance of the alternatives presented to us in life situations. But
it is precisely with respect to content, that is, with respect to knowledge about
situations, that the citizen is not a specialist.

It turns out, therefore, that although content is used applicatively only by
the specialist, logical form is the same when used by specialist or nonspecialist;
it must be used applicatively if used at all. This means that all subjects, if
logically organized, must be studied with respect to both their logical form or
structure and their specific content. Except by the specialist, the content is used
interpretively and associatively, but the logical form of the subject (mathematics, chemistry, physics, history) is used applicatively, and this means only that
the logical form of a subject matter is used applicatively to regulate our interpretations. When this occurs, we are thinking critically.

The discussion of the various uses of school learnings has been admittedly schematic and abstract. It may be helpful, therefore, to examine in some
detail a task that confronts us so commonly that we forget its importance as a
test of schooling—the task of reading a newspaper or magazine.

NOTE

1. See William York Tindall, *The Literary Symbol* (New York: Columbia University Press, 1955). Beginning the section called "Burial of the Dead," T. S. Eliot wrote in *The Waste Land* (*Collected Poems of T. S. Eliot, 1909–1935* [New York: Harcourt, Brace & World, Inc., 1936]):

> April is the cruelest month, breeding
> Lilacs out of the dead land, mixing
> Memory and desire, stirring
> Dull roots with spring rain.

What can we recall explicitly that gives these lines their haunting appropriateness? Grover Smith devoted twenty-six pages, in his *T. S. Eliot's Poetry and Plays* (Chicago: University of Chicago Press, 1950), to the sources of meaning of this section of the poem.

Curriculum
Development and the
Language of
Instruction

The Hidden Curriculum and the Nature of Conflict

Michael W. Apple is a distinguished scholar in the critical theory of education and one of the major writers in the new sociology of education. His
books have received widespread attention in England and in America.

The selection that follows is from chapter 5, "The Hidden Curriculum
and the Nature of Conflict," of Apple's book *Ideology and Curriculum*
(Routledge & Kegan Paul, 1979). In it, Apple argues that public school
curricula tend to stress hegemonic (dominant) social values. Furthermore,
these curricula are designed to get students to accept existing social values,
rules, and institutions as predetermined, "neutral," and unchangeable,
rather than as changing, fluid, and open to dialectic challenge by students or
their teachers. The "hidden curriculum" of most schools, Apple says, is
composed of "consensus" values and attitudes that dominant social groups
wish to impose on all others. Tacit (silent) rules as to what behaviors and
attitudes are acceptable are imbedded in all school curricula. Students are
encouraged to conform to and accept rather than enter into conflict with the

dominant social values. Apple concludes that students need to be taught how to counter hegemonic social values in school curricula.

Key Concept: the "hidden curriculum"

Before proceeding, . . . it is important to note that in order for the school to continue to perform in a relatively smooth manner its complex historical roles in the maximization of the production of technical knowledge and in the socialization of students into the normative structure required by our society, it has to do something else which is related to and helps underpin both roles. It has to make legitimate a basically technical perspective, a tension of consciousness that responds to the social and intellectual world in an acritical fashion. That is, the school needs to make all this seem natural. A society based on technical cultural capital and individual accumulation of economic capital needs to seem as if it were the only possible world. Part of the school's role, in other words, is to contribute to the distribution of what the critical theorists of the Frankfurt School might call purposive-rational patterns of rationality and action.

This is an important element in ideological hegemony, for, . . . in order for students' definitions of situations (like those taught in their initial school experience) to be maintained, these definitions must be ongoingly confirmed. This confirmation must entail a continuation of the patterns of interaction that dominated kindergarten, of course. But, since students, as they get older, now verbally reason with some facility, and can think through aspects of their social and cultural conditions, the curriculum content itself becomes even more important. There needs to be continuous and increasingly sophisticated *justification* for acceptance of the distinctions and social rules they learned earlier. This justification needs to *set the ideological limits* of such thinking by embodying 'appropriate' ways in which students can begin to reason through the logic of why the institutions and the culture they interact with everyday are in fact legitimate. This requires that institutions, commonsense rules, and knowledge be seen as relatively pregiven, neutral, and basically unchanging because they all continue to exist by 'consensus.' Thus, the curriculum should stress hegemonic assumptions, ones which ignore the actual working of power in cultural and social life and which point to the naturalness of acceptance, institutional beneficence, and a positivistic vision in which knowledge is divorced from the real human actors who created it. The key to uncovering this, I believe, is the treatment of *conflict* in the curriculum.

CONFLICT AND THE HIDDEN CURRICULUM

The fact that schools normally seem neutral and are usually *overtly* insulated from political processes and ideological argumentation has both positive and negative qualities. The insulation has served to defend the school against

98

*Chapter 6
Curriculum
Development
and the
Language of
Instruction*

whims and fads that can often have a destructive effect upon educational practice. It also, however, can make the school rather unresponsive to the needs of local communities and a changing social order. The pros and cons of the schools as a 'conservative' institution have been argued fervently for the last ten years or so, at least. Among the most articulate of the spokespeople have been Edgar Z. Friedenberg and the late Jules Henry. Aside from the discussions of the teaching of work related norms, the covert teaching of an achievement and marketplace ethic and the probable substitution of a 'middle class' and often 'schizophrenic' value system for a student's own biographical meanings have been some of the topics most usually subject to analysis. As we saw, a good deal of the focus has been on what Jackson has so felicitously labeled the 'hidden curriculum'—that is, on the norms and values that are implicitly, but effectively, taught in schools and that are not usually talked about in teachers' statements of end or goals. . . .

It has become increasingly evident that the formal corpus of school knowledge found in, say, most history books and social studies texts and materials has, over the years, presented a somewhat biased view of the true nature of the amount and possible use of internecine strife in which groups in this country and others have engaged. Our side is good; their side is bad. 'We' are peace loving and want an end to strife; 'they' are warlike and aim to dominate. The list could be extended considerably especially in racial and class matters.[1] Yet, we must go beyond this type of analysis, often even beyond the work of the revisionist historians, political scientists, students of political socialization, and educators to get at many of the roots of the teaching of this dominant orientation. I shall examine here two specific areas—social studies and science. In so doing, I shall point out that the presentation of these two areas (among others) in schools both mirrors and fosters an ideology that is oriented to a static perspective: in the social studies, on the positive and even essential functions of social conflict; and in science, on the nature of scientific work and argumentation and on what has been called 'revolutionary' science. The view presented of science, especially, in the schools is particularly interesting since it is essentially an archetype of the ideological position on conflict I wish to illuminate.

Two tacit assumptions seem to be prominent in teaching and in curricular materials. The first centers around a negative position on the nature and uses of conflict. The second focuses on men and women as recipients of values and institutions, not on men and women as creators and recreators of values and institutions. These assumptions act as basic guidelines that order experiences.

BASIC RULES AND TACIT ASSUMPTIONS

The concept of hegemony implies that fundamental patterns in society are held together by tacit ideological assumptions, rules if you will, which are not usually conscious, as well as economic control and power. These rules serve to organize and legitimate the activity of the many individuals whose interaction makes up a social order. Analytically it is helpful to distinguish two types of

Michael W.
Apple

rules—constitutive or basic rules and preference rules.[2] Basic rules are like the rules of a game; they are broad parameters in which action takes place. Preference rules, as the name suggests, are the choices one has within the rules of the game. Take chess, for instance. There are basic ground rules (which are not usually brought to a level of awareness) that make chess different from, say, checkers or other board games or even nonboard games. And within the game of chess, one has choices of the moves to make within this constitutive framework. Pawn's choices involve moving forward (except in 'taking' an opponent), rooks move forward or side to side, and so forth. If an opponent's pawn were to jump over three men to put you in check, then he obviously would not be following the 'rules of the game;' nor would he be following the tacitly accepted rules if he, say, swept all your men from the board and shouted 'I win!'

On the very broadest level, one of the constitutive rules most predominant in our society involves the notion of trust. When we drive down the street, we trust that the car approaching from the opposite direction will stay in its lane. Unless there is some outward manifestation of deviance from this rule, we never even bring to a level of conscious awareness how this basic rule of activity organizes our lives.[3] A similar rule is the one that posits the legitimate bounds of conflict. The rules of the game implicitly set out the boundaries of the activities people are to engage or not to engage in, the types of questions to ask, and the acceptance or rejection of other people's activities.[4] Within these boundaries, there are choices among a range of activities. We can use the courts, but not bomb; we can argue, but not duel; and so forth. A basic assumption seems to be that conflict among groups of people is *inherently* and fundamentally bad and we should strive to eliminate it *within* the established framework of institutions, rather than seeing conflict and contradiction as the basic 'driving forces' in society.

While some of the better schools and classrooms are alive with issues and controversy, the controversies usually exhibited in schools concern choices *within* the parameters of implicitly held rules of activity. Little attempt is made to focus on the parameters themselves.

The hidden curriculum in schools serves to reinforce basic rules surrounding the nature of conflict and its uses. It posits a network of assumptions that, when internalized by students, establishes the boundaries of legitimacy. This process is accomplished not so much by explicit instances showing the negative value of conflict, but by nearly the total absence of instances showing the importance of intellectual and normative conflict in subject areas. The fact is that these assumptions are obligatory for the students, since at no time are the assumptions articulated or questioned. By the very fact that they are tacit, that they reside not at the roof but the root of our brains, their potency as aspects of hegemony is enlarged. . . .

Social studies and science as they are taught in the large majority of schools provide some of the most explicit instances of the hidden teaching. I have chosen these areas for two reasons. First, there has been built up a rather extensive and important literature concerned with the sociology of the disciplines of scientific endeavor. This literature deals rather insightfully with the 'logic in use' of scientists (that is, what scientists seem actually to do) as op-

100

*Chapter 6
Curriculum
Development
and the
Language of
Instruction*

posed to the 'reconstructed logic' of scientists (that is, what philosophers of science and other observers say scientists do) that is normally taught in schools.[5] Second, in social studies the problems we discuss can be illuminated rather clearly by drawing upon selected Marxian notions to show that the commonsense views of social life often found in the teaching of social studies are not inevitable. Let us examine science initially. In so doing, I also want to propose, . . . an alternate or, rather, a broader view of scientific endeavor that should be considered by educators and, especially, curriculum workers, if they are, at the very least, to focus on the ideological assumptions inherent in much that is taught in our educational institutions. . . .

What is intriguing is the nearly complete lack of treatment of or even reference to conflict as a social concern or as a category of thought in most available social studies curricula or in most classrooms observed. Of the more popular materials, only those developed under the aegis of the late Hilda Taba refer to it as a key concept. However, while the Taba Social Studies Curriculum overtly focuses on conflict, and while this focus in itself is a welcome sight, its orientation is on the serious consequences of sustained conflict rather than on the many positive aspects also associated with conflict itself. Conflict again is viewed as 'dysfunctional,' even though it is pictured as being ever present.[6]

As was noted previously, to a large extent society as it exists, in *both* its positive and negative aspects, is held together by implicit commonsense rules and paradigms of thought, by hegemony as well as by overt power. Social studies materials such as this (and there are many others to which I have not referred) can contribute to the reinforcing and tacit teaching of certain dominant basic assumptions and, hence, a pro-consensus and anti-dissension belief structure.

This view is being countered somewhat by a portion of the content now being taught under the rubric of Black and Women's Studies. Here, struggle and conflict on a communal basis are often explicitly and positively focused upon.[7] While many curriculists may find such overt espousal of community goals somewhat antithetical to their own inclinations, the fact that there has been an attempt to present a comparatively realistic outlook on the significant history and uses of conflict in the progress of social classes and groups, through the civil rights and black power movements for instance, must be recognized. Even those who would not applaud or would applaud only a rather safe or conservative view on this subject should realize the potency and positive value of just such a perspective for developing a group consciousness and a cohesiveness not heretofore possible. This point will be made again in my more general discussion of the uses of conflict in social groups.

To say, however, that most Black Studies curricula exhibit this same perspective would be less than accurate. One could also point to the by now apparent presentation of Black historical material where those Blacks are presented who stayed within what were considered to be the legitimate boundaries (constitutive rules) of protest or progressed in accepted economic, athletic, scholarly, or artistic fields. Usually, one does not find reference to Malcolm X, Marcus Garvey, or others who offered a potent critique of existing modes of economic and cultural control and activity. However, it is the *massiveness* of the tacit presentation of the consensus perspective that must be stressed, as well as its occurrence in the two areas examined in this chapter.

It is not sufficient, though, for our purposes to 'merely' illuminate how the hidden currriculum obligates students to experience certain encounters with basic rules. It is essential that an alternative view be posited and that the uses of social conflict that I have been mentioning be documented.

It is possible to counter the consensus orientation with a somewhat less consensus bound set of assumptions, assumptions that seem to be as empirically warranted, if not more so, as those to which I have raised objections. For instance, some social theorists have taken the position that 'society is not primarily a smoothly functioning order of the form of a social organism, a social system, or a static social fabric.' Rather, continuous change in the elements *and* basic structural form of society is a dominant characteristic. Conflicts are the systematic products of the changing structure of a society and by their very nature tend to lead to progress. The 'order' of society, hence, becomes the regularity of change. The 'reality' of society is conflict and flux, not a 'closed functional system.'[8] It has been stated that the most significant contribution to the understanding of society made by Marx was his insight that a major source of change and innovation is internal conflict.[9] In essence, therefore, conflicts must be looked at as a basic and often beneficial dimension of the dialectic of activity we label society. . . .

I have been proposing an alternative outlook on the presence and uses of conflict in social groups. It is feasible for it to be used as a more objective foundation for designing curricula and guiding teaching so that the more static hidden curriculum students encounter can be counterbalanced to some extent. The explicit focusing on conflict as a legitimate category of conceptualization and as a valid and essential dimension of collective life could enable the development by students of a more viable and potent political and intellectual perspective from which to perceive their relation to existing economic and political institutions. At the least, such a perspective gives them a better understanding of the tacit ideological assumptions that act to structure their own activity.

PROGRAMMATIC CONSIDERATIONS

There are a number of programmatic suggestions that can be made that could at least partially serve to counterbalance the hidden curriculum and selective tradition most evident in science and social studies as representatives of the formal corpus of school knowledge. While these are by their very nature still rather tentative and only partial, they may prove important.

A more balanced presentation of some of the espoused values of science is essential, especially that relating to organized skepticism. The historical importance to the scientific communities of the overriding skeptical outlook needs to be recognized and focused upon.

The history of science can be seen as a continuing dialectic of controversy and conflict between advocates of competing research programs and para-

102

*Chapter 6
Curriculum
Development
and the
Language of
Instruction*

digms, between accepted answers and challenges to these 'truths.' As such, science itself could be presented with a greater historical orientation documenting the conceptual revolutions necessary for significant breakthroughs to occur.

Rather than adhering to a view of science as truth, the balanced presentation of science as truth-until-further-notice, as a process of continual change, could prevent the crystallization of attitude. In this connection also, the study of how conceptual revolutions in science have proceeded would contribute to a less positive perspective on consensus as the only mode of progress.

To this point can be added a focus upon the moral uses and dilemmas of science. For example, personalizing the history of science through cases such as Oppenheimer, Watson, and, intriguingly, the controversy surrounding the Velikovsky case, would indeed be helpful.[10] When taken together with a serious analysis of, say, the role of women in science and medicine, these suggestions would help to eliminate the bias of present curricula by introducing the idea of personal and interpersonal controversy and conflict.[11]

In the social studies, a number of suggestions can be made. The comparative study of revolution, say the American, French, Russian, Portuguese, and Chinese, would serve to focus upon the properties of the human condition that cause and are ameliorated by interpersonal conflict. This suggestion is made more appropriate when coupled with the fact that in many countries revolution is the legitimate (in a quite real sense of the word) mode of procedure for redressing grievances. To this could be added studies of economic and cultural imperialism.[12]

A more realistic appraisal and presentation of the uses of conflict in the legal and economic rights movement of Blacks, Indians, women, workers, and others would no doubt assist in the formation of a perspective that perceives these and similar activities as legitimate models of action. The fact that laws *had* to be broken and were then struck down by the courts later is not usually focused upon in social studies curricula. Yet, it was through these types of activities that a good deal of progress was and is made. Here community and 'movement' studies of how changes have been effected is an interesting process, one that should prove of considerable moment. This points to how critical it is that things like serious labor history be taught in schools. All too often we minimize the history of the concrete struggles workers had to engage in and the sacrifices they made. At the same time, students can be led to ground their own family and personal experiences in the history of class and ethnic group as well. Numerous bibliographies on topics such as labor history, the struggles of women, Blacks, and others are available to assist us in countering the selective tradition here.[13]

Beyond these suggestions for specific programmatic changes, one further area should be noted. Sociological 'paradigms' also attempt to account for the commonsense reality in which students and teachers dwell. Schools are integrally involved in this reality and its internalization. It might be wise to consider engaging students in the articulation and development of paradigms of activity within their everyday lives at school. Such involvement could enable students to come to grips with and amplify crucial insights into their own conditionedness and freedom. Such insights could potentially alter the original paradigm and the commonsense reality itself. It would also make possible to a greater degree a concrete and meaningful educational encounter for students with the process of value and institutional recreation. Social action curricula and student rights struggles, though limited in their usefulness because of the serious danger of 'incorporation,' could be quite helpful here in giving students a sense of their own possible competence in challenging hegemonic conditions in certain areas.[14]

CONCLUSIONS

Research on political socialization of children seems to indicate the importance of the president and the police as points of contact between children and the structures of authority and legitimacy in a society.[15] For instance, there is a strongly personal initial bond between the child and these representatives of the structures of authority. As the child matures, these very personal ties are transferred to more anonymous institutions such as Congress or to political activities such as voting. The tendency to lift impersonal institutions to high esteem may be quite an important source of the relative stability and durability of the structures of authority in industrial societies.[16]

Yet it is not quite certain that this formulation really answers the questions one could raise concerning political and social stability. The foundation of political (broadly conceived) leanings and relations to political and social structures is in a belief system that itself rests upon basic patterns of assumptions 'determined' by social and economic activity. Such rules for activity (and thought as a fundamental form of this activity) are probably more important to a person's relation to his or her life-world than we realize. We have been examining one of these constitutive ideological assumptions.

It has been my contention that the schools systematically distort the functions of social conflict in collectivities. The social, intellectual, and political manifestations of this distortion are manifold. They may contribute significantly to the ideological underpinnings that serve to fundamentally orient individuals toward an unequal society.

Students in most schools and in urban centers in particular are presented with a view that serves to legitimate the existing social order since change, conflict, and men and women as creators as well as receivers of values and institutions are systematically neglected. I have pointed to the massiveness of the presentation. Now something else must be stressed once again—the fact that these meaning structures are obligatory. Students receive them from persons who are 'significant others' in their lives, through their teachers, other role models in books and elsewhere. To change this situation, students' perceptions of to whom they are to look as holders of 'expert knowledge' must be radically altered. In ghetto areas, a partial answer is, perhaps, instituting a more radical perspective in the schools. This change can be carried out only by political activity. As has been mentioned before, it may very well be that to divorce an educator's educational existence from his or her other political existence is to forget that as an act of influence, education is also an inherently political act. Yet with this political sensitivity must also come a fair measure of economic and

104

*Chapter 6
Curriculum
Development
and the
Language of
Instruction*

cultural understanding that speaks to the power of these ideological meanings, that situates them back into the actual social processes which generated them.

Thus, that these assumptions exist should not surprise us given the argument about the 'inner logic' of a particular economic and ideological form. The selective tradition I have analyzed . . . is a 'natural' outgrowth of the relations between our extant cultural and economic institutions. When a society 'requires,' at both an economic and a cultural level, the maximization (not distribution) of the production of technical knowledge, then the science that is taught will be divorced from the concrete human practices that sustain it. When a society 'requires,' at an economic level, the 'production' of agents who have internalized norms which stress engaging in often personally meaningless work, acceptance of our basic political and economic institutions as stable and always beneficent, a belief structure resting on consensus, and a positivistic and technical logic, then we would expect that the formal and informal curricula, the cultural capital, in schools will become aspects of hegemony. The inner logic of these tensions and expectations will set the limits, the constitutive rules, that will become our common sense. Any other response will seem unnatural, which is exactly the point both Williams and Gramsci have maintained.

The overt and covert teaching of these views of science and social life combine with and justify earlier socialization. Both make it quite difficult for one to be at all aware of the ideological saturation that goes on. For if the 'facts' of the world do rest on our theories of them, then the world people see, the economic and cultural meanings they give to it, will be defined in such a way as to be self-justifying. Meanings are given about the way the world 'really is' and the economic and cultural interests that determine *why* it is this way are legitimated as well. The ideological function is circular. Power and knowledge are here again intimately and subtly linked through the roots of our common sense, through hegemony.

One of the primary tasks . . . has been to present lenses that are alternative to those that normally legitimate many of the activities and encounters curriculists design for students. It will become clearer as this volume progresses that the curriculum field itself has limited its own forms of consciousness so that the political and ideological assumptions that undergird a good deal of its normal patterns of activity are as hidden as those that students encounter in schools.[17] I have pointed to the possibilities inherent in a more realistic approach to the nature of conflict as one alternative 'form of consciousness.' . . .

Without an analysis and greater understanding of these latent assumptions, educators run the very real risk of continuing to let ideological values work through them. A conscious advocacy of a more realistic outlook on and teaching of the dialectic of social change would, no doubt, contribute to preparing students with the political and conceptual tools necessary to deal with the dense reality they must face. However, can we accomplish the same for curriculists and other educators? Can we illuminate the political and conceptual tools needed to face the unequal society in which they also live? The most fruitful way to begin this task is to document what their conceptual and political tools do *now:* Do they again maintain a false consensus? How do they act as aspects of hegemony? What are their latent ideological functions? With a firmer grasp on the way schools assist in the creation of hegemony through the 'socialization' of students, it is this task—how hegemony operates in the heads of educators—to which we shall now turn.

NOTES

1. See, for example, Edith F. Gibson, 'The Three D's: Distortion, Deletion, Denial,' *Social Education*, XXXIII (April, 1969), 405–9 and Sidney M. Willhelm, *Who Needs the Negro?* (Cambridge, Mass.: Schenkman, 1970).
2. Helen McClure and George Fischer, 'Ideology and Opinion Making: General Problems of Analysis' (New York: Columbia University Bureau of Applied Social Research, July, 1969, mimeographed).
3. The language of 'rules of activity' is less analytically troublesome than the distinction often made between thought and action, since it implies that the distinction is somewhat naive and enables action—perceptual, conceptual, and bodily—to be the fundamental category of an individual's response to his or her situation. While we often use rules of activity and assumptions interchangeably, the point should be made that assumptions usually connote a less inclusive category of phenomena and are actually indicative of the existence of these socially sedimented rules and boundaries that seem to affect even our very perceptions. Further work on such rules can be found in the ethnomethodological literature and, of course, in the later Wittgenstein. See, for example, Harold Garfinkel, *Studies in Ethnomethodology* (Englewood Cliffs, N.J.: Prentice-Hall, 1967) and Ludwig Wittgenstein, *Philosophical Investigations* (New York: Macmillan, 1953).
4. In essence, the 'system' that many individuals decry is *not only* an ordered interrelationship of institutions, but a framework of fundamental assumptions that act in a dialectical relationship with these institutions.
5. Michael W. Apple, 'Community, Knowledge and the Structure of Disciplines,' *The Educational Forum*, XXXVII (November, 1972), 75–82.
6. Maxine Durkin, *et al.*, *The Taba Social Studies Curriculum: Communities Around Us* (Reading, Mass.: Addison-Wesley, 1969), p. v.
7. Nathan Hare, 'The Teaching of Black History and Culture in the Secondary Schools,' *Social Education*, XXXIII (April, 1969), 385–8, and Preston Wilcox, 'Education for Black Liberation,' *New Generation*, L1 (Winter 1969), 20–1.
8. Ralf Dahrendorf, *Class and Class Conflict in Industrial Societies* (Stanford: Stanford University Press, 1959), p. 27. For concrete studies of conflict both within and among classes in corporate society, see R. W. Connell, *Ruling Class, Ruling Culture* (Cambridge University Press, 1977) and Nicos Poulantzas, *Classes in Contemporary Capitalism* (London: New Left Books, 1975).
9. Jack Walker, 'A Critique of the Elitist Theory of Democracy,' *Apolitical Politics*, Charles A. McCoy and John Playford, eds (New York: Crowell, 1967), pp. 217–18.
10. Michael Mulkay, 'Some Aspects of Cultural Growth in the Natural Sciences,' *Social Research*, XXXVI (Spring, 1969), 22–52.
11. See, for example, Mary Roth Walsh, *Doctors Wanted. No Women Need Apply* (New Haven: Yale, 1977), Edward T. James, Janet Wilson James and Paul S. Boyer, *Notable American Women 1607–1950* (Cambridge, Mass.: Belknap Press, 1971), and H. J. Mozans, *Woman in Science* (Cambridge, Mass.: Massachusetts Institute of Technology, 1974).
12. See, for example, Ariel Dorfman and Armand Mattelart, *How to Read Donald Duck* (New York: International General, 1975) and Martin Carnoy, *Education as Cultural Imperialism* (New York: David McKay, 1974). One of the more interesting books for children which deals with some of these issues is Pal Rydlberg, *et al. The History Book* (Culver City, California: Peace Press, 1974).
13. Among the available bibliographies are *Women in U.S. History: An Annotated Bibliography* (Cambridge, Mass.: Common Women Collective, 1976) and Jim O'Brien, *et al.*

106

*Chapter 6
Curriculum
Development
and the
Language of
Instruction*

A Guide to Working Class History (2nd edn: Somerville, Mass.: New England Free Press, n.d.).

14. The proposals for social action curriculum by Fred Newmann are interesting here. See his *Education for Citizen Action* (Berkeley: McCutchan, 1975). For a discussion of some of the problems with such proposals, see Michael W. Apple, 'Humanism and the Politics of Educational Argumentation,' *Humanistic Education: Visions and Realities*, Richard Weller, ed. (Berkeley: McCutchan, 1977), pp. 315–30.

15. David Easton and Jack Dennis, *Children in the Political System* (New York: McGraw-Hill, 1969), p. 162.

16. Ibid., pp. 271–6.

17. Dwayne Huebner, 'Politics and the Curriculum,' *Curriculum Crossroads*, A. Harry Passow, ed. (New York: Teachers College Press, 1962), p. 88.

6.2 ISRAEL SCHEFFLER

Educational Slogans

Israel Scheffler is a distinguished philosopher of education and science. His contributions to the clarification of discourse on education have brought him widespread recognition among British and American educators. His many books include *The Anatomy of Inquiry: Philosophical Studies in the Theory of Science* (Alfred A. Knopf, 1963); *Conditions of Knowledge: An Introduction to Epistemology and Education* (Scott, Foresman, 1965); and *In Praise of the Cognitive Emotions and Other Essays in the Philosophy of Education* (Routledge, 1991).

The selection that follows is from chapter 2, "Educational Slogans," in Scheffler's *The Language of Education* (Charles C. Thomas, 1960). In it, Scheffler argues that educational slogans "are altogether unsystematic" and that they are used to rally people to causes in the field of education rather than to prove theories or to define ideas. One of the problems Scheffler finds with educational slogans as they are used in discourse about education is that those who believe in particular slogans may use them as if they were "operational doctrines in their own right." The "practical movements" that give birth to slogans also need to be critiqued. In this selection, Scheffler discusses the ways in which educational slogans are used and provides examples to illustrate the problems with slogans.

Key Concept: educational slogans

*E*ducational slogans are clearly unlike definitions in a number of ways. They are altogether unsystematic, less solemn in manner, more popular, to be repeated warmly or reassuringly rather than pondered gravely. They do not figure importantly in the exposition of educational theories. They have no standard form and they make no claim either to facilitate discourse or to explain the meanings of terms. We speak of definitions as clarifying, but not of slogans; slogans may be rousing, but not definitions.

Slogans in education provide rallying symbols of the key ideas and attitudes of educational movements. They both express and foster community of spirit, attracting new adherents and providing reassurance and strength to veterans. They are thus analogous to religious and political slogans and, like

108

*Chapter 6
Curriculum
Development
and the
Language of
Instruction*

these, products of the party spirit. Since slogans make no claim to facilitate communication or to reflect meanings, some of the main points of the last chapter are here irrelevant. No one defends his favorite slogan as a helpful stipulation or as an accurate reflection of the meanings of its constituent terms. It is thus idle to criticize a slogan for formal inadequacy or for inaccuracy in the transcription of usage.

There is, nevertheless, an important analogy with definitions, that needs to be discussed. Slogans, we have said, provide rallying symbols of the key ideas and attitudes of movements, ideas, and attitudes that may be more fully and literally expressed elsewhere. With the passage of time, however, slogans are often increasingly interpreted more literally both by adherents and by critics of the movements they represent. They are taken more and more as literal doctrines or arguments, rather than merely as rallying symbols. When this happens in a given case, it becomes important to evaluate the slogan both as a straightforward assertion and as a symbol of a practical social movement, without, moreover, confusing the one with the other. In the need for this dual evaluation lies the analogy mentioned between slogans and definitions.

In education, such dual evaluation is perhaps even more important than in the case of political and religious slogans, for, at least in Western countries, educators are not subject to the discipline of an official doctrine and are not organized in creedal units as are religious and political groups.[1] Educational ideas formulated in careful, and often difficult, writings soon become influential among teachers in popularized versions. No official discipline or leadership preserves the initial doctrines or some elaboration of them, seeing to it that they take precedence over popular versions at critical junctures, as is familiar in religion and politics. Educational slogans often evolve into operational doctrines in their own right, inviting and deserving criticism as such. It is important to remember, at this point, that though such criticism is fully warranted, it needs to be supplemented by independent criticism of the practical movements giving birth to the slogans in question, as well as of their parent doctrines. We may summarize by saying that what is required is a critique both of the literal and the practical purport of slogans; parent doctrines must, furthermore, be independently evaluated.

The example of John Dewey's educational influence is instructive. His systematic, careful, and qualified statements soon were translated into striking fragments serving as slogans for the new progressive tendencies in American education. Dewey himself criticized the uses to which some of his ideas were put,[2] and his criticisms had the effect of inviting reconsideration and reflection. He was, after all, the acknowledged intellectual leader of the movement. Increasingly, however, progressive slogans have taken on a life of their own. They have been defended as literal statements and attacked as such. Critics, in particular, have often begun by attributing the literal defects of progressive slogans to Dewey's parent doctrines and gone on to imply that the progressive movement has thereby been shown unworthy in its aims and operation.

That the liberal purport and practical purport of slogans require independent criticism may be illustrated by consideration of the slogan, "We teach children, not subjects." In view of the fact that this and closely analogous formulas have sometimes been treated as literal statements, and not merely as rallying symbols of the progressive movement, let us examine the statement literally. Does it make sense?

Israel Scheffler

Suppose I told you I had been teaching my son all afternoon yesterday. You would have a perfect right to ask, "What have you been teaching him?" You would not necessarily expect some single type of answer, such as the name of some academic subject. If, instead of saying, "Mathematics," I were to answer, "How to play first base," or "To be polite," or "The importance of being earnest," you would be satisfied. But, suppose, in answer to your question, I said, "Oh, nothing in particular, I've just been teaching him, that's all," you would, I think, be at a loss to understand how we spent the afternoon. It would be as if you had asked me, "What did you have for dinner?" and got the reply, "Oh, nothing, I've just had dinner, but had nothing *for* dinner."

I might, of course, say reasonably in the latter case, "I can't recall," or "I don't know the name of the dish," or "I don't think I can describe it to you." But in each such case, I am acknowledging that your question has some true answer naming or describing some food, though I am, for one or another reason, not supplying it. To say, however, "I had nothing *for* dinner, just had dinner," is to deny that your question has such a true answer in this case, and it is this denial that makes the assertion impossible to understand. Analogously, to revert to the teaching example, I might, of course, say, "I can't recall the name of the book," or "I don't know the name of the swimming stroke," or even "I don't think I can describe it to you now" (suppose it is a complicated chess strategy). If, however, I said none of these things but insisted rather that I had been teaching the boy nothing, you would fail to understand me, or, at least, fail to take me as uttering a literal truth.

This case must be distinguished from another in which you ask me, "What have you taught him?" that is, "What have you been successful in teaching him?" In answer to this question, it is quite possible for me to say, "Nothing." It is quite possible for me to have been teaching algebra to someone to whom I have been unsuccessful in teaching algebra. I have taught him nothing, though I have been teaching him algebra, I have been trying to get him to learn algebra but he has failed to learn. To ask, however, in the words of our original question, "What have you been teaching him?" is not to ask, "What is it that you have been successful in teaching him?" It is rather to ask, "What have you been trying to get him to learn?" As to this question, if I answered, "Nothing; I have just been teaching him, but have not been trying to get him to learn anything at all," you would, I think, be really puzzled. It would be as bad as if I had said, "I spent yesterday afternoon teaching swimming," and in response to your question, "To whom?" I had replied, "Oh, to no one; just teaching swimming, that's all." If no one teaches anything unless he teaches it to someone, it is equally true that no one can be engaged in teaching anyone without being engaged in teaching him something.

Let us return now to the statement, "We teach children, not subjects." If we take 'subjects' as a general word without restriction to academic subjects, it appears that the statement is not interpretable as both literal and true, since it seems to say, quite literally, "We teach children, but there isn't anything that we try to get them to learn." We have, indeed, previously seen that a denial that anything is taught is legitimate where the question concerns the success of

110

*Chapter 6
Curriculum
Development
and the
Language of
Instruction*

teaching rather than its intent. But this fact is surely of no help in interpreting the slogan before us, as the resulting statement in such an interpretation would be, "We teach children, but we are not successful in teaching them anything." The latter statement, unlikely in any event, would hardly be claimed true by proponents of any educational movement. Taken literally, the slogan is a clear failure, and cannot be used as a serious premise in any argument.

To reach this conclusion, however, is not to evaluate the practical purport of the slogan, the aims it symbolized, the educational tendencies with which it was associated. What, in fact, was its practical purport? Briefly, its point was to direct attention to the child, to relax educational rigidity and formalism, to free the processes of schooling from undue preoccupation with adult standards and outlooks and from mechanical modes of teaching, to encourage increased imagination, sympathy and understanding of the child's world on the part of the teacher. To know the educational context in which such a practical message took shape is to grasp the relevance of its emphasis. Conversely, the relevance of the message cannot be seen without reference to the context. The story is a long one but a quotation from a recent study will serve to indicate the outstanding features. Citing Joseph Rice's report on the American public schools in 1892, based on a tour of 36 cities in which Rice talked with 1,200 teachers, L. A. Cremin writes:[3]

> "Rice's story bore all the earmarks of the journalism destined to make 'muckraking' a household word in America. In city after city public apathy, political interference, corruption, and incompetence were conspiring to ruin the schools ... A principal in New York, asked whether students were allowed to move their heads, answered: 'Why should they look behind when the teacher is in front of them?' A Chicago teacher, rehearsing her pupils in a 'concert drill,' harangued them with the command: 'Don't stop to think, tell me what you know!' In Philadelphia, the 'ward bosses' controlled the appointment of teachers and principals; in Buffalo, the city superintendent was the single supervising officer for seven hundred teachers. With alarming frequency the story was the same: political hacks hiring untrained teachers who blindly led their innocent charges in singsong drill, rote repetition, and meaningless verbiage."

Given such a situation, the relevance of a renewed educational emphasis on the world of the child is obvious. It is, moreover, easy to see that a positive evaluation of this emphasis, representing the practical purport of our slogan,[4] is altogether independent of the criticisms we made of its literal sense. That is, one commits no logical error in accepting these criticisms and at the same time applauding the emphasis of the slogan. Whether or not one is to applaud this emphasis is a separate question, requiring consideration of practical and moral issues in relation to some given context. It is, finally, clear that the practical relevance of a slogan, as well as the applause accorded to it, may vary with context quite independently of its literal purport. In the case of the slogan before us, many feel, indeed, that its practical message is presently less urgent than it once may have been, that it is either irrelevant or considerably less warranted in the current educational situation. This variation in the fortunes of the slogan's practical purport is a function of changing times and changing problems; it cannot result from the failure of the slogan as a literal doctrine, which is invariant.

One important corollary is that doctrines that contradict each other as literal statements may nevertheless, in their practical purport, represent abstractly compatible emphases which may, to be sure, vary independently in relevance and moral warrant from context to context. That is, there may be no cause for supposing that we have an irreconcilable conflict of practical proposals of which we must flatly reject at least one. This point may be illustrated by considering a statement that has acquired the typical status of a slogan in education, the statement that there can be no teaching without learning. As there can be no selling without buying, so there can be no teaching without learning. A recent writer[5] has argued against this statement, asking us to consider as a counterexample the case of a teacher who has tried his best to teach his pupils a certain lesson but has failed to get them to learn it. Shall we say that such a man has not, in fact, been teaching, has not earned his pay, has not fulfilled his responsibility? Surely this case shows that there can be teaching without learning.

If we take the two statements, "There can be no teaching without learning," and "There can be teaching without learning," simply as literal doctrines, we must agree that they are contradictory. Further, we must agree that the counterexample produced against the first of these statements is effective in showing it to be false. If we have an actual case before us of teaching without learning, then we must reject the doctrine that denies the existence of such cases. The counterexample does, moreover, represent a real case of teaching without learning. Here, in short, does seem to be a flat contradiction between two statements, one of which is wrong.

It is, furthermore, easy to see why the statement, "There can be no teaching without learning," sounds so plausible as a literal doctrine, though it is in fact false. For though in some uses of the verb 'to teach' it does not imply success, in others it does. We have already noted the difference between asking, "What have you been teaching him?" ("What have you been trying to get him to learn?") and "What have you taught him?" ("What have you been successful in teaching him?"). The first question, we may say, contains an "intentional" use of the verb, while the second contains a "success" use.[6] It is clear that if the pupil I have been teaching has in fact not learned anything, I may reply to the second question (but not to the first) by saying, "Nothing." For the second question, that is, unless my pupil has learned something, I cannot say I have taught him anything, i.e., there can (here and in all "success" uses) indeed be no teaching without learning.

Some further illustrations may be helpful, especially since the distinction between "success" and "intentional" uses is important and will recur in later discussions. Clearly, if I have been teaching my nephew how to catch a baseball, he may still not have learned, and may in fact never learn, how to catch a baseball. I have, of course, been trying to get him to learn how to catch a baseball, but I need not have succeeded. Generally, then, we may say that the schema "X has been teaching Y how to . . ." does not imply success. Suppose, however, that I have taught my nephew how to catch a baseball. If I have indeed taught him, then he must, in fact, have learned how. Were I to say,

112

*Chapter 6
Curriculum
Development
and the
Language of
Instruction*

"Today I taught him how to catch a baseball but he hasn't learned and never will," I would normally be thought to be saying something puzzling. We may, then, say that the schema "X taught Y how to . . ." does imply success. This schema represents a "success" use of 'to teach' whereas the earlier schema does not, representing rather an "intentional" use of the verb.

It should be noted, incidentally, that not every use of the simple past tense of the verb implies success, though the above "success" schema contains such a form. It is, for example, true that some teachers taught mathematics last year to some students who learned nothing of mathematics. It should further be noticed that "success" uses of the verb 'to teach' do not eliminate distinctions of relative proficiency. To have been successful in teaching implies no more than that students have learned in relevant ways, not that they have become masters. We may ask rhetorically, in traffic, "Who taught *him* to drive?" suggesting that, though he has learned, he is not very good at it. It is minimal achievement, sufficient to warrant us in saying that learning has occurred at all, that is normally implied by "success" uses of the verb 'to teach.'

Finally, we should make note of the fact that 'to teach' is not exceptional in having both "success" and "intentional" uses. Indeed, many verbs relating to action have both uses inasmuch as what is done is often described in terms of trying to reach a goal, the attainment of which defines the success of the try. To say a man is building a house does not mean he has succeeded or ever will. He is, of course, doing something with a certain intention and certain hopes and beliefs; he is, in short, trying to bring it about or make it true that there be a house built by himself. It may, further, be normally understood that what he is doing in this attempt is reasonably considered effective. But from the fact that someone is building a house it cannot be inferred that there is (or will be) some house built by him. He may have been building ("intentional" use) until the flood came and wiped away his work, and he then never completed the job. He may thus never have built ("success" use) the house that he had been building ("intentional" use). Or, better, there may never exist any house built ("success" use) by him, though he has, in fact, been house-building ("intentional" use).

If now, with respect to the verb 'to teach,' we recognise that it has both "intentional" and "success" uses, we see that for the latter uses, there can, indeed, be no teaching without learning. If one's examples are all drawn from such uses, the doctrine that there can be no teaching without learning seems entirely plausible. Nevertheless, the general way in which it is expressed leaves the doctrine open to falsification through a single counterexample, such as has been discussed above. Thus we return, after a long digression, to the conclusion we reached earlier: taken as literal doctrines, the statements, "There can be no teaching without learning," and "There can be teaching without learning" are contradictory, hence irreconcilable, and it is the first statement, moreover, that must be rejected.

If, however, we examine the practical purport of these two statements, it becomes clear that, though their practical emphases are not equally relevant and warranted in every context, neither are they opposed as exclusive alternatives. Rather, they relate to different practical aims that are perfectly compatible. The practical purport of the statement "There can be no teaching without learning" is closely related to that of the slogan "We teach children, not subjects," that is, to turn the attention of the teacher toward the child. But we have here a distinctive emphasis on the child's learning as the intended *result* of teaching, the point being to improve the effectiveness of teaching by referring it to its actual as compared with its intended results. This emphasis hardly strikes anyone today as being either very original or very controversial. It seems rather taken for granted in quite prosaic contexts. Imagine someone saying to a soap manufacturer, "Look here, you'd really do a better job if you systematically studied your product and tried to improve it. You can't really call yourself a soap manufacturer unless you produce good soap, and you can't do that unless you look at what you're turning out and make sure that it is up to par." Such a little speech would seem rather out of place in our consumer-oriented world. Soap makers are looking at their products anyway (not, perhaps, always to make better soap, but at least to make soap more attractive to buyers). No soap maker supposes that, apart from their contribution to his final product, his manufacturing processes have any intrinsic value.

But teachers often have supposed something dangerously like this. They often assume that, apart from their effects on students, their teaching in just the way they habitually do has intrinsic value, and is therefore self-justifying. Instead of achieving attainable improvements through deliberate effort, they thus tend to deny that any improvements are needed or possible so long as they continue to teach as before. When such educational inertia is widespread, as it seemed to many observers to be when our slogan gained currency, the practical purport of the slogan may seem urgent, indeed, revolutionary. To speak, moreover, of teaching as selling and of learning as buying, to suggest that teaching be compared with business methods improvable by reference to effects on the consumer, was to signal strikingly the intent to support reform of teaching.

In part because such reform has become widespread, the practical purport of our slogan appears to many current observers irrelevant or less warranted. Indeed, it has seemed to such observers that the pendulum has in many places swung too far in the direction of orientation to the child's world and preoccupation with the effects of teaching on this world. The schools have, in some respects, been described as too much concerned with their consumers. Teachers, feeling the weight of each student's adjustment and personality conflicts resting on their tired shoulders, have in many instances tried to do too much—to become parents, counselors, and pals as well as teachers. They have (understandably, given such aspirations coupled with the emphasis on consequences) felt harried and guilty at not being able to do all that their charges require, accepting meanwhile the responsibility for all failures in learning upon themselves.[7]

If someone should want to help the morale of such teachers, he would hardly keep repeating the old message under the new conditions. Rather, he would want to say, "Stop feeling guilty, give up your attempts at omnipotence, stop paying so much attention to the inner problems and motivations of your students. Do your very best in teaching your subject and testing your students and when you've done that, relax with an easy conscience." This represents just the practical purport of the statement, "There *can* be teaching without learning." It is this emphasis which seems to many current writers relevant and warranted in the present situation.

Both emphases, however—that of the present statement and that of its opposite—are abstractly compatible in spite of the fact that they may be un-

114

*Chapter 6
Curriculum
Development
and the
Language of
Instruction*

equally relevant or warranted in specific educational contexts. It is, thus, possible to hold (and, indeed, to urge) that teaching ought to be appraised and modified in the light of its effects on learners, and at the same time to believe (and to stress) that there are limits to what the teacher can do, with the best will in the world: whatever he does, he may still fail to achieve the desired learning on the part of his pupils.

In given situations, however, it may be considered more important to maintain the teacher's morale by stressing the limits of his responsibility than to try to improve teaching by stressing the need to examine effects. Whether we say "Try to improve!" or "Don't worry, you've done your best!" is indeed, in this way, a function of the context. But these emphases are not, in general, irreconcilable, nor do they require a flat rejection of the one or the other. They may, in fact, occur together and they may alternate in urgency. To sum up, when slogans are taken literally, they deserve literal criticism. We need, independently however, to evaluate their practical purport in reference to their changing contexts, as well as the parent doctrines from which they have sprung. We must, moreover, avoid assuming that when slogans are in literal contradiction to each other, they represent practical proposals that are in irreconcilable conflict.

NOTES

1. I am, it should be obvious, not arguing for the desirability of such disciplined organization, but only suggesting that its lack renders more urgent the dual criticism of slogans.
2. Dewey, J.: *Experience and Education.* New York, The Macmillan Company, 1938.
3. Cremin, L. A.: The progressive movement in American education: a perspective, *Harvard Educational Review,* 27:251, (Fall) 1957.
4. By the relevance of a slogan's practical purport, I mean its applicability within the context of its use on a particular occasion. In speaking of the evaluation or warrant of this practical purport, I refer to the question whether or not such application ought indeed to be made. To illustrate, compare the case of imperatives. Consider the imperative, 'Put on the light!', uttered on a given occasion. It is relevant on that occasion only if the light is not already on. Even if it is relevant, however, we may still ask whether or not the light ought to be put on.
5. Broudy, H. S. *Building a Philosophy of Education.* Englewood Cliffs, N.J., Prentice-Hall, Inc., 1954, p. 14. Broudy writes, "Many educators rather glibly pronounce the dictum: 'If there is no learning, there is no teaching.' This is a way of speaking because no educator really believes it to be true, or if he did he would in all honesty refuse to take most of his salary. There is a difference between successful teaching and unsuccessful teaching, just as there is a difference between successful surgery and unsuccessful surgery . . . To teach is deliberately to try to promote certain learnings. When other factors intrude to prevent such learnings, the teaching fails. Sometimes the factors are in the teacher; sometimes in the pupil; sometimes in the very air both breathe, but as long as the effort was there, there was teaching."
6. I am indebted to the treatment of achievement words in Ryle, G.: *The Concept of Mind.* London, Hutchinson's University Library, 1949. See also Anscombe, G.E.M.: *Intention.* Oxford, Basil Blackwell, 1957.
7. See Freud, A.: The rôle of the teacher, *Harvard Educational Review,* 22:229, (Fall) 1952, and Riesman, D.: Teachers amid changing expectations, *Harvard Educational Review,* 24:106, (Spring) 1954.

PART THREE

Schools in a Multicultural Society

CHAPTER 7 The Struggle for Freedom in Education

7.1 BOOKER T. WASHINGTON

The Atlanta Exposition Address, September 18, 1895

Booker T. Washington (1856–1915), who was born into slavery, founded the Tuskegee Normal and Industrial Institute in Alabama in 1881. At the Tuskegee Institute he emphasized industrial, skilled trade education rather than traditional college-level liberal arts studies. Washington pursued this policy because he believed that the majority of African Americans needed industrial and artisan skills to escape the sharecropper system of dependent agriculture in the post–Civil War South. He was able to influence many powerful conservative whites to support his program at the institute. Washington also founded the National Negro Business League in 1900. He owned several newspapers, and his ideas carried much weight among other Black-owned publishing enterprises of his day. Washington's most famous articulation of his educational philosophy was given to a business convention on September 18, 1895, in Atlanta, Georgia. This speech, called "The Atlantic Exposition Address," is reprinted in the following selection.

Washington was severely critiqued for his educational position, which focused on economic empowerment and practical skills and less so on intellectual empowerment. Black intellectual leader W. E. B. Du Bois was a notable critic of Washington's views, and he called for the development of an African American intellectual elite that would be able to argue and struggle for African American rights with the white American elite. Actually, many contemporary sociologists agree that both Washington's and Du Bois's social agendas for African American freedpersons were correct—both greater numbers of skilled Black workers *and* a Black American intelligentsia were necessary for African Americans to attain their constitutional rights in the late nineteenth and twentieth centuries.

Key Concept: practical education and "intercultural understanding" as the path to liberation

"Cast down your bucket where you are. . . ."

*O*ne-third of the population of the South is of the Negro race. No enterprise seeking the material, civil, or moral welfare of this section can disregard this element of our population and reach the highest success. I but convey to you, Mr. President and Directors, the sentiment of the masses of my race when I say that in no way have the value and manhood of the American Negro been more fittingly and generously recognized than by the managers of this magnificent Exposition at every stage of its progress. It is a recognition that will do more to cement the friendship of the two races than any occurrence since the dawn of freedom.

Not only this, but the opportunity here afforded will awaken among us a new era of industrial progress. Ignorant and inexperienced, it is not strange that in the first years of our new life we began at the top instead of at the bottom; that a seat in Congress or the State Legislature was more sought than real estate or industrial skill; that the political convention or stump speaking had more attractions than starting a dairy farm or truck garden.

A ship lost at sea for many days suddenly sighted a friendly vessel. From the mast of the unfortunate vessel was seen a signal: "Water, water, we die of thirst." The answer from the friendly vessel at once came back, "Cast down your bucket where you are." A second time the signal, "Water, water, send us water," ran up from the distressed vessel and was answered, "Cast down your bucket where you are." And a third and fourth signal for water was answered "Cast down your bucket where you are." The captain of the distressed vessel, at last heeding the injunction, cast down his bucket and it came up full of fresh, sparkling water from the mouth of the Amazon River.

To those of my race who depend on bettering their condition in a foreign land, or who underestimate the importance of cultivating friendly relations with the Southern white man who is their next-door neighbor, I would say: Cast down your bucket where you are; cast it down in making friends, in every manly way, of the people of all races by whom we are surrounded. Cast it down in agriculture, mechanics, in commerce, in domestic service, and in the professions. And in this connection it is well to bear in mind that whatever other sins the South may be called upon to bear, when it comes to business pure and simple, it is in the South that the Negro is given a man's chance in the commercial world, and in nothing is this Exposition more eloquent than in emphasizing this chance. Our greatest danger is that, in the great leap from slavery to freedom, we may overlook the fact that the masses of us are to live by the productions of our hands and fail to keep in mind that we shall prosper in the proportion as we learn to dignify and glorify common labor, and put brains and skill into the common occupations of life; shall prosper in proportion as we learn to draw the line between the superficial and the substantial, the ornamental gewgaws of life and the useful. No race can prosper till it learns that there is as much dignity in tilling a field as in writing a poem. It is at the bottom of life we must begin, and not at the top. Nor should we permit our grievances to overshadow our opportunities.

To those of the white race who look to the incoming of those of foreign birth and strange tongue and habits for the prosperity of the South, were I permitted I would repeat what I say to my own race, "Cast down your bucket where you are." Cast it down among the 8,000,000 Negroes whose habits you know, whose fidelity and love you have tested in days when to have proved treacherous meant the ruin of your firesides. Cast down your bucket among these people who have, without strikes and labor wars, tilled your fields, cleared your forests, builded your railroads and cities, and brought forth treasures from the bowels of the earth and helped make possible this magnificent representation of the progress of the South. Casting down your bucket among my people, helping and encouraging them as you are doing on these grounds, and, with education of head, hand and heart, you will find that they will buy your surplus land, make blossom the waste places in your fields, and run your factories.

While doing this, you can be sure in the future, as in the past, that you and your families will be surrounded by the most patient, faithful, law-abiding, and unresentful people that the world has seen. As we have proved our loyalty to you in the past, in nursing your children, watching by the sickbed of your mothers and fathers, and often following them with tear-dimmed eyes to their graves, so in the future, in our humble way, we shall stand by you with a devotion that no foreigner can approach, ready to lay down our lives, if need be, in defense of yours; interlacing our industrial, commercial, civil, and religious life with yours in a way that shall make the interests of both races one. In all things that are purely social we can be as separate as the fingers, yet one as the hand in all things essential to mutual progress.

There is no defense or security for any of us except in the highest intelligence and development of all. If anywhere there are efforts tending to curtail the fullest growth of the Negro, let these efforts be turned into stimulating, encouraging and making him the most useful and intelligent citizen. Effort or means so invested will pay a thousand percent interest. These efforts will be twice blessed—"blessing him that gives and him that takes."

There is no escape, through law of man or God, from the inevitable:

The laws of changeless justice bind
Oppressor with oppressed,
And close as sin and suffering joined
We march to fate abreast.

Nearly sixteen million hands will aid you in pulling the load upward, or they will pull against you the load downward. We shall constitute one-third and more of the ignorance and crime of the South, or one-third its intelligence and progress; we shall contribute one-third to the business and industrial prosperity of the South, or we shall prove a veritable body of death, stagnating, depressing, retarding every effort to advance the body politic.

Gentlemen of the Exposition: As we present to you our humble effort at an exhibition of our progress, you must not expect overmuch. Starting thirty years ago with ownership here and there in a few quilts and pumpkins and chickens (gathered from miscellaneous sources), remember: the path that has led us from these to the invention and production of agricultural implements, buggies, steam engines, newspapers, books, statuary, carving, paintings, the management of drugstores and banks, has not been trodden without contact with thorns and thistles. While we take pride in what we exhibit as a result of our independent efforts, we do not for a moment forget that our part in this exhibition would fall far short of your expectations but for the constant help that has come to our educational life, not only from the Southern states, but especially from Northern philanthropists who have made their gifts a constant stream of blessing and encouragement.

The wisest among my race understand that the agitation of questions of social equality is the extremest folly, and that progress in the enjoyment of all the privileges that will come to us must be the result of severe and constant struggle rather than of artificial forcing. No race that has anything to contribute to the markets of the world is long in any degree ostracized. It is important and right that all privileges of the laws be ours, but it is vastly more important that we be prepared for the exercise of those privileges. The opportunity to earn a dollar in a factory just now is worth infinitely more than the opportunity to spend a dollar in an opera house.

In conclusion, may I repeat that nothing in thirty years has given us more hope and encouragement and drawn us so near to you of the white race as this opportunity offered by the Exposition; and here bending, as it were, over the altar that represents the results of the struggles of your race and mine, both starting practically empty-handed three decades ago, I pledge that, in your effort to work out the great and intricate problem which God has laid at the doors of the South, you shall have at all times the patient, sympathetic help of my race. Only let this be constantly in mind that, while from representations in these buildings of the product of field, of forest, of mine, of factory, letters and art, much good will come—yet by far above and beyond material benefits, will be that higher good, that let us pray God will come, in a blotting out of sectional differences and racial animosities and suspicions, in a determination to administer absolute justice, in a willing obedience among all classes to the mandates of law. This, coupled with material prosperity, will bring into our beloved South a new heaven and a new earth.

7.2 W. E. B. DU BOIS

The Talented Tenth

W. E. B. Du Bois (1868–1963) was a renowned intellectual leader during the first half of the twentieth century. In 1895 he became the first African American to be awarded a Ph.D. from Harvard University. Du Bois took a position as professor of classics at Wilberforce University in Ohio while pursuing his doctoral studies. He also taught at the University of Pennsylvania in Philadelphia, Pennsylvania, where he published his well-known study *The Philadelphia Negro: A Sociological Study* (1899), and at Atlanta University in Atlanta, Georgia. In 1900 he attended the Pan African Congress in London, where he made his famous statement, "The problem of the twentieth century is the problem of the color line." Du Bois was one of the founders of the National Negro Committee, which became the National Association for the Advancement of Colored People (NAACP). He edited the NAACP's *Crisis* magazine for 24 years, and he became one of the most prominent figures in the struggle for civil liberties in the United States in the twentieth century.

In 1903 Du Bois published *The Souls of Black Folk,* a book that brought him critical acclaim and a wide reading audience. In that same year, Du Bois wrote the selection that follows, "The Talented Tenth," and included it in a book of essays entitled *The Negro Problem.* In "The Talented Tenth," Du Bois argues for the development of a Black educational elite that would be able to articulate the interests of African Americans on an equal basis with the white intellectual establishment.

Key Concept: the "talented tenth," and the need to develop an African American intellectual elite

The Negro race, like all races, is going to be saved by its exceptional men. The problem of education, then, among Negroes must first of all deal with the Talented Tenth; it is the problem of developing the Best of this race that they may guide the Mass away from the contamination and death of the Worst, in their own and other races. Now the training of men is a difficult and intricate task. Its technique is a matter for educational experts, but its object is for the vision of seers. If we make money the object of man-training, we shall develop money-makers but not necessarily men; if we make technical skill the object of education, we may possess artisans but not, in nature, men. Men we shall have only as we make manhood the object of the work of the schools—intelligence, broad sympathy, knowledge of the world that was and is, and of the relation of men to it—this is the curriculum of that Higher Education which must underlie true life. On this foundation we may build bread winning, skill of hand and quickness of brain, with never a fear lest the child and man mistake the means of living for the object of life.

If this be true—and who can deny it—three tasks lay before me; first to show from the past that the Talented Tenth as they have risen among American Negroes have been worthy of leadership; secondly, to show how these men may be educated and developed; and thirdly, to show their relation to the Negro problem.

You misjudge us because you do not know us. From the very first it has been the educated and intelligent of the Negro people that have led and elevated the mass, and the sole obstacles that nullified and retarded their efforts were slavery and race prejudice; for what is slavery but the legalized survival of the unfit and the nullification of the work of natural internal leadership? Negro leadership, therefore, sought from the first to rid the race of this awful incubus that it might make way for natural selection and the survival of the fittest. In colonial days came Phillis Wheatley and Paul Cuffee striving against the bars of prejudice; and Benjamin Banneker, the almanac maker, voiced their longings when he said to Thomas Jefferson, "I freely and cheerfully acknowledge that I am of the African race, and in colour which is natural to them, of the deepest dye; and it is under a sense of the most profound gratitude to the Supreme Ruler of the Universe, that I now confess to you that I am not under that state of tyrannical thraldom and inhuman captivity to which too many of my brethren are doomed, but that I have abundantly tasted of the fruition of those blessings which proceed from that free and unequalled liberty with which you are favored, and which I hope you will willingly allow, you have mercifully received from the immediate hand of that Being from whom preceedeth every good and perfect gift.

"Suffer me to recall to your mind that time, in which the arms of the British crown were exerted with every powerful effort, in order to reduce you to a state of servitude; look back, I entreat you, on the variety of dangers to which you were exposed; reflect on that period in which every human aid appeared unavailable, and in which even hope and fortitude wore the aspect of inability to the conflict, and you cannot but be led to a serious and grateful sense of your miraculous and providential preservation, you cannot but acknowledge, that the present freedom and tranquility which you enjoy, you have mercifully received, and that a peculiar blessing of heaven.

"This, sir, was a time when you clearly saw into the injustice of a state of Slavery, and in which you had just apprehensions of the horrors of its condition. It was then that your abhorrence thereof was so excited, that you publicly held forth this true and invaluable doctrine, which is worthy to be recorded and remembered in all succeeding ages: 'We hold these truths to be self evident, that all men are created equal; that they are endowed with certain inalienable rights, and that among these are life, liberty and the pursuit of happiness.' "

Then came Dr. James Derham, who could tell even the learned Dr. Rush something of medicine, and Lemuel Haynes, to whom Middlebury College gave a honorary A.M. in 1804. These and others we may call the Revolutionary group of distinguished Negroes—they were persons of marked ability, leaders of a Talented Tenth, standing conspicuously among the best of their time. They strove by word and deed to save the color line from becoming the line between the bond and free, but all they could do was nullified by Eli Whitney and the Curse of Gold. So they passed into forgetfulness.

But their spirit did not wholly die; here and there in the early part of the century came other exceptional men. Some were natural sons of unnatural fathers and were given often a liberal training and thus a race of educated mulattoes sprang up to plead for black men's rights. There was Ira Aldridge, whom all Europe loved to honor; there was that Voice crying in the Wilderness, David Walker, and saying:

"I declare it does appear to me as though some nations think God is asleep, or that he made the Africans for nothing else but to dig their mines and work their farms, or they cannot believe history, sacred or profane. I ask every man who has a heart, and is blessed with the privilege of believing—Is not God a God of justice to all his creatures? Do you say he is? Then if he gives peace and tranquility to tyrants and permits them to keep our fathers, our mothers, ourselves and our children in eternal ignorance and wretchedness to support them and their families, would he be to us a God of Justice? I ask, O, ye Christians, who hold us and our children in the most abject ignorance and degradation that ever a people were afflicted with since the world began—I say if God gives you peace and tranquility, and suffers you thus to go on afflicting us, and our children, who have never given you the least provocation—would He be to us a God of Justice? If you will allow that we are men, who feel for each other, does not the blood of our fathers and of us, their children, cry aloud to the Lord of Sabaoth against you for the cruelties and murder with which you have and do continue to afflict us?"

This was the wild voice that first aroused Southern legislation in 1829 to the terrors of abolitionism.

In 1831 there met that first Negro convention in Philadelphia, at which the world gaped curiously but which bravely attacked the problems of race and slavery, crying out against persecution and declaring that "Laws as cruel in themselves as they were unconstitutional and unjust, have in many places been enacted against our poor, unfriended and unoffending brethren (without a shadow of provocation on our part), at whose bare recital the very savage draws himself up for fear of contagion—looks noble and prides himself because he bears not the name of Christian." Side by side this free Negro movement, and the movement for abolition, strove until they merged into one strong stream. Too little notice has been taken of the work which the Talented Tenth among Negroes took in the great abolition crusade. From the very day that a Philadelphia colored man became the first subscriber to Garrison's "Liberator," to the day when Negro soldiers made the Emancipation Proclamation possible, black leaders worked shoulder to shoulder with white men in a movement, the success of which would have been impossible without them. There was [Robert] Purvis and [Charles Lenox] Remond, [James] Pennington and Highland Garnett, Sojourner Truth and Alexander Crummell, and above all, Frederick Douglass—what would the abolition movement have been without them? They stood as living examples of the possibilities of the Negro race, their own hard experiences and well wrought culture said silently more than all the drawn periods of orators—they were the men who made American slavery impossible. As Maria Weston Chapman once said, from the school of anti-slavery agitation "a throng of authors, editors, lawyers, orators and accomplished gentlemen of color have taken their degree! It has equally implanted hopes and aspirations, noble thoughts, sublime purposes, in the hearts of both races. It has prepared the white man for the freedom of the black man, and it has made the black man scorn the thought of enslavement, as does a white man, as far as its influence has extended. Strengthen that noble influence! Before its organization, the country only saw here and there in slavery some faithful Cudjoe or Dinah, whose strong natures blossomed even in bondage, like a fine plant beneath a heavy stone. Now, under the elevating and cherishing influence of the American Anti-Slavery Society, the colored race, like the white, furnished Corinthian capitals for the noblest temples."

Where were these black abolitionists trained? Some, like Frederick Douglass were self-trained, but yet trained liberally; others, like Alexander Crummel and [James] McCune Smith, graduated from famous foreign universities. Most of them rose up through the colored schools of New York and Philadelphia and Boston, taught by college-bred men like [John Brown] Russworm, of Dartmouth, and college-bred white men like [Elias] Neau and [Anthony] Benezet.

After emancipation came a new group of educated and gifted leaders: [John Mercer] Langston, [Blanche K.] Bruce and [Robert Brown] Elliott, [Richard Theodore] Greener, [Dr. Daniel Hale] Williams and [Daniel A.] Payne. Through political organization, historical and polemic writing and moral regeneration, these men strove to uplift their people. It is the fashion of to-day to sneer at them and to say that with freedom Negro leadership should have begun at the plow and not in the Senate—a foolish and mischievous lie; two hundred and fifty years that black serf toiled at the plow and yet that toiling was in vain till the Senate passed the war amendments; and two hundred and fifty years more the half-free serf of to-day may toil at his plow, but unless he have political rights and righteously guarded civic status, he will still remain the poverty-stricken and ignorant plaything of rascals, that he now is. This all sane men know even if they dare not say it.

And so we come to the present—a day of cowardice and vacillation, of strident wide-voiced wrong and faint hearted compromise; of double-faced dallying with Truth and Right. Who are to-day guiding the work of the Negro people? The "exceptions" of course. And yet so sure as this Talented Tenth is pointed out, the blind worshippers of the Average cry out in alarm: "They are exceptions, look here at death, disease and crime—these are the happy rule." Of course they are the rule, because a silly nation made them the rule. Because for three long centuries this people lynched Negroes who dared to be brave, raped black women who dared to be virtuous, crushed dark-hued youth who dared to be ambitious, and encouraged and made to flourish servility and lewdness and apathy. But not even this was able to crush all manhood and chastity and aspiration from black folk. A saving remnant continually survives and persists, continually aspires, continually shows itself in thrift and ability and character. Exceptional it is to be sure, but this is its chiefest promise; it shows the capability of Negro blood, the promise of black men. Do Americans ever stop to reflect that there are in this land a million men of Negro blood, well-educated, owners of homes, against the honor of whose womanhood no breath was ever raised, whose men occupy positions of trust and usefulness, and who, judged by any standard, have reached the full measure of the best type of modern European culture? Is it fair, is it decent, is it Christian to ignore these facts of the Negro problem, to belittle such aspiration, to nullify such leadership and seek to crush these people back into the mass out of which by toil and travail, they and their fathers have raised themselves?

Can the masses of the Negro people be in any possible way more quickly raised than by the effort and example of this aristocracy of talent and character? Was there ever a nation on God's fair earth civilized from the bottom upward? Never; it is, ever was and ever will be from the top downward that culture filters. The Talented Tenth rises and pulls all that are worth the saving up to their vantage ground. This is the history of human progress; and the two historical mistakes which have hindered that progress were the thinking first that no more could ever rise save the few already risen; or second, that it would better the unrisen to pull the risen down.

How then shall the leaders of the struggling people be trained and the hands of the risen strengthened? There can be but one answer: The best and most capable of their youth must be schooled in the colleges and universities of the land. We will not quarrel as to just what the university of the Negro should teach or how it should teach it—I willingly admit that each soul and each race-soul needs its own peculiar curriculum. But this is true: A university is a human invention for the transmission of knowledge and culture from generation to generation, through the training of quick minds and pure hearts, and for this work no other human invention will suffice, not even trade and industrial schools.

All men cannot go to college but some men must; every isolated group or nation must have its yeast, must have for the talented few centers of training where men are not so mystified and befuddled by the hard and necessary toil of earning a living, as to have no aims higher than their bellies, and no God greater than Gold. This is true training, and thus in the beginning were the favored sons of the freedmen trained. Out of the colleges of the North came, after the blood of war, Ware, Cravath, Chase, Andrews, Bumstead and Spence to build the foundations of knowledge and civilization in the black South. Where ought they to have begun to build? At the bottom, of course, quibbles the mole with his eyes in the earth. Aye! truly at the bottom, at the very bottom; at the bottom of knowledge, down in the very depths of knowledge there where the roots of justice strike into the lowest soil of Truth. And so they did begin; they founded colleges, and up from the colleges shot normal schools, and out from the normal schools went teachers, and around the normal teachers clustered other teachers to teach the public schools; the college trained in Greek and Latin and mathematics, 2,000 men; and these men trained full 50,000 others in morals and manners, and they in turn taught thrift and the alphabet to nine millions of men, who to-day hold $300,000,000 of property. It was a miracle—the most wonderful peace-battle of the 19th century, and yet to-day men smile at it, and in fine superiority tell us that it was all a strange mistake; that a proper way to found a system of education is to gather the children and buy them spelling books and hoes; afterward men may look about for teachers, if haply they may find them; or again they would teach men Work, but as for Life—why, what has Work to do with Life, they ask vacantly.

Was the work of these college founders successful; did it stand the test of time? Did the college graduates, with all their fine theories of life, really live? Are they useful men helping to civilize and elevate their less fortunate fellows? Let us see. Omitting all institutions which have not actually graduated students from a college course, there are to-day in the United States thirty-four institutions giving something above high school training to Negroes and designed especially for this race.

Three of these were established in border States before the War; thirteen were planted by the Freedman's Bureau in the years 1864–1869; nine were established between 1870 and 1880 by various church bodies; five were established after 1881 by Negro churches, and four are state institutions supported by United States' agricultural funds. In most cases the college departments are small adjuncts to high and common school work. As a matter of fact six institutions—Atlanta, Fisk, Howard, Shaw, Wilberforce and Leland, are the important Negro colleges so far as actual work and number of students are concerned. In all these institutions, seven hundred and fifty Negro college students are enrolled. . . . In addition to these students in the South, Negroes have attended Northern colleges for many years. As early as 1826 one was graduated from Bowdoin College, and from that time till to-day nearly every year has seen elsewhere, other such graduates. They have, of course, met much color prejudice. Fifty years ago very few colleges would admit them at all. Even to-day no Negro has ever been admitted to Princeton, and at some other leading institutions they are rather endured than encouraged. Oberlin was the great pioneer in the work of blotting out the color line in colleges, and has more Negro graduates by far than any other Northern college. . . .

The most interesting question, and in many respects the crucial question, to be asked concerning college-bred Negroes, is: Do they earn a living? It has been intimated more than once that the higher training of Negroes has resulted in sending into the world of work, men who could find nothing to do suitable to their talents. Now and then there comes a rumor of a colored college man working at menial service, etc. Fortunately, returns as to occupations of college-bred Negroes, gathered by the Atlanta conference, are quite full—nearly sixty per cent of the total number of graduates.

This enables us to reach fairly certain conclusions as to the occupations of all college-bred Negroes. Of 1,312 persons reported . . . over half are teachers, a sixth are preachers, another sixth are students and professional men; over 6 per cent are farmers, artisans and merchants, and 4 per cent are in government services. . . .

These figures illustrate vividly the function of the college-bred Negro. He is, as he ought to be, the group leader, the man who sets the ideals of the community where he lives, directs its thoughts and heads its social move-ments. It need hardly be argued that the Negro people need social leadership more than most groups; that they have no traditions to fall back upon, no long established customs, no strong family ties, no well defined social classes. All these things must be slowly and painfully evolved. The preacher was, even before the war, the group leader of the Negroes, and the church their greatest social institution. Naturally this preacher was ignorant and often immoral, and the problem of replacing the older type by better educated men has been a difficult one. Both by direct work and by direct influence on other preachers, and on congregations, the college-bred preacher has an opportunity for reformatory work and moral inspiration, the value of which cannot be overestimated.

It has, however, been in the furnishing of teachers that the Negro college has found its peculiar function. Few persons realize how vast a work, how mighty a revolution has been thus accomplished. To furnish five millions and more of ignorant people with teachers of their own race and blood, in one generation, was not only a very difficult undertaking, but a very important one, in that, it placed before the eyes of almost every Negro child an attainable ideal. It brought the masses of the blacks in contact with modern civilization, made black men the leaders of their communities and trainers of the new generation. In this work college-bred Negroes were first teachers, and then teachers of teachers. And here it is that the broad culture of college work has been of peculiar value. Knowledge of life and its wider meaning, has been the point of the Negro's deepest ignorance, and the sending out of teachers whose training has not been simply for bread winning, but also for human culture, has been of inestimable value in the training of these men.

In earlier years the two occupations of preacher and teacher were practi-cally the only ones open to the black college graduate. Of later years a larger diversity of life among his people, has opened new avenues of employment. Nor have these college men been paupers and spendthrifts; 557 college-bred Negroes owned in 1899, $1,342,862.50 worth of real estate, (assessed value) or $2,411 per family. The real value of the total accumulations of the whole group is perhaps about $10,000,000 or $5,000 a piece. Pitiful, is it not, beside the fortunes of oil kings and steel trust, but after all is the fortune of the millionaire the only stamp of true and successful living? Alas! it is, with many, and there's the rub.

The problem of training the Negro is to-day immensely complicated by the fact that the whole question of the efficiency and appropriateness of our present systems of education, for any kind of child, is a matter of active debate, in which final settlement seems still afar off. Consequently it often happens that persons arguing for or against certain systems of education for Negroes, have these controversies in mind and miss the real question at issue. The main question, so far as the Southern Negro is concerned, is: What under the present circumstance, must a system of education do in order to raise the Negro as quickly as possible in the scale of civilization? The answer to this question seems to me clear: It must strengthen the Negro's character, increase his knowl-edge and teach him to earn a living. Now it goes without saying, that it is hard to do all these things simultaneously or suddenly, and that at the same time it will not do to give all the attention to one and neglect the others; we could give black boys trades, but that alone will not civilize a race of ex-slaves; we might simply increase their knowledge of the world, but this would not necessarily make them wish to use this knowledge honestly; we might seek to strengthen character and purpose, but to what end if this people have nothing to eat or to wear? A system of education is not one thing, nor does it have a single definite object, nor is it a mere matter of schools. Education is that whole system of human training within and without the school house walls, which molds and develops men. If then we start out to train an ignorant and unskilled people with a heritage of bad habits, our system of training must set before itself two great aims—the one dealing with knowledge and character, the other part seeking to give the child the technical knowledge necessary for him to earn a living under the present circumstances. These objects are accomplished in part by the opening of the common schools on the one, and of the industrial schools on the other. But only in part, for there must also be trained those who are to teach these schools—men and women of knowledge and culture and technical skill who understand modern civilization, and have the training and aptitude to impart it to the children under them. There must be teachers, and teachers of teachers, and to attempt to establish any sort of a system of common and industrial school training, without *first* (and I say *first* advisedly) without *first* providing for the higher training of the very best teachers, is simply throwing your money to the winds. School houses do not teach themselves—piles of brick and mortar and machinery do not send out *men*. It is the trained living human soul, cultivated and strengthened by long study and thought, that breathes the real breath of life into boys and girls and makes them human, whether they be black or white, Greek, Russian or American. Nothing, in these latter days, has so dampened the faith of thinking Negroes in recent educational movements, as the fact that such movements have been accompanied by ridicule and denouncement and decrying of those very institutions of higher training which made the Negro public school possible, and make Negro industrial schools thinkable. It was Fisk, Atlanta, Howard and Straight, those colleges born of the faith and sacrifice of the abolitionists, that placed in the black schools of the South the 30,000 teachers and more, which some, who depreciate the work of these higher schools, are using to teach their own new experiments. If Hampton, Tuskegee and the hundred other industrial schools prove in the future to be as successful as they deserve to be, then their success in training black artisans for the South, will be due primarily to the white colleges of the North and the black colleges of the South, which trained the teachers who to-day conduct these institutions. . . .

I would not deny, or for a moment seem to deny, the paramount necessity of teaching the Negro to work, and to work steadily and skillfully; or seem to depreciate in the slightest degree the important part industrial schools must play in the accomplishment of these ends, but I *do* say, and insist upon it, that it is industrialism drunk with its vision of success, to imagine that its own work can be accomplished without providing for the training of broadly cultured men and women to teach its own teachers, and to teach the teachers of the public schools.

But I have already said that human education is not simply a matter of schools; it is much more a matter of family and group life—the training of one's home, of one's daily companions, of one's social class. Now the black boy of the South moves in a black world—a world with its own leaders, its own thoughts, its own ideas. In this world he gets by far the larger part of his life training, and through the eyes of the dark world he peers into the veiled world beyond. Who guides and determines the education which he receives in his world? His teachers here are the group leaders of the Negro people—the physicians and clergymen, the trained fathers and mothers, the influential and forceful men about him of all kinds; here it is, if at all, that the culture of the surrounding world trickles through and is handed by the graduates of the higher schools. Can such culture training of group leaders be neglected? Can we afford to ignore it? Do you think that if the leaders of thought among Negroes are not trained and educated thinkers, that they will have no leaders? On the contrary a hundred half-trained demagogues will still hold the places they so largely occupy now, and hundreds of vociferous busy-bodies will multiply. You have no choice; either you must help furnish this race from within its own ranks with thoughtful men of trained leadership, or you must suffer the evil consequences of a headless misguided rabble.

I am an earnest advocate of manual training and trade teaching for black boys, and for white boys, too. I believe that next to the founding of Negro colleges the most valuable addition to Negro education since the war, has been industrial training for black boys. Nevertheless, I insist that the object of all true education is not to make men carpenters, it is to make carpenters men; there are two means of making the carpenter a man, each equally important: the first is to give the group and community in which he works, liberally trained teachers and leaders to teach him and his family what life means; the second is to give him sufficient intelligence and technical skill to make him an efficient workman; the first object demands the Negro college and college-bred men—not a quantity of colleges, but a few of excellent quality; not too many college-bred men, but enough to leaven the lump, to inspire the masses, to raise a good system of common schools, well-taught, conveniently located and properly equipped. . . .

What is the chief need for the building up of the Negro public school in the South? The Negro race in the South needs teachers to-day above all else. This is the concurrent testimony of all who know the situation. . . . [I]t is safe to say that the Negro has not one-tenth his quota in college studies. How baseless, therefore, is the charge of too much training! We need Negro teachers for the Negro common schools, and we need first-class normal schools and colleges to train them. This is the work of higher Negro education and it must be done.

Further than this, after being provided with group leaders of civilization, and a foundation of intelligence in the public schools, the carpenter, in order to be a man, needs technical skill. This calls for trade schools. Now trade schools are not nearly such simple things as people once thought. The original idea was that the "Industrial" school was to furnish education, practically free, to those willing to work for it; it was to "do" things—i.e.: become a center of productive industry, it was to be partially, if not wholly, self-supporting, and it was to teach trades. Admirable as were some of the ideas underlying this scheme, the whole thing simply would not work in practice; it was found that if you were to use time and material to teach trades thoroughly, you could not at the same time keep the industries on a commercial basis and make them pay. Many schools started out to do this on a large scale and went into virtual bankruptcy. . . .

[M]odern industry has taken great strides since the war, and the teaching of trades is no longer a simple matter. Machinery and long processes of work have greatly changed the work of the carpenter, the ironworker and the shoemaker. A really efficient workman must be today an intelligent man who has had good technical training in addition to thorough common school, and perhaps even higher training. To meet this situation the industrial schools began a further development; they established distinct Trade Schools for the thorough training of better class artisans, and at the same time they sought to preserve for the purpose of general education, such of the simpler processes of elementary trade learning, as were best suited therefor. In this differentiation of the Trade School and manual training, the best of the industrial schools simply followed the plain trend of the present educational epoch. . . .

Thus, again, in the manning of trade schools and manual training schools we are thrown back upon the higher training as its source and chief support. There was a time when any aged and wornout carpenter could teach in a trade school. But not so to-day. Indeed the demand for college-bred men by a school like Tuskegee, ought to make Mr. Booker T. Washington the firmest friend of higher training. Here he has as helpers the son of a Negro senator, trained in Greek and the humanities, and graduated at Harvard; the son of a Negro congressman and lawyer, trained in Latin and mathematics, and graduated at Oberlin; he has as his wife, a woman who read Virgil and Homer in the same class room with me; he has as college chaplain, a classical graduate of Atlanta University; as teacher of science, a graduate of Fisk; as teacher of history, a graduate of Smith—indeed some thirty of his chief teachers are college graduates, and instead of studying French grammars in the midst of weeds, or buying pianos for dirty cabins, they are at Mr. Washington's right hand helping him in a noble work. And yet one of the effects of Mr. Washington's propaganda has been to throw doubt upon the expedience of such training for Negroes, as these persons have had.

Men of America, the problem is plain before you. Here is a race transplanted through the criminal foolishness of your fathers. Whether you like it or not the millions are here, and here they will remain. If you do not lift them up, they will pull you down. Education and work are the levers to uplift a people. Work alone will not do it unless inspired by the right ideals and guided by intelligence. Education must not simply teach work—it must teach Life. The Talented Tenth of the Negro race must be made leaders of thought and missionaries of culture among their people. No others can do this work and Negro colleges must train men for it. The Negro race, like all other races, is going to be saved by its exceptional men.

A Talk to Teachers

James Baldwin (1924–1987) was a widely known twentieth-century African American essayist, novelist, and playwright. Born and raised in the Harlem ghettos in New York City, he became one of the most eloquent voices in the struggle for civil rights in the United States. His works, which reflect his own experience as a Black American writer and which focus on themes relating to the struggle for human rights, include *Go Tell It on the Mountain* (1953), his first novel and a best-seller; the play *The Amen Corner* (1965); and a collection of essays entitled *Notes of a Native Son* (1955), which attracted much critical attention and public acceptance in both Europe and America. In November 1962 he wrote a long essay on the Black Muslim separatist movement and the civil rights struggle in general; it was republished as a book under the title *The Fire Next Time* (1963).

On October 16, 1963, Baldwin agreed to give a talk to approximately 200 New York City teachers at one of their professional in-service meetings. The topic he chose to speak on was "The Negro Child—His Self Image." Baldwin delivered the talk extemporaneously, but he permitted it to be recorded. Because Baldwin was a major voice in the civil rights struggle at the time, his remarks were published in the December 21, 1963, edition of *Saturday Review* under the title "A Talk to Teachers." The following selection is from that talk.

Key Concept: a child's right to critically challenge social reality

*L*et's begin by saying that we are living through a very dangerous time. . . . We are in a revolutionary situation, no matter how unpopular that word has become in this country. The society in which we live is desperately menaced, not by Khrushchev [premier of the Soviet Union], but from within. So any citizen of this country who figures himself as responsible—and particularly those of you who deal with the minds and hearts of young people—must be prepared to "go for broke." Or to put it another way, you must understand that in the attempt to correct so many generations of bad faith and cruelty, when it is operating not only in the classroom but in society, you will meet the most fantastic, the most brutal, and the most determined resistance. There is no point in pretending that this won't happen.

Now, . . . I beg you to let me leave that and go back to what I think to be the entire purpose of education in the first place. It would seem to me that when a child is born, if I'm the child's parent, it is my obligation and my high duty to civilize that child. Man is a social animal. He cannot exist without a society. A society, in turn, depends on certain things which everyone within that society takes for granted. Now, the crucial paradox which confronts us here is that the whole process of education occurs within a social framework and is designed to perpetuate the aims of society. Thus, for example, the boys and girls who were born during the era of the Third Reich, when educated to the purposes of the Third Reich, became barbarians. The paradox of education is precisely this—that as one begins to become conscious one begins to examine the society in which he is being educated. The purpose of education, finally, is to create in a person the ability to look at the world for himself, to make his own decisions, to say to himself this is black or this is white, to decide for himself whether there is a God in heaven or not. To ask questions of the universe, and then learn to live with those questions, is the way he achieves his own identity. But no society is really anxious to have that kind of person around. What societies really, ideally, want is a citizenry which will simply obey the rules of society. If a society succeeds in this, that society is about to perish. The obligation of anyone who thinks of himself as responsible is to examine society and try to change it and to fight it—at no matter what risk. This is the only hope society has. This is the only way societies change.

Now, if what I have tried to sketch has any validity, it becomes thoroughly clear, at least to me, that any Negro who is born in this country and undergoes the American educational system runs the risk of becoming schizophrenic. On the one hand he is born in the shadow of the stars and stripes and he is assured it represents a nation which has never lost a war. He pledges allegiance to that flag which guarantees "liberty and justice for all." He is part of a country in which anyone can become President, and so forth. But on the other hand he is also assured by his country and his countrymen that he has never contributed anything to civilization—that his past is nothing more than a record of humiliations gladly endured. He is assured by the republic that he, his father, his mother, and his ancestors were happy, shiftless, watermelon-eating darkies who loved Mr. Charlie and Miss Ann, that the value he has as a black man is proven by one thing only—his devotion to white people. If you think I am exaggerating, examine the myths which proliferate in this country about Negroes.

Now all this enters the child's consciousness much sooner than we as adults would like to think it does. As adults, we are easily fooled because we are so anxious to be fooled. But children are very different. Children, not yet aware that it is dangerous to look too deeply at anything, look at everything, look at each other, and draw their own conclusions. They don't have the vocabulary to express what they see, and we, their elders, know how to intimidate them very easily and very soon. But a black child, looking at the world around him, though he cannot know quite what to make of it, is aware that there is a reason why his mother works so hard, why his father is always on edge. He is aware that there is some reason why, if he sits down in the front of the bus, his father or mother slaps him and drags him to the back of the bus.

He is aware that there is some terrible weight on his parents' shoulders which menaces him. And it isn't long—in fact it begins when he is in school—before he discovers the shape of his oppression.

Let us say that the child is seven years old and I am his father, and I decide to take him to the zoo, or to Madison Square Garden, or to the U.N. Building, or to any of the tremendous monuments we find all over New York. We get into a bus and we go from where I live on 131st Street and Seventh Avenue downtown through the park and we get into New York City, which is not Harlem. Now, where the boy lives—even if it is a housing project—is in an undesirable neighborhood. If he lives in one of those housing projects of which everyone in New York is so proud, he has at the front door, if not closer, the pimps, the whores, the junkies—in a word, the danger of life in the ghetto. And the child knows this, though he doesn't know why.

I still remember my first sight of New York. It was really another city when I was born—where I was born. We looked down over the Park Avenue streetcar tracks. It was Park Avenue, but I didn't know what Park Avenue meant *downtown*. The Park Avenue I grew up on, which is still standing, is dark and dirty. No one would dream of opening a Tiffany's on that Park Avenue, and when you go downtown you discover that you are literally in the white world. It is rich—or at least it looks rich. It is clean—because they collect garbage downtown. There are doormen. People walk about as though they owned where they were—and indeed they do. And it's a great shock. It's very hard to relate yourself to this. You don't know what it means. You know—you know instinctively—that none of this is for you. You know this before you are told. And who is it for and who is paying for it? And why isn't it for you?

Later on when you become a grocery boy or messenger and you try to enter one of those buildings a man says, "Go to the back door." Still later, if you happen by some odd chance to have a friend in one of those buildings, the man says, "Where's your package?" Now this by no means is the core of the matter. What I'm trying to get at is that by this time the Negro child has had, effectively, almost all the doors of opportunity slammed in his face, and there are very few things he can do about it. He can more or less accept it with an absolutely inarticulate and dangerous rage inside—all the more dangerous because it is never expressed. It is precisely those silent people whom white people see every day of their lives—I mean your porter and your maid, who never say anything more than "Yes Sir" and "No Ma'am." They will tell you it's raining if that is what you want to hear, and they will tell you the sun is shining if *that* is what you want to hear. They really hate you—really hate you because in their eyes (and they're right) you stand between them and life. I want to come back to that in a moment. It is the most sinister of the facts, I think, which we now face.

There is something else the Negro child can do, too. Every street boy—and I was a street boy, so I know—looking at the society which has produced him, looking at the standards of that society which are not honored by anybody, looking at your churches and the government and the politicians, understands that this structure is operated for someone else's benefit—not for his. And there's no room in it for him. If he is really cunning, really ruthless, really strong—and many of us are—he becomes a kind of criminal. He becomes a kind of criminal because that's the only way he can live. Harlem and every ghetto in this city—every ghetto in this country—is full of people who live outside the law. They wouldn't dream of calling a policeman. They wouldn't, for a moment, listen to any of those professions of which we are so proud on the Fourth of July. They have turned away from this country forever and totally. They live by their wits and really long to see the day when the entire structure comes down.

The point of all this is that black men were brought here as a source of cheap labor. They were indispensable to the economy. In order to justify the fact that men were treated as though they were animals, the white republic had to brainwash itself into believing that they were, indeed, animals and *deserved* to be treated like animals. Therefore it is almost impossible for any Negro child to discover anything about his actual history. The reason is that this "animal," once he suspects his own worth, once he starts believing that he is a man, has begun to attack the entire power structure. This is why America has spent such a long time keeping the Negro in his place. What I am trying to suggest to you is that it was not an accident, it was not an act of God, it was not done by well-meaning people muddling into something which they didn't understand. It was a deliberate policy hammered into place in order to make money from black flesh. And now, in 1963, because we have never faced this fact, we are in intolerable trouble.

The Reconstruction, as I read the evidence, was a bargain between the North and South to this effect: "We've liberated them from the land—and delivered them to the bosses." When we left Mississippi to come North we did not come to freedom. We came to the bottom of the labor market, and we are still there. Even the Depression of the 1930s failed to make a dent in Negroes' relationship to white workers in the labor unions. Even today, so brainwashed is this republic that people seriously ask in what they suppose to be good faith, "What does the Negro want?" I've heard a great many asinine questions in my life, but that is perhaps the most asinine and perhaps the most insulting. But the point here is that people who ask that question, thinking that they ask it in good faith, are really the victims of this conspiracy to make Negroes believe they are less than human.

In order for me to live, I decided very early that some mistake had been made somewhere. I was not a "nigger" even though you called me one. But if I was a "nigger" in your eyes, there was something about *you*—there was something *you* needed. I had to realize when I was very young that I was none of those things I was told I was. I was not, for example, happy. I never touched a watermelon for all kinds of reasons. I had been invented by white people, and I knew enough about life by this time to understand that whatever you invent, whatever you project, is you! So where we are now is that a whole country of people believe I'm a "nigger," and I *don't*, and the battle's on! Because if I am not what I've been told I am, then it means that *you're* not what you thought *you* were *either!* And that is the crisis.

It is not really a "Negro revolution" that is upsetting this country. What is upsetting the country is a sense of its own identity. If, for example, one managed to change the curriculum in all the schools so that Negroes learned more about themselves and their real contributions to this culture, you would be liberating not only Negroes, you'd be liberating white people who know nothing about their own history. And the reason is that if you are compelled to lie about one aspect of anybody's history, you must lie about it all. If you have to lie about my real role here, if you have to pretend that I hoed all that cotton just because I loved you, then you have done something to yourself. You are mad.

Now let's go back a minute. I talked earlier about those silent people—the porter and the maid—who, as I said, don't look up at the sky if you ask them if it is raining, but look into your face. My ancestors and I were very well trained. We understood very early that this was not a Christian nation. It didn't matter what you said or how often you went to church. My father and my mother and my grandfather and my grandmother knew that Christians didn't act this way. It was as simple as that. And if that was so there was no point in dealing with white people in terms of their own moral professions, for they were not going to honor them. What one did was to turn away, smiling all the time, and tell white people what they wanted to hear. But people always accuse you of reckless talk when you say this.

All this means that there are in this country tremendous reservoirs of bitterness which have never been able to find an outlet, but may find an outlet soon. It means that well-meaning white liberals place themselves in great danger when they try to deal with Negroes as though they were missionaries. It means, in brief, that a great price is demanded to liberate all those silent people so that they can breathe for the first time and *tell* you what they think of you. And a price is demanded to liberate all those white children—some of them near forty—who have never grown up, and who never will grow up, because they have no sense of their identity.

What passes for identity in America is a series of myths about one's heroic ancestors. It's astounding to me, for example, that so many people really appear to believe that the country was founded by a band of heroes who wanted to be free. That happens not to be true. What happened was that some people left Europe because they couldn't stay there any longer and had to go someplace else to make it. That's all. They were hungry, they were poor, they were convicts. Those who were making it in England, for example, did not get on the *Mayflower*. That's how the country was settled. Not by Gary Cooper. Yet we have a whole race of people, a whole republic, who believe the myths to the point where even today they select political representatives, as far as I can tell, by how closely they resemble Gary Cooper. Now this is dangerously infantile, and it shows in every level of national life. When I was living in Europe, for example, one of the worst revelations to me was the way Americans walked around Europe buying this and buying that and insulting everybody—not even out of malice, just because they didn't know any better. Well, that is the way they have always treated me. They weren't cruel, they just didn't know you were alive. They didn't know you had any feelings.

What I am trying to suggest here is that in the doing of all this for 100 years or more, it is the American white man who has long since lost his grip on reality. In some peculiar way, having created this myth about Negroes, and the myth about his own history, he created myths about the world so that, for example, he was astounded that some people could prefer Castro, astounded that there are people in the world who don't go into hiding when they hear the word "Communism," astounded that Communism is one of the realities of the twentieth century which we will not overcome by pretending that it does not exist. The political level in this country now, on the part of people who should know better, is abysmal.

The Bible says somewhere that where there is no vision the people perish. I don't think anyone can doubt that in this country today we are menaced—intolerably menaced—by a lack of vision.

It is inconceivable that a sovereign people should continue, as we do so abjectly, to say, "I can't do anything about it. It's the government." The government is the creation of the people. It is responsible to the people. And the people are responsible for it. No American has the right to allow the present government to say, when Negro children are being bombed and hosed and shot and beaten all over the deep South, that there is nothing we can do about it. There must have been a day in this country's life when the bombing of four children in Sunday School would have created a public uproar and endangered the life of a Governor Wallace. It happened here and there was no public uproar.

I began by saying that one of the paradoxes of education was that precisely at the point when you begin to develop a conscience, you must find yourself at war with your society. It is your responsibility to change society if you think of yourself as an educated person. And on the basis of the evidence—the moral and political evidence—one is compelled to say that this is a backward society. Now if I were a teacher in this school, or any Negro school, and I was dealing with Negro children, who were in my care only a few hours of every day and would then return to their homes and to the streets, children who have an apprehension of their future which with every hour grows grimmer and darker, I would try to teach them—I would try to make them know—that those streets, those houses, those dangers, those agonies by which they are surrounded, are criminal. I would try to make each child know that these things are the results of a criminal conspiracy to destroy him. I would teach him that if he intends to get to be a man, he must at once decide that he is stronger than this conspiracy and that he must never make his peace with it. And that one of his weapons for refusing to make his peace with it and for destroying it depends on what he decides he is worth. I would teach him that there are currently very few standards in this country which are worth a man's respect. That it is up to him to begin to change these standards for the sake of the life and the health of the country. I would suggest to him that the popular culture—as represented, for example, on television and in comic books and in movies—is based on fantasies created by very ill people, and he must be aware that these are fantasies that have nothing to do with reality. I would teach him that the press he reads is not as free as it says it is—and that he can do something about that, too. I would try to make him know that just as American history is longer, larger, more various, more beautiful, and more terrible than anything anyone has ever said about it, so is the world larger, more daring, more beautiful and more terrible, but principally larger—and that it belongs to him. I would teach him that he doesn't have to be bound by the expediencies of any given Administration, any given policy, any given time—that he has the right and the necessity to examine everything. I would try to show him that one has not learned anything about Castro when one says, "He is a Communist." This is a way of *not* learning something about Castro, something about Cuba, something, in fact, about the world. I would suggest to him that he is living, at the moment, in an enormous province. America is not the world and if America is going to become a nation, she must find a way—and this child must help her to find a way—to use the tremendous potential and tremendous energy which this child represents. If this country does not find a way to use that energy, it will be destroyed by that energy.

Struggle for Public Policy: Black Children Since 1950

Meyer Weinberg (b. 1920) was a professor of history in the Graduate School of Education as well as the director of the Center for Equal Education at Northwestern University. He has also been a professor of history at the City Colleges of Chicago and the editor of the journal *Integrated Education*. Throughout his career, Weinberg has been a leader in the fight for human rights in education.

The selection that follows is from what many consider to be one of the most important books ever published on the history of race and education. The selection is from chapter 3, "Struggle for Public Policy: Black Children Since 1950," of Weinberg's *A Chance to Learn: The History of Race and Education in the United States* (Cambridge University Press, 1977). In it, Weinberg traces African Americans' struggle for freedom in the years just prior to the historic *Brown v. Board of Education* decision in 1954 and the efforts to achieve school desegregation in the United States from *Brown* to the 1970s. He documents the historic leadership of Thurgood Marshall, chief counsel for the plaintiffs. He builds on the prior scholarship of African American scholars as well as on his close study of the arguments in the *Brown* decision and the historic events during and after the case. Weinberg's narrative embodies a convincing argument for social justice in America.

Key Concept: Black children and the struggle for equality of education

Midcentury marked a turning point in the history of black America. The movement for equality came under black leadership, embraced unprecedented numbers of Negroes, and became national in scope. A persistent black initiative forced a reformulation of public policies in education.

During the 1930s depression and discrimination had driven Negro living standards to new depths. Inequalities of schooling between black and white children in the South reached their widest extent in almost a century. Segregation spread in southern and northern cities. Yet a counter-movement began in the midst of despair. As earlier, political strength was a condition for impetus toward equality. In northern cities, the Negro vote became a counter for political change. New Deal welfare policies relieved significantly extensive unemployment among blacks. In 1936, in a wholesale switch away from the Republican party, Negroes became strong supporters of the Roosevelt administration. The emerging industrial union movement in the Congress of Industrial Organizations enrolled hundreds of thousands of blacks, giving "black and white workers a sense of common interest, of solidarity, that transcended racial lines."

World War II sped the process of transformation. Racial discrimination continued in employment, the armed forces, education, and public accommodations, but black protest was insistent. Membership in the NAACP grew almost ninefold between 1940 and 1946, from 50,556 to nearly 450,000. The group's branches increased threefold to 1,073. Negroes turned to demonstrative actions. The grandest of them was the projected March on Washington, organized in 1941 by A. Philip Randolph, a black labor leader. To head off the protest, President Roosevelt agreed to act against job discrimination and created by executive order the Fair Employment Practices Committee. "The Negro masses," as Dalfiume observes, "simply did not support a strategy of moderating their grievances for the duration of the war." Blacks hastened to point out parallels between Nazi racial doctrines and American racial practices.

In 1944, the U.S. Supreme Court struck down the "white primary" law of Texas, invalidating the single most important means of disfranchising the Negro voter. During the next dozen years, the number of registered Negro voters in the South rose nearly fivefold, from 250,000 to almost 1.25 million. The Negro vote seemed to be a significant element in the 1948 election of President Truman. A number of state and local measures were enacted on behalf of equal use of public accommodations and fair employment.

Southern schooling had undergone few important changes during the war. In 1946, Du Bois could write:

> The majority of Negro children in the United States, from 6 to 18, do not have the opportunity to learn to read and write. We know this is true in the country districts of Mississippi, Louisiana and a half dozen other southern states. But even in the towns and cities of the South, the Negro schools are so crowded and ill-equipped that no thorough teaching is possible.

TEACHER AND PARENT DEMANDS FOR EQUALIZATION

A new dynamic was introduced into black education when Negro teachers began taking on a new role during the late thirties and wartime. During the war, blacks became more numerous in the ranks of teachers in northern schools. Historically self-restrained from taking public action, even on behalf of their own group interests, they now began to respond publicly. They filed lawsuits demanding salary equalization with white teachers in a test of the doctrine of separate-but-equal. Courts responded almost uniformly in their favor. By 1948, of twenty-seven cases only four were lost. These victories introduced major strains into the structure of southern schools, based as they were on malappropriation of funds for whites that belonged to Negro students. If equal expenditures became a fact, white privilege would exist no longer.

The court victories engendered, in Jones's phrase, a "contagion" among black teachers throughout the South. State authorities moved quickly to create single salary schedules. They provided for state subsidies to those local school districts that pleaded an inability to meet the new requirement, lest impecunious districts be tempted to avoid creating expensive duplicate facilities by ending segregation.

Teacher equalization was often moderated by southern judges. On the one hand, they rejected school board complaints that they could not afford equalization; on the other hand, courts did not grant immediate relief to the teachers, but set up a time schedule over which equalization was to be achieved, thus, some believe, acting to coerce the Negro teachers into softening their demands.

School boards resorted to a "professional rating scale." Salaries were to be set in accordance with the judgment of the subject's supervisors, who presumably would employ defensible professional criteria. Black teachers' salaries most often turned out to be lower than their experience and training warranted. Court challenges to the new system were by and large fruitless. It proved almost impossible for the aggrieved to demonstrate that the assigned salary was set unprofessionally. To fend off suits by black teachers, one school district in Florida provided that any teacher dissatisfied with his or her placement could take the National Teacher Examination and permit the salary to be raised or lowered in accordance with the test score. The test was notorious among black teachers for its uncanny success in yielding low grades to Negro teachers. Consequently, few took up the dare.

The salary gap between black and white teachers narrowed nevertheless. In the dozen years after 1939, the average Negro salary increased from 52.5 percent to 87.2 percent of the average white salary. Black teachers' organizations had developed "a new aggressiveness" that paid off.

Black parents and, in some cases, students, also began to rebel against planned inequality and to demand equalization of facilities and programs. "At that time," NAACP counsel Thurgood Marshall recalled, "the best strategy seemed to be an attack against the segregation system by law suits seeking absolute and complete equalization of curricula, faculty, and physical equipment of the white and Negro schools on the theory that the extreme cost of maintaining two 'equal' school systems would eventually destroy segregation." A number of lawsuits were filed attacking material inequalities and asking for equalization although separate. Some cases were won; their number was not large but their import was. Perhaps 200 cases were filed against southern schools. Neither disfranchisement nor violence could be used to silence protest now. The currents of the time were against both. Southern state governments tried to deflect the movement by a rapid but highly spotty program of improvement of black school facilities.

Increased expenditure on black schools might put off one threat, but it intensified another:

A modernized physical plant and an increase in the quantity and quality of education mean greater diversity of offerings. Herein lies the danger and real significance of the new legal requirements affecting equality of educational opportunities at the physical and curriculum levels for the social system of the South. New offerings in the schools mean an increase in the number of professionally and technically trained persons at all levels—persons who, once trained, will enter the competitive labor market and thereby earn a greater share of the labor dollar.

Yet the white South of the 1940s and early 1950s was far from ready either to yield its privileges or invest seriously in equalization.

Over the period 1939–1951, in six southern states the black-white gap in current expenditures per pupil narrowed from 57.3 percent to 30.3 percent, although the absolute magnitude of the change was slight. The size of the gap in actual dollars was reduced from $53.85 to $50.12. Discrimination persisted. In seven southern states, by 1951, black children in metropolitan areas received only 76 percent of white allocations; in rural areas, 62 percent. In North Carolina, the figures were 95 and 79 percent; in Mississippi, 51 and 33 percent. Between 1940 and 1952, the value of black school buildings rose, reducing the black-white disparity from four-fifths to slightly more than one-half.

Mississippi, with at least one-tenth of all black children in the South, illustrated some of the dimensions of the challenge of equalization. During the 1953–1954 school year, 95 percent of all the one-teacher schools in the state were black schools. Nearly two-thirds of the state's black children attended schools with three or fewer teachers; only one-sixth of the white children attended such schools. Willie Morris said of the black schools in Yazoo City in 1948: "There were no school buses for Negroes, no indoor plumbing, and no central heating." In Attala County, James Meredith was going to school. "I walked to school over four miles each way, every day for eleven years," he said. "Throughout these years, the white school bus passed us each morning. There was no Negro school bus." By 1952, two years after Meredith graduated from high school, some black students were being bused in Mississippi, but many fewer, proportionately, than whites.

Late in 1953, Mississippi legislators began serious exploration of equalization. In 1954, Walter Sillers, speaker of the state house of representatives, acknowledged that "the cost to equalize will be high because in the past we actually have not maintained a dual system of schools, financially. We have maintained a white system."

Among black leaders there was a deep reluctance to abandon the effort to equalize separate schools. About 1948, recounts the historian Kelly, the matter of strategy was raised by Thurgood Marshall, chief counsel for the NAACP Legal Defense Fund: "At this stage of the game, . . . if the school boards in key southern states had shown a general disposition to accept any kind of gradualist program combining more adequate schools with some primary and secondary desegregation, the Association might well have agreed to cooperate, at least for a time." No such overtures were forthcoming, and so the legal attack turned in a new direction. Segregation, as the source of inequality, was to become the target of a sustained legal campaign.

THE LEGAL CHALLENGE TO SEGREGATION

Between 1938 and 1952, the U.S. Supreme Court decided six cases involving inequalities in higher education. These were *Gaines* (1938), *Sipuel* (1948), *Fisher* (1949), *Sweatt* (1950), *McLaurin* (1950), and *Gray* (1952). In each case, provisions for black students were found to be constitutionally objectionable. The Court shuttled between remedies of equalizing separate facilities and outright desegregation. In *McLaurin*, where a Negro was admitted to a previously all-white university, the plaintiff was forced to sit apart, near the door of a lecture room. The court held that this act of segregation of itself impaired McLaurin's equal opportunity to gain an education. This was a virtual declaration that segregation was incompatible with equal treatment. Lawyers for the NAACP Legal Defense Fund seized on the opening. In mid-1950, they began a wholesale attack on segregation as such in elementary and secondary school cases. Until this time, the LDF had argued such cases only on the basis of equalization of separate facilities.

The decision to challenge segregation was historic. In 1934, Horace Mann Bond concluded an important work on the education of black children without proposing that segregation be ended. Indeed, as he recalled later, in 1934 "the institution of racial segregation appeared to be an immutable feature of the American social order." Just sixteen years later, perspectives had altered sharply. A new sense of collective identity among Negroes had emerged from World War II. A readiness and a drive to protest against discrimination emboldened the NAACP to take a more forward position. Black teachers and parents in the South, even the rural South, drew lines with unprecedented daring. In 1954 Lewis found that Negroes as a whole were "developing a new sense of personal dignity and group pride ... more akin to the pride of an integrating cultural minority than to pride as such." The managers of the segregated southern system were growing less secure in their conviction that segregation was the surest protection for their privileges.

The new legal strategy required for success close support by black communities. The earlier strategy of challenging unequal facilities in higher education drew very little community support. Few Negroes had been personally involved and, therefore, the effort seemed somewhat abstract. In the late 1940s, when the LDF and the NAACP turned to the common schools, community interest rose.

In Summerton, South Carolina, black parents in 1949 petitioned the school board to relieve severe overcrowding in the black high school. When no action resulted, an NAACP lawyer drew up a formal petition that was signed by 107 parents and children. After a period of inaction, in 1950 a formal lawsuit was entered, requesting not equal facilities but the end of segregated schools altogether. A year later, black high school students in Farmville, Virginia, carried on a strike against deplorable conditions at the school. At first the Negro Parent-Teacher Association supported demands for a new, although separate, high school. After an NAACP lawyer suggested the attack be on separation as such, parents agreed. The school board was petitioned to stop segregating. It refused. In May 1951, parents entered a lawsuit challenging segregation.

In Topeka, Kansas, black plaintiffs acknowledged material equality of black and white schools, but challenged segregation. And in Wilmington, Delaware, a state court granted parents' request that their children be admitted to a superior white school until both schools were equalized. In Washington, D.C., parents challenged the principle of segregation. All five cases were heard together by the U.S. Supreme Court in 1952–1955. They are known as the *School Segregation* cases.

The NAACP Legal Defense Fund, whose staff Marshall headed, represented the plaintiffs. Robert Carter, an LDF lawyer who handled the Topeka case and now a federal judge in New York, told the Court in 1952: "It is the gravamen of our complaint . . . that . . . we have been deprived of the equal protection of the laws where the statute requires appellants to attend public elementary schools on a segregated basis, because the act of segregation in and of itself denies them equal educational opportunities which the Fourteenth Amendment secures."

When counsel for the defendants demonstrated that various southern states were narrowing the racial gap in per student expenditures, LDF attorneys denied equality would ever be gained by this route. Thus, Spottswood Robinson explained that "even though Virginia could spend $26 millions—an enormous sum by Virginia standards—all that we succeed in doing is moving from a present 61 cents to 79 cents per Negro student for each dollar that is invested in buildings and sites for white students."

In the 1953 hearings, the NAACP submitted a long historical brief designed to show the role of segregated education in creating an official caste system in the United States:

> Controlling economic and political interests in the South were convinced that the Negro's subjugation was essential to their survival, and the Court in *Plessy* v. *Ferguson* had ruled that such subjugation through public authority was sanctioned by the Constitution. . . . Without the sanction of *Plessy* v. *Ferguson*, archaic and provincial notions of racial superiority could not have injured and disfigured an entire region for so long a time.

The rights of the aggrieved children "to learn and grow" and "to be treated as entire citizens of the society into which they have been born" were at stake. In the oral argument, LDF attorney James Nabrit inquired "whether under our Constitution the federal government is authorized to classify Negroes in the District of Columbia as untouchables for the purpose of educating them for living in a democracy."

On May 17, 1954, the Court handed down a unanimous opinion in *Brown* v. *Board of Education of Topeka* (347 U.S. 483). The central contention of the plaintiffs was upheld: "In the field of public education the doctrine of 'separate but equal' has no place. Separate educational facilities are inherently unequal. . . .

We hold that the plaintiffs and others similarly situated . . . are, by reason of the segregation complained of, deprived of equal protection of the laws guaranteed by the Fourteenth Amendment.

The court witheld any immediate orders regarding implementation. It announced that it would hold hearings later in the year before deciding upon specific measures of relief.

The *Brown* decision was hailed as initiating a new era in American history. Du Bois wrote: "I have seen the Impossible happen. It did happen on May 17, 1954." Much remained to be done against discrimination in travel, public accommodations, health, and elsewhere. Yet *Brown* was hailed as a "great victory," by black leaders and the black press, although Muse notes: "There was no dancing in the streets. The significance was not quickly grasped by the Negro masses."

As he had done so often in his long life, Du Bois summed up both sides of the black equation of anticipation and fear. In an address delivered in February 1955, he spoke of *Brown's* possible long-run effect on American democracy. The decision confronted "Negroes with a cruel dilemma." On the one hand, "they want their children educated. That is a must, else they continue in semislavery." On the other hand, "with successfully mixed schools they know what their children must suffer for years from southern white teachers, from white hoodlums who sit beside them and under school authorities from janitors to superintendents who hate and despise them. They know, dear God, how they know." He predicted that most of the best black teachers would lose their jobs "because they will not and cannot teach what many white folks will want taught."

A large cultural price for the end of segregation would have to be paid by blacks. Du Bois wrote: "They must eventually surrender race solidarity and the idea of American Negro culture to the concept of world humanity, above race and nation. This is the price of liberty. This is the cost of oppression."

"Eventually" was a long way off. Du Bois was by no means urging an end to a study of black history and culture. He wrote: "Much teaching of Negro history will leave the [desegregated] school and with it that brave story of Negro resistance. This teaching will be taught more largely in the home or in the church where, under current Christian custom, segregation by race and class will remain until the last possible moment." (Seven years earlier in the *Chicago Defender,* Du Bois had predicted that within another generation every American college and university would offer a standard course in Negro culture.)

In April 1955, the Supreme Court conducted a five-day hearing on the implementation of *Brown.* Nearly a year had elapsed since the decision. The Court had collected numerous suggestions from plaintiffs, defendants, and other interested parties, including attorneys general from each of the southern states.

The temper of the hearing was curious. Counsel for the plaintiffs was full of foreboding; the opposition was deferential but defiant. One issue was paramount: would the Court set a deadline for desegregation? Without a definite date, no specific commitment to action would follow.

Counsel for Clarendon County, South Carolina, warned: "I think if you ordered the trustees tomorrow to comply or else, that that would destroy the public school system of South Carolina." In Virginia, warned another lawyer, "an integrated system of public schools would require more than a court decree. It would require an evolutionary change in the attitude of people in Virginia, both Negro and white." The attorney general of Texas told the Court: "Texas loves its Negro people." His colleague added that "Texas enjoys harmonious relationships and has made excellent progress in economic, educational, and social advancement." Counsel for the District of Columbia informed the justices that "we have always had a school system which largely, though in two halves, was perfectly equal side by side." In reply to charges the South created and enforced a caste system, a North Carolina attorney explained: "Race consciousness is not race prejudice. It is not race hatred. It is not intolerance. It is a deeply ingrained awareness of a birthright held in trust for posterity."

These protestations of good faith and high moral ground, mixed with practical reminders of the power dominance of whites in the South, were expected by the LDF legal staff. What was disturbing was the possibility that the Court would be impressed by such arguments. In that case, the Court would effectively negate *Brown* by depending on the good faith of local authorities, who, in matters tinged by race, had historically demonstrated bad faith. *Brown* would, then, remain a vague declaration of general rights which no specific child could claim as a basis for action. An order that proclaimed gradualism as an operative principle would necessarily confer constitutional rights on some and withhold them from most others.

This problem had been anticipated even before the *Brown* proceedings started. In April 1952, Howard University held a national conference on "The Courts and Racial Integration in Education," attended by most, if not all, the LDF attorneys who later argued the *Brown* case before the Supreme Court. At the conference, James M. Nabrit, Jr., stressed that "the Constitution gives the Negro the fundamental right to enjoy *now* all benefits offered by the state, without any limitations based on race." Before the Court, during the first round of hearings late in 1952, the same point was made more than once. Jack Greenberg, an LDF attorney, held "that if constitutional rights are being denied our respondents, they are entitled to those rights as quickly as those rights can be made available." During the 1953 hearings, Thurgood Marshall told the Court that desegregation could be accomplished within a year: "If they don't have staff enough to do these administrative things, the sovereign states can hire more people to do it."

During the 1955 hearings, Marshall spoke extensively on the issue. He warned against allowing the pace of desegregation to be left up to the states, Should this happen, Marshall pointed out, "then the Negro in this country would be in a horrible shape. He, as a matter of fact, would be as bad, if not worse off than under the 'separate but equal' doctrine for this reason." District court judges would tend to accept school board pleas for more time, and the right to a desegregated education would be nullified. "This is a national Constitution," said Marshall. "There is no place for local option in our Constitution." Various justices continued to speak of the difficulties and complexities of desegregation. To this, Marshall replied, exasperated: "This Court is not dealing with the complexities, this Court is dealing with whether or not race can be used [in school assignments]."

Most of all, the plaintiffs wanted a definite court order installing desegregation in the litigated districts by September 1955. Marshall stated: "If we cannot get that, then we say that the least that would do us any good at all would be a decree which included four items: (1) That this Court make the clearest declaration that not only those statutes but others are in violation of the Fourteenth Amendment. We think it is necessary for that to be put in the decree. (2) That they start immediately to desegregate. (3) File reports. (4) That it must end at a certain day." Justice Frankfurter objected that the Court had to take into account "certain unalterable facts of life that cannot be changed even by this Court"; he referred to administrative problems. Marshall replied that gradual desegregation could never be effective. Further, he expressed shock "at arguments of the impotency of our government to enforce its Constitution." Without a decree that included a time limit, he concluded, "there will be no protection whatsoever for the decision of this Court rendered on May 17."

On the last day of the final hearing, in April 1955, Marshall repeated the plaintiffs' view, adding a charge of racism, although the target of the charge was not clear. "This time limit becomes a part of the effectiveness . . . of the May 17 decision," he told the Court. "But," he continued, "I don't believe any argument has ever been made to this Court to postpone the enforcement of a constitutional right." He then added: "The argument is never made until Negroes are involved." Essentially, only Negroes were being asked to forgo their rights.

The position of the national administration on a deadline was expressed in testimony by Solicitor General Simon E. Sobeloff. He opposed placing any general deadline at all in the final decree. On the other hand, he advocated instructing the district judges to inform school districts they must produce a plan within ninety days; extension could be given if necessary. "The thing ought not to be left hanging in the air indefinitely."

Seven weeks later the Supreme Court decided *Brown II* (349 U.S. 294). The cases were remanded to the respective U.S. District Courts to fashion specific decrees. "At stake," wrote the Court, "is the personal interest of the plaintiffs in admission to public schools as soon as practicable on a nondiscriminatory basis." Defendants, the Court held, will be required to "make a prompt and reasonable start toward full compliance." The district courts were to facilitate the admission of the plaintiffs "to public schools on a racially nondiscriminatory basis with all deliberate speed." The Supreme Court thus failed to set either a general deadline, as plaintiffs' lawyers had urged, or even a flexible deadline for the guidance of district judges.

In the retrospective opinion of at least one LDF lawyer, Robert L. Carter, *Brown II* was "a grave mistake." The clear implication of the deliberate speed formula "was movement toward compliance on terms that the white South could accept." In agreeing to less than immediate enforcement of every child's constitutional right, Carter wrote, "the Warren Court sacrificed individual and immediate vindication of the newly discovered right to desegregated education." Justice Hugo Black said much the same thing some years later. *Brown II* weakened *Brown I* in several respects; it strengthened it in none. . . .

In many southern states, material inequality continued under segregation or token desegregation, while states spent tax moneys to fight desegregation and finance private white segregated schools. In Virginia, during 1961–1962, public funds amounting to $2,060,859 in tuition grants were transferred to white children who wished to avoid attending a desegregated school. In 1963–1964, Louisiana granted a total of $3,500,000. The transfer of public school property to private schools was authorized by law in seven states and tuition grants in eight states. Segregation was financed by public finds, thereby compelling "the Negro taxpayer to pay for insulting himself."

Unequal Achievement

Before 1954, the myth of equal-though-separate was believed by few persons familiar with the facts of southern education. Yet direct evidence of comparative achievement disparities by race was not available. One reason for this is the earlier deliberate failure to gather statistics on Negro learning. In the public schools of the District of Columbia, for example, before 1954 achievement tests were given to white but not Negro children.

Texas, the largest southern state, was not untypical. In 1953–1954, the state's association of school administrators surveyed the quality of Texas education. Based on a study of 80 percent of the state's school children, the academic achievement of white pupils was ranked "very satisfactory"; that of Negro pupils was classed as "unsatisfactory." Governor Allen Shivers said "we still have a long way to go in obtaining separate but equal schools." In 1956, while three out of five white fourth-graders in Dallas were at or above grade level in reading achievement—the pivot of school success—only one of eight Negro children was so classified. In Houston during 1961 white first-graders averaged grade *B*; Negro first-graders averaged *C*. Three years later, 40 percent of the students in Houston's all-Negro Texas Southern University were taking, the school's dean of arts and sciences said, courses to supply them with knowledge they should have learned in high school. An investigator for the U.S. Commission on Civil Rights recalled, in 1964, that eight years earlier the average Negro eighth-grader in Houston had lagged behind the average white eighth-grader nearly a year and a half in spelling and three and a third years in reading (paragraph meaning). He did not report later data.

In Tennessee, the usual pattern held. Negro sixth-graders in Nashville were more than two years behind white children. Knoxville superintendent Thomas N. Johnson reported that Negro children were almost one and one-half years behind white children. In Memphis, Negro eighth-graders lagged two years and two months behind whites in achievement. A study for the U.S. Commission on Civil Rights commented that the state's educators frequently complained that Negro students lagged, on the average, from one and one-half to two grade levels.

The conclusion reached in 1962 by a similar study covering Virginia could apply more or less to the other southern states: "Negro education in Negro schools is not equal to the education provided whites, either in tangible aspects or, more importantly, in intangibles. Officially, very little is being done to improve the quality of this education. At present the educational opportunity of white and Negro children in the state is not [even] comparable."

During the years 1954–1964, southern educators in desegregated schools responded to achievement differentials by initiating or expanding ability grouping and tracking systems. This was the case in the District of Columbia, Saint Louis, Baltimore, and Wilmington, Delaware. When the tracking plan was first introduced for District of Columbia tenth graders in 1956, the 1,118 white and 2,822 black children were distributed as follows:

> *College preparatory course*
> 315 (86.7 percent) of whites
> 50 (13.7 percent) of blacks
> *Terminal course*
> 685 (30.7 percent) of whites
> 1,453 (69.3 percent) of blacks
> *Basic course*
> 158 (10.7 percent) of whites
> 1,319(89.3 percent) of blacks

The college preparatory track was virtually all white; the basic track was overwhelmingly black. Little was tried to narrow the achievement gap, and less was accomplished. Before desegregation, the offering of special classes, including provisions for "slow learners," was common in the white schools of the District of Columbia, "but the Negro side of the school system had relatively few because of the lack of funds allocated for the purpose." School authorities claimed that tracking was a means of improving student performance by moving to higher tracks. Seven years after initiation of tracking, 96.9 percent of junior high school students in the District of Columbia were still in the track they had occupied two years earlier. . . .

THE LAW AND THE JUDICIARY

Neither *Brown* nor the Civil Rights Act of 1964 dealt with urban-style segregation. A common defense of northern school boards when charged with segregation during the 1950s and early 1960s was to point to residential segregation as the real culprit. Yet as one legal expert contended in 1965: "In every case of racially imbalanced schools sufficient responsibility can be ascribed to government to satisfy the requirement that stems from the equal protection clause's proscription of unequal treatment by government." No grand legal principle to this effect could have been proclaimed by any high court. Yet pragmatically, just such a structure of legal reasoning came into being by the opening of the 1970s. It took two main avenues: (1) state actions against so-called de facto segregation and (2) federal lower court actions against deliberate efforts to sustain de facto segregation.

During the decade after 1962, several northern states adopted legislative, judicial, or administrative standards that permitted or required the disestablishment of segregation, whatever its origin. The novelty lay in creating a positive obligation for school boards to desegregate, regardless of how the segregation originated. This was held by the supreme courts of California, Illinois, Massachusetts, Pennsylvania, and Washington. By administrative action, New York adopted the same policy. A number of other states adopted regulations that fell short of binding requirements.

In the federal courts, plaintiffs had the difficult assignment of proving conscious intent by school boards. Because the segregative techniques were often seemingly neutral, proving intent was not feasible.

CHAPTER 8 The Critical Perspective on the Struggle for Freedom in Education

8.1 PAULO FREIRE AND DONALDO MACEDO

Literacy and Critical Pedagogy

In the selection that follows, from *Literacy: Reading the Word and the World* (Bergin & Garvey, 1987), Paulo Freire and Donaldo Macedo demonstrate how achieving literacy is a political action and how people create the power to control their own lives through their own words—through their own expression of the contradictions and realities with which they have to deal in their cultural worlds. The authors argue that literacy "cannot be viewed as simply the development of skills aimed at acquiring the dominant standard language." They argue instead that a human being's decision to choose to become literate is a choice to take power and control over his or her own life. They further state that literacy as a concept must be situated in the context of the struggle for human liberation from established systems of cultural reproduction. Literacy must involve the critical reexamination of all of a society's social arrangements and institutions on the part of those who choose to become literate.

Paulo Freire (b. 1921) teaches in the Graduate Schools of Education at Harvard University. He has also taught at the Catholic University of São Paulo, and he has been a consultant to the World Council of Churches in Geneva, Switzerland. A pioneer in critical pedagogy, whose theories on the social forces that prevent people from fulfilling their potentials have inspired a vast critical literature in the field of education, Freire helped to establish the Institute of Cultural Action (IDAC), and he has participated in adult literacy campaigns in several Third World countries.

Donaldo Macedo (b. 1950) is an associate professor of linguistics at the University of Massachusetts–Boston. The book that Macedo coauthored with Freire and from which the following selection comes is considered a critical contribution to the struggle for human freedom.

Key Concept: literacy and human liberation

Within the last decade, the issue of literacy has taken on a new importance among educators. Unfortunately, the debate that has emerged tends to recycle old assumptions and values regarding the meaning and usefulness of literacy. The notion that literacy is a matter of learning the standard language still informs the vast majority of literacy programs and manifests its logic in the renewed emphasis on technical reading and writing skills.

. . . [L]iteracy cannot be viewed as simply the development of skills aimed at acquiring the dominant standard language. This view sustains a notion of ideology that systematically negates rather than makes meaningful the cultural experiences of the subordinate linguistic groups who are, by and large, the objects of its policies. For the notion of literacy to become meaningful it has to be situated within a theory of cultural production and viewed as an integral part of the way in which people produce, transform, and reproduce meaning. Literacy must be seen as a medium that constitutes and affirms the historical and existential moments of lived experience that produce a subordinate or a lived culture. Hence, it is an eminently political phenomenon, and it must be analyzed within the context of a theory of power relations and an understanding of social and cultural reproduction and production. By "cultural reproduction" we refer to collective experiences that function in the interest of the dominant groups, rather than in the interest of the oppressed groups that are the object of its policies. We use "cultural production" to refer to specific groups of people producing, mediating, and confirming the mutual ideological elements that emerge from and reaffirm their daily lived experiences. In this case, such experiences are rooted in the interests of individual and collective self-determination.

This theoretical posture underlies our examination of how the public school systems in the ex-Portuguese colonies in Africa have developed educational policies aimed at stamping out the tremendously high illiteracy rate inherited from colonialist Portugal. These policies are designed to eradicate the

152

*Chapter 8
The Critical
Perspective on
the Struggle for
Freedom in
Education*

colonial educational legacy, which had as its major tenet the total de-Africanization of these people. Education in these colonies was discriminatory, mediocre, and based on verbalism. It could not contribute anything to national reconstruction because it was not constituted for this purpose. Schooling was antidemocratic in its methods, in its content, and in its objectives. Divorced from the reality of the country, it was, for this very reason, a school for a minority and thus against the majority.

Before the independence of these countries in 1975, schools functioned as political sites in which class, gender, and racial inequities were both produced and reproduced. In essence, the colonial educational structure served to inculcate the African[1] natives with myths and beliefs that denied and belittled their lived experiences, their history, their culture, and their language. The schools were seen as purifying fountains where Africans could be saved from their deep-rooted ignorance, their "savage" culture, and their bastardized language, which, according to some Portuguese scholars, was a corrupted form of Portuguese "without grammatical rules (they can't even be applied)."

This system could not help but reproduce in children and youth the profile that the colonial ideology itself had created for them, namely that of inferior beings, lacking in all ability.

On the one hand, schooling in these colonies served the purpose of deculturating the natives; on the other hand, it acculturated them into a predefined colonial model. Schools in this mold functioned "as part of an ideological state apparatus designed to secure the ideological and social reproduction of capital and its institutions, whose interests are rooted in the dynamics of capital accumulation and the reproduction of the labor force." This educated labor force in the ex-Portuguese colonies was composed mainly of low-level functionaries whose major tasks were the promotion and maintenance of the status quo. Their role took on a new and important dimension when they were used as intermediaries to further colonize Portuguese possessions in Africa. Thus, colonial schools were successful to the extent that they created a petit-bourgeois class of functionaries who had internalized the belief that they had become "white" or "black with white souls," and were therefore superior to African peasants, who still practiced what was viewed as barbaric culture.

This assimilation process penetrated the deepest level of consciousness, especially in the bourgeois class. For instance, with respect to becoming "white," we are reminded of an anecdote about a black Cape Verdian so preoccupied with his blackness that he paid a well-respected white Cape Verdian to issue him a decree proclaiming him white. The man jokingly wrote for him on a piece of paper "Dja'n branco dja," meaning "I have thereby been declared white."

After independence and in the reconstruction of a new society in these countries, schools have assumed as their major task the "decolonization of mentality," as it is termed by Aristides Pereira, and which Amilcar Cabral called the "re-Africanization of mentality." It is clear that both Pereira and Cabral were well aware of the need to create a school system in which a new mentality cleansed of all vestiges of colonialism would be formulated; a school system that would allow people to appropriate their history, their culture, and their language; a school system in which it was imperative to reformulate the programs of geography, history, and the Portuguese language, changing all the reading texts that were so heavily impregnated with colonialist ideology. It was an absolute priority that students should study their own geography and not that of Portugal, the inlets of the sea and not Rio Tejo. It was urgent that they study their history, the history of the resistance of their people to the invader and the struggle for their liberation, which gave them back the right to make their own history—not the history of the kings of Portugal and the intrigues of the court.

The proposal to incorporate a radical pedagogy in schools has met a lukewarm reception in these countries. We want to argue that the suspicion of many African educators is deeply rooted in the language issue (African versus Portuguese) and has led to the creation of a neocolonialist literacy campaign under the superficially radical slogan of eliminating illiteracy in the new republics. The difficulties of reappropriating African culture have been increased by the fact that the means for such struggle has been the language of the colonizer. As we will argue . . . , the present literacy campaign in these nations concerns itself mainly with the creation of functional literates in the Portuguese language. No longer based on the cultural capital of subordinate Africans, the program has fallen prey to positivistic and instrumental approaches to literacy concerned mainly with the mechanical acquisition of Portuguese language skills. . . .

APPROACHES TO LITERACY

Almost without exception, traditional approaches to literacy have been deeply ingrained in a positivistic method of inquiry. In effect, this has resulted in an epistemological stance in which scientific rigor and methodological refinement are celebrated, while "theory and knowledge are subordinated to the imperatives of efficiency and technical mastery, and history is reduced to a minor footnote in the priorities of 'empirical' scientific inquiry." In general, this approach abstracts methodological issues from their ideological contexts and consequently ignores the interrelationship between the sociopolitical structures of a society and the act of reading. In part, the exclusion of social and political dimensions from the practice of reading gives rise to an ideology of cultural reproduction, one that views readers as "objects." It is as though their conscious bodies were simply empty, waiting to be filled by that word from the teacher. Although it is important to analyze how ideologies inform various reading traditions, . . . we will limit our discussion to a brief analysis of the most important approaches to literacy, linking them to either cultural reproduction or cultural production.

The Academic Approach to Reading

The purpose assigned to reading in the academic tradition is twofold. First, the rationale for this approach "derives from classical definitions of the

154

*Chapter 8
The Critical
Perspective on
the Struggle for
Freedom in
Education*

well-educated man—thoroughly grounded in the classics, articulate in spoken and written expression, actively engaged in intellectual pursuits." This approach to reading has primarily served the interests of the elite classes. In this case, reading is viewed as the acquisition of predefined forms of knowledge and is organized around the study of Latin and Greek and the mastery of the great classical works. Second, since it would be unrealistic to expect the vast majority of society to meet such high standards, reading was redefined as the acquisition of reading skills, decoding skills, vocabulary development, and so on. This second rationale served to legitimize a dual approach to reading: one level for the ruling class and another for the dispossessed majority. According to Giroux (*Theory and Resistance*): "This second notion is geared primarily to working class students whose cultural capital is considered less compatible, and thus inferior in terms of complexity and value, with the knowledge and values of the dominant class."

This twofold academic approach to reading is inherently alienating in nature. On the one hand, it ignores the life experience, the history, and the language practice of students. On the other, it overemphasizes the mastery and understanding of classical literature and the use of literary materials as "vehicles for exercises in comprehension (literal and interpretative), vocabulary development, and word identification skills." Thus, literacy in this sense is stripped of its sociopolitical dimensions; it functions, in fact, to reproduce dominant values and meaning. It does not contribute in any meaningful way to the appropriation of working-class history, culture, and language.

The Utilitarian Approach to Reading

The major goal of the utilitarian approach is to produce readers who meet the basic reading requirements of contemporary society. In spite of its progressive appeal, such an approach emphasizes the mechanical learning of reading skills while sacrificing the critical analysis of the social and political order that generates the need for reading in the first place. This position has led to the development of "functional literates," groomed primarily to meet the requirements of our ever more complex technological society. Such a view is not simply characteristic of the advanced industrialized countries of the West; even within the Third World, utilitarian literacy has been championed as a vehicle for economic betterment, access to jobs, and increase of the productivity level. As it is clearly stated by UNESCO, "Literacy programs should preferably be linked with economic priorities. [They] must impart not only reading and writing, but also professional and technical knowledge, thereby leading to a fuller participation of adults in economic life."

This notion of literacy has been enthusiastically incorporated as a major goal by the back-to-basics proponents of reading. It has also contributed to the development of neatly packaged reading programs that are presented as the solution to difficulties students experience in reading job application forms, tax forms, advertisement literature, sales catalogs, labels, and the like. In general, the utilitarian approach views literacy as meeting the basic reading demand of an industrialized society. As Giroux points out:

> Literacy within this perspective is geared to make adults more productive workers and citizens within a given society. In spite of its appeal to economic mobility, functional literacy reduces the concept of literacy and the pedagogy in which it is suited to the pragmatic requirements of capital; consequently, the notions of critical thinking, culture and power disappear under the imperatives of the labor process and the need for capital accumulation.

Cognitive Development Approach to Reading

While the academic and utilitarian approaches to reading emphasize the mastery of reading skills and view the readers as "objects," the cognitive development model stresses the construction of meaning whereby readers engage in a dialectical interaction between themselves and the objective world. Although the acquisition of literacy skills is viewed as an important task in this approach, the salient feature is how people construct meaning through problem-solving processes. Comprehension of the text is relegated to a position of lesser importance in favor of the development of new cognitive structures that can enable students to move from simple to highly complex reading tasks. This reading process is highly influenced by the early work of John Dewey and has been shaped in terms of the development of Piagetian cognitive structures. Under the cognitive development model, reading is seen as an intellectual process, "through a series of fixed, value-free, and universal stages of development."

The cognitive development model thus avoids criticism of the academic and utilitarian views of reading and fails to consider the content of what is read. Instead, it emphasizes a process that allows students to analyze and critique issues raised in the text with an increasing level of complexity. This approach, however, is rarely concerned with questions of cultural reproduction. Since students' cultural capital—i.e., their life experience, history, and language—is ignored, they are rarely able to engage in thorough critical reflection, regarding their own practical experience and the ends that motivate them in order, in the end, to organize the findings and thus replace mere opinion about facts with an increasingly rigorous understanding of their significance.

The Romantic Approach to Reading

Like the cognitive development model, the romantic approach is based on an interactionist approach with a major focus on the construction of meaning; however, the romantic approach views meaning as being generated by the reader and not occurring in the interaction between reader and author via text. The romantic mode greatly emphasizes the affective and sees reading as the fulfillment of self and a joyful experience. One writer praised "the intimate reliving of fresh views of personality and life implicit in the work (of literature); the pleasure and release of tensions that may flow from such an experi-

156

*Chapter 8
The Critical
Perspective on
the Struggle for
Freedom in
Education*

ence ... the deepening and broadening of sensitivity to the sensuous quality and emotional impact of day-to-day living."

In essence, the romantic approach to reading presents a counterpoint to the authoritarian modes of pedagogy which view readers as "objects." However, this seemingly liberal approach to literacy fails to make problematic class conflict, gender, or racial inequalities. Furthermore, the romantic model completely ignores the cultural capital of subordinate groups and assumes that all people have the same access to reading, or that reading is part of the cultural capital of all people. This failure to address questions of cultural capital or various structural inequalities means that the romantic model tends to reproduce the cultural capital of the dominant class, to which reading is intimately tied. It is presumptuous and naive to expect a student from the working class, confronted and victimized by myriad disadvantages, to find joy and self-affirmation through reading alone. But more important is the failure of the romantic tradition to link reading to the asymmetrical relations of power within the dominant society, relations of power that not only define and legitimate certain approaches to reading but also disempower certain groups by excluding them from such a process.

We have argued thus far that all of these approaches to literacy have failed to provide a theoretical model for empowering historical agents with the logic of individual and collective self-determination. While these approaches may differ in their basic assumptions about literacy, they all share one common feature: they all ignore the role of language as a major force in the construction of human subjectivities. That is, they ignore the way language may either confirm or deny the life histories and experiences of the people who use it. This becomes clearer in our analysis of the role of language in the literacy programs.

THE ROLE OF LANGUAGE IN LITERACY

... Educators must develop radical pedagogical structures that provide students with the opportunity to use their own reality as a basis of literacy. This includes, obviously, the language they bring to the classroom. To do otherwise is to deny students the rights that lie at the core of the notion of an emancipatory literacy. The failure to base a literacy program on the native language means that oppositional forces can neutralize the efforts of educators and political leaders to achieve decolonization of mind. Educators and political leaders must recognize that "language is inevitably one of the major preoccupations of a society which, liberating itself from colonialism and refusing to be drawn into neo-colonialism, searches for its own recreation. In the struggle to re-create a society, the reconquest by the people of their own world becomes a fundamental factor." It is of tantamount importance that the incorporation of the students' language as the primary language of instruction in literacy be given top priority. It is through their own language that they will be able to reconstruct their history and their culture.

In this sense, the students' language is the only means by which they can develop their own voice, a prerequisite to the development of a positive sense of self-worth. As Giroux elegantly states, the students' voice "is the discursive means to make themselves 'heard' and to define themselves as active authors of their world." The authorship of one's own world, which would also imply one's own language, means what Mikhail Bakhtin defines as "retelling a story in one's own words."

Although the concept of voice is fundamental in the development of an emancipatory literacy, the goal should never be to restrict students to their own vernacular. This linguistic constriction inevitably leads to a linguistic ghetto. Educators must understand fully the broader meaning of student's "empowerment." That is, empowerment should never be limited to what Arnowitz describes as "the process of appreciating and loving oneself." In addition to this process, empowerment should also be a means that enables students "to interrogate and selectively appropriate those aspects of the dominant culture that will provide them with the basis for defining and transforming, rather than merely serving, the wider social order." This means that educators should understand the value of mastering the standard dominant language of the wider society. It is through the full appropriation of the dominant standard language that students find themselves linguistically empowered to engage in dialogue with the various sectors of the wider society. What we would like to reiterate is that educators should never allow the students' voice to be silenced by a distorted legitimation of the standard language. The students' voice should never be sacrificed, since it is the only means through which they make sense of their own experience in the world.

... Educators must develop an emancipatory literacy program informed by a radical pedagogy so that the students' language will cease to provide its speakers the experience of subordination and, moreover, may be brandished as a weapon of resistance to the dominance of the standard language.

As we stated earlier, the linguistic issues raised [here] are not limited to developing countries of Africa and Latin America. The asymmetrical power relations in reference to language use are also predominant in highly industrialized societies. For instance, the U.S. English movement in the United States headed by the ex-California senator S. I. Hayakawa points to a xenophobic culture that blindly negates the pluralistic nature of U.S. society and falsifies the empirical evidence in support of bilingual education, as has been amply documented. These educators ... fail to understand that it is through multiple discourses that students generate meaning of their everyday social contexts. Without understanding the meaning of their immediate social reality, it is most difficult to comprehend their relations with the wider society.

By and large, U.S. English proponents base their criticism of bilingual education on quantitative evaluation results, which are "the product of a particular model of social structure that gear the theoretical concepts to the pragmatics of the society that devised the evaluation model to begin with." That is, if the results are presented as facts determined by a particular ideological framework, these facts cannot in themselves get us beyond that framework. We would warn educators that these evaluation models can provide answers that are correct and nevertheless without truth. A study that concludes that linguis-

158

*Chapter 8
The Critical
Perspective on
the Struggle for
Freedom in
Education*

tic minority students in the United States perform way below other main-stream students in English is correct, but such an answer tells us very little about the material conditions with which these linguistic- and racial-minority students work in the struggle against racism, educational tracking, and the systematic negation of their histories. . . .

We believe that the answer lies not in the technical questions of whether English is a more elaborate and viable language of instruction. This position would point to an assumption that English is in fact a superior language. We want to propose that the answer rests in a full understanding of the ideological elements that generate and sustain linguistic, racial, and sex discrimination. . . .

The new literacy programs must be largely based on the notion of emancipatory literacy, in which literacy is viewed "as one of the major vehicles by which 'oppressed' people are able to participate in the sociohistorical transformation of their society." In this view, literacy programs should be tied not only to mechanical learning of reading skills but, additionally, to a critical understanding of the overall goals for national reconstruction. Thus, the reader's development of a critical comprehension of the text, and the sociohistorical context to which it refers, becomes an important factor in our notion of literacy. The act of learning to read and write, in this instance, is a creative act that involves a critical comprehension of reality. The knowledge of earlier knowledge, gained by the learners as a result of analyzing praxis in its social context, opens to them the possibility of a new knowledge. The new knowledge reveals the reason for being that is behind the facts, thus demythologizing the false interpretations of these same facts. Thus, there is no longer any separation between thought-language and objective reality. The reading of a text now demands a reading within the social context to which it refers.

Literacy, in this sense, is grounded in a critical reflection on the cultural capital of the oppressed. It becomes a vehicle by which the oppressed are equipped with the necessary tools to reappropriate their history, culture, and language practices. It is, thus, a way to enable the oppressed to reclaim "those historical and existential experiences that are devalued in everyday life by the dominant culture in order to be both validated and critically understood."

NOTE

1. By African we mean to refer to African natives belonging to African countries that were colonized by Portugal. For the sake of economy of terms, we have selected this term, but we want to point out that we are aware of the great linguistic and cultural diversity that exists in Africa.

Radical Excesses and Post-Modernism

"Postmodernism" and "deconstructionism" are two leading concepts in the critical theoretical debate over the social purposes of education. The postmodernist movement was founded by Jacques Derrida and Michel Foucault. Derrida used the term *deconstruction* to make the point that all human knowledge is situated in a matrix, or web, of racial, cultural, gender, and social class relations. Postmodernists tend to believe that reason itself is politicized in such a matrix to the extent that people always reason from some politicized situation in life. Postmodernists also maintain that dominant social class, gender, and cultural forces in society exercise effective control over the lives of subordinate social groups, such as cultural minorities, women, and low-income or unemployed persons. When postmodernists turn to educational issues, they argue that teachers must play a socially transformative role in their classrooms by helping students to "deconstruct" the dominant group's vision of social reality and justice and to replace dominant conceptions of knowledge with visions of social reality based on their own experience of it.

In the following selection, Benjamin R. Barber explores the assumptions of critical theory and attacks them from a liberal perspective. Barber is concerned that postmodernism and deconstructionism may become new orthodoxies whose adherents will resist fundamental questioning of their theoretical framework. This selection illustrates the advantages of critical, reasoned analysis of ideas.

Barber (b. 1939) is the Walt Whitman Professor of Political Science and the director of the Walt Whitman Center for the Culture and Politics of Democracy at Rutgers University. *An Aristocracy of Everyone: The Politics of Education and the Future of America* (Oxford University Press, 1992), from which the following selection is taken, is his eighth book.

Key Concept: a critique of pedagogical radicals and present-day progressive educators

Chapter 8
The Critical
Perspective on
the Struggle for
Freedom in
Education

*T*raditional orthodoxies have too often been replaced with new coun-terorthodoxies, no less noxious for being novel, no less inimical to democracy for being offered on behalf of the powerless. Orthodoxy cannot be fought with counterorthodoxy. The challenge is to overcome not to replace dogma, and this requires a critical spirit. I have argued that too many critics of political correct-ness have drawn a phony picture of neutrality that is oblivious to the realities of power in the modern school and university—particularly when seen from the perspective of the powerless. But pedagogical radicals at times outcarica-ture their critics and have themselves been oblivious to several of the most insidious modern sophistries, including a species of reductionism that lurks in their own "deconstruction" of traditional academic rationality. They have sometimes acceded to the temptation to intimidate, to suppress, and to silence not merely the powerful without but the doubtful within. They have been quick to assert as dogma convictions they do not wish to see subjected to critical questioning. And they have all too easily confounded their psychic longing for values with an actual argument on behalf of values.

Powerlessness is a justification for rebellion, but it is not a license for mindlessness. The reality of being without a voice can become part of a good argument, but it is not the same thing as a good argument; it certainly does not exempt the powerless and the voiceless from the obligation to offer good rea-sons. Indeed, this is precisely why there is both a need and a right to be heard—a right secured only through an education in liberty. This right, how-ever, is not necessarily the same thing as the right to stop others from talking or the right to cease listening. Reason can be a smoke screen for interest, but the argument that it is a smoke screen itself depends on reason—or we are caught up in an endless regression in which each argument exposing the dependency of someone else's argument on arbitrariness and self-interest is in turn shown to be self-interested and arbitrary.

Let us consider the principal sins of the present generation of progressive educators justifiably concerned with the future of democracy—sins more of exaggeration than of attitude. Some of the problem is plain old silliness: the utterly serious and therefore utterly comical insistence on certain campuses that "seminars" be called "ovulars" or the caricatured transformation of Chris-topher Columbus from a silent movie saint into a silent movie villain, to be known henceforth exclusively as a torturer, plunderer, and proto-imperialist. The instinct of the sympathetic moderate here can only be to cry, "Whoa! Slow down!" In traversing the terra infirma of modern education, I have expressed a cautious solidarity with the progressives who have devoted themselves to in-stitutionalizing in the schools the 1960's critique of establishment education of the 1990s. Yet by trying to negotiate several sharp curves at too great a velocity, some seem in recent years to have skidded off the tracks. In their under-standing haste to arrive at more democratic schools, their grasp on the mean-ing of democracy has sometimes looked shaky. In their devotion to a public education that can encompass a new and radically heterogenous American public, their feel for the public character of public education has been weak-ened. Impatience has prompted them to travel at reckless speeds; and so, at what we might fancifully call the curve of critical doubt, they have plunged into a gorge of hyperskepticism, where every argument turns relentlessly on itself and where the demand to ground values reasonably becomes a relativization of all values. At the sharp turn of difference, they have fallen into the ravine of hyperpluralism, where overdifferentiation destroys the possibility of integration and community.

I want to examine here these two perils of the current reform movement. Doubt is a powerful vehicle of learning, but moving at too high a speed can also undermine the process. Diversity is a condition of freedom for all, but when it runs off the rails it can rob the "all" of common identity and ultimately destroy the liberty of individuals.

HYPERSKEPTICISM: PRUDENT DOUBT OR FATAL NIHILISM?

All thoughtful inquiry, and hence all useful education, starts with questioning. All usable knowledge, and thus all practical science, starts with the provisional acceptance of answers. Education is a dialectic in moderation in which probing and accepting, questioning and answering, must achieve a delicate balance. Stories must be told, queried, retold, revised, questioned, and retold still again—much as the American story has been. In periods of rebellion, academic no less than social, when challenging authority means questioning answers, there is an understandable tendency toward skepticism, even cynicism. Michael Wood has characterized Jacques Derrida's approach to method as "a patient and intelligent suspicion," which is a useful description of one moment in a student's democratic education.

The methodologies deployed by critics of power and convention in the academy do not always find the dialectical center, however, and are subject to distortion by hyperbole. Sometimes they seem to call for all questions and no answers, all doubt and no provisional resting places. This radicalism has many virtues as scholarship, but as pedagogy far fewer. In its postmodern phase, where the merely modern is equated with something vaguely reactionary and post-modernism means a radical battering down of all certainty, this hyperskeptical pedagogy can become self-defeating.

Skepticism is an essential but slippery and thus dangerously problematic teaching tool. It demystifies and decodes; it denies absolutes; it cuts through rationalization and hypocrisy. Yet it is a whirling blade, an obdurate reaper hard to switch off at will. It is not particularly discriminating. It doesn't necessarily understand the difference between rationalization and reason, since its effectiveness depends precisely on conflating them. It can lead to a refusal to judge or to take responsibility or to impose norms on conduct. If, as Derrida has insisted, "the concept of making a charge itself belongs to the structure of phallogocentrism" (the use of reason and language as forms of macho domination), there can be no responsibility, no autonomy, no morals, no freedom. Like a born killer who may be a hero in wartime but, unable to discriminate between war and peace, becomes a homocidal maniac when the war ends for everyone else, radical skepticism lacks a sense of time and place, a sense of elementary propriety.

162

*Chapter 8
The Critical
Perspective on
the Struggle for
Freedom in
Education*

The questions this poses for pedagogy are drawn in the recondite language of literary postmodernism and deconstruction, but are of the first importance for education. Does the art of criticism doom the object of critical attention to displacement by the self-absorbed critic? In other words, does criticizing books replace reading them? Can the art of questioning be made self-limiting, or do critics always become skeptics? Are skeptics in turn doomed by their negative logic to be relativists? Must relativists melt down into nihilists? Conservatives have worried that this particularly slippery slope cannot be safely traversed at all, and thus have worried about a pedagogy that relies on a too-critical mode of radical questioning. They prefer to think of education as instilling the right values and teaching authoritative bodies of knowledge to compliant students for whom learning is primarily a matter of absorbing information. When these conservatives appeal to the ancients, it is the rationalist Plato to whom they turn, rather than the subversive Socrates.

Yet pedagogical progressives actually confirm the conservatives' fears when they themselves tumble happily down the slope, greasing it as they go with an epistemology that denies the possibility of any stopping place, any objectivity, any rationality, any criterion of reasonableness or universalism whatsoever. Asked to choose between dogma and nihilism, between affirming hegemonic authority and denying all authority, including the authority of reason, of science, and of open debate, what choice does the concerned teacher have but despair? Where she seeks a middling position, she is offered orthodoxy or nihilism. Where she seeks moderation in her students—a respect for rationality but an unwillingness to confound it with or measure it by somebody's power, or eloquence, or status—she is informed that all appeals to rationality are pretense. . . .

There is little new or surprising in skepticism's consuming appetite. Cynicism has been a tendency of philosophy from the start, and its inclination to move from intelligent suspicion to wholesale paranoia is well documented. In *The Republic* Socrates had to contend with Thrasymachus, who saw behind every claim on behalf of truth or justice a sneaky rationalization of somebody's stealthily concealed interest. Socrates showed that Thrasymachus started with a prudent if furtive suspicion but ended as a moral bankrupt, a sellout to the brute argument of force, unable to defend any notion of virtue or justice. For many of the same reasons, the Sophists of ancient Athens who followed Thrasymachus were understood to be tireless interrogators who could ask, "Yes, but why?" until people with beliefs dropped of exhaustion or surrendered, running out of reasonable "becauses" long before their tormentors ran out of probing "whys."

From their earliest encounters with belief (the claims of subjectivity), knowledge (the claims of intersubjectivity), and truth (the claims of objectivity), pedagogy and scholarship have tried to balance the need to ask questions with the need to offer well-grounded if tentative answers. Since an answer is at least a provisional suspension of questioning, it interrupts the critical process and also suspends the critical element in learning. But unless questioning stops and is at some point provisionally satisfied, there is no knowledge worth the name—neither subjective beliefs, intersubjective values, nor objective truths (however small the *t* in truth).

The pedagogy of questioning naturally and properly takes the standpoint of suspicion. It looks behind appearances and beneath surfaces, and thus has a penchant for reductionism: turning the immediate into the mediated, turning the observed into the intuited, turning apparent universals into actual particulars, turning putative reasons into sham rationalizations, turning claims to truth into rationalizations of interest—looking always for a concealed reality behind *prima facie* events. . . . To reductionists, things are never quite what they seem. Suspicious of truth as an external "empirical" thing or an inherently meaningful text or an uncontested object, they reduce such entities to the conditions (psychological, historical, material) by which they are produced and the interests of those who produce them.

The author of a book, argues Foucault, a reductionist here who sees behind the smoke screen of "reason" a hundred hidden varieties of coercion, is not some vessel of art or creative genius but merely "an ideological product." A book is less a work of literature imbued with truth and beauty or with standards to which human conduct might be made to conform (the old-fashioned view) than a product of its readers or its critics; an emanation of the class, gender, and status of the background that produced the writer or his audience. As David Hume, skeptic and critic of objectivist ethics, said long before deconstruction seized on such arguments, a value is not a symbol for some objective right or eternal good, it is merely a token of someone's preference. To say "It is good" is merely a disguised way of saying "I like it." And whereas (when we allow that objective standards exist) we can presumably assess and argue rationally about human conduct, preferences are purely subjective, and all we can say about them is that at most they exist. The assertion "Cruelty is good" takes a form inviting debate and argument, and may elicit the counterassertion "No, it is evil," which can in turn be debated in historical, moral, and philosophical terms. On the other hand, the descriptive sentence "Cruelty feels good to me" cannot be contested at all other than in terms of its descriptive accuracy ("Does it *really* feel good to you?"). To someone who says "I like being cruel," neither "No, you don't" nor "But cruelty is evil" is an appropriate response. The reductive language of what philosophers call "noncognitivism" makes ethics radically subjective, and it soon vanishes as a subject of moral discourse. . . .

Reducing supposed objective goods to subjective preferences and reducing claims about truth to statements about power and interest are two related forms of a very ancient and very useful but also very risky skepticism. For millennia, both skepticism and reductionism lived as parasites off the host philosophy—which, fortunately, had its own affirmative business to attend to (understanding human conduct in an often unintelligible cosmos). In the last hundred years or so, these two have more or less consumed the philosophical tradition that sustained them. The same thing has happened in literature, as the critic came first to deny the meaning of literature, then to displace it with the activities of the critics. Criticism is now seemingly severed from literature in many universities, leading and independent existence as literary theory in English departments that teach not literature and the art of reading, but theory and the art of criticism. Social scientists and humanists in many other departments, especially those understandably dissatisfied with traditional academe and its spurious appeals to neutrality and universalism, are taking their cue

164

*Chapter 8
The Critical
Perspective on
the Struggle for
Freedom in
Education*

from literary theorists and deploying reductive post-modern critiques against the establishment. This has certain virtues as a tactic but ultimately is poor strategy and bad pedagogy.

. . . As Edmund Burke once noted, those who destroy everything are certain to remedy some grievance. The annihilation of all values will undoubtedly rid us of hypocritical ones or the ones misused by hypocrites. We can prevent the powerful from using reason to conceal their hegemony by burning the cloak—extirpating reason from political and moral discourse. However, those who come after can hardly complain that they feel naked or that their discourse, absent such terms as reason, legitimacy, and justice, seems incapable of establishing an affirmative pedagogy or a just politics.

Just how crucially such seemingly abstruse issues impact on actual college curricula is unpleasantly evident in this approving portrait of literature and culture in a recent issue of the *Bulletin of the American Association of University Professors*:

> Cultural studies moves away from "history of ideas" to a contested history of struggles for power and authority, to complicated relations between "center" and "margin," between dominant and minority positions. Literature is no longer investigated primarily as the masterworks of individual genius, but as a way of designating specialized practices of reading and writing and cultural production. . . . The renaming of "literature" as "culture" is thus not just a shift in vocabulary. It marks a rethinking of what is experienced as cultural materials . . . [including] media, MTV, popular culture, newspapers, magazines, advertising, textbooks, and advice materials. But the shift also marks the movement away from the study of an "object" to the study of a practice, the practice called "literary study" or "artistic production," the practice of criticism.

How slippery this particular slope has become! What begins as a sound attempt to show that art is produced by real men and women with agendas and interests attached to things like their gender, race, and economic status ends as the nihilistic denial of art as object. What beings as a pedagogically useful questioning of the power implications of truth ends as the cynical subverting of the very possibility of truth. What begins as a prudent unwillingness to accept at face value "objective" knowledge, which is understood to be, at least in part, socially constructed, ends as the absurd insistence that knowledge is exclusively social and can be reduced entirely to the power of those who produce it. What begins as an educationally provocative inquiry into the origins of literature in the practice of literary production ends in the educationally insidious annihilation of literature and its replacement by criticism—the practice, it turns out ever so conveniently, of those asking the questions! Thus does the whirling blade of skepticism's latest reductive manifestations, post-modernism and deconstruction, cut and cut and go on cutting until there is nothing left. Thus does the amiable and pedagogically essential art of criticism somehow pass into carnage.

As epistemology, this is what post-moderns would, in their mimitable jargon, call logocidal—deadly to reason and discourse. As pedagogy it is suicidal, above all to those already deprived of power and voice by the social forms and educational strategies supposedly being deconstructed. It is hard to tell what service a teacher does a ninth grader just learning to read books when she informs him that there is no difference between Emily Dickinson and MTV, both being simply cultural products of interested artisans pushing their particular ideological interests. To make his point about the relativism of cultural values, Houston A. Baker, the current president of the Modern Language Association, tells us there is no more difference between high culture and pop culture than between a hoagie and a pizza. What he means is that there is no more difference between Shakespeare and Virginia Woolf than between Virginia Woolf and a pepperoni slice with extra cheese. This is to say, as John Stuart Mill quipped about Jeremy Bentham's reductionist utilitarianism, that there is no difference between pushpin and poetry.

These are more than theoretical points: Rutgers has offered social science courses not only on film but on MTV, and Duke University teaches Louis L'Amour alongside Shakespeare and George Eliot, not because popular writing deserves a place in the curriculum along with high culture (it does), but in the belief that the distinction between pop and high culture is spurious, an invention of elites trying to maintain their cultural hegemony. Yet without the aspiration to excellence, however contested the end products, "culture" loses its normative and directing power and becomes a cipher; no distinctions can be made between the "culture of pinball machines," "the drug culture," and "skinhead culture," on the one hand, and "Italian Renaissance culture," "the culture of Benin civilization," and "Harlem Renaissance culture," on the other. . . .

Like all fundamental political and social terms, culture is inherently and necessarily normative. That is why we argue about it, why it is contested. That is what makes multiculturalism worth debating. To annul the power of the word "culture" as a standard of human organization, aesthetic and intellectual evolution, and general excellence does nothing to enhance cultural pluralism or learning in the name of liberty and respect. On the contrary, it creates the impression that there are no standards of excellence whatsoever other than the bogus claims advanced by elites.

The confusion of multiculturalists on this question is evident in their ambivalence over whether to take some significant credit for Western civilization by showing its roots in Egyptian and African sources (thereby paying tribute to its many achievements), as does Martin Bernal in *Black Athena,* or to reject it altogether in favor of a radical "Afrocentric" view that celebrates Africa and subjects Western culture to a not so benign neglect, as scholars like Molefi Asante have done. If Western culture manifests certain virtues, if culture implies standards (however contested) and is more than just a collection of artifacts, then the sources of "Western" civilization are worth fighting over. If not, why bother contest their origins at all?

Sometimes multiculturalists want it both ways, sounding a little like the storied defense attorney who, without taking a breath, managed to argue, "My client is innocent, your honor; he never took the jewels, and besides, he didn't know they belonged to anyone, and anyway they were fake." With the same all-encompassing logic, the Afrocentric multiculturalist at times seems to say, "Western civilization is worthless, dangerous, a colonizing imperium with pretended virtues it never lives up to; and besides, it was originally *OUR* creation,

166

Chapter 8
The Critical
Perspective on
the Struggle for
Freedom in
Education

a product of an Egypt we can prove was Black, and anyway Black Africa had a great culture of its own, which we can see reflected in the values of so-called Western civilization *IT* actually produced." Critics have suggested that Afrocentrists are not really multiculturalists at all, but monocultural zealots of a civilization other than Europe's. Perhaps a response in keeping with the moderation offered earlier would be to see Afrocentrism as a stage on the way to a more genuine multiculturalism, itself a stage on the way to appreciating America as a culture defined precisely by its diversity and multiculturalism. This eliminates the harsh attack on Western culture, which is of more use to conservative critics looking to dismiss multiculturalism than to multicultured educators.

Conservatives (who surely have to be congratulating themselves privately on their good fortune in being tossed so splendid a provocation!) have repeatedly expressed their horror over the Stanford march led by the Reverend Jesse Jackson not so long ago in which students protesting traditional curricula chanted, "Hey, hey, ho, ho, Western Culture has got to go!" (although it was the course labeled as such rather than the generic entity they were protesting). As new expressions of anti-Western monocultural intolerance, such slogans are reprehensible. But they are also implicit in the reductionist perspective, which denies "culture" any status other than that of "ideological product." By transforming normative truths subject to rational debate that are embodied in the books, conventions, and institutions that constitute a civilization into an unwholesome product of vested interests, the skeptic undermines not civilization but civility, not rationalization but reason, not dogma but the possibility of consensus and thus community. Along the way, in impugning the inherent authority of the idea of culture, he also manages to impugn the authority of the non-Western civilizations to which his multiculturalism supposedly pays homage.

Questioning should challenge objectivity but also be capable of redeeming it. Criticism finds its pedagogical legitimacy in its powers of redemption: the power to save virtue from hypocrisy, truth from its counterfeits, reason from rationalization. Anything else pushes skepticism over the brink and gives to subjectivism the aspect of narcissism. In philosophy, this narcissism is called solipsism, a term suggesting a self so absorbed in the mysteries of its capacity to sense and make sense (or nonsense) of the world that it ceases to perceive anything but itself. This is a matter of the eye being distracted from the object to which the finger points to the finger itself, until the whole world resembles nothing so much as a finger.

. . . [A]dvocates of the new hyperskepticism . . . are genuine reformers struggling against the dogmas of what they see as a hypocritical establishment. They seek more equality, more justice, better education for all. They want not just to expose the hypocrisies of power, but to tame and equalize it. They want to reclaim true justice from its hypocritical abusers. They chase shadows in the valley of cynicism but trust they are on the path that leads to redemption.

Yet the instruments of revolution they have chosen are more suited to the philosophical terrorist than the pedagogical reformer. Radical skepticism, reductionism, solipsism, nihilism, subjectivism, and cynicism will not help American women gain a stronger voice in the classroom; will not lift Americans of color from the prison of ignorance and despair to which centuries of oppression, broken families, and ghettoized schools have relegated them; will not provide a firm value foundation for the young in equality, citizenship, and justice. How can such reformers think they will empower the voiceless by proving that voice is always a function of power? How can they believe the ignorant will be rescued from illiteracy by showing that literacy is an arbitrary form of cultural imperialism? How do they think the struggle for equality and justice can be waged with an epistemology that denies standing to reasons and normative rational terms such as justice and equality?

. . . [R]eason is an ideal that can teach us how to live in comity and free ourselves from the incivility that always attends reasons' failure. When reason is polluted by interest and power, the remedy is not to jettison but to cleanse it. The remedy for hypocrisy is not less but more reason. Rationalization is evidence of reason abused, not proof that there is no reason. The object of questioning is to test and strengthen rather than to annihilate the idea of the rational.

Education is a training in the middle way between the dogmatic belief in absolutes and the cynical negation of all belief. On the fringes where dogma or nihilism prevail, force is always master. Well-taught students learn to suspect every claim to truth and then to redeem truth provisionally by its capacity to withstand pointed questioning. They learn that somewhere between Absolute Certainty and Permanent Doubt there is a point of balance that permits knowledge to be provisionally accepted and applied (science, modestly understood, for example) and allows conduct to be provisionally evaluated in a fashion that makes ethics, community, and democracy possible. There is much illusion in this fragile middle ground. Civilization, Yeats reminded us, it tied together by a hoop of illusion. It would be dangerous to pretend that the illusion is real, but it is fatal to dispense with it altogether. Justice and democracy are the illusions that permit us to live in comity. Truth and knowledge are the illusions that permit us to live commodiously. Art and literature are the illusions that make commodious living worthwhile. Deconstruction may rid us of all our illusions and thus seem a clever way to think, but it is no way at all to live.

The educator's art is to prompt questions that expose our illusions and at the same time to tether illusion to provisional moorings. The teacher must know how to arouse but also how to mollify the faculty of doubt. Her special art is moderation. She will question whether the statements "This is good! This is beautiful! This is justice!" mean something more than "I control the discourse! I define art! I am justice." But her aim will be to distinguish the counterfeit from the real rather than to expunge the very ideas of the good, the beautiful, and the right. There are illusions and there are illusions. "We the People" as a description of a slave-holding society is an illusion that needs to be exposed; "We the People" as an aspiration that permitted, even encouraged, the eventual abolition of slavery is an illusion worth keeping, even worth fighting for, along with such illusions as natural right and human reason on which the concept relies. The ability to discern the difference between these two forms of illusion is what good education teaches. Such judgment can come neither from inculcating fixed canons nor from deconstructing all canons.

The educator cannot teach when offered only the choice between dogma and nothingness; between orthodoxy and meaninglessness; between some-

168

*Chapter 8
The Critical
Perspective on
the Struggle for
Freedom in
Education*

one's covert value hegemony and the relativism of all values. The first business of educational reformers in schools and universities—multiculturalists, feminists, progressives—ought to be to sever their alliance with esoteric post-modernism; with literary metatheory (theory about theory); with fun-loving, self-annihilating hyperskepticism. As pedagogy these intellectual practices court catastrophe. . . . They give to people whose very lives depend on the right choices a lesson in the impossibility of judgment. They tell emerging citizens looking to legitimize their preferences for democracy that there is no intellectually respectable way to ground political legitimacy.

CHAPTER 9 Women and Education

9.1 ELIZABETH CADY STANTON

Eighty Years and More (1815–1897): Reminiscences of Elizabeth Cady Stanton

Elizabeth Cady Stanton (1815–1902) was a leader in the fight for women's rights in the United States. Along with Lucretia Mott and others, Stanton led the call for the Seneca Falls (New York) Convention, which convened on July 19–20, 1848. This event is credited as being the official launching of the organized women's rights movement in the United States. Stanton read a "Declaration of Sentiments" before the Seneca Falls Convention, in which she listed the wrongs inflicted on women by then-existing laws and customs. She demanded suffrage and property rights for women as well as the right of women to divorce for good cause.

In the following selection from Stanton's autobiography, *Eighty Years and More (1815–1897): Reminiscences of Elizabeth Cady Stanton* (T. Fisher Unwin, 1898), we see the beginnings of her commitment as a girl and as a young woman to engage in the struggle for the rights of women. Her writing captures the spirit of her time and of her schooling.

Key Concept: education of girls in the nineteenth century

169

SCHOOL DAYS

When I was eleven years old, two events occurred which changed considerably the current of my life. My only brother, who had just graduated from Union College, came home to die. A young man of great talent and promise, he was the pride of my father's heart. We early felt that this son filled a larger place in our father's affections and future plans than the five daughters together. Well do I remember how tenderly he watched my brother in his last illness, the sighs and tears he gave vent to as he slowly walked up and down the hall, and, when the last sad moment came, and we were all assembled to say farewell in the silent chamber of death, how broken were his utterances as he knelt and prayed for comfort and support. I still recall, too, going into the large darkened parlor to see my brother, and finding the casket, mirrors, and pictures all draped in white, and my father seated by his side, pale and immovable. As he took no notice of me, after standing a long while, I climbed upon his knee, when he mechanically put his arm about me and, with my head resting against his beating heart, we both sat in silence, he thinking of the wreck of all his hopes in the loss of a dear son, and I wondering what could be said or done to fill the void in his breast. At length he heaved a deep sigh and said: "Oh, my daughter, I wish you were a boy!" Throwing my arms about his neck, I replied: "I will try to be all my brother was."

Then and there I resolved that I would not give so much time as heretofore to play, but would study and strive to be at the head of all my classes and thus delight my father's heart. All that day and far into the night I pondered the problem of boyhood. I thought that the chief thing to be done in order to equal boys was to be learned and courageous. So I decided to study Greek and learn to manage a horse. Having formed this conclusion I fell asleep. My resolutions, unlike many such made at night, did not vanish with the coming light. I arose early and hastened to put them into execution. They were resolutions never to be forgotten—destined to mold my character anew. As soon as I was dressed I hastened to our good pastor, Rev. Simon Hosack, who was always early at work in his garden.

"Doctor," said I, "which do you like best, boys or girls?"

"Why, girls, to be sure; I would not give you for all the boys in Christendom."

"My father," I replied, "prefers boys; he wishes I was one, and I intend to be as near like one as possible. I am going to ride on horseback and study Greek. Will you give me a Greek lesson now, doctor? I want to begin at once."

"Yes, child," said he, throwing down his hoe, "come into my library and we will begin without delay."

He entered fully into the feeling of suffering and sorrow which took possession of me when I discovered that a girl weighed less in the scale of being than a boy, and he praised my determination to prove the contrary. The old grammar which he had studied in the University of Glasgow was soon in my hands, and the Greek article was learned before breakfast.

Then came the sad pageantry of death, the weeping of friends, the dark rooms, the ghostly stillness, the exhortation to the living to prepare for death, the solemn prayer, the mournful chant, the funeral cortège, the solemn, tolling bell, the burial. How I suffered during those sad days! What strange undefined fears of the unknown took possession of me! For months afterward, at the twilight hour, I went with my father to the new-made grave. Near it stood two tall poplar trees, against one of which I leaned, while my father threw himself on the grave, with outstretched arms, as if to embrace his child. At last the frosts and storms of November came and threw a chilling barrier between the living and the dead, and we went there no more.

During all this time I kept up my lessons at the parsonage and made rapid progress. I surprised even my teacher, who thought me capable of doing anything. I learned to drive, and to leap a fence and ditch on horseback. I taxed every power, hoping some day to hear my father say: "Well, a girl is as good as a boy, after all." But he never said it. When the doctor came over to spend the evening with us, I would whisper in his ear: "Tell my father how fast I get on," and he would tell him, and was lavish in his praises. But my father only paced the room, sighed, and showed that he wished I were a boy; and I, not knowing why he felt thus, would hide my tears of vexation on the doctor's shoulder.

Soon after this I began to study Latin, Greek, and mathematics with a class of boys in the Academy, many of whom were much older than I. For three years one boy kept his place at the end of the class, and I always stood next. Two prizes were offered in Greek. I strove for one and took the second. How well I remember my joy in receiving that prize. There was no sentiment of ambition, rivalry, or triumph over my companions, nor feeling of satisfaction in receiving this honor in the presence of those assembled on the day of the exhibition. One thought alone filled my mind. "Now," said I, "my father will be satisfied with me." So, as soon as we were dismissed, I ran down the hill, rushed breathless into his office, laid the new Greek Testament, which was my prize, on his table and exclaimed: "There, I got it!" He took up the book, asked me some questions about the class, the teachers, the spectators, and, evidently pleased, handed it back to me. Then, while I stood looking and waiting for him to say something which would show that he recognized the equality of the daughter with the son, he kissed me on the forehead and exclaimed, with a sigh, "Ah, you should have been a boy!"

My joy was turned to sadness. I ran to my good doctor. He chased my bitter tears away, and soothed me with unbounded praises and visions of future success. He was then confined to the house with his last illness. He asked me that day if I would like to have, when he was gone, the old lexicon, Testament, and grammar that we had so often thumbed together. "Yes, but I would rather have you stay," I replied, "for what can I do when you are gone?" "Oh," said he tenderly, "I shall not be gone; my spirit will still be with you, watching you in all life's struggles." Noble, generous friend! He had but little on earth to bequeath to anyone, but when the last scene in his life was ended, and his will was opened, sure enough there was a clause saying: "My Greek lexicon, Testament, and grammar, and four volumes of Scott's commentaries, I will to Elizabeth Cady." I never look at these books without a feeling of thankfulness that in childhood I was blessed with such a friend and teacher. . . .

An important event in our family circle was the marriage of my oldest sister, Tryphena, to Edward Bayard of Wilmington, Delaware. He was a graduate of Union College, a classmate of my brother, and frequently visited at my father's house. At the end of his college course, he came with his brother Henry to study law in Johnstown. A quiet, retired little village was thought to be a good place in which to sequester young men bent on completing their education, as they were there safe from the temptations and distracting influences of large cities. In addition to this consideration, my father's reputation made his office a desirable resort for students, who, furthermore, not only improved their opportunities by reading Blackstone, Kent, and Story, but also by making love to the Judge's daughters. We thus had the advantage of many pleasant acquaintances from the leading families in the country, and, in this way, it was that four of the sisters eventually selected most worthy husbands.

Though only twenty-one years of age when married, Edward Bayard was a tall, fully developed man, remarkably fine looking, with cultivated literary taste and a profound knowledge of human nature. Warm and affectionate, generous to a fault in giving and serving, he was soon a great favorite in the family, and gradually filled the void made in all our hearts by the loss of the brother and son.

My father was so fully occupied with the duties of his profession, which often called him from home, and my mother so weary with the cares of a large family, having had ten children, though only five survived at this time, that they were quite willing to shift their burdens to younger shoulders. Our eldest sister and her husband, therefore, soon became our counselors and advisers. They selected our clothing, books, schools, acquaintances, and directed our reading and amusements. Thus the reins of domestic government, little by little, passed into their hands, and the family arrangements were in a manner greatly improved in favor of greater liberty for the children.

The advent of Edward and Henry Bayard was an inestimable blessing to us. With them came an era of picnics, birthday parties, and endless amusements; the buying of pictures, fairy books, musical instruments and ponies, and frequent excursions with parties on horseback. Fresh from college, they made our lessons in Latin, Greek, and mathematics so easy that we studied with real pleasure and had more leisure for play. Henry Bayard's chief pleasures were walking, riding, and playing all manner of games, from jack-straws to chess, with the three younger sisters, and we have often said that the three years he passed in Johnstown were the most delightful of our girlhood. . . .

As my father's office joined the house, I spent there much of my time, when out of school, listening to the clients stating their cases, talking with the students, and reading the laws in regard to woman. In our Scotch neighborhood many men still retained the old feudal ideas of women and property. Fathers, at their death, would will the bulk of their property to the eldest son, with the proviso that the mother was to have a home with him. Hence it was not unusual for the mother, who had brought all the property into the family, to be made an unhappy dependent on the bounty of an uncongenial daughter-in-law and a dissipated son. The tears and complaints of the women who came to my father for legal advice touched my heart and early drew my attention to the injustice and cruelty of the laws. As the practice of the law was my father's business, I could not exactly understand why he could not alleviate the sufferings of these women. So, in order to enlighten me, he would take down his books and show me the inexorable statutes. The students, observing my interest, would amuse themselves by reading to me all the worst laws they could find, over which I would laugh and cry by turns. One Christmas morning I went into the office to show them, among other of my presents, a new coral necklace and bracelets. They all admired the jewelry and then began to tease me with hypothetical cases of future ownership. "Now," said Henry Bayard, "if in due time you should be my wife, those ornaments would be mine; I could take them and lock them up, and you could never wear them except with my permission. I could even exchange them for a box of cigars, and you could watch them evaporate in smoke."

With this constant bantering from students and the sad complaints of the women, my mind was sorely perplexed. So when, from time to time, my attention was called to these odious laws, I would mark them with a pencil, and becoming more and more convinced of the necessity of taking some active measures against these unjust provisions, I resolved to seize the first opportunity, when alone in the office, to cut every one of them out of the books; supposing my father and his library were the beginning and the end of the law. However, this mutilation of his volumes was never accomplished, for dear old Flora Campbell, to whom I confided my plan for the amelioration of the wrongs of my unhappy sex, warned my father of what I proposed to do. Without letting me know that he had discovered my secret, he explained to me one evening how laws were made, the large number of lawyers and libraries there were all over the State, and that if his library should burn up it would make no difference in woman's condition. "When you are grown up, and able to prepare a speech," said he, "you must go down to Albany and talk to the legislators; tell them all you have seen in this office—the sufferings of these Scotchwomen, robbed of their inheritance and left dependent on their unworthy sons, and, if you can persuade them to pass new laws, the old ones will be a dead letter." Thus was the future object of my life foreshadowed and my duty plainly outlined by him who was most opposed to my public career when, in due time, I entered upon it.

Until I was sixteen years old, I was a faithful student in the Johnstown Academy with a class of boys. Though I was the only girl in the higher classes of mathematics and the languages, yet, in our plays, all the girls and boys mingled freely together. In running races, sliding downhill, and snowballing, we made no distinction of sex. True, the boys would carry the school books and pull the sleighs up hill for their favorite girls, but equality was the general basis of our school relations. I dare say the boys did not make their snowballs quite so hard when pelting the girls, nor wash their faces with the same vehemence as they did each other's, but there was no public evidence of partiality. However, if any boy was too rough or took advantage of a girl smaller than himself, he was promptly thrashed by his fellows. There was an unwritten law and public sentiment in that little Academy world that enabled us to study and play together with the greatest freedom and harmony.

From the academy the boys of my class went to Union College at Schenectady. When those with whom I had studied and contended for prizes for five years came to bid me good-by, and I learned of the barrier that prevented me from following in their footsteps—"no girls admitted here"—my vexation and mortification knew no bounds. I remember, now, how proud and handsome the boys looked in their new clothes, as they jumped into the old stage coach and drove off, and how lonely I felt when they were gone and I had nothing to do, for the plans for my future were yet undetermined. Again I felt more keenly than ever the humiliation of the distinctions made on the ground of sex.

My time was now occupied with riding on horseback, studying the game of chess, and continually squabbling with the law students over the rights of women. Something was always coming up in the experiences of everyday life, or in the books we were reading, to give us fresh topics for argument. They would read passages from the British classics quite as aggravating as the laws. They delighted in extract from Shakespeare, especially from "The Taming of the Shrew," an admirable satire in itself on the old common law of England. I hated Petruchio as if he were a real man. Young Bayard would recite with unction the famous reply of Milton's ideal woman to Adam: "God thy law, thou mine." The Bible, too, was brought into requisition. In fact it seemed to me that every book taught the "divinely ordained" headship of man; but my mind never yielded to this popular heresy.

GIRLHOOD

Mrs. Willard's Seminary at Troy was the fashionable school in my girlhood, and in the winter of 1830, with upward of a hundred other girls, I found myself an active participant in all the joys and sorrows of that institution. When in family council it was decided to send me to that intellectual Mecca, I did not receive the announcement with unmixed satisfaction, as I had fixed my mind on Union College. The thought of a school without boys, who had been to me such a stimulus both in study and play, seemed to my imagination dreary and profitless.

The one remarkable feature of my journey to Troy was the railroad from Schenectady to Albany, the first ever laid in this country. The manner of ascending a high hill going out of the city would now strike engineers as stupid to the last degree. The passenger cars were pulled up by a train, loaded with stones, descending the hill. The more rational way of tunneling through the hill or going around it had not yet dawned on our Dutch ancestors. At every step of my journey to Troy I felt that I was treading on my pride, and thus in a hopeless frame of mind I began my boarding-school career. I had already studied everything that was taught there except French, music, and dancing, so I devoted myself to these accomplishments. As I had a good voice I enjoyed singing, with a guitar accompaniment, and, having a good ear for time, I appreciated the harmony in music and motion and took great delight in dancing. The large house, the society of so many girls, the walks about the city, the novelty of everything made the new life more enjoyable than I had anticipated. To be sure I missed the boys, with whom I had grown up, played with for years, and later measured by intellectual powers with, but, as they became a novelty, there was new zest in occasionally seeing them. After I had been there a short time, I heard a call one day: "Heads out!" I ran with the rest and exclaimed, "What is it?" expecting to see a giraffe or some other wonder from Barnum's Museum. "Why, don't you see those boys?" said one. "Oh," I replied, "is that all? I have seen boys all my life." When visiting family friends in the city, we were in the way of making the acquaintance of their sons, and as all social relations were strictly forbidden, there was a new interest in seeing them. As they were not allowed to call upon us or write notes, unless they were brothers or cousins, we had, in time, a large number of kinsmen.

There was an intense interest to me now in writing notes, receiving calls, and joining the young men in the streets for a walk, such as I had never known when in constant association with them at school and in our daily amusements. Shut up with girls, most of them older than myself, I heard many subjects discussed of which I had never thought before, and in a manner it were better I had never heard. The healthful restraint always existing between boys and girls in conversation is apt to be relaxed with either sex alone. In all my intimate association with boys up to that period, I cannot recall one word or act for criticism, but I cannot say the same of the girls during the three years I passed at the seminary in Troy. My own experience proves to me that it is a grave mistake to send boys and girls to separate institutions of learning, especially at the most impressible age. The stimulus of sex promotes alike a healthy condition of the intellectual and the moral faculties and gives to both a development they never can acquire alone.

Mrs. Willard, having spent several months in Europe, did not return until I had been at the seminary some time. I well remember her arrival, and the joy with which she was greeted by the teachers and pupils who had known her before. She was a splendid-looking woman, then in her prime, and fully realized my idea of a queen. I doubt whether any royal personage in the Old World could have received her worshipers with more grace and dignity than did this far-famed daughter of the Republic. She was one of the remarkable women of that period, and did a great educational work for her sex. She gave free scholarships to a large number of promising girls, fitting them for teachers, with a proviso that, when the opportunity arose, they should, in turn, educate others. . . .

After the restraints of childhood at home and in school, what a period of irrepressible joy and freedom comes to us in girlhood with the first taste of liberty. Then is our individuality in a measure recognized and our feelings and opinions consulted; then we decide where and when we will come and go, what we will eat, drink, wear, and do. To suit one's own fancy in clothes, to buy what one likes, and wear what one chooses is a great privilege to most young people. To go out at pleasure, to walk, to ride, to drive, with no one to say us nay or question our right to liberty, this is indeed like a birth into a new world of happiness and freedom. This is the period, too, when the emotions rule us, and we idealize everything in life; when love and hope make the present an ecstasy and the future bright with anticipation.

Then comes that dream of bliss that for weeks and months throws a halo of glory round the most ordinary characters in every-day life, holding the strongest and most common-sense young men and women in a thraldom from which few mortals escape. The period when love, in soft silver tones, whispers his first words of adoration, painting our graces and virtues day by day in living colors in poetry and prose, stealthily punctuated ever and anon with a kiss or fond embrace. What dignity it adds to a young girl's estimate of herself when some strong man makes her feel that in her hands rest his future peace and happiness! Though these seasons of intoxication may come once to all, yet they are seldom repeated. How often in after life we long for one more such rapturous dream of bliss, one more season of supreme human love and passion!

After leaving school, until my marriage, I had the most pleasant years of my girlhood. With frequent visits to a large circle of friends and relatives in various towns and cities, the monotony of home life was sufficiently broken to make our simple country pleasures always delightful and enjoyable. An entirely new life now opened to me. The old bondage of fear of the visible and the invisible was broken and, no longer subject to absolute authority, I rejoiced in the dawn of a new day of freedom in thought and action.

My brother-in-law, Edward Bayard, ten years my senior, was an inestimable blessing to me at this time, especially as my mind was just then opening to the consideration of all the varied problems of life. To me and my sisters he was a companion in all our amusements, a teacher in the higher departments of knowledge, and a counselor in all our youthful trials and disappointments. He was of a metaphysical turn of mind, and in the pursuit of truth was in no way trammeled by popular superstitions. He took nothing for granted and, like Socrates, went about asking questions. Nothing pleased him more than to get a bevy of bright young girls about him and teach them how to think clearly and reason logically.

One great advantage of the years my sisters and myself spent at the Troy Seminary was the large number of pleasant acquaintances we made there, many of which ripened into lifelong friendships. From time to time many of our classmates visited us, and all alike enjoyed the intellectual fencing in which my brother-in-law drilled them. He discoursed with us on law, philosophy, political economy, history, and poetry, and together we read novels without number. The long winter evenings thus passed pleasantly, Mr. Bayard alternatively talking and reading aloud Scott, Bulwer, James, Cooper, and Dickens, whose works were just then coming out in numbers from week to week, always leaving us in suspense at the most critical point of the story. Our readings were varied with recitations, music, dancing, and games. . . .

As I had become sufficiently philosophical to talk over my religious experiences calmly with my classmates who had been with me through the Finney revival meetings, we all came to the same conclusion—that we had passed through no remarkable change and that we had not been born again, as they say, for we found our tastes and enjoyments the same as ever. My brother-in-law explained to us the nature of the delusion we had all experienced, the physical conditions, the mental processes, the church machinery by which such excitements are worked up, and the impositions to which credulous minds are necessarily subjected. As we had all been through that period of depression and humiliation, and had been oppressed at times with the feeling that all our professions were arrant hypocrisy and that our last state was worse than our first, he helped us to understand these workings of the human mind and

reconciled us to the more rational condition in which we now found ourselves. He never grew weary of expounding principles to us and dissipating
the fogs and mists that gather over young minds educated in an atmosphere
of superstition.

We had a constant source of amusement and vexation in the students in
my father's office. A succession of them was always coming fresh from college
and full of conceit. Aching to try their powers of debate on graduates from the
Troy Seminary, they politely questioned all our theories and assertions. However, with my brother-in-law's training in analysis and logic, we were a match
for any of them. Nothing pleased me better than a long argument with them on
woman's equality, which I tried to prove by a diligent study of the books they
read and the games they played. I confess that I did not study so much for a
love of the truth or my own development, in these days, as to make those
young men recognize my equality. I soon noticed that, after losing a few games
of chess, my opponent talked less of masculine superiority. Sister Madge
would occasionally rush to the defense with an emphatic "Fudge for these
laws, all made by men! I'll never obey one of them. And as to the students with
their impertinent talk of superiority, all they need is such a shaking up as I
gave the most disagreeable one yesterday. I invited him to take a ride on
horseback. He accepted promptly, and said he would be most happy to go.
Accordingly I told Peter to saddle the toughest-mouthed, hardest-trotting car-
riage horse in the stable. Mounted on my swift pony, I took a ten-mile canter as
fast as I could go, with that superior being at my heels calling, as he found
breath, for me to stop, which I did at last and left him in the hands of Peter, half
dead at his hotel, where he will be laid out, with all his marvelous masculine
virtues, for a week at least. Now do not waste your arguments on these prigs
from Union College. Take each, in turn, the ten-miles' circuit on 'Old Boney'
and they'll have no breath left to prate of woman's inferiority. You might argue
with them all day, and you could not make them feel so small as I made that
popinjay feel in one hour. I knew 'Old Boney' would keep up with me, if he
died for it, and that my escort could neither stop nor dismount, except by
throwing himself from the saddle."

"Oh, Madge!" I exclaimed; "what will you say when he meets you
again?"

"If he complains, I will say 'the next time you ride see that you have a
curb bit before starting.' Surely, a man ought to know what is necessary to
manage a horse, and not expect a woman to tell him."

Our lives were still further varied and intensified by the usual number
of flirtations, so called, more or less lasting or evanescent, from all of which
I emerged, as from my religious experiences, in a more rational frame of
mind. We had been too much in the society of boys and young gentlemen,
and knew too well their real character, to idealize the sex in general. In
addition to our own observations, we had the advantage of our brother-in-
law's wisdom. Wishing to save us as long as possible from all matrimonial
entanglements, he was continually unveiling those with whom he associated, and so critically portraying their intellectual and moral condition that
it was quite impossible, in our most worshipful moods, to make gods of any
of the sons of Adam.

However, in spite of all our own experiences and of all the warning words of wisdom from those who had seen life in its many phases, we entered the charmed circle at last, all but one marrying into the legal profession, with its odious statute laws and infamous decisions. And this, after reading Blackstone, Kent, and Story, and thoroughly understanding the status of the wife under the old common law of England, which was in force at that time in most of the States of the Union.

How Schools Shortchange Girls: A Study of Major Findings on Girls and Education

The American Association of University Women (AAUW) is an organization of college and university graduates that was founded in 1881 to work for the advancement of women. In 1990 the AAUW Educational Foundation's Eleanor Roosevelt Fund commissioned the Wellesley College Center for Research on Women to do an in-depth study and to report on the treatment of girls from early childhood through grade 12. The completed study, which is based on the analysis of several years of empirical research on the status of girls in American schools, was published in 1992. *The AAUW Report: How Schools Shortchange Girls* will be a major source of reliable information on how girls are treated in school for several years to come. The data in the report are to be used to help advise educators and government policymakers on educational policy issues relating to equality of educational opportunities for girls and young women in school.

The selection that follows is from the AAUW's executive summary of their findings, and it includes the association's recommendations for action to improve the quality of opportunities for girls and young women in school. There are many implications for educational policymakers and for classroom teachers in the findings of the AAUW report. The call for gender fairness in the education of all American children is in earnest. The report's recommendations, such as that girls be taught assertive and affiliative skills as well as verbal and mathematical skills, cover several areas of concern.

Key Concept: gender equity in the schools

*F*or those who believe that equitable education for all young Americans is the greatest source of a nation's strength, The AAUW Report: How Schools Short-change Girls, will not be reassuring. Commissioned by the AAUW Educational Foundation and developed by the Wellesley College Center for Research on Women, the study challenges the common assumption that girls and boys are treated equally in our public schools.

Ironically, AAUW's first national study—undertaken in 1885—was initiated to dispel the commonly accepted myth that higher education was harmful to women's health. This latest report presents the truth behind another myth—that girls and boys receive equal education.

While most of us are painfully aware of the crisis in American education, few understand or acknowledge the inequities that occur daily in classrooms across the country. Didn't we address that problem in Title IX of the 1972 Education Amend-ments, which prohibits discrimination in educational institutions receiving federal funds? Many of us worked hard to ensure that this legislation would be passed. Its passage, however, did not solve the problem.

This report is a synthesis of all the available research on the subject of girls in school. It presents compelling evidence that girls are not receiving the same quality, or even quantity, of education as their brothers.

The implications of the report's findings are enormous. Women and children are swelling the ranks of the poor, at great cost to society. Yet our education policymakers are failing to address the relationship between education and the cycle of poverty. The shortchanging of girls is not even mentioned in the current educational restructuring debate.

A well-educated work force is essential to the country's economic development, yet girls are systematically discouraged from courses of study essential to their future employability and economic well-being. Girls are being steered away from the very courses required for their productive participation in the future of America, and we as a nation are losing more than one-half of our human potential. By the turn of the century, two out of three new entrants into the work force will be women and minori-ties. This work force will have fewer and fewer decently paid openings for the unskilled. It will require strength in science, mathematics, and technology—subjects girls are still being told are not suitable for them.

The AAUW Report *presents a base for a new and enlightened education pol-icy—a policy that will ensure that this nation will provide the best possible education for all its children. It provides policymakers with impartial data on the ways in which our school system is failing to meet the needs of girls and with specific strategies that can be used to effect change. The wealth of statistical evidence must convince even the most skeptical that gender bias in our schools is shortchanging girls—and compromis-ing our country.*

The AAUW Educational Foundation is proud to present The AAUW Report: How Schools Shortchange Girls, *made possible through the generosity of the many supporters of the Eleanor Roosevelt Fund. This report is destined to add a new dimen-sion to the education debate. The evidence is in, and the picture is clear: shortchanging girls—the women of tomorrow—shortchanges America.*

Alice McKee, President
AAUW Educational Foundation

The invisibility of girls in the current education debate suggests that girls and boys have identical educational experiences in school. Nothing could be further from the truth. Whether one looks at achievement scores, curriculum design, or teacher-student interaction, it is clear that sex and gender make a difference in the nation's public elementary and secondary schools.

The educational system is not meeting girls' needs. Girls and boys enter school roughly equal in measured ability. Twelve years later, girls have fallen behind their male classmates in key areas such as higher-level mathematics and measures of self-esteem. Yet gender equity is still not a part of the national debate on educational reform.

Neither the *National Education Goals* issued by the National Governors Association in 1990 nor *America 2000*, the 1991 plan of the President and the U.S. Department of Education to "move every community in America toward these goals," makes any mention of providing girls equitable opportunities in the nation's public schools. Girls continue to be left out of the debate—despite the fact that for more than two decades researchers have identified gender bias as a major problem at all levels of schooling.

Schools must prepare both girls and boys for full and active roles in the family, the community, and the work force. Whether we look at the issues from an economic, political, or social perspective, girls are one-half of our future. We must move them from the sidelines to the center of the education-reform debate.

A critical step in correcting educational inequities is identifying them publicly. The *AAUW Report: How Schools Shortchange Girls* provides a comprehensive assessment of the status of girls in public education today. It exposes myths about girls and learning, and it supports the work of the many teachers who have struggled to define and combat gender bias in their schools. The report challenges us all—policymakers, educators, administrators, parents, and citizens—to rethink old assumptions and act now to stop schools from shortchanging girls.

Our public education system is plagued by numerous failings that affect boys as negatively as girls. But in many respects girls are put at a disadvantage simply because they are girls. *The AAUW Report* documents this in hundreds of cited studies.

When our schools become more gender-fair, education will improve for all our students—boys as well as girls—because excellence in education cannot be achieved without equity in education. By studying what happens to girls in school, we can gain valuable insights about what has to change in order for each student, every girl and every boy, to do as well as she or he can.

WHAT THE RESEARCH REVEALS

What Happens in the Classroom?

- Girls receive significantly less attention from classroom teachers than do boys.

- African American girls have fewer interactions with teachers than do white girls, despite evidence that they attempt to initiate interactions more frequently.
- Sexual harassment of girls by boys—from innuendo to actual assault—in our nation's schools is increasing.

A large body of research indicates that teachers give more classroom attention and more esteem-building encouragement to boys. In a study conducted by Myra and David Sadker, boys in elementary and middle school called out answers eight times more often than girls. When boys called out, teachers listened. But when girls called out, they were told to "raise your hand if you want to speak." Even when boys do not volunteer, teachers are more likely to encourage them to give an answer or an opinion than they are to encourage girls.

Research reveals a tendency, beginning at the preschool level, for educators to choose classroom activities that appeal to boys' interests and to select presentation formats in which boys excel. The teacher-student interaction patterns in science classes are often particularly biased. Even in math classes, where less-biased patterns are found, psychologist Jacquelynne Eccles reports that select boys in each math class she studied received particular attention to the exclusion of all other students, female and male.

Teaching methods that foster competition are still standard, although a considerable body of research has demonstrated that girls—and many boys as well—learn better when they undertake projects and activities cooperatively rather than competitively.

Researchers, including Sandra Damico, Elois Scott, and Linda Grant, report that African American girls have fewer interactions with teachers than do white girls, even though they attempt to initiate interactions more often. Furthermore, when African American girls do as well as white boys in school, teachers often attribute their success to hard work while assuming that the white boys are not working up to their potential.

Girls do not emerge from our schools with the same degree of confidence and self-esteem as boys. The 1990 AAUW poll, *Shortchanging Girls, Shortchanging America,* documents a loss of self-confidence in girls that is twice that for boys as they move from childhood to adolescence. Schools play a crucial role in challenging and changing gender-role expectations that undermine the self-confidence and achievement of girls.

Reports of boys sexually harassing girls in schools are increasing at an alarming rate. When sexual harassment is treated casually, as in "boys will be boys," both girls and boys get a dangerous, damaging message: "girls are not worthy of respect; appropriate behavior for boys includes exerting power over girls."

What Do We Teach Our Students?

- The contributions and experiences of girls and women are still marginalized or ignored in many of the textbooks used in our nation's schools.

- Schools, for the most part, provide inadequate education on sexuality and healthy development despite national concern about teen pregnancy, the AIDS crisis, and the increase of sexually transmitted diseases among adolescents.
- Incest, rape, and other physical violence severely compromise the lives of girls and women all across the country. These realities are rarely, if ever, discussed in schools.

Curriculum delivers the central message of education. It can strengthen or decrease student motivation for engagement, effort, growth, and development through the images it gives to students about themselves and the world. When the curriculum does not reflect the diversity of students' lives and cultures, it delivers an incomplete message.

Studies have shown that multicultural readings produced markedly more favorable attitudes toward nondominant groups than did the traditional reading lists, that academic achievement for all students was linked to use of nonsexist and multicultural materials, and that sex-role stereotyping was reduced in students whose curriculum portrayed males and females in nonstereotypical roles. Yet during the 1980s, federal support for reform regarding sex and race equity dropped, and a 1989 study showed that of the ten books most frequently assigned in public high school English courses only one was written by a woman and none by members of minority groups.

The "evaded" curriculum is a term coined in this report to refer to matters central to the lives of students that are touched on only briefly, if at all, in most schools. The United States has the highest rate of teenage childbearing in the Western industrialized world. Syphilis rates are now equal for girls and boys, and more teenage girls than boys contract gonorrhea. Although in the adult population AIDS is nine times more prevalent in men than in women, the same is not true for young people. In a District of Columbia study, the rate of HIV infection for girls was almost three times that for boys. Despite all of this, adequate sex and health education is the exception rather than the rule.

Adolescence is a difficult period for all young people, but it is particularly difficult for girls, who are far more likely to develop eating disorders and experience depression. Adolescent girls attempt suicide four to five times as often as boys (although boys, who choose more lethal methods, are more likely to be successful in their attempts).

Perhaps the most evaded of all topics in schools is the issue of gender and power. As girls mature they confront a culture that both idealizes and exploits the sexuality of young women while assigning them roles that are clearly less valued then male roles. If we do not begin to discuss more openly the ways in which ascribed power—whether on the basis of race, sex, class, sexual orientation, or religion—affects individual lives, we cannot truly prepare our students for responsible citizenship.

How Do Race/Ethnicity and Socioeconomic Status Affect Achievement in School?

- Girls from low-income families face particularly severe obstacles. Socio-economic status, more than any other variable, affects access to school resources and educational outcomes.
- Test scores of low-socioeconomic-status girls are somewhat better than for boys from the same background in the lower grades, but by high school these differences disappear. Among high-socioeconomic-status students, boys generally outperform girls regardless of race/ethnicity.
- Too little information is available on differences among various groups of girls. While African Americans are compared to whites, or boys to girls, relatively few studies or published data examine differences by sex *and* race/ethnicity.

All girls confront barriers to equal participation in school and society. But minority girls, who must confront racism as well as sexism, and girls from low-income families face particular severe obstacles. These obstacles can include poor schools in dangerous neighborhoods, low teacher expectations, and inadequate nutrition and health care.

Few studies focus on issues affecting low-income girls and girls from minority groups—unless they are pregnant or drop out of school. In order to develop effective policies and programs, a wide range of issues—from course-taking patterns to academic self-esteem—require further examination by sex, race/ethnicity, and socioeconomic status.

How Are Girls Doing in Math and Science?

- Differences between girls and boys in math achievement are small and declining. Yet in high school, girls are still less likely than boys to take the most advanced courses and be in the top-scoring math groups.
- The gender gap in science, however, is *not* decreasing and may, in fact, be increasing.
- Even girls who are highly competent in math and science are much less likely to pursue scientific or technological careers than are their male classmates.

Girls who see math as "something men do" do less well in math than girls who do not hold this view. In their classic study, Elizabeth Fennema and Julia Sherman reported a drop in both girls' math confidence and their achievement in the middle school years. The drop in confidence *preceded* the decline in achievement.

Researcher Jane Kahle found that boys come to science classes with more out-of-school familiarity and experience with the subject matter. This advantage is furthered in the classroom. One study of science classrooms found that

79 percent of all student-assisted science demonstrations were carried out by boys.

We can no longer afford to disregard half our potential scientists and science-literate citizens of the next generation. Even when girls take math and science courses and do well in them, they do not receive the encouragement they need to pursue scientific careers. A study of high school seniors found that 64 percent of the boys who had taken physics and calculus were planning to major in science and engineering in college, compared to only 18.6 percent of the girls who had taken the same subjects. Support from teachers can make a big difference. Studies report that girls rate teacher support as an important factor in decisions to pursue scientific and technological careers.

Tests: Stepping Stones or Stop Signs?

- Test scores can provide an inaccurate picture of girls' and boys' abilities. Other factors such as grades, portfolios of student work, and out-of-school achievements must be considered in addition to test scores when making judgments about girls' and boys' skills and abilities.
- When scholarships are given based on the Scholastic Aptitude Test (SAT) scores, boys are more apt to receive scholarships than are girls who get equal or slightly better high school grades.
- Girls and boys with the same Math SAT scores do not do equally well in college—girls do better.

In most cases tests reflect rather than cause inequities in American education. The fact that groups score differently on a test does not necessarily mean that the test is biased. If, however, the score differences are related to the validity of the test—for example, if girls and boys know about the same amount of math but boys' test scores are consistently and significantly higher—then the test is biased.

A number of aspects of a test—beyond that which is being tested—can affect the score. For example, girls tend to score better than boys on essay tests, boys better than girls on multiple-choice items. Even today many girls and boys come to a testing situation with different interests and experiences. Thus a reading-comprehension passage that focuses on baseball scores will tend to favor boys, while a question testing the same skills that focuses on child care will tend to favor girls.

Why Do Girls Drop Out and What Are the Consequences?

- Pregnancy is not the only reason girls drop out of school. In fact, less than half the girls who leave school give pregnancy as the reason.
- Dropout rates for Hispanic girls vary considerably by national origin: Puerto Rican and Cuban American girls are more likely to drop out than are boys from the same cultures or other Hispanic girls.

• Childhood poverty is almost inescapable in single-parent families headed by women without a high school diploma: 77 percent for whites and 87 percent for African Americans.

In a recent study, 37 percent of the female dropouts compared to only 5 percent of the male dropouts cited "family-related problems" as the reason they left high school. Traditional gender roles place greater family responsibilities on adolescent girls than on their brothers. Girls are often expected to "help out" with caretaking responsibilities; boys rarely encounter this expectation.

However, girls as well as boys also drop out of school simply because they do not consider school pleasant or worthwhile. Asked what a worthwhile school experience would be, a group of teenage girls responded, "School would be fun. Our teachers would be excited and lively, not bored. They would act caring and take time to understand how students feel. . . . Boys would treat us with respect. If they run by and grab your tits, they would get into trouble."

Women and children are the most impoverished members of our society. Inadequate education not only limits opportunities for women but jeopardizes their children's—and the nation's—future.

9.3 BELL HOOKS

Ecstasy: Teaching and Learning Without Limits

The following selection, from *Teaching to Transgress: Education as the Practice of Freedom* (Routledge, 1994), captures the spirit and imagination of a truly committed feminist scholar and teacher. It speaks well to the issues confronting aspiring young women artists and scholars while addressing the possibilities of committed teaching for affirmative learning experiences for both women and men. The selection is a testimony to the possibilities of teaching to enhance students' faith in themselves and their work. It is an autobiographical account entailing true engagement in critical thinking about teaching.

The author of *Teaching to Transgress,* bell hooks (she prefers to sign her name with lowercase letters), addresses the key concept of "engaged pedagogy"—teaching with commitment to one's bravest hopes. Hooks speaks to the heavy personal emotional stresses produced by a teacher's commitment to impassioned teaching without limits. In her concept of "engaged pedagogy," she advocates intellectual as well as emotional involvement of the teacher with the students in the classroom. She addresses the issue of creativity in teachers and asserts that engaged teachers try to spark creative dialogue between themselves and their students. She believes that engaged teachers must be concerned about the lives of their students beyond the classroom setting.

Hooks is the Distinguished Professor of English at City College in New York City. She taught for several years at Oberlin College in Ohio, where she earned great regard from her students. She is an actively publishing feminist scholar whose ideas speak to the affirmation and fulfillment of the aspirations of all persons.

Key Concept: "engaged pedagogy"

On a gorgeous Maine summer day, I fell down a hill and broke my wrist severely. As I was sitting in the dirt, experiencing the most excruciating pain, more intense than any I had ever felt in my life, an image flashed across the screen of my mind. It was one of me as a young girl falling down another hill. In both cases, my falling was related to challenging myself to move beyond limits. As a child it was the limits of fear. As a grown woman, it was the limits of being tired—what I call "bone weary." I had came to Skowhegan to give a lecture at a summer art program. A number of nonwhite students had shared with me that they rarely have any critique of their work from scholars and artists of color. Even though I felt tired and very sick, I wanted to affirm their work and their needs, so I awakened early in the morning to climb the hill to do studio visits.

Skowhegan was once a working farm. Old barns had been converted into studios. The studio I was leaving, after having had an intense discussion with several young black artists, female and male, led into a cow pasture. Sitting in pain at the bottom of the hill, staring in the face of the black female artist whose studio door I had been trying to reach, I saw such disappointment. When she came to help me, she expressed concern, yet what I heard was another feeling entirely. She really needed to talk about her work with someone she could trust, who would not approach it with racist, sexist, or classist prejudice, someone whose intellect and vision she could respect. That someone did not need to be me. It could have been any teacher. When I think about my life as a student, I can remember vividly the faces, gestures, habits of being of all the individual teaches who nurtured and guided me, who offered me an opportunity to experience joy in learning, who made the classroom a space of critical thinking, who made the exchange of information and ideas a kind of ecstasy.

Recently, I worked on a program at CBS on American feminism. I and other black women present were asked to name what we felt helps enable feminist thinking and feminist movement. I answered that to me "critical thinking" was the primary element allowing the possibility of change. Passionately insisting that no matter what one's class, race, gender, or social standing, I shared my beliefs that without the capacity to think critically about our selves and our lives, none of us would be able to move forward, to change, to grow. In our society, which is so fundamentally anti-intellectual, critical thinking is not encouraged. Engaged pedagogy has been essential to my development as an intellectual, as a teacher/professor because the heart of this approach to learning is critical thinking. Conditions of radical openness exist in any learning situation where students and teachers celebrate their abilities to think critically, to engage in pedagogical praxis.

Profound commitment to engaged pedagogy is taxing to the spirit. After twenty years of teaching, I have begun to need time away from the classroom. Somehow, moving around to teach at different institutions has always prevented me from having that marvelous paid sabbatical that is one of the material rewards of academic life. This factor, coupled with commitment to teaching, has meant that even when I take a job that places me on a part-time schedule, instead of taking time away from teaching, I lecture elsewhere. I do this because I sense such desperate need in students—their fear that no one really cares whether they learn or develop intellectually.

My commitment to engaged pedagogy is an expression of political activism. Given that our educational institutions are so deeply invested in a banking system, teachers are more rewarded when we do not teach against the grain. The choice to work against the grain, to challenge the status quo, often has negative consequences. And that is part of what makes that choice one that is not politically neutral. In colleges and universities, teaching is often the least valued of our many professional tasks. It saddens me that colleagues are often suspicious of teachers whom students long to study with. And there is a tendency to undermine the professorial commitment of engaged pedagogues by suggesting that what we do is not as rigorously academic as it should be. Ideally, education should be a place where the need for diverse teaching methods and styles would be valued, encouraged, seen as essential to learning. Occasionally students feel concerned when a class departs from the banking system. I remind them that they can have a lifetime of classes that reflect conventional norms.

Of course, I hope that more professors will seek to be engaged. Although it is a reward of engaged pedagogy that students seek courses with those of us who have made a wholehearted commitment to education as the practice of freedom, it is also true that we are often overworked, our classes often overcrowded. For years, I envied those professors who taught more conventionally, because they frequently had small classes. Throughout my teaching career my classes have been too large to be as effective as they could be. Over time, I've begun to see that departmental pressure on "popular" professors to accept larger classes was also a way to undermine engaged pedagogy. If classes became so full that it is impossible to know students' names, to spend quality time with each of them, then the effort to build a learning community fails. Throughout my teaching career, I have found it helpful to meet with each student in my classes, if only briefly. Rather than sitting in my office for hours waiting for individual students to choose to meet or for problems to arise, I have preferred to schedule lunches with students. Sometimes, the whole class might bring lunch and have discussion in a space other than our usual classroom. At Oberlin, for instance, we might go as a class to the African Heritage House and have lunch, both to learn about different places on campus and gather in a setting other than our classroom.

Many professors remain unwilling to be involved with any pedagogical practices that emphasize mutual participation between teacher and student because more time and effort are required to do this work. Yet some version of engaged pedagogy is really the only type of teaching that truly generates excitement in the classroom, that enables students and professors to feel the joy of learning.

I was reminded of this during my trip to the emergency room after falling down that hill. I talked so intensely about ideas with the two students who were rushing me to the hospital that I forgot my pain. It is this passion for ideas, for critical thinking and dialogical exchange that I want to celebrate in the classroom, to share with students.

Talking about pedagogy, thinking about it critically, is not the intellectual work that most folks think is hip and cool. Cultural criticism and feminist theory are the areas of my work that are most often deemed interesting by students and colleagues alike. Most of us are not inclined to see discussion of pedagogy as central to our academic work and intellectual growth, or the practice of teaching as work that enhances and enriches scholarship. Yet it has been the mutual interplay of thinking, writing and sharing ideas as an intellectual and teacher that creates whatever insights are in my work. My devotion to that interplay keeps me teaching in academic settings, despite their difficulties.

When I first read *Strangers in Paradise: Academics from the Working Class*, I was stunned by the intense bitterness expressed in the individual narratives. This bitterness was not unfamiliar to me. I understood what Jane Ellen Wilson meant when she declared, "The whole process of becoming highly educated was for me a process of losing faith." I have felt that bitterness most keenly in relation to academic colleagues. It emerged from my sense that so many of them willingly betrayed the promise of intellectual fellowship and radical openness that I believe is the heart and soul of learning. When I moved beyond those feelings to focus my attention on the classroom, the one place in the academy where I could have the most impact, they became less intense. I became more passionate in my commitment to the art of teaching.

Engaged pedagogy not only compels me to be constantly creative in the classroom, it also sanctions involvement with students beyond that setting. I journey with students as they progress in their lives beyond our classroom experience. In many ways, I continue to teach them, even as they become more capable of teaching me. The important lesson that we learn together, the lesson that allows us to move together within and beyond the classroom, is one of mutual engagement.

I could never say that I have no idea of the way students respond to my pedagogy; they give me constant feedback. When I teach, I encourage them to critique, evaluate, make suggestions and interventions as we go along. Evaluations at the end of a course rarely help us improve the learning experience we share together. When students see themselves as mutually responsible for the development of a learning community, they offer constructive input.

Students do not always enjoy studying with me. Often they find my courses challenge them in ways that are deeply unsettling. This was particularly disturbing to me at the beginning of my teaching career because I wanted to be liked and admired. It took time and experience for me to understand that the rewards of engaged pedagogy might not emerge during a course. Luckily, I have taught many students who take time to reconnect and share the impact of our working together on their lives. Then the work I do as a teacher is affirmed again and again, not only by the accolades extended to me but by the career choices students make, their habits of being. When a student tells me that she struggled with the decision to do corporate law, joined such and such a firm, and then at the last minute began to reconsider whether this was what she felt called to do, sharing that her decision was influenced by the courses she took with me, I am reminded of the power we have as teachers as well as the awesome responsibility. Commitment to engaged pedagogy carries with it the willingness to be responsible, not to pretend that professors do not have the power to change the direction of our students' lives.

. . . After twenty years of teaching, I can confess that I am often most joyous in the classroom, brought closer here to the ecstatic than by most of life's experiences.

PART FOUR

The American Constitutional Tradition and Education

CHAPTER 10 *Brown v. Board of Education*

10.1 U.S. SUPREME COURT

Brown v. Board of Education of Topeka, Kansas

In 1954 the United States Supreme Court issued a truly historic, constitutionally groundbreaking interpretation of the meaning of the "equal protection of the laws" clause of the Fourteenth Amendment to the Constitution of the United States. In the decision of *Brown v. Board of Education of Topeka, Kansas,* the Court held that "in the field of public education the doctrine of 'separate but equal' has no place. Separate educational facilities are inherently unequal." Seventeen states had used the "separate but equal" principle first enunciated in *Plessy v. Ferguson* (1896) to pass laws requiring the segregation of students of differing racial backgrounds in the public schools of those states. The *Brown* decision declared such segregation unconstitutional. What gave even greater historical importance to *Brown* was that the Court found "for Linda Brown and *all similarly situated persons*" (emphasis added by editor). This phrase made the decision a class action decision, the first time the "equal protection of the laws" clause was applied to all segregated persons.

In the years following the *Brown* decision, Hispanic Americans, Native Americans, Asian Americans, and all American women benefited from the powerful, clear finding for "Linda Brown and all similarly situated persons."

Furthermore, during the 20 years after *Brown*, laws were passed by Congress that improved the educational opportunities of *all* Americans.

Key Concept: educational equality

Mr. Chief Justice Warren delivered the opinion of the Court.

These cases come to us from the States of Kansas, South Carolina, Virginia, and Delaware. They are premised on different facts and different local conditions, but a common legal question justifies their consideration together in this consolidated opinion.

In each of the cases, minors of the Negro race, through their legal representatives, seek the aid of the courts in obtaining admission to the public schools of their community on a nonsegregated basis. In each instance, they had been denied admission to schools attended by white children under laws requiring or permitting segregation according to race. This segregation was alleged to deprive the plaintiffs of the equal protection of the laws under the Fourteenth Amendment. In each of the cases other than the Delaware case, a three-judge federal district court denied relief to the plaintiffs on the so-called "separate but equal" doctrine announced by this Court in *Plessy* v. *Ferguson*. . . . Under that doctrine, equality of treatment is accorded when the races are provided substantially equal facilities even though these facilities be separate. In the Delaware case, the Supreme Court of Delaware adhered to that doctrine, but ordered that the plaintiffs be admitted to the white schools because of their superiority to the Negro schools.

The plaintiffs contend that segregated public schools are not "equal" and cannot be made "equal," and that hence they are deprived of the equal protection of the laws. Because of the obvious importance of the question presented, the Court took jurisdiction. Argument was heard in the 1952 Term, and reargument was heard this Term on certain questions propounded by the Court.

Reargument was largely devoted to the circumstances surrounding the adoption of the Fourteenth Amendment in 1868. It covered exhaustively consideration of the Amendment in Congress, ratification by the states, then existing practices in racial segregation, and the views of proponents and opponents of the Amendment. This discussion and our own investigation convince us that, although these sources cast some light, it is not enough to resolve the problem with which we are faced. At best, they are inconclusive. The most avid proponents of the post–War Amendments undoubtedly intended them to remove all legal distinctions among "all persons born or naturalized in the United States." Their opponents, just as certainly were antagonistic to both the letter and the spirit of the Amendments and wished them to have the most limited effect. What others in Congress and the state legislatures had in mind cannot be determined with any degree of certainty.

An additional reason for the inconclusive nature of the Amendment's history, with respect to segregated schools, is the status of public education at that time. In the South, the movement toward free common schools, supported by general taxation, had not yet taken hold. Education of white children was largely in the hands of private groups. Education of Negroes was almost non-existent, and practically all of the race were illiterate. In fact, any education of Negroes was forbidden by law in some states. Today, in contrast, many Negroes have achieved outstanding success in the arts and sciences as well as in the business and professional world. It is true that public education had already advanced further in the North, but the effect of the Amendment on Northern States was generally ignored in the congressional debates. Even in the North, the conditions of public education did not approximate those existing today. The curriculum was usually rudimentary; ungraded schools were common in rural areas; the school term was but three months a year in many states; and compulsory school attendance was virtually unknown. As a consequence, it is not surprising that there should be so little in the history of the Fourteenth Amendment relating to its intended effect on public education.

In the first cases in this Court construing the Fourteenth Amendment, decided shortly after its adoption, the Court interpreted it as proscribing all state-imposed discriminations against the Negro race. The doctrine of "separate but equal" did not make its appearance in this court until 1896 in the case of *Plessy* v. *Ferguson, supra,* involving not education but transportation. American courts have since labored with the doctrine for over half a century. In this Court, there have been six cases involving the "separate but equal" doctrine in the field of public education. In *Cumming* v. *County Board of Education . . .* and *Gong Lum* v. *Rice . . .* , the validity of the doctrine itself was not challenged. In more recent cases, all on the graduate school level, inequality was found in that specific benefits enjoyed by white students were denied to Negro students of the same educational qualifications. *Missouri* ex rel. *Gaines* v. *Canada; Sipuel* v. *Oklahoma; Sweatt* v. *Painter; McLaurin* v. *Oklahoma State Regents.* In none of these cases was it necessary to reexamine the doctrine to grant relief to the Negro plaintiff. And in *Sweatt* v. *Painter, supra,* the Court expressly reserved decision on the question whether *Plessy* v. *Ferguson* should be held inapplicable to public education.

In the instant cases, that question is directly presented. Here, unlike *Sweatt* v. *Painter,* there are findings below that the Negro and white schools involved have been equalized, or are being equalized, with respect to buildings, curricula, qualifications and salaries of teachers, and other "tangible" factors. Our decision, therefore, cannot turn on merely a comparison of these tangible factors in the Negro and white schools involved in each of the cases. We must look instead to the effect of segregation itself on public education.

In approaching this problem, we cannot turn the clock back to 1868 when the Amendment was adopted, or even to 1896 when *Plessy* v. *Ferguson* was written. We must consider public education in the light of its full development and its present place in American life throughout the Nation. Only in this way can it be determined if segregation in public schools deprives these plaintiffs of the equal protection of the laws.

Today, education is perhaps the most important function of state and local governments. Compulsory school attendance laws and the great expenditures for education both demonstrate our recognition of the importance of education to our democratic society. It is required in the performance of our most basic public responsibilities, even service in the armed forces. It is the very foundation of good citizenship. Today it is a principal instrument in awakening the child to cultural values, in preparing him for later professional training, and in helping him to adjust normally to his environment. In these days, it is doubtful that any child may reasonably be expected to succeed in life if he is denied the opportunity of an education. Such an opportunity, where the state has undertaken to provide it, is a right which must be made available to all on equal terms.

We come then to the question presented: Does segregation of children in public schools solely on the basis of race, even though the physical facilities and other "tangible" factors may be equal, deprive the children of the minority group of equal educational opportunities? We believe that it does.

In *Sweatt* v. *Painter, supra*, in finding that a segregated law school for Negroes could not provide them equal educational opportunities, this Court relied in large part on "those qualities which are incapable of objective measurement but which make for greatness in a law school." In *McLaurin* v. *Oklahoma State Regents, supra*, the Court, in requiring that a Negro admitted to a white graduate school be treated like all other students, again resorted to intangible considerations: " . . . his ability to study, to engage in discussions and exchange views with other students, and, in general, to learn his profession." Such considerations apply with added force to children in grade and high schools. To separate them from others of similar age and qualifications solely because of their race generates a feeling of inferiority as to their status in the community that may affect their hearts and minds in a way unlikely ever to be undone. The effect of this separation on their educational opportunities was well stated by a finding in the Kansas case by a court which nevertheless felt compelled to rule against the Negro plaintiffs:

> Segregation of white and colored children in public schools has a detrimental effect upon the colored children. The impact is greater when it has the sanction of the law; for the policy of separating the races is usually interpreted as denoting the inferiority of the Negro group. A sense of inferiority affects the motivation of a child to learn. Segregation with the sanction of law, therefore, has a tendency to retard the educational and mental development of Negro children and to deprive them of some of the benefits they would receive in a racially integrated school system.

Whatever may have been the extent of psychological knowledge[1] at the time of *Plessy* v. *Ferguson*, this finding is amply supported by modern authority. Any language in *Plessy* v. *Ferguson* contrary to this finding is rejected.

We conclude that in the field of public education the doctrine of "separate but equal" has no place. Separate educational facilities are inherently unequal. Therefore, we hold that the plaintiffs and others similarly situated for whom the actions have been brought are, by reason of the segregation complained of, deprived of the equal protection of the laws guaranteed by the Fourteenth Amendment. This disposition makes unnecessary any discussion whether such segregation also violates the Due Process Clause of the Fourteenth Amendment.

Because these are class actions, because of the wide applicability of this decision, and because of the great variety of local conditions, the formulation of decrees in these cases presents problems of considerable complexity. On reargument, the consideration of appropriate relief was necessarily subordinated to the primary question—the constitutionality of segregation in public education. We have now announced that such segregation is a denial of the equal protection of the laws. In order that we may have the full assistance of the parties in formulating decrees, the cases will be restored to the docket, and the parties are requested to present further argument.

NOTE

1. The decision in *Brown* v. *Board of Education* was justified in part on psychological and sociological grounds. This line of argument helped Chief Justice Warren obtain a unanimous decision, but it did not provide the strongest legal foundation for attacking segregation.

Twenty Years After "Brown": Where Are We Now?

Marian Wright Edelman is the president of the Children's Defense Fund and a well-known scholar on the history of school desegregation since *Brown v. Board of Education of Topeka, Kansas* (1954). In 1974 she published an excellent synthesis and interpretation of United States Supreme Court decisions of several key cases that established the interpretive parameters for what the Court had meant in *Brown.* She also published an earlier version of her scholarship on school desegregation, "Southern School Desegregation: 1954–1973," *The Annals of the American Academy of Political and Social Science* (vol. 407, 1973, pp. 32–42). Edelman has led a distinguished life of leadership and example in the cause of human rights, and she is widely recognized for her efforts.

The selection that follows, from the *New York University Education Quarterly* (Summer 1974), was published 20 years after the initial *Brown* decision. Edelman's call for action for social justice in the field of education is as necessary and meaningful today as it was in 1974. In interpreting the first 20 years after *Brown,* she argues that effective racial integration is the most just manner through which to ensure equality of educational opportunity.

Key Concept: school integration

*I*n May of 1954, rewarding the hope and toil of decades, the Supreme Court's decision in *Brown v. Board of Education* seemed a great, transforming event. (1) A great event it was. Whether it would work the transformation it promised remained to be seen. For, after all, the Fourteenth Amendment itself had promised much but accomplished little over almost a century.

In the spring of 1964, a decade after *Brown* and a decade ago, the achievement of school desegregation seemed almost as far off as ever. We asked ourselves: When will the law be enforced? When will the law be obeyed? But, behind those questions lay another: What *was* the law? Without a clear understanding of what the law was—and without a solid political coalition to rally behind a clear view of the law—enforcement and obedience could only become more problematic.

That was the situation on the tenth anniversary of *Brown*. And, I believe, that is the situation today, on the twentieth anniversary. Despite all of the progress during the intervening years, we are standing at a crossroads again, where the future is opaque and the tasks before us difficult.

DOES DESEGREGATION REQUIRE INTEGRATION?

The comparison with 1964 is instructive. At that time, concerned with enforcement and obedience, we lawyers focused on the Supreme Court's "all deliberate speed" formula. There was much debate about the chain of causation. Had the Court's formula opened the door for—indeed, encouraged—Southern resistance and federal foot-dragging? Or, was Southern resistance and federal inaction inevitable at first? Was "all deliberate speed" a corruption of the rule of law, or was it a statesmanlike recognition that desegregation could only be a slow process? (2) This debate on *Brown's* tenth anniversary was interesting; but, in a way, it missed a basic problem underlying the lack of progress in the fifties and early sixties.

The problem was that for ten long years the Supreme Court had not decided even one major case to define just what school "desegregation" meant. "All deliberate speed" was all the less speedy because no one knew what we were supposed to be inching toward. The effect was corrosive.

In 1955, only one year after *Brown*, a Southern federal court had raised the most central issue, going to the heart of school desegregation. In the case of *Briggs v. Elliott* (3), a District Court in South Carolina had argued that the Constitution forbids segregation but "does not require integration." *Brown*, according to the *Briggs* court, did not imply that a state must "mix persons of different races in the schools or . . . deprive them of the right of choosing the schools they attend." One might have thought the Supreme Court would respond. But it did not. In 1958, it convened a special session to announce that, whatever the resistance, a judicial desegregation order must be obeyed. (4) But what sort of desegregation were the lower courts entitled to order? The Court did not say. It maintained its silence up to 1964.

Finally, in the year of *Brown's* tenth anniversary, it did signal that the time for delay had run out (5); and a year later it stated that "delays in desegregating school systems are no longer tolerable." (6) But, still, it gave no real clue what "desegregating school systems" implied.

With no lead to follow, and with no answer to the issue posed in *Briggs v. Elliott*, the lower courts did little for ten years. They issued decrees permitting a few token, though courageous, black children voluntarily to attend "white" schools. And they struck down the most egregious Southern pupil placement laws that preserved the segregatory assignment system. But no affirmative duty to integrate was put in their place.

By 1964, a conservative scholar, Alexander Bickel, could predict that "the end result of desegregation" would simply be "a school system in which there is residential zoning, either absolute or modified by some sort of choice or transfer scheme." The most ever to be expected, he said, was that Southern school districts would settle "into conditions of substantial *de facto* segregation, alleviated by a number of successful integrated situations. In other words, essentially Northern conditions. . . . This," he concluded, "is the likely—and anticlimactic—outcome of all the litigating and striving." (2)

The years between 1964 and 1974 would seem to have proved Bickel wrong. The Supreme Court has spoken at last. Freedom-of-choice plans in the South have been swept aside and effective dismantling of formally dual school systems has been mandated by *Green v. County School Board.* (7) And both busing and assignment on an explicitly integrative basis—cutting across neighborhood lines—have been upheld in *Swann v. Charlotte-Mecklenburg Board of Education* as reasonable means to achieve that end. (8)

It might seem, then, that we have solved the problem of what *is* law. We might suppose that the central issue has now been resolved: Integration *is* required in America. It might appear, once again, that the only remaining problem is one of enforcement and obedience to the law.

BREAKDOWN IN ENFORCEMENT

Without doubt, enforcement and obedience are major problems now. They no longer stem from the "all deliberate speed" formula. That formula was finally buried in 1969 in *Alexander v. Holmes County Board of Education.* (9) Rather, delay 1974-style stems from federal government foot-dragging—even hostility. It is not an altogether unfamiliar phenomenon. During *Brown's* first ten years, we felt the deadening effect of President Eisenhower's refusal even to endorse the principle of desegregation and President Kennedy's excessive caution in the face of pressure from Southern Democrats. But, in the middle and late sixties, we learned what an important, powerful weapon enforcement by the federal government can be. Vigorous court action by the Justice Department and, particularly, vigorous endorsement of desegregation guidelines by the Department of Health, Education and Welfare under the Civil Rights Act of 1964, boosted by the Elementary and Secondary Education Act of 1965 pouring large sums of federal aid into local school coffers, helped to produce the first really substantial progress toward school desegregation in the South. Now that the Nixon Administration has cut back enforcement across the board, the chilling effect is all too plain. (10)

One solution might be to exert new pressure on the now-vulnerable Administration to mend its ways. Another might be to invoke more vigorously the Supreme Court's *Alexander* decision, repudiating Justice Department requests for delay in enforcing court decrees. Yet another solution might be to implement the recent District Court decision in *Adams v. Richardson*, ordering the Department of Health, Education and Welfare to resume desegregation enforcement under the 1964 Civil Rights Act. (11) All of these efforts focusing on enforcement are important. But the present problem is deeper than that.

The present breakdown in enforcement and obedience to the law is tied—as it was in 1964—to a new and troubling uncertainty as to the substance of the law. What is uncertain is the extent of applicability of the principles originally set forth in *Brown v. Board of Education.* The law grows incrementally, by analogy to past cases, with little regard for overriding principle. But, if that is the case, the growth of the law may be stopped at any point. And, today, as new and different issues of school desegregation present themselves, some question whether *Brown* still has the life left in it to meet them. For the principles of *Brown* appear almost as susceptible to limitation as to expansion.

One might ask: How can that be? Hasn't *Briggs v. Elliott* been discredited? Hasn't it been held that desegregation demands effective integration? The answer is: Yes, those paramount issues of the sixties have been resolved. But they were resolved in the context of Southern school districts, very recently separated by law into "white" schools and "black" schools. It has been established that unconstitutional segregation must be remedied by integration. But the issue we face now is a more basic one: What *is* unconstitutional segregation?

The problem lies not just in the familiar distinction between *de jure* and *de facto* segregation. It is a problem of having had to spend too long just beginning to dismantle the most egregious forms of school segregation. Anything seems tame by comparison. And now it is being suggested that the job is finished. New questions assume key importance. What does *de jure* segregation mean in the North? How blatant must it be? How long do its effects last? Are we approaching a time when courts will say that the "taint"—even in the South—has been dissipated and that the remedy of affirmative integration is no longer required? Is anything short of the most extreme form of segregation really harmful to children? If the harm is not so great, should the remedy be less strict?

There are those who say that *Brown v. Board of Education* suggests no answer to these questions, that *Brown* is now "obsolete." (12) And there are those who would declare that America's schools have been "desegregated" without being fully integrated. Thus the prediction by Professor Bickel ten years ago—that we would end up with the nationwide institution of *de facto* school segregation—has still to be finally disproved.

Once again, as the Supreme Court draws back from "activism" and as the civil rights coalition of the sixties comes apart, the law threatens to come unhinged. It is our job to put it right once more, to build the doctrine we once thought secure, and, in my view, to reestablish integration in our schools as the basic goal.

I recognize that there are those, black and white, who quarrel with this goal. As one who grew up in segregated and unequal schools, themselves the product of power inequities between whites and blacks grounded in the deep racism still pervasive in all America, I hold the strong view that real integration is the best goal and the best strategy for achieving nondiscriminatory, quality, and responsive education for black children and all children. I reject bargaining off constitutional rights for other necessary steps toward building a good educational system for our children including community control and "compensatory" educational measures which black and white parents should demand for the good of their youngsters anyway. We should never forget the power and political realities with which we live and the problem posed to segregation of resources and power along with segregation of schools. Those people who have resisted real integration have also fought equalization and will fight empowerment of minority communities to control their own lives, which they are entitled to do regardless of segregation or desegregation. While desegregation is not *the* answer to all the difficult problems of schooling today—inequitable financing schemes, misclassification and tracking, unresponsive and sometimes hostile teachers are some others—can there be doubt that the root of some of these problems is founded in the racial (and class) discrimination which *Brown* attempted to address? . . .

SEGREGATION BY MANIPULATION

Yet the definition of *de jure* segregation is probably the most unsettled aspect of desegregation doctrine today. Often, integrationists seek to short-circuit this problem. They argue that courts should simply hold now that all *de facto* segregation is unconstitutional, making the definition of *de jure* segregation unimportant.

This approach offers the great advantage of clarity. In time, we may hope that it will prevail. But, at present, such a holding would require a great doctrinal and psychological leap. For years, lower courts have refused to go so far, so fast. The Supreme Court has not only avoided the issue; recently, when the claim was presented in far too sweeping form, it summarily rejected it. Thus the game of defining *de jure* segregation, in my opinion, must be played through to its conclusion.

For the time being, there is no need even to concede the validity of the *de jure/de facto* distinction. Indeed, there is no such thing as *de facto* school segregation of the pure type. Governmental involvement of one sort or another can usually be found in the history of segregated residential patterns; and, after all, it is a governmental agency that bases school assignments on neighborhoods *known* to be segregated-in-fact. (14) What we face are varying kinds and degrees of governmental responsibility for assignment by race. Until the Court rigidly confines the meaning of *de jure* segregation to *certain* kinds and degrees of governmental responsibility, *de facto* segregation has no meaning of its own. And, until that time, there is no reason to ask the courts to take the leap of declaring all *de facto* segregation unconstitutional. At present, the Court has not so confined the meaning of *de jure* segregation. And yet it has defined it in such a way that confusion and uncertainty now prevail and will for some while.

For nineteen years after *Brown*, the Court heard argument only in cases from school districts that had very recently been openly segregated by statute. *De jure* segregation in that context was too clear to be questioned. Finally, just last year, the Court took a case from the North, from Denver. In the *Keyes* case, it began at long last to define the broader meaning of *de jure* segregation. Its decision was important not only for the North. It also could be controlling in cases from the South if it is ever held that the "taint" of Southern segregation by statute has been dissipated.

What the Court did in *Keyes* was barely to inch forward from the Southern paradigm of *de jure* segregation. Specifically the Court held that segregation-in-fact is unconstitutional if it is the product of "segregatory intent" on the part of governmental authorities. Some thought this is a victory. For the Court went beyond the pure form of Southern segregation. But the formula of "segregatory intent" presents all sorts of problems. It is itself hard to define. And, depending on its definition, it may be difficult to prove and narrow in impact.

Despite the lack of a recently mandated statutory segregation and despite protestations that the Denver school board was simply following a "neutral" neighborhood school policy, the Court held that sufficient "segregatory intent" had been shown in the board's "manipulations" of its neighborhood policy to increase the segregation than would have resulted from a truly "neutral" approach.

The occasions for "manipulation" of a neighborhood policy are present every time any school board draws a zoning line, or locates a new school, or determines the size of a new school, or closes an old school, or adopts a voluntary transfer plan. (13) The *Keyes* opinion recognizes most of these occasions, and more. Certainly, the myriad decisions involved in administering a neighborhood school policy offer litigators many opportunities for investigation and many opportunities to make a showing of *de jure* segregation.

But what kind of showing? Is it enough, for example, simply to show that the location of new schools *resulted* in increased segregation? Must that result have been *foreseeable* or *known* to the school board? Or must there be a showing of a *desire* for increased segregation—a conscious segregatory policy—underlying such "manipulative" decisions? If so, can it be inferred from a pattern of decisions producing segregatory results? Or must it be proved independently?

If particular "manipulations" of a neighborhood policy can be explained *only* as serving a segregatory purpose, "segregatory intent" would seem clear. But what if they can be explained as serving other purposes as well? That probably is the most typical case. Is an inference of "segregatory intent" still possible? Must the segregatory purpose be "dominant"?

The *Keyes* opinion raises all these problems, but does not resolve any of them conclusively. For, in a way, *Keyes* was an easy case for the Supreme Court. The District Court had already found that the Denver school board had pursued a "policy of deliberate racial segregation" in one section of the city. That finding was not contested; and the Supreme Court did not examine it. Rather, the Court simply held that once there has been such a finding as to one part of the city, the burden is on the school board to show that it did not act with "segregatory intent" in the rest of the city and that the board could not meet its burden at that stage simply by showing that its actions served some end in addition to segregation. But the Court said nothing about how litigants may make the crucial, initial showing of "deliberate" segregation.

Thus *Keyes* does not close the door to nationwide integration. Nor does it open the door wide. At best, *Keyes* leaves it swinging ajar, uneasily and uncertainly. In the short run—and, in matters of school desegregation, that unfortunately means the next five or ten years—litigators will have to press carefully for an elaboration of the *Keyes* standard that is both clear and expansive.

There is one dialectic that will confront our efforts, whether in the short-run attempt to expand the meaning of *de jure* segregation or in the long-run assault on the citadel of *de facto* segregation, once defined. That is the dialectic of fairness in rules of selection versus fairness in fact.

The rhetoric of equal protection law, as applied to racial discrimination, has purported to separate the two rigidly. It has focused largely on fairness in governmental rules of selection—rules of selection for juries, for voting rights, for employment, for use of public facilities, for school assignments. Courts have suggested that so long as those rules of selection are held to be fair, it is improper to inquire into their results. So long as the rule used to select jurors is fair, courts will not concern themselves with the actual representation of minorities. So long as the rule used to select employees is fair, courts will not worry about the number of minority employees hired. And so long as the actions that determine school assignments are fair—or, in *Keyes*, are not infected by "segregatory intent"—courts insist that they will not mandate actual integration.

In theory, this rigid distinction corresponds to the powerful American ideology of equal opportunity. But, in practice, the distinction is untenable. The fairness of a rule of selection—whether for juries or employment or school assignments—cannot be assessed in total blindness to results achieved.

In the law of employment discrimination, it has repeatedly been held that a showing of a discriminatory effect is enough to establish, *prima facie*, that the criteria used for hiring are discriminatory. And, in the law of jury discrimination, it has been held that even though a rule of selection may appear fair on its face, a court must look to the results it achieves to determine if it is being applied discriminatorily. In the law of school desegregation, too, the courts have examined the results of apparently "neutral" policies of school assignment, at least in Southern school districts once segregated by statute. They must be urged to do so in all cases. (14)

It is the task of litigators now to persuade the courts that the element of "segregatory intent" is something that can be inferred from results, as well as proved independently. More importantly, we must persuade the courts that the very meaning of "segregatory intent" is tied to the actual segregation resulting from governmental action. "Segregatory intent" must be broader than the *desire* for segregation. We are not dealing with first degree murder cases. We should not be looking for "malice aforethought." The Constitution, after all, is meant to protect, not to punish.

In other areas of the law, more comparable to constitutional law, one is held to "intend" particular results if he simply *knew* that those results would follow his act. Such knowledge is inferred if a reasonable man would have been substantially certain that the results would, in fact, occur. Similarly, it should be enough to show "segregatory intent" that increased segregation was substantially certain to follow a "manipulation" of a neighborhood school policy, and that any reasonable member of the school board should have known it. Such a showing usually would not be too difficult. (15)

Such a definition of "segregatory intent" may have a more sweeping impact than the *Keyes* Court had in mind. If the Court were to accept it, it might feel that it must balance the harm done by the intended, increased segregation against the value of other intended results of the particular "manipulation" of the neighborhood policy. But such a balancing act would lead us directly to the basic issue of *de facto* segregation. For once a court starts balancing segregation against other values as those, for example, allegedly served by a neighborhood policy, it matters little whether it is dealing with the *increased* segregation resulting from a "manipulation" of the policy or with the basic segregation inherent in the policy itself.

We should endeavor to lead the courts through this step-by-step progression to the basic issue at stake. If, in the end, defining *de jure* segregation becomes more a matter of weighing the costs and benefits of the *results* of a neighborhood policy than a matter of searching out "segregatory intent," that is entirely appropriate.

Violations of the First Amendment rights need not generally be "intentional" before they are unconstitutional. Nor Fourth Amendment rights. Nor Fifth Amendment rights. Why should the right to the equal protection of the laws under the Fourteenth Amendment be somehow different? When the courts apply the equal protection clause to apportionment laws, they do not look for "intent" to discriminate against certain voters. Rather, they look to the extent of the inequality that *results* from the apportionment laws. Why should *racial* discrimination be treated more leniently?

In time, then, if all goes well, the question of "intention" may drop away. For, in view of residential patterns in our cities, segregation is the substantially certain result of any neighborhood policy. By *Brown's* thirtieth anniversary, the Court may see that its job, finally, is to decide whether the values served by a neighborhood school policy justify the resulting segregation. Our job will be to show that there can be no such justification. I feel strongly that there is not. . . .

THE PROBLEM OF REMEDY

But even if we do manage to establish that the "taint" of segregation is not soon dissipated, that *de jure* segregation is not confined to narrowly "intentional" segregatory acts, and that a segregated education is indeed an inferior education, we shall face one last uncertainty at the core of desegregation law. This is the uncertainty of remedy. Unlike the others, this one is not the product of anything the Supreme Court has yet said or done. Rather, it is the product of something the Court did not do and of what one fears the Court may do in the future.

In a word, the problem of remedy may be the problem of busing. Busing—or rather a particular kind of busing (of white children to black schools, of too many black children to white schools)—is not very popular today. Even though we have spent ever increasing energy and resources getting more buses for more children every decade, totally unrelated to desegregation, the present opposition to it stems from a more basic opposition to further integration or from a dislike of sending one's children to a "distant," "unfamiliar," and often "inferior" school (the fact that usually gives rise to the necessity to desegregate in the first place). After all, you cannot expect our children to suffer what "their" children are forced to suffer! The fact is that "busing" has become a symbol, a separate political issue of its own, created by the Southerners with Mr. Nixon's help, to achieve the basic end of resegregating the nation's schools. It drove liberal politicians in 1972 to speak the language of "quality education," as if it were irreconcilable or separable from nondiscriminatory or desegregated education! And it may have contributed to the now-tattered mandate the President received that year. If the Court, as is said, "follows the election returns," the busing remedy may be in for trouble. Because busing is *not* a separate issue, but is tied to the only possibility for real desegregation, the effect of a pull-back by the Court could be devastating.

Since the *Green* decision in 1968 the Court had held that, once a condition of *de jure* school segregation or its "vestiges" are found in a school district, the remedy must be a total one, a "root and branch" dismantling of the segregated system. In *Swann*, the Court held that this remedy could include busing, within the reasonable discretion of the trial judge. Both *Green* and *Swann* arose in Southern school districts that had recently been openly and thoroughly segregated by statute. Last year, in the *Keyes* decision, the Court took a major step forward despite the election returns. It held that the "root and branch" remedial requirement, including busing, applies no less in a Northern city where *de jure* segregation is the result of many, discrete segregatory "manipulations," rather than of a statutory "dual system."

One might think, after *Keyes*, that the busing remedy presents no separate doctrinal problems. That may be correct—insofar as it is established that "root and branch" desegregation must follow any finding of *de jure* segregation. But must "root and branch" desegregation include busing? And how much busing must there be?

When we step back for a moment, we see a troubling uncertainty in the very decision once hailed as a great victory: *Swann v. Charlotte-Mechklenburg Board of Education*. The Court there stated that desegregation plans "cannot be limited to the walk-in school." It required that transportation of students at least be considered. But it did not *require* any particular degree of busing. To the contrary, it suggested a vague, uncertain *limit* on the busing remedy.

The limit on the remedy, the *Swann* Court said, "will vary with many factors," including the time and distance to be traveled, the directness of the route, and the age of the students. "The reconciliation of competing values," it said, "is . . . a difficult task with many sensitive facets but fundamentally no more so than remedial measures courts of equity have traditionally employed." This left matters somewhat up in the air. But, within months, the author of the *Swann* opinion—Chief Justice Burger—was complaining publicly that the opinion had been read too broadly. He said, in a memorandum opinion, that a desegregation plan might "trespass the limits on school bus transportation indicated in *Swann*" and suggested that a most important limit was that of time to be traveled to school. (16)

The transportation time sanctioned in *Swann* was about one hour round-trip. Lower courts have upheld plans involving similarly limited traveling time. But no one can be sure whether one hour is an outer limit or not. It is not clear how serious a limitation this might be, as I suspect that most of the busing in the nation falls within this reasonable limit and practice. Contrary to the misinformation and fears inflamed by opponents of desegregation, courts have not been ordering busing in amounts which broke with past practice or which could be considered unreasonable. Even in the metropolitan remedy proposed in Richmond, in only one of the six sub-districts would busing time have reached one hour. I would, nonetheless, like the time flexibility to remain and not have rigid lines drawn. After all, there is precedent for much longer busing time stemming from efforts to maintain segregation.

The Court's decision not to decide on clear guidelines for the busing remedy—but just the same to insist that there are limits—may have put some desegregation plans into doubt and may have influenced another non-decision by the Court: its equally-divided silence in the Richmond metropolitan cross-district busing case. (17) Of course, the Court is considering this issue again this year in the Detroit case. (18) One hopes that the opinion it issues may not simply compound the current confusion.

That there is confusion and that it could end up limiting, rather than expanding, opportunities for school integration was made clear in Mr. Justice Powell's separate opinion in last year's *Keyes* decision. He agreed that busing is "one tool of school desegregation"; but, he said, the "crucial issue is when, under what circumstances, and to what extent such transportation may appropriately be ordered." He then argued that tight restrictions should be imposed in the future, raising the spectre of "white flight" and even questioning the use of a "root and branch" remedy for separate, discrete segregative acts.

We may be walking on a minefield in the dark. But, if we look and not leap too far, we should be able to expect success. For, so long as we hold the courts to the obligation of "root and branch" desegregation, the busing remedy will be indispensable and no arbitrary limits can be imposed on it. If, on the other hand, the courts abandon the standard of "root and branch" desegregation, then all desegregation's future may be extremely difficult.

AFFIRMATIVE ACTION

Perhaps not too difficult. There is still the possibility of voluntary action by particular local communities to adopt plans for "root and branch" dismantling of even *de facto* school segregation. Many communities have taken such action. The lower state and federal courts have unanimously upheld their action. The Supreme Court has not spoken. In *Swann*, it did strongly indicate that voluntary desegregation, using "benign" racial classifications and busing, is permissible. But not until this very year did it even take a case involving such classifications.

The case, of course, is *DeFunis v. Odegaard*. (19) It involves an affirmative effort by a state law school to admit minority students. It may be distinguishable from voluntary school desegregation. But the basic principles involved are the same.

The DeFunis case is important in one other respect which should be mentioned in closing. It revealed for all to see that the civil rights coalition of the sixties may be coming apart. But it should not be surprising that the willingness to share and sacrifice becomes thinner the closer one's own perceived interests are affected. Civil rights groups, educators, some unions, some Jewish groups, and many other organizations supported the state law school's affirmative admissions program. But the AFL-CIO, several Jewish groups, and a few "ethnic" organizations and some academics opposed it in amicus briefs to the Court.

If, in fact, the coalition of the sixties does break apart, the effect could be more devastating than any of the doctrinal uncertainties I have discussed up to now. There is no simple preventive medicine to be applied. The issues of the seventies *are* difficult ones for many who supported civil rights before. The danger simply shows that our task now is less a legal one than a political and leadership one.

If the sixties were the time of eradicating egregious segregation, the seventies are the time of seeking real equality. This will be much harder because it involves an equalization of sacrifice in order to overcome the past inequality of sacrifice imposed on some minorities. It may even mean that some individuals may have a more difficult time in the process during the interim of trying to ensure fairness in the process for all groups and all individuals. It also means that many institutions, unusually timid in the past, who have condemned and practiced overt or covert discrimination, must go beyond adopting paper policies to implementing affirmative programs to desegregate that will be controversial. But any reform, racial or nonracial, is controversial. What is needed is nondefensive leadership with a commitment to real equality.

This account of the state of school desegregation on *Brown's* twentieth anniversary may not be encouraging. Some might prefer to celebrate the achievements of the past ten years and leave developments in the next ten for discussion at the thirtieth anniversary. But, if that occasion, ten years hence, is to be a pleasant one, we must realistically assess where we stand now, perhaps stressing the dangers. For, if we are to avoid them, we must first see them clearly.

The *Quarterly* was unable to grant the author's request for use of full legal citations in the published version of her paper. Cases are noted only at the point of first reference, and the initial page of the proceedings is provided. References to related legal principals established by the courts are omitted. However, interested readers may request a copy of Mrs. Edelman's original manuscript containing complete citation.

—Editor [of *New York University Education Quarterly*]

NOTES

1. Brown v. Board of Education, 347 U.S. 483 (1954).
2. H. H. Quint, *Profile in Black and White*, Westport, Conn.: Greenwood, 1973; A. Bickel, "The Decade of School Desegregation: Progress and Prospects," *Columbia Law Review* 64 (1964): 193–229.

3. Briggs v. Elliott, 132 F. Supp. 776 (E.D.S.C. 1955).
4. Cooper v. Aaron, 358 U.S. 1 (1958).
5. Griffin v. Prince Edward County Board of Education, 377 U.S. 218 (1964).
6. Bradley v. School Board of Richmond, 382 U.S. 103 (1965).
7. Green v. County School Board, 391 U.S. 450 (1968).
8. Swann v. Charlotte-Mecklenburg Board of Education, 402 U.S. 1 (1971).
9. Alexander v. Holmes County Board of Education, 396 U.S. 19 (1969).
10. See Marian W. Edelman, "Southern School Desegregation, 1954–1973: A Judicial-Political Overview," *Annals of the American Academy of Political and Social Science* 407 (1973): 32–42.
11. Adams v. Richardson, 351 F. Supp. 636 (D.D.C. 1972).
12. E.g., A. Bickel, *The Supreme Court and the Idea of Progress,* New York: Harper & Row, 1970.
13. See O. M. Fiss, "Racial Imbalance in the Public Schools: The Constitutional Concepts," *Harvard Law Review* 78 (1964): 564–617.
14. Just this Term, the Court indicated that it would look to results in the context of a Northern city: Mayor of Philadelphia v. Educational Equality League, 42 U.S.L.W. 4405 (1975).
15. See O. M. Fiss, "The Charlotte-Mecklenburg Case—Its Significance for Northern School Desegregation," *University of Chicago Law Review* 38 (1971): 697–709; Note, "School Desegregation after Swann: A Theory of Government Responsibility," *University of Chicago Law Review* 39 (1972): 421–447.
16. Winston Salem/Forsyth County Board of Education v. Scott, 404 U.S. 1221 (1971).
17. Bradley v. School Board of Richmond, 412 U.S. 937 (1973).
18. Milliken v. Bradley, cert. granted, 42 U.S.L.W. 3306 (11/20/73).
19. DeFunis v. Odegaard, cert. granted, 42 U.S.L.W. 3129 (9/11/73).

A Dream Realized: Brown v. Board of Education of Topeka

Frank Aquila, a professor emeritus at Indiana University--Purdue University at Indianapolis, has examined each of the major United States Supreme Court decisions related to school desegregation since the Court first handed down its historic decision in *Brown v. Board of Education of Topeka, Kansas.* Jn the selection that follows, Aquila and Thomas Black provide a contextual analysis of the federal judicial decisions leading up to *Brown,* and then summarize the constitutional issues involved in *Brown.* Their work enables the reader to quickly understand the chain of reasoning that led to the Supreme Court's decision in *Brown I* (1954). The selection also contains a summary of the Court's arguments in *Brown II,* which was the Court's implementation ruling about one year after the initial finding. Black and Aquila briefly discuss the specific ramifications of this ruling for the lower federal courts. They note particularly the Court's use of the phrases "with all deliberate speed" and "a prompt and reasonable start" to the school desegregation process as guiding principles for local school boards. The authors clearly show that the Court intended for the constitutional principles enunciated in *Brown I* to be upheld by all lower federal courts.

Key Concept: school desegregation

BROWN v. BOARD OF EDUCATION OF TOPEKA [I]
347 U.S. 483 (Argued Dec. 9, 1952; reargued Dec. 8, 1953; decided May 17, 1954)

BACKGROUND: Four cases originating from Kansas, South Carolina, Virginia, and Delaware, each based on different facts and different local conditions, were consolidated in one opinion because each involved common legal questions.

The first case, from Kansas, *Brown v. Board of Education* 98 F. Supp. 797 (1951), involved black children of elementary school age who sought to enjoin the enforcement of a Kansas statute which permitted, but did not require, cities with a population of more than 15,000 to maintain separate school facilities for black and white students. The Topeka Board of Education opted to establish segregated elementary schools. The federal district court found that segregation in public education has a detrimental effect upon black children, but denied relief because the two separate schools were substantially equal, and because of past Supreme Court authority. Moreover, the district court held that segregation alone, absent substantial inequalities, is not per se unconstitutional. This case and the other two federal court cases bypassed the normal appellate route and came before the Supreme Court on direct appeal pursuant to a United States statute.

The South Carolina case, *Briggs v. Elliot*, 98 F. Supp. 529 (1951), involved both high school and elementary school age children who sought to enjoin the enforcement of state constitutional and statutory segregation provisions. The federal district court denied the injunction but found the black schools to be inferior to the white schools and ordered state officials to equalize the former. The Supreme Court vacated that judgment for the purpose of obtaining the district court's views concerning the progress made in the equalization program. 342 U.S. 350. On remand, the district court found that substantial equality had been achieved. 103 F. Supp. 920 (1952).

In the Virginia case, *Davis v. County School Board*, 103 F. Supp. 337 (1952), black high school age students sought to enjoin the enforcement of the state constitutional provision permitting public school desegregation. The district court upheld the segregation provisions and ordered the school board to equalize the separate school systems with due diligence.

In *Gebhart v. Beltor*, 91 A.2d 137 (1952) the Delaware case, elementary and high school children sought to enjoin the enforcement of mandatory segregation provisions in the Delaware Constitution and statutory code. The lower state court held that segregation results in an inferior education for black children, that the black schools were not substantially equal, and ordered the white schools to admit the black children. The Supreme Court of Delaware affirmed the lower court's ruling but the segregation provisions were not held invalid or unconstitutional. The state sought to overturn this decision in the Supreme Court.

In each of the federal cases, the school children sought to be admitted to state-supported public schools on a non-segregated basis, and in each case they were denied admittance. The basis on which the petitioners claimed relief was that they were denied equal protection of the laws under the Fourteenth Amendment. The "separate but equal" doctrine of *Plessy v. Ferguson*, 163 U.S. 537 (1896), and subsequent cases relying on *Plessy* were applied in each case. Although the black children were admitted to the white school in the *Gebhart* case it was only because there were substantial inequalities between the two schools. In essence, the *Gebhart* case also applied the fiction, but due to the situation in the Delaware School system, the separate public schools were not, in fact, equal.

Much data and statistical information was compiled and became a part of the record from which the Supreme Court could clearly determine the inequality of the separate schools. In each case counsel for the black children used the testimony of school officials and private citizens to draw startling contrasts between physical facilities, curricula, and quality of instruction. Moreover, in several cases per capita tax expenditures for white schools versus black schools showed a wide disparity. Comparisons of the number of pupils per schools, room and teacher, and physical facilities in terms of water fountains, restrooms, auditoriums and gymnasiums also clearly revealed gaping differences.

In addition to stressing the physical and intangible inequalities between the separate schools, testimony from social psychologists, educationalists and sociologists indicated that segregation itself is detrimental in that it produces harmful effects upon the emotional, physical and financial status of those segregated. (See the discussions in the Selected Bibliography section.)

Armed with the above-mentioned data and statistical evidence, the segregation cases were thoroughly argued before the court in the 1951 term. A decision was not rendered. Reargument was set and heard in the 1954 term based on five questions propounded by the court.

The first question was whether Congress contemplated the abolition of public school segregation when the Fourteenth Amendment was framed, adopted and ratified. If there was no such contemplation, the second question was whether Congress could abolish public school segregation under the express power granted it under section five of the Fourteenth Amendment; or, in light of future conditions not contemplated by the framers in 1865, whether the judiciary could construe the amendment as abolishing educational segregation. If neither alternative could eliminate segregation in public schools, the third question considered whether it was within the judiciary's power to abolish it anyway. The relevancy of these three questions was apparent and pivotal since the proponents of segregation in public schools strongly argued that such segregation was common and accepted at the time of the amendment's adoption, so there could have been no intention on the part of the framers to interfere with this social practice (see the Bickel article for an excellent analysis of the congressional intent in adopting the Fourteenth Amendment and the Supreme Court's application of that intent (or lack of) to the present cases). The last two questions dealt with the method of enforcement in the event that the court should find segregated education a denial of equal protection.

COURT RULING: After stating the facts and the legal issues involved in the segregation cases, a unanimous court, speaking through Chief Justice Earl Warren, addressed the circumstances surrounding the adoption of the Fourteenth Amendment. Much historical evidence and research was presented to the court on reargument, but the opinion disposes of these materials quite summarily by stating " . . . although these sources cast some light, it is not enough to resolve the problem with which we are faced. At best, they are inconclusive" (at p. 489). The evidence was inconclusive since the understanding of the Congress, the states and the framers could not be authoritatively determined, because of the status of public education at the time the amendment was adopted.

In the South, the movement toward free common schools, supported by general taxation, had not yet taken hold. Education of white children was largely in the hands of private groups. Education of Negroes was almost non-existent, and practically all of the race was illiterate. In fact, any education of Negroes was forbidden by law in some states (at pp. 489–90).

As a consequence of the very rudimentary stage of public education at that time, it was no surprise to the Court that there was so "little in the history of the Fourteenth Amendment relating to its intended effect on public education" (at p. 490).

Therefore, as the Supreme Court viewed the problem, the question before it was not what the understanding was in regard to segregation in 1868 when the amendment was ratified, or even in 1896 when *Plessy v. Ferguson* was written. Instead, "We must consider public education in light of its full development and its present place in American life throughout the nation. Only in this way can it be determined if segregation in public schools deprives these plaintiffs of the equal protection of the laws" (at pp. 492–93).

Viewed in this context, the court proceeded to its conclusion. Emphasizing that education is today perhaps the most important function of state and local governments, that compulsory education laws demonstrate society's recognition of the importance of education to a democratic people, that education is the very foundation of good citizenship and that in today's modern age it is doubtful that any child may reasonably expect to succeed in life if s/he is denied the opportunity of an education, the court concluded that such an opportunity, where the state undertakes to provide it, is a right which must be available to all on equal terms. Segregation of children in public schools based solely on race, even though the physical facilities and other "intangible" factors may be equal, deprives the minority children of equal educational opportunities.

In holding that racial segregation in public schools violates equal protection of the laws, the court relied on the professional education segregation cases of *Sweatt v. Painter,* 339 U.S. 629 (1950), and *McLaurin v. Oklahoma State Regents,* 339 U.S. 637 (1950). The court stressed the importance of the "qualities which are incapable of measurement" in comparing the educational advantages afforded by segregated schools. These intangible considerations "apply with equal force to children in grade and high schools. To separate them from others of similar age and qualifications solely because of their race generates a feeling of inferiority as to their status in the community that may affect their hearts and minds in a way unlikely ever to be undone." Reference was also made to the finding by the federal district court in the Kansas case (*Brown*):

The impact (of segregation) is greater when it has the sanction of the law. For the policy of separating the races is usually interpreted as denoting inferiority of the Negro group. A sense of inferiority affects the motivation of a child to learn. Segregation with the sanction of law, therefore, has a tendency to retard the educational and mental development of Negro children and to deprive them of some of the benefits they would receive in a racially integrated school system.

The court stated that whatever might have been the extent of "psychological knowledge" at the time of *Plessy v. Ferguson*, this finding as to the retarding educational effect of enforced segregation was amply supported by modern authority and that only the language in *Plessy* contrary to this finding is rejected.

The court concluded by stating that in the field of public education the doctrine of "separate but equal" has no place. The crux of the opinion was stated in a single sentence of dramatic force: "Separate educational facilities are inherently unequal" (p. 495). The segregation cases were then restored to the docket in order for the court to hear further argument on the issue of enforcement—questions four and five.

BOLLING v. SHARPE, 372 U.S. 497 (1954)

In a companion case to the four state segregation cases the court dealt with segregation in the public schools of the District of Columbia. Here, the Supreme Court reached the same conclusion, but via a different route. The Fourteenth Amendment is not applicable to the District of Columbia because it is not a state. But the District, as a subdivision of the federal government, is subject to the limitations imposed by the due process clause of the Fifth Amendment. Referring to prior decisions, the court stated that the liberty secured by due process could not be restricted except for a proper governmental objective. The court, therefore, held that "segregation in public education is not reasonably related to any proper governmental objective, since this imposes on Negro children . . . a burden that constitutes an arbitrary deprivation of their liberty in violation of the Due Process clause" (p. 500).

The decision in *Brown* applies only to segregation in state supported schools, and does not require the states to establish school districts in such a way as to ensure racial integration. In certain areas a normal program of districting for school purposes will have the effect of a segregation program. Nothing in *Brown* can be interpreted to interfere with the establishment of school districts along geographical lines. The court recognized these ministerial problems when it decided to hear further argument on the relief and remedies to be proscribed in implementing the court's decision.

Selected Law Review Articles

1. "The Desegregation Cases: Criticism of the Social Scientists Role," Kenneth B. Clark, 5 *Villanova L. Rev.* 224 (1959).

Clark discusses specific fundamental criticisms of the social scientist's role as well as the authors in the segregation cases. Criticism from southern states and senators charge that the decision in *Brown* violates states' rights and that there is an attempt to substitute psychological and sociological theories for the law. The author believes such criticisms are motivated by political considerations.

Clark refers to criticisms leveled at him by Professor Cahn of New York University Law School [*see* "Jurisprudence," 30 *N.Y.U.L. Rev.* 150 (1955)] and Ernest van den Haag, a doctor in the social science field. [*See also* K. B. Clark, the *Social Scientist, the Brown Decision, and Contemporary Confusion*, where the author argues his position and replies to critics. *See also:* Van den Haag, "Social Science Testimony in Desegregation Cases—A reply to Professor Kenneth Clark," 6 *Villanova L. Rev.* 69 (1960), and Pittman, "The Blessings of Liberty v. The Blight of Equality" 42 *N.C.L.* Rev. 86 (1963) and Gregor, "The Law, Social Science, and School Segregation: An Assessment," 14 W. *Res. L. Rev.* 621 (1963)].

2. "The Chief Justice, Racial Segregation and the Friendly Critics, "Ira Michael Heyman, 49 *California Law Review* 104 (1961).

Heyman discusses, analyzes, and refutes criticism leveled by two renowned scholars of the *Brown* decision. Both the scholars abhor segregation and their criticism is directed at the theoretical and legal underpinnings of the decision. Professor Herbert Wechsler asserts that there is no legal basis for the court to stamp out segregation [*see* Wechsler, "Toward Neutral Principles of Constitutional Law," 73 *Harvard L. Rev.* 1 (1959)]; and Professor Louis Pollak, who also agrees with the court's action, believes that the opinion of the chief justice was intellectually insufficient and asserts that the court's decision was based on the ground that segregation "harms" blacks by making them feel inferior. [*See* Pollak, "Racial Discrimination and Judicial Integrity: A Reply to Professor Wechsler," 108 *V. Pa. L. Rev.* 1 (1959) and Pollak, "The Supreme Court Under Fire," 6 *J. Pub. L.* 428 (1957)]. Both critics are dissatisfied with that interpretation and interpret the opinion as making "harm" the sole basis of the unconstitutionality of public school segregation. Heyman believes that the criticisms are unjustified. He asserts that *Brown*, when properly read, establishes the proposition that the Fourteenth Amendment invalidates laws employing racial classifications in the field of public education whether or not blacks are made to feel inferior.

3. "The Original Understanding and the Segregation Decision," Alexander M. Bickel, 69 *Harvard Law Review* 1 (1955).

Bickel reviews, analyzes and discusses the congressional record of the debates and hearings surrounding the framing and adoption of the Fourteenth Amendment in order to ascertain the intent of the framers, with regard to segregation.

He concludes that it is clear that the Fourteenth Amendment was not expected to apply to segregation in 1866. He also believes that the inquiry into the Congressional understanding in 1866 should not stop at the immediate impact of the enactment on conditions then present. Another inquiry should be made into the Congressional intent of the long-range effect under future circumstances. The Supreme Court in the segregation cases recognized this second inquiry in question two of the five propounded in the 1952 term. Because of the general language used in Section 1 of the amendment, it appears that it is to apply to all state discrimination whether based on race or not. Bickel believes the adopters had this in mind and it was their intent to subject the amendment to a "Latitudinarian" construction. It was also their belief, according to the author, that the construction and interpretation of the amendment was to come from Congress under its powers under Section 5.

The language of the Fourteenth Amendment was a compromise between several competing groups. The language had both the "sweep and appearance" of a careful enumeration of rights, and it had a "ring to assuage the prejudices of the people." The author believes that there was an "awareness on the part of (the framers) that it was a constitution they were writing, which led to a choice of language capable of growth."

The author concludes that "the record of history, properly understood, left the way open to, in fact invited, a decision based on the moral and material state of the nation in 1954, not 1866."

4. "Segregation and its Impact on Educational and Psychological Development," Edmond Cahn.

It is difficult to state that the critical element in the segregation cases was the court's endorsement of the finding that state-imposed segregation "has a tendency to retard the educational and mental development of Negro children." The reliance on social science evidence—and the quality of those data; then and now—have been criticized.

Professor Edmond Cahn, distinguished professor of jurisprudence at New York University of Law School, believes that it is incorrect to think that the *Brown* decision was "caused by the testimony and opinions of the scientists." Cahn also comments that "I would not have the constitutional rights of Negroes—or of other Americans—rest of any such flimsy foundation as some of the scientific demonstrations in these records. . . . (Behavioral science findings) have an uncertain expectancy of life." [See "Jurisprudence," 30 *N.Y.U.L. Rev.* 150 (1955)].

There has also been disagreement in the court's decision when it stated that segregation "generates a feeling of inferiority." The disagreement stems from the basis of such a conclusion—whether the critical elements in establishing the conclusion comes from social science data, judicial notice, history, the stereotypical assumption of black inferiority, which provided the underpinnings for the general system of segregation or the black communities perception of the stigma imposed by segregation. Professor Cahn emphasized "the most familiar and universally accepted standards of right and wrong" as demonstrating that "racial segregation under government auspices inevitably inflicts humiliation," and that "official humiliation of innocent law-abiding citizens is psychologically injurious and morally evil." However, as commonsensical as this may sound, it is doubtful that the court can properly rest a decision on "universal" moral standards without added support from empirical data or history.

5. "The Lawfulness of the Segregation Decision," C.L. Black, Jr., 69 *Yale L. J* 421 (1960).

Professor Black defends the "lawfulness" of *Brown* by emphasizing that the southern cultural tradition during the period of enforced segregation makes it clear that "segregation is a massive intentional disadvantaging of the Negro race, as such, by state law." Moreover, "If a whole race or people finds itself confined within a system which is set up and continued for the very purpose of keeping it in an inferior station, and if the question is then solemnly propounded whether such a race is being treated 'equally,' I think we ought to exercise one of the sovereign prerogatives of philosophers—that of laughter." Black felt that the segregation system clearly fit that description. He added: "Segregation is historically and contemporaneously associated in a functioning complex with practices which are indisputably and grossly discriminatory . . . The purpose and impact of segregation in the Southern regional culture," he noted, were "matters of common notoriety, matters not so much for judicial notice as for the background knowledge of educated men who live in the world." At the time of *Brown*, Southern segregation was not "mutual separation of whites and Negroes," but rather "one in-group enjoying full normal communal life and one out-group that is barred from this life and forced into an inferior life of its own."

6. "Toward Neutral Principles of Constitutional Law," Herbert Weschler, 73 *Harvard L. Rev* 1 (1959).

Professor Herbert Wechsler argues:

For me, assuming equal facilities, the question posed by state-enforced segregation is not one of discrimination at all. Its human and its constitutional dimensions lie entirely elsewhere, in the denial by the state of freedom to associate, a denial that impinges in the same way on any groups or races that may be involved.

He asked:

Given a situation where the state must practically choose between denying the association to those individuals who wish it or imposing it on those who would avoid it, is there a basis in neutral principles for holding that the Constitution demands that the claims for association should prevail?

7. "Racial Discrimination and Judicial Integrity: A Reply to Professor Weschler," Pollak, 108 *J. Pa. L. Rev.* 1 (1959).

In reply to Weschler's article, Pollak writes:

We start from the base point that in the United States "All legal restrictions which curtail the civil rights of a single racial group are immediately suspect." *Korematsu v. United States, 323 U.S. 214 (1944)*. Certainly legislation cased in such terms is not entitled to the ordinary presumptions of validity. On the contrary there is special need for "a searching judicial inquiry into the legislative judgment in situations where prejudice against discrete and insular minorities may tend to curtail the operation of those political processes ordinarily to be relied on to protect minorities." We could not, therefore, sustain the reasonableness of these racial distinctions and the absence of harm said to flow from them, unless we were prepared to say that no factual case can be made the other way. . . . To the extent that implementation of this decision forces racial mingling on school children against their will, or against the will of their parents, this consequence follows because the community through its political processes has chosen and may continue to choose compulsory education—just as, from time to time, the nation has, through federal legislation, adopted the principle of coerced association implicit in a draft army. In neither instance can the coercion be said to emanate from (the Supreme Court) or from the Constitution. In any event, parents sufficiently disturbed at the prospect of having their children educated in democratic fashion in company with their peers are presumably entitled to fulfill their educational responsibilities in other ways.

8. "The Effects of Segregation and the Consequences of Desegregation," Appellant's Brief, *37 Minn. L. Rev. 427* (1953).

At trial in several of the segregation cases, psychologists, psychiatrists, and social scientists testified as to the harmful effects of state-imposed segregation on Negro school children. On appeal, appellants filed, as an appendix to their brief, a statement to this effect drafted by 32 sociologists, anthropologists, and psychiatrists who worked in the area of American race relations. . . .

BROWN v. BOARD OF EDUCATION (II) 349 U.S. 294 (1955)

BACKGROUND: *Brown* II implemented the Supreme Court's decision on *Brown* I, which held that racial segregation by the state in its public school facilities was a denial of the equal protection prohibited by the Fourteenth Amendment.

Whether *Brown I* is viewed as prohibiting segregation because it is an impermissible racial classification, or because it does educational damage to blacks, or because of the inherent inequality of segregated education, or because of any combination of these factors—the causes of segregation would appear to be immaterial. Whether a state requires segregation by law, or merely accepts it, the same invalid classification, the injury, or inequality takes place.

In *Brown II*, the Supreme Court reversed the lower courts' judgements (except in *Gebhart v. Belton*) and remanded to the lower courts to take such proceedings and enter such orders and decrees consistent with the two Brown opinions.

COURT RULING: The court began by reaffirming the principle in *Brown*, that racial discrimination in public education is unconstitutional, and stated that "all provisions of federal, state or local law requiring or permitting such discrimination must yield" to the decisions in the two *Brown* cases (at p. 298).

Because of the "complexities arising from the transition to a system of public education freed of racial discrimination," the court heard further argument. The states which required or permitted educational segregation were given the opportunity to present their views and solutions on the implementation of *Brown*.

The decree implementing the *Brown* principle instructed the lower courts that the local school boards should retain primary responsibility for "elucidating, assessing and solving" the varied local school problems of the period of transition. In framing their mandates the lower courts are to "consider whether the action of school authorities constitutes good faith implementation of the governing constitutional principles" (p. 299).

Though "it should go without saying that the vitality of these constitutional principles cannot be allowed to yield simply because of disagreement with them" (at p. 300), the public interest in overcoming a variety of obstacles in making the transition may permit delay in granting a remedy. Here, as a court of equity, the Supreme Court is balancing the interests of the opposing groups in its attempt to formulate a workable remedy that will affect a large number of people. Such a delay in effecting a remedy is a valid exercise of equitable powers and has been applied in other Supreme Court decisions. The court is "shopping for" the available relief and "adjusting and reconciling public and private needs" by not requiring immediate desegregation (at p. 300).

However, in every case, the local school boards are required to make "a prompt and reasonable start" toward compliance with *Brown*. Once a start has been made, additional time may be granted "to carry out the ruling in an effective manner." Once the "prompt and reasonable start" has been made, the state official or school boards must show that additional time is necessary, that it is in the public interest, and that it is "consistent with good faith compliance at the earliest practicable date" (at p. 300). In determining how much delay should be granted the courts should consider problems related to "administration, arising from the physical condition of the school plant, the school transportation system, personnel, revision of school districts and attendance areas into compact units to achieve a system of determining admission to the public schools on a nonracial basis, and revision of local laws and regulations which may be necessary in solving the problems (at p. 300–1).

During the period of transition, the courts are to retain jurisdiction of the cases and are to "enter such orders and decrees consistent with this opinion as are necessary and proper to admit to public schools on a racially nondiscriminatory basis with all deliberate speed the parties to these cases" (at p. 301). The Supreme Court's decision in *Brown II* can be summed up as follows: (1) The local school boards are required to implement *Brown* in good faith; i.e., they are required to do everything reasonable in eliminating public school segregation. (2) The lower courts, because of their proximity to local conditions and possible need for further hearings, will retain jurisdiction of the cases in order to see that *Brown* is carried out. The lower courts are to consider administrative obstacles in implementation and the competing interests involved. (3) The school boards must make this good faith implementation promptly and reasonably. (4) After the start toward desegregation is made, additional time may be granted to effect desegregation if the defendants (school boards) prove that the additional time is necessary, is in the public interest, and is consistent with its good faith compliance or beginning. Community hostility will not be grounds for an additional delay in desegregating the school system because it is not consistent with good faith compliance. (5) The standards of "with all deliberate speed" and "a prompt and reasonable start" serve as guiding principles in any desegregation plan that could potentially override a recalcitrant school board.

A New Educational Decision: Is Detroit the End of the School Bus Line?

Biloine Whiting Young and Grace Billings Bress have both done considerable scholarship and service in the area of equality of educational opportunity. Young, who has taught English at the University of Illinois, has been the director of the U.S. Binational Center in Cali, Colombia, and the director of the Illinois Television Project for the Gifted. Her articles have appeared in many publications, including the *Modern Language Journal* and *Phi Delta Kappan.* Bress, who has taught English at Harvard University and at the University of Minnesota, has been active in the Minnesota Association for Children with Learning Disabilities and has worked to implement an open enrollment program for minority students at Kenwood Elementary School in Minneapolis, Minnesota. She is the author of a 64-page annotated bibliography of desegregation research.

In April 1975, 21 years after *Brown v. Board of Education of Topeka, Kansas* (1954), Young and Bress published in *Phi Delta Kappan* a synthesis and interpretation of the ramifications of *Milliken v. Bradley* (1974) for school systems and the school desegregation effort. (This case is now referred to as *Milliken v. Bradley I,* because a second *Milliken v. Bradley* decision was handed down by the Supreme Court in 1977.) The case involved whether or not it was possible to achieve racial balance in the Detroit, Michigan, public schools, and if so, how. The selection that follows is from Young and Bress's article. In it, the authors examine the debate in the mid-1970s over the effectiveness of school desegregation and evaluate the research on the effects of school desegregation as of early 1975. They also discuss the limitations of the research on school desegregation conducted from 1966 through 1974. They argue that the Detroit decision had the effect of throwing the responsibility of how to achieve effective educational outcomes for all children back onto the shoulders of the public schools. Their analysis of the use of social science findings in the national debate over efforts to achieve racial balance in American schools was a greatly needed contribution to the literature.

Key Concept: racial integration in schools

*I*n the summer of 1974, 20 years after its landmark *Brown v. Board of Education* decision, the U.S. Supreme Court again aroused bitter controversy with a school desegregation ruling. On July 25, 1974, the High Court ruled 5 to 4 that the 53 suburban school districts clustering around Detroit could not be legally compelled to merge with the Detroit district in order to improve the racial balance of the 70%-black Detroit public schools. The Court stated that no evidence had been offered to show that the 53 suburban districts had been guilty of segregation or discrimination in their treatment of black students; therefore, the suburbs need not, in effect, be "punished" by a mandatory two-way racial exchange with Detroit.

Civil rights activists, hoping for a decision that would have required the largely white, middle-class suburbs to share the responsibility for educating the urban black poor, argue that this decision effectively locks the problems of unequal educational opportunity inside America's increasingly black cities.

Other observers applaud the Detroit ruling (the case is officially titled *Milliken v. Bradley*) as a reaffirmation of the judicial essence of the earlier *Brown* decision; namely, that the law must be applied to all Americans in a color-blind fashion; that race is not a constitutionally valid basis for differentiating among school children; and that a legal wrong must be proved before a remedy (however socially desirable) may be ordered.

The writers of this article support the second interpretation. Further, we believe that the Detroit decision, by setting limits on court-ordered busing, may force a reappraisal of the causes and cures of poor academic performance of minorities and thus lead to genuine educational solutions far more productive for black achievement than the largely symbolic, political gesture of busing for racial balance.

Integration as a remedy for low black achievement became a part of American educational philosophy with the *Brown* suit. Early in 1951 an NAACP lawyer approached Kenneth B. Clark to ask "whether psychologists had any findings which were relevant to the effects of racial segregation on the personality development of Negro children."[1] Clark was not able to provide the NAACP lawyers with precisely the social science support that they were looking for to buttress their legal arguments: "The available studies had so far not isolated this single variable [segregated schools] from the total social complexity of racial prejudice, discrimination, and segregation. It was therefore not possible to testify on the psychologically damaging effects of segregated schools alone."[2]

Nevertheless, that was precisely the intent of the evidence presented to the Court as expert testimony reflecting current social science scholarship. Its aim was to prove that dual, segregated schools lowered the self-esteem and motivation of Negro children and were thus responsible for their poor academic achievement. The remedy proposed—school integration—thus became weighted with a very heavy load of expectations: School integration was to make up for all the psychological and intellectual damage imposed on black children by the crushing burden of Southern racist ideology.

Clark and the other social scientists were, in effect, assuring the Court that school integration alone would raise Negro children's self-concepts, motivation, and academic performance to match these characteristics in white children. This optimistic assumption makes up the first and most important part of the "integration hypothesis" that soon became a central tenet of American educational theory.

The second part of the "integration hypothesis" was that integration would improve race relations. This assumption derives from "contact theory" (based on psychologist Gordon Allport's work), which assumes that once different groups of people are brought together in "equal status" contact they will like and respect each other better than before contact.

Although the grounds for these assumptions were largely theoretical, the integration hypothesis soon became a part of the conventional wisdom. As a result, legal, educational, and political decisions on desegregation were often made first and the "evidence" to support them was sought later.[3]

"I don't think politicians make these decisions *because* psychologists have produced the data," explains Leon Kamin, chairman of Princeton's psychology department. "They make decisions for other reasons, and then they find scientists who willingly provide the data to help sell those decisions. . . . I think, in 1954, when the politicians were making what could be called liberal decisions about desegregation, they turned to social scientists to point out, 'Here is evidence that scientifically supports us.' I think that evidence was very poor. . . ."[4]

Sociologist David Armor explains: "Integration was the policy first, and most social scientists then went about filling in the pro-integration evidence after the fact."[5] David K. Cohen, Harvard professor of education and social policy, agrees. Writing on the "evidence of the educational impact of desegregation," he says flatly, "There had been none at the time of *Brown*."[6]

For a decade after *Brown*, desegregation was still considered essentially a Southern problem. Most Americans understood equal educational opportunity to mean providing all public school children with comparable facilities, teachers, materials, etc., in unitary systems. Scholarly and political perception of the problem changed significantly in 1966 with the publication of the Coleman Report, which revealed that most Northern school children were attending "racially imbalanced" (though not legally dual) schools. In describing this situation, the word "segregation" was inappropriately extended beyond the specific Southern de jure meaning to include this Northern de facto imbalance, an imbalance owing to different socioeconomic as well as racial concentrations in different neighborhoods. The use of the same term to describe both situations conveyed the assumption that the problem in the North was identical to the Southern situation and equally immoral as well as illegal.

The Coleman Report was a giant survey of schools, teachers, and students authorized by the Civil Rights Act of 1964 to bring back evidence "concerning the *lack* of availability of equal educational opportunities for individuals by reason of race, color, religion, or national origin in public educational institutions at all levels in the United States" (emphasis added). Congress, irritated by the South's foot-dragging in implementing the *Brown* decision to desegregate its schools, assumed that school resources and facilities for whites and blacks were unequal and wanted documentation of this inequality in order to speed up integration.

The Coleman researchers had expected to find direct evidence of large inequalities in educational facilities in schools attended by children from different majority and minority groups, and they believed this "input" inequality would be statistically related to the "output" of student achievement. To their surprise, they found that facilities and other school inputs were almost identical for majority-black and majority-white schools. As two Harvard analysts, Frederick Mosteller and Daniel Moynihan, put it six years later, "[We] believe that in 1966 the nation had come much closer to achieving this classical notion of equality of educational opportunity than most of us realized then or realize now."[7]

By this time, however, the original meaning of equal educational opportunity had given way to the concept of equal educational results. The Coleman Report deliberately shifted the meaning of the phrase "equality of educational opportunity" from school inputs (the economic resources going into a school) to focus on school outputs or student achievement (the "results" of "opportunity"). Thus equal educational opportunity was reinterpreted to mean equal educational results in terms of group averages of achievement for all races, ethnic groups, and classes.[8]

The director of the study, James S. Coleman, justified this enormous change of meaning: " . . . [T]he major virtue of the study . . . lay in the fact that it did *not* accept that [earlier] definition [of equality of opportunity as meaning inputs], and by refusing to do so, has had its major impact in *shifting* policy attention from its traditional focus on comparison of inputs . . . to a focus on output and the effectiveness of inputs for bringing about changes in output."[9]

This dramatic change of meaning, insisted upon by the Coleman researchers, was apparently prompted by their concern at finding that the achievement gap between majority and minority pupils was a national phenomenon and not uniquely Southern. Similar inputs were apparently not producing similar outputs. At each grade level, the percentage of black students scoring below the white average was roughly constant: 85%. The achievement gap existed even at the beginning of school, in the fall of first grade. It did not narrow as schooling went on, but in fact widened so that by sixth grade the gap was more than a year and by twelfth grade it was more than three years.

The Coleman Report provided ambiguous data on the academic results of school integration. Overall, the researchers found very little difference among the average scores of black students in all-black schools, in majority-black schools, in half-white and half-black schools, and in majority-white schools. However, observing that black children in majority-white schools scored slightly higher (about two points on an achievement test of 50 questions) than other black children in all-black or majority-black schools, the researchers concluded that the integrated school environment was responsible for the difference. They asserted that if black students were to be moved to majority-white schools, their academic performance would increase correspondingly and causally: "If a minority pupil from a home without much educational strength is put with schoolmates with strong educational backgrounds, his achievement is likely to increase."[10]

"Quite the contrary," disagrees Henry S. Dyer of the Educational Testing Service. "There is nothing whatever in the Coleman analysis that can justify such an inference. The Coleman study contains no data at all on the effects that might accrue from 'putting' minority pupils with different kinds of schoolmates."[11]

Dyer's point concerns the important difference between cross-sectional and longitudinal studies. The Coleman Report, like the earlier social science evidence on which the integration hypothesis of *Brown* depended, utilized a cross-sectional survey, taken at one time, comparing the test scores of different groups of children in different educational environments. The Coleman Report was not a longitudinal experiment measuring the performance of the same children over a period of time. Cross-sectional surveys cannot test or prove causation. The most that can emerge from a cross-sectional survey is a correlation that produces a hypothesis to be tested by longitudinal experiment.

These (and other) criticisms of the Coleman Report either were not understood or were ignored by journalists sympathetic to the integration hypothesis repeated in the summary of the Coleman Report. News stories reported as proved what was still a hypothesis. With popular acceptance of the Coleman Report, the educational goal of "equality of opportunity" became transformed into a political demand for "equality of educational results." This shift in goals led directly to the massive busing programs undertaken in our major cities.

Nathan Glazer was the first prominent social scientist to challenge the academic and social assumptions of the integration hypothesis on the basis of longitudinal studies of real-life integration. In 1972 he wrote, " . . . [M]uch integration through transportation has been so disappointing in terms of raising achievement that it may well lead to a reevaluation of the earlier research whose somewhat tenuous results raised what begin to look like false hopes. . . ." He found the claims for reduction of racial tension equally unfounded and concluded, "If, then, judges are moving toward a forcible reorganization of American education because they believe this will improve relations between the races, they are acting neither on evidence nor on experience but on faith."[12]

Several months later, a long-standing dispute between Thomas Pettigrew, one of the most active spokesmen for those who believed integration would significantly improve minority achievement, and David Armor, a former pupil and Harvard colleague, erupted in the pages of *The Public Interest*. Armor claimed, on the basis of longitudinal studies, that induced integration did not raise minority achievement and, in fact, increased tensions and conflict.[13] Pettigrew countered with a rebuttal in a later issue. Although the results of the debate were inconclusive, the publication of Armor's research brought further into the open the growing disagreement among scholars about the validity of the integration hypothesis.[14]

Other researchers evaluated additional data. Jeffrey Leech, writing in the *Indiana Law Review* in 1973, surveyed a number of longitudinal studies on the effect of induced integration and warned, "The federal judiciary should examine its recent push toward massive busing in light of more current sociological evidence which indicates that busing to achieve integration may in fact produce no education gains, may hinder the psychological development of black children, and may intensify racial misunderstanding."[15]

In April, 1974, *The New York Times*'s Tom Wicker admitted, "There is little evidence to show that the educational test scores of minority children have been improved in those districts that have been integrated."

David K. Cohen concluded in the November-December, 1974, issue of *Society:* " . . . [E]vidence on the educational impact of desegregation (there had been none at the time of *Brown*) began to flow as schools integrated. Sometimes it showed modest gains and sometimes it showed no change over expectations, but it never showed that desegregated schools came close to eliminating achievement differences between blacks and whites." (In their reanalysis of the Coleman data in 1972, Pettigrew, Cohen, and Riley had estimated that "assigning Negro students to mostly white classes would raise their verbal ability about 1.94 points. This is less than one-sixth of the difference between average Negro and white achievement in these schools at grade 12."[16])

Ironically, Kenneth Clark, architect of the social science evidence used in the *Brown* case, himself now apparently rejects the use of social science findings in court proceedings. Commenting on recent studies that appear to contradict the integration hypothesis, Clark said in 1972, "Courts and political bodies . . . should decide questions of school spending and integration, not on the basis of uncertain research findings, but on the basis of the constitutional and equity rights of human beings."[17]

Some complex and unexamined psychological conflicts may be inhibiting black academic effort. A *Wall Street Journal* article on Evanston Township High School, integrated for 90 years, reports that "the average black sophomore score[s] in the eighth percentile, meaning that 92 out of 100 students in the entire county [do] better than he [does]," while white students average in the 88th percentile.

" 'No way I'm going to do things The Man's way,' says Ben, a black senior who says he is failing most of his courses and doesn't particularly care. Teachers say Ben isn't untypical. 'Many of the black kids feel it's just not hip to study and they put pressure on others to conform,' notes Lucia Peele, a high school guidance counselor who also is black."[18]

As integration's *lack* of significant effect on black achievement becomes documented, some advocates have shifted the basis of their arguments to the second desired goal of the integration hypothesis: better race relations. When test scores for both whites and blacks in Pasadena declined after induced integration (despite a 50% greater expenditure, adjusted for inflation), a fourth-grade teacher dismissed these results: "Test scores are meaningless. Look instead at the smiling faces—all colors—of the kids in my classroom, playing together, working together."[19]

However, by junior high, separate black and white peer-group cultures have formed in many racially balanced schools. Black and white students at Evanston Township High have separate lounges and do not share each others' facilities. The black senior class president of Berkeley High School told Senator Mondale's subcommittee that "the only true existence of integration of Berkeley High is in the hallways when the bell rings. Everybody, you know, passes through the hallways. That is the only time I see true integration at Berkeley High."[20]

The existence of separate racial and class-cultural peer groups in schools has not received the serious investigation it deserves, due, in large part, to a defensiveness which insists that there are no differences worth investigating. The principal of a 90%-black elementary school in Portland, Oregon, caused an uproar when he spoke openly about what he termed "the group pressure against learning created by the black students" in his school. "This school has a strong pecking order in which physical prowess and the ability to socialize according to the rules of urban black culture are the main determinants of status," he said. "Most white students, even those strong enough to defend themselves physically, aren't used to the social ritual of a black school—the dancing, the clothing, the jive. Whites may be accepted but they do not become leaders."[21] The special problems and conflicting loyalties of middle-class black students in racially polarized situations have been largely ignored.

It has become difficult to gather evidence of integration's assumed positive effects on race relations, because opposition has developed to the use of psychological tests to measure racial attitudes among school children. The Department of Health, Education, and Welfare dropped a planned evaluation of attitudes in response to protests of teachers, principals, and parents to the use of such tests.[22]

Although there is some tentative evidence that race relations in schools in Southern rural and middle-sized city systems may be better than in Northern large-city school systems, at least two national surveys, the Carnegie Commission's and *The New York Times*'s, reported increased racial hostility, intimidation, and violence in racially balanced schools throughout the country.

One of the very few scholars whose work is respected by all "sides" is Harvard's Nancy St. John. Unlike a number of desegregation experts who have taken on advocate roles, she has consistently refused to testify in court proceedings, believing that "public hearings or trials are not the best setting for constructive discussion of the intricacies of these matters."[23] St. John has compiled what is probably the most objective assessment of integration's academic and social effects on black children.

She suggests that integration benefits black children differentially rather than uniformly, tending to produce good results for those who are male and are "already advantaged"—by reason of enjoying good mental health, confidence, middle-class family status, high academic ability, etc.—and tending to produce negative results in black children who are female and who do not share the above-mentioned characteristics. In general, she finds, "children of low socioeconomic status can expect to be academically and socially threatened by desegregation." Her summary of available evidence is a plea for educators and judges to think about each child in a desegregation program as an individual rather than as a token to be deposited here or there for political purposes. She urges that integration be viewed in relation to the requirements of the individual child, believing that rigid integration plans too often ignore the individual characteristics and needs of individual children, ciphering them by numbers and skin color alone into that inhuman abstraction, "the racial and socioeconomic mix."

She writes, "Social scientists, lawyers, and educators tend to . . . search for the ideal racial mix for children generally, rather than for this child or that. In their zeal for one valued principle, they often ignore others and forget that integration, however important, is only one component of quality education, and not necessarily, for all children at all stages, the most important component."[24]

Twenty-one years after *Brown*, the South's dual, segregated school systems have been abolished and the stigma of legally imposed racial assignment to separate black and white schools is gone forever. For some blacks, the years since *Brown* have produced greater opportunities and rewards. Increasing numbers of black families have moved into the middle class, thus expanding the life choices available to their children.

For other blacks—the poor, the unskilled, the unmotivated—there has not been much improvement. For these, attaining competence in basic skills—reading, writing, spelling, and arithmetic—has been an insurmountable obstacle to further education and better job opportunities. Prematurely discouraged with the results of the sixties's inadequately monitored innovations (many of which were oversold), many city school systems have, in effect, given up on the goal of producing equal educational results through "equalizing upwards," i.e., by raising the achievement of poor and minority students to meet the white average. Perhaps without realizing it, they are attempting to "equalize down" by discouraging excellence. Some New York City schools have eliminated courses like calculus, enriched English, etc., that attract primarily a high-achieving white middle-class enrollment.

"There is no doubt that our classes for the intellectually gifted would have been totally segregated . . . if we had continued them," says the superintendent of Community School District 22. Another district has banned all classes for academically talented children on the ground that they would not have the "correct" racial balance.[25]

The Office of Education tried, unsuccessfully, to establish separate achievement norms for black and white students so that schools with heavily black enrollments could compare their students' test scores with national black averages rather than with the higher white norms.

Unanticipated at the time of *Brown*, the phenomenon of "resegregation" has occurred following mandatory desegregation when the class-cultural environment of a school becomes chaotic and hostile to intellectual achievement. Middle-class parents (including middle-class blacks) remove their children from these environments to private schools or the suburbs, thus increasing the racial and class imbalance in city schools which well-intentioned theorists had intended to stabilize.

The New York State Board of Regents has now disavowed the use of enrollment quotas and black-white ratios to measure equal opportunity as a result of studies showing New York's schools to be more segregated after 15 years of efforts at integration than before.[26] In 1968, 72.1% of minority children in the state attended schools that were more than half minority. Today the figure is 75%. Half of the black and Hispanic children in New York State attend schools that are over 90% minority.[27]

The problem of "white flight" is slowly being perceived more as one of class than of race. The over-representation of blacks in the disorganized lower class (with its antisocial behavioral life-style, the "culture of poverty") has obscured and confused this fact. Americans have traditionally been reluctant to admit to the existence of class differences in U.S. society, much less to class conflicts. It is not surprising, then, that public discussion of the problems of inner-city schools repeats the tired and out-of-date rhetoric of race when the issues now are class-cultural differences between middle and lower class (not stable working class) in values, life-style, learning style, social behavior norms, language, etc. Since desegregation of their schools, Southern whites have discovered, agreeably and with some surprise, that not all blacks are lower class; as busing to achieve racial balance has moved North, Northern whites are discovering, with some dismay, that not all blacks are middle class.

Many inner-city classrooms are becoming a battleground between the middle-class values of the teacher and the lower-class and often anti-intellectual values of increasing percentages of the children. The current ideological disarray among educators and academics who find much to complain about "middle-class-ness" further compounds the problems that inner-city schools face in reaching and teaching their mainly lower-class clientele while still preserving the classroom order and intellectual challenge required to keep middle-class families from moving their children out.

Black academic successes which have run counter to the prevailing ideology have been largely ignored—most notably the success of Dunbar High School, which was brought to national attention by Thomas Sowell, an economist who is black. Dunbar was an all-black high school in Washington, D.C., that for 85 years consistently came in first in citywide tests given in both black and white schools. It produced large numbers of well-educated graduates whose outstanding achievements enriched American society. These graduates included America's first black general, the first black cabinet member, the discoverer of blood plasma, and the first black senator since Reconstruction. Dunbar's success was not the result of its racial segregation (except as it may have contributed to a competitive desire to make a black high school the best), but because students, parents, and faculty, in miserably inadequate facilities, enthusiastically supported and worked for the academic goals of the school. Although at least 88% of the students came from homes of nonprofessionals, they subscribed to an ethic based on work and achievement. There was no self-defeating assumption that high academic performance was a value antithetical to blacks.[28]

Dunbar, for 85 years, proved that blacks can achieve in the public schools. Race, in relation to achievement, was irrelevant. What was important was the motivation, the belief in excellence.

For 20 years the national remedy for low minority achievement has been busing for integration—the faith that if the correct racial mix can be provided in a classroom, problems of low achievement and racial tensions will disappear. Such a "solution" now appears to have been dangerously simplistic, creating expectations it has, so far, been unable to satisfy. Further, mandatory busing has contributed to the racial and economic segregation of our cities on a scale undreamed of in 1954, to the extent that in many there are no longer enough white pupils to integrate.

The Detroit ruling now ends the search for more white faces and throws the challenge back on the schools to find genuine solutions rather than inadequate and largely symbolic remedies which distract attention from learning problems that need real—not symbolic—solutions. Educators must free their thinking of the racist notion that there is something magical in whiteness—that without it a black or a red or a brown child cannot learn. Once this mythic heritage of white superiority is abandoned, educators can address themselves to an analysis of the strengths, weaknesses, and needs of each school system, school, classroom, and, ultimately, each child—no matter his color or that of his seatmates—to determine which of the many resources, including integration, are most applicable to his learning needs.

At bottom, learning and achievement are individual matters. As Martin Mayer insists, opportunity does not mean results: "The best that can be given is opportunity; the burden will continue to rest on the Negro community because there is no way to transfer it. Governments cannot legislate and courts cannot mandate results."[29] Schools can provide the educational technology and committed teachers. The responsibility rests on the black community to lead its young away from the suicidal belief that excellence and achievement somehow involve a disloyal collaboration with a white enemy.

A number of black leaders have already taken up this important charge. Toni Morrison, writing in *The New York Times Magazine,* calls on black people to recommit themselves to their traditional ethic of pride in work and excellence. "Before black life rearranged itself into elusive symbols of dashikis, pimp hats, and kentecloth bikinis, we had a hold on life, an attitude which was most dramatically expressed in one particular area . . . it concerned work and the way we worked. There was a *press toward excellence* in the execution of just about everything we tackled . . . I mean the pride in work well done for its own sake. . . . Perhaps doing a good job these days is too much like pleasing the enemy. But at one time it was different . . ." (emphasis added).

Jesse Jackson, speaking before the convention of the National Urban League, sounded a similar exhortation to blacks to prove their equality by achieving excellence. "Mrs. Mary Bethune survived because she was excellent. George Washington Carver survived because he was excellent. Roland Hayes survived because he was excellent. . . ."

While there is a danger that the concept of "excellence" as an energizing factor may become merely another simplistic slogan, it may also, in the long run, turn out to be the most honest and effective catalyst. The words of James Cheek, president of Howard University, are a good beginning: "Black Americans and this university community must value excellence and quality more than we have ever in the past.... We must ... make being black synonymous with being excellent, to endow that which is black with an unmatched quality, and to express a dedication and a devotion that will be the envy of all men everywhere."

An abstract appeal to excellence, however, is not a realistic solution for children and young people who are already having trouble in school. Cornell's Urie Bronfenbrenner has suggested that learning intervention which produces the most sizable and lasting cognitive gains focuses on the mother and young child in the home environment rather than on the older child in school. He believes that for maximum success, mother and child intervention should begin in the child's second year of life. If he is right, then even so bold a public school commitment as California's new decision to concentrate most of its educational resources on the 4- to 8-year-old population will still not be reaching the children and their mothers early enough. Early mother and child intervention and the effects of prenatal nutrition on childhood development are two important research areas which may hold answers to problems that the public schools have so far failed to solve.

NOTES

1. Kenneth B. Clark, *Prejudice and Your Child* (Boston: Beacon Press, 1955), p. 210.
2. Ibid., p. 193.
3. See David Armor, "The Evidence on Busing," *The Public Interest*, Summer, 1972, for a very useful summary of the history of desegregation theory.
4. Leon Kamin, "The Misuse of IQ Testing," *Change*, October, 1973, pp. 40, 41.
5. Michael Kramer, "Bus Stop," *New York Magazine*, August 21, 1972, pp. 6, 7.
6. David K. Cohen, "Segregation, Desegregation, and *Brown*," *Society*, November-December, 1974.
7. Frederick Mosteller and Daniel P. Moynihan, eds., *On Equality of Educational Opportunity: Papers Deriving from the Harvard University Faculty Seminar on the Coleman Report* (New York: Random House, 1972), pp. 11, 12.
8. Ibid., p. 6.
9. Ibid., pp. 149, 150.
10. James S. Coleman, et al., *Equality of Educational Opportunity Report*, 1966, p. 22.
11. Henry S. Dyer, "School Factors and Equal Educational Opportunity," *Harvard Educational Review*, Winter, 1968, p. 53.
12. Nathan Glazer, "Is Busing Necessary?" *Commentary*, March, 1972, p. 51.
13. Armor, op.cit.
14. Harvard's James Q. Wilson has formulated two "laws" that help explain how two credentialed scholars can disagree so sharply about the same set of "facts." In a coda to the acrimonious public debate between Pettigrew and Armor, Wilson commented (*The Public Interest*, Winter 1973, p. 133): " ... [A]fter having looked at the results of countless social science evaluations of public policy programs, I have formulated two general laws which cover all cases with which I am familiar: *First Law:* All policy interventions in social problems produce the intended effect—*if* the research is carried out by those implementing the policy or their friends. *Second Law:*

No policy intervention in social problems produces the intended effect—*if* the research is carried out by independent third parties, especially those skeptical of the policy." Wilson explains, "These laws may strike the reader as a bit cynical but they are not meant to be. Rarely does anyone deliberately fudge the results of a study to conform to pre-existing opinions. What is frequently done is to apply very different standards of evidence and method."

15. Jeffrey J. Leech, "Busing as a Judicial Remedy: A Socio-Legal Reappraisal," *Indiana Law Review*, May, 1973, pp. 710, 712.

16. Mosteller and Moynihan, op. cit., pp. 358, 359.

17. *The New York Times*, June 11, 1972.

18. David M. Elsner, "A Problem at Evanston High," *The Wall Street Journal*, April 16, 1974.

19. Earl C. Gottschalk, Jr., "Pasadena's Plight," *The Wall Street Journal*, July 2, 1974, p. 1.

20. *Hearings Before the Select Committee on Equal Educational Opportunity of the U.S. Senate*, Part 9A, San Francisco and Berkeley, Calif., pp. 4058, 1059.

21. Roy C. Rist, "Busing White Children into Black Schools: A Study in Controversy," *Integrated Education*, July, 1974, pp. 13–18.

22. Leonard Buder, "U.S. Drops Survey of Pupils' Attitudes on Race Relations," *The New York Times*, March 19, 1974, p. 1.

23. Personal communication from Nancy St. John.

24. Nancy St. John, "Desegregation: Voluntary or Mandatory?" *Integrated Education*, January-February, 1972, pp. 9, 10.

25. Gene I. Maeroff, "Bright and Slow Classes Resulting in Segregation," *The New York Times*, May 22, 1974, p. 1.

26. On February 20, 1975, the New York Board of Regents softened their opposition to the use of ethnic ratios. In a prefatory statement, the board said, " ... [M]any responsible people, black and white, do not regard the massive transportation of pupils out of their neighborhoods for purposes of achieving racial balance to be productive in the education of [their] children. To determine compliance ... on integration principally by use of quantitative measures is to use a method which by itself offers no assurance that the educational opportunity of each child is protected." The regents went on to define an integrated school as one in which "the racial composition of the student body reflects the pupil population of the school district without necessarily attempting to be proportionate to it. ... What constitutes a reflection of the population of a school district will depend upon the circumstances in specific situations." (From *The New York Times*, February 21, 1975, p. 1)

27. *The New York Times*, January 26, 1975.

28. Thomas Sowell, "Black Excellence: The Case of Dunbar High School," *The Public Interest*, Spring, 1972, pp. 3–21.

29. Martin Mayer, "The Sham of Instant Equality," *The New Republic*, April 1, 1972, pp. 14, 15.

CHAPTER 11 Law and the Schools

11.1 THOMAS R. ASCIK

The Courts and Education

Thomas R. Ascik is an attorney who has focused on the study of how federal court decisions in the United States have affected educational policy in several areas of concern. He has served as a senior research associate in the Law and Public Management Division of the National Institute of Education, which is under the direction of the Department of Education.

In the following selection, which is from "The Courts and Education," *The World and I* (March 1986), Ascik explores the major educational issues and cases that the United States Supreme Court has ruled on in the past half century. He reviews the reasoning that the Court has used in cases relating to (1) public aid to nonpublic schools (the private school "choice" issue); (2) spiritual values in public schools; and (3) the rights of teachers and students. In a section of the original article not included here, Ascik explores the Supreme Court's role in school desegregation.

Key Concept: the United States Supreme Court and public education

*T*he Supreme Court said in 1960 that "the vigilant protection of constitutional freedoms is nowhere more vital than in the community of American schools." Starting with the cases of *Everson v. Board of Education* (1947) and *Brown v. Board of Education* (1954), and continuing with one precedent-shattering case after another, the Supreme Court has applied the concept of constitutional rights to nearly every aspect of American education. Although the United States has been flooded by studies and reports severely critical of the nation's public schools, the historic changes in education wrought by the Supreme Court over the past four decades have hardly been mentioned.

Most critical are those rulings in which the Supreme Court has applied the Constitution to education without prior precedent. These have particularly affected public aid to nonpublic schools, prayer and spiritual values in public schools, racial segregation, and teacher and student rights. In these four areas, the Court, on its own initiative, has broken with the past and established comprehensive national educational policies.

PUBLIC AID TO NONPUBLIC SCHOOLS

The authority of any branch of the federal government to intervene in state public policies regarding religion traditionally has been governed by the doctrine of the 1833 case of *Barron v. Baltimore*. In this case, concerning city damage to private property, Chief Justice John Marshall, speaking for a unanimous Supreme Court, ruled that the Court had no jurisdiction over the case because the Bill of Rights placed no restrictions on the actions of city or state governments. The framers of the Bill of Rights had not "intended them to be limitations on the powers of the state governments," explained Marshall.

In the 1920s and 1930s, however, the Court abandoned *Barron v. Baltimore* and began developing perhaps the most important judicial doctrine of this century: the "incorporation" of the Bill of Rights into the Fourteenth Amendment. That amendment, ratified in 1868, made federal citizenship preeminent over state citizenship and declared in its most important parts that "no state shall . . . deprive any person of life, liberty, or prosperity, without due process of law; nor deny to any person within its jurisdiction the equal protection of the laws." By incorporating the various rights guaranteed by the Bill of Rights into these Fourteenth Amendment guarantees, the Court gave itself power to overturn state law dealing with almost all areas covered by the ten amendments of the Bill of Rights.

The Court ruled in the 1947 case of *Everson v. Board of Education*, for instance, that the First Amendment's clause prohibiting laws "respecting an establishment of religion" was binding on the states. In this most important Supreme Court education case, except for *Brown v. Board of Education* (1954), the Court was construing the Establishment Clause for the first time. At stake was the constitutionality of a New Jersey statute requiring local school boards to provide free transportation, along established routes, to children attending nonprofit, private (including religiously affiliated) schools.

More significant than the specific ruling in the case was the Court's construction of the First Amendment's Establishment Clause. Declared the Court:

> The "establishment of religion" clause of the First Amendment means at least this: Neither a state nor the Federal Government can set up a church. Neither can it pass laws which aid one religion, aid all religions, or prefer one religion over

another. Neither can it force nor influence a person to go to or to remain away from a church against his will or force him to profess a belief or disbelief in any religion. No person can be punished for entertaining or professing religious beliefs or disbeliefs, for church attendance or nonattendance. No tax in any amount, large or small, can be levied to support any religious activities or institutions, whatever they may be called, or whatever form they may adopt to teach or practice religion. Neither a state nor the Federal Government can, openly or secretly, participate in the affairs of any religious organizations or groups and vice versa. In the words of Jefferson, the clause against establishment of religion by law was intended to erect "a wall of separation between Church and State." . . . That Amendment requires the state to be neutral in its relations with groups of religious believers and nonbelievers.

Until this declaration, the most widely held view of the meaning of the Establishment Clause was that it prohibited government preference of one religion over another. When the Supreme Court concluded that states cannot "pass laws which aid one religion, aid all religions, or prefer one religion over another," it introduced for the first time the notion that the Establishment Clause forbade not only government preference of one religion over another but also government preference of religion over nonreligion.

More than twenty years passed before the Court heard its next significant case concerning government aid to religious schools, *Board of Education v. Allen.* In *Allen,* the Court examined a challenge to a New York statute that required local school boards to purchase textbooks (in secular subjects only) and loan them, without charge, to all children enrolled in grades seven through twelve of public or private schools. The books were not limited to those actually in use in the public schools but could include those "designated for use" in the public schools or otherwise approved by the local board of education.

The Court applied *Everson* to the case and decided that the provision of textbooks, like transportation, was permissible means to the accomplishment of the legitimate state objective of secular education of all children. Religious schools participated in the public interest because "they pursue two goals, religious instruction and secular education." Parochial schools, the Court said, "are performing, in addition to their sectarian function, the task of secular education." This was the birth of the "secular-sectarian" distinction that has defined religious schools as partly serving the public good (the secular subjects in the curriculum) and partly not (religious instruction).

Various cases followed that further defined the principles laid down in *Everson,* including a case dealing with the question of reimbursement to non-public schools for their expenditures on teachers of secular subjects and secular institutional materials (*Lemon v. Kurtzman* [1971]). In *Lemon,* the Court ruled the reimbursements unconstitutional because of the danger a teacher under religious control could pose to the separation of the religious from the secular. In *Committee for Public Education and Liberty v. Nyquist* (1973), maintenance and repair grants to nonpublic schools were judged to have the primary effect of advancing religion because the buildings maintained and repaired were not restricted to secular purposes. Also in this case, tuition reimbursements and tuition tax deductions were rejected by the Court as being effectively indistinguishable from aid to the schools themselves: "The effect of the aid is unmistakably to provide desired financial support for nonpublic sectarian institutions." Furthermore, said the Court, states could not "encourage or reward" parents for sending their children to religious schools because this advances religion. Finally, the plan failed the "politically divisive" test because it had the "grave potential" of stimulating "continuing political strife over religion."

Separate strong dissents were filed by Chief Justice Warren Burger and by Justices William Rehnquist and Byron White. Burger thought that there was a definitive difference between government aid to individuals and direct aid to religious institutions. He wrote: "The private individual makes the decision that may indirectly benefit church-sponsored schools; to that extent the state involvement with religion is substantially attenuated." Rehnquist argued that, if the Court could uphold the constitutionality of exempting churches from taxation, then it should similarly uphold the constitutionality of exempting parents from taxation for certain educational expenses. White contended that the Court was ruling as unconstitutional schemes that had "any effect" of advancing religion, whereas the test was properly one of "primary effect."

The Thirty-Years War between the Supreme Court and those states seeking to give public aid to their private schools may have ended with the Supreme Court's 1983 decision in *Mueller v. Allen*. In an opinion written by Justice Rehnquist, a majority of the Court upheld a Minnesota law allowing a deduction on state income taxes for tuition, textbooks, and transportation expenses incurred in the education of students in elementary or secondary schools—public or nonpublic.

Rehnquist decided that the deduction had a secular purpose of "ensuring that the state's citizenry is well-educated" regardless of the type of schools attended. Minnesota also had "a strong public interest" in assuring the survival of religious and nonreligious private schools because such schools relieve the public schools of the financial burden of educating a certain percentage of the youth population and because private schools provide "a wholesome competition" for public schools. Furthermore, the primary effect of the law was not the advancement of religion, Rehnquist concluded, in the most important part of his opinion.

Minnesota's plan was distinguished from the tax deductions in *Nyquist* because "the deduction is available for educational expenses incurred by all parents, including those whose children attend public schools and those whose children attend nonsectarian private schools or sectarian private schools." Rehnquist cited the Court's 1981 decision in the *Widmar v. Vincent* ruling that if a state university makes its facilities available for use by student groups, it must allow student religious groups to use the facilities on an equal basis. In keeping with the *Widmar* decision, Minnesota was here providing benefits on an equal basis to a "broad spectrum of citizens," and this nondiscriminatory breadth was "an important index of secular effect."

Having thus distinguished *Nyquist*, the Court was then able to say that there is a significant difference, in terms of the Establishment Clause, between providing aid to parents and providing it directly to schools despite the reality that "financial assistance provided to parents ultimately has an economic effect comparable to that of aid given directly to the schools attended by their children." Religious schools received public funds "only as a result of numerous, private choices of individual parents of school-age children," and this exercise of parental choice caused the financial benefits flowing to religious schools to be much "attentuated."

Implications

The *Mueller* decision and the *Widmar* decision requiring state universities to give "equal access" to student religious groups may signal an emerging Supreme Court view of the relationship of church to state and a possible end to the struggle between the states and the Court over public aid for nonpublic education. In *Mueller,* the Court accepted the principle that parents whose children attended religious schools could receive benefits so long as public school parents were equally eligible for benefits. This principle, allowing a state to accommodate its citizens with religious purposes on an equal basis with those pursuing secular purposes, received strong bipartisan support in Congress in 1984. By significant majorities, both Houses passed the "equal access" bill requiring elementary and secondary schools to allow student religious clubs to use their facilities on an equal basis with other student clubs. This was nothing more than the extension of *Widmar* to elementary and secondary schools.

In the United States, religion has always been the major motivation for the formation and continuation of private schools. Without the *Everson* doctrine, therefore, there would be many more U.S. private schools.

SPIRITUAL VALUES IN PUBLIC SCHOOLS

The Supreme Court addressed prayer in schools in the 1962 case of *Engle v. Vital,* a constitutional challenge to the mandated daily recitation of a nondenominational prayer in a New York State school district that said:

> Almighty God, we acknowledge our dependence upon Thee, and we beg Thy blessings upon us, our parents, our teachers, and our country.

The prayer had been carefully crafted in consultation with a wide range of Jewish and Christian leaders and officially recommended (in 1951 and 1955) to the state's school districts by the New York State Board of Regents as part of its "Statement on Moral and Spiritual Training in the Schools." In the lower state courts and the New York Court of Appeals (the highest court of New York), the constitutional challenge to the prayer had been rejected with the caveat that no student could be compelled to recite the prayer. Twenty-three other states joined New York in its petition to have the Supreme Court uphold the constitutionality of the prayer. This, however, the Court did not do.

In what might have been unique for such an important case, Justice Hugo Black, writing for the Court, referred to no previous Supreme Court decision as precedent. Instead, he explained the decision by means of an essay on the history of the separation of church and state. Significantly, almost all of the history considered was preconstitutional—the history of religion in England and the writings of various men, especially Madison and Jefferson, at the time of the ratification of the Constitution and of the Bill of Rights. Justice Potter Stewart, the sole dissenter, argued that the case brought the Free Exercise Clause into consideration in two ways. First, the lack of compulsion meant that the state was not interfering with the free exercise of anyone's religion. Second, the children who wanted to pray were denied the free exercise of their religion, Stewart contended, and they were denied the "opportunity of sharing the spiritual heritage of our Nation." History is relevant, Stewart argued, but not "the history of an established church in sixteenth century England or in eighteenth century America." Instead, the relevant history was the "history of the religious traditions of our people, reflected in countless practices of the institutions and officials of our government."

A year later in the companion cases of *Abington v. Schempp* and *Murray v. Curlett*, the Court struck down state laws requiring the reading of the Bible in public schools. In *Schempp*, the Unitarian plaintiffs challenged a Pennsylvania state law, passed in 1949, requiring the reading of ten verses from the Bible, without comment or interpretation, in the public schools at the beginning of each day. Upon written request, parents could excuse their children from the readings. The plaintiffs had bypassed the Pennsylvania Supreme Court and sued in federal district court, where the law was struck down in a decision based primarily on the *Everson* decision.

In *Murray*, militant atheist Madlyn Murray and her son challenged a 50-year-old rule of the Baltimore School Board requiring the reading of the Lord's Prayer each day in the city's public schools. As in Pennsylvania, parents could excuse their children from the practice. Murray did not request that her son be excused but brought the suit claiming that the rule violated religious liberty by "placing a premium on belief as against nonbelief." The Maryland Supreme Court appealed to the U.S. Supreme Court, and eighteen other states joined Maryland's defense of its customs.

The Supreme Court ruled in favor of Murray. *Engle* and especially *Everson* formed the basis of the decision. The Court quoted the *Everson* statement that neither the states nor the federal government "can pass laws which aid one religion, aid all religions, or prefer one religion over another." Once more the Supreme Court was ruling that the influence of religion must be absolutely segregated from the affairs of state. Finally, the Court invented a test for the establishment of religion: a law is constitutional only if it has "a secular legislative purpose and a primary effect that neither advances nor inhibits religion." According to these principles, the practices in these cases were unconstitutional because they were indisputably exercises of which both purpose and effect were religious. The Court denied that its decision advanced what amounted to a religion of secularism but gave no reason for its denial.

In *Epperson v. Arkansas* (1968), the Supreme Court added a new wrinkle to its judicial attitude toward religion: a law may be unconstitutional, stated the

Court, if the legislative motive for passing the law was religious. Since 1928, an Arkansas law prohibited the teaching of evolution in its public schools. The law had never been enforced. In 1965, however, a high school biology teacher, confronted with newly adopted biology textbooks that taught evolution, maintained that she was caught between opposing duties and sued to have the law declared void. In a two-sentence opinion, the Arkansas Supreme Court turned back the challenge by concluding that the law was a "valid exercise of the state's power to specify the curriculum in its public schools."

In addition to the question of religious influence in public schools, at least four other profound issues were involved here: the content of the school curriculum, the authority of states over their public schools, the authority and ability of the federal judiciary to prescribe or proscribe parts of the curriculum, and the growing legal movement to have the federal courts promulgate some First Amendment-based rights of academic freedom. In its resolution of the *Epperson* case, the Supreme Court confined itself to two rationales. The first and more important rationale for the decision was the principle of the *Everson, Engle,* and *Schempp* cases. There was no relationship between church and state, the Court said; instead there was a wall. Such a statue clearly violated the "purpose" of the *Schempp* two-part test. The purpose of the statute was clearly religious, and the state did not have the right to make its decisions about school curricula "based upon reasons that violate the First Amendment." In its strongest statement yet about the *Everson* neutrality principle, the Court emphasized that government must treat religion and nonreligion equally, for "the First Amendment mandates government neutrality between religion and religion, and between religion and nonreligion."

As its second rationale, the Court quoted the statement in *Shelton v. Tucker,* that "the vigilant protection of constitutional freedoms is nowhere more vital than in the community of American schools," and the statement in *Keyishian v. Board of Regents* that the First Amendment will not tolerate "a pall of orthodoxy over the classroom."

Through *Epperson v. Arkansas,* the Court brought the results of constitutional litigation affecting higher education to elementary and secondary schools. To Arkansas's claim that it had constitutional power over its public schools, the Supreme Court declared that the Bill of Rights is applicable everywhere, and constitutional powers are not superior to constitutional rights. Said the Court: "Fundamental values of freedom of speech and inquiry and of belief" are at stake here. Quoting *Keyishian,* "It is much too late to argue that the State may impose upon the teachers in its schools any conditions that it chooses, however restrictive they may be of constitutional guarantees." With this concern for the academic freedom (free speech) of teachers, the Court invented independent rights for teachers to control the curriculum of public schools.

Implications

No court has ever doubted the authority of the states to prescribe moral and spiritual instruction in their public schools. The New York State Board of

Regents was exercising that authority when it composed the prayer that became the issue in *Engle*. Today there is a growing consensus that more character training is needed in public schools. Historically, almost all systematic codes of Western morality or developed notions of character have been based on religion.

The effect of these Supreme Court decisions has been to prevent religion from influencing the education of those attending public schools. These decisions have forced those who believe that education cannot be separated from religion and who cannot afford private schools to attend institutions whose governing values are antagonistic to their own. In his concurrence in *Epperson*, Justice Black strongly implied that, if the wall of separation meant that nonreligion may influence the curriculum of public schools but religion may not, then the wall might very well be interfering with the free exercise of religion of some of those in attendance. This is, of course, a step beyond governmental neutrality between religion and nonreligion. Under governmental neutrality, the schools are merely indifferent to the values of religious people.

If any statement about the relationship of religion to education is itself a religious statement, then public education that does not discriminate against anyone is impossible under a system of absolute separation of church and state. The only alternative is the opportunity for individuals to exempt themselves at those times when the values presented or implied are antagonistic to their own. But the Court has rejected this principle of voluntariness. So the dilemma grows.

In his dissent in *Schempp*, Justice Stewart said government and religion must necessarily interact. Until *Everson*, they had at least been interacting throughout American history without any of the persecution that the court said it was trying to prevent with the *Engle* decision. In fact, it was *Everson* that launched an unprecedented era of church-state conflict in the U.S., chiefly in the context of education. American history before *Everson* dealt with interaction; since *Everson* it has been the history of conflict. It may be that neutrality is impossible. . . .

THE RIGHTS OF TEACHERS AND STUDENTS

The first important case applying the constitutional principle of free speech to the field of education was *Shelton v. Tucker* (1960). One of the most important First Amendment cases, it was decided by a narrow five to four margin. An Arkansas statute required prospective teachers at public schools or colleges to disclose every organization to which he or she had belonged or contributed regularly in the preceding five years. Some teachers who refused to do so, challenged the statue as a deprivation of their "rights to personal association, and academic liberty, protected by the Due Process Clause of the Fourteenth Amendment from invasion by state action."

In overruling the Arkansas Supreme Court, which had upheld the statute, The Supreme Court said that this case differed from that group of First Amendment cases in which the Court had invalidated state statutes because the statutes did not really serve a legitimate governmental purpose. Here, there was "no question of the relevance of a State's inquiry into the fitness and competence of its teachers." Nevertheless, without any discussion at all, the Court immediately reached two definitive conclusions:

1. It declared that teachers had "a right of free association, a right closely allied to freedom of speech and a right which, like free speech, lies at the foundation of a free society."
2. Rather than consider the issue of the permissible qualifications that a state may place on public employment, or the question of the uniqueness of teachers as public employees, the Court asserted that a constitutionally protected "personal freedom" of teachers was at stake here. At stake were "freedom of speech. . . . freedom of inquiry. . . . freedom of association. . . . the free spirit of teachers. . . . the free play of the spirit. . . . the free[dom] to inquire, to study, and to evaluate."

Consequently, "the vigilant protection of constitutional freedoms is nowhere more vital than in the community of American schools." This last statement and the two conclusions upon which it is based have presaged most of the substance of other key cases.

The Court found that a teacher could have many associations that would have no bearing upon the teacher's competence or fitness. Therefore, "The statute's comprehensive interference with associational freedom goes far beyond what might be justified in the exercise of the State's legitimate inquiry into the fitness and competency of its teachers." The four dissenters all joined two separate dissents written by Justices John Harlan and Felix Frankfurter. Their similar arguments had two main points. First, there was no evidence that the information collected had ever been abused or used in a discriminatory manner. Secondly, this was a reasonable and not excessive way for the state to exercise its conceded right to inquire into the fitness of its teachers.

That a major change had been effected in the attitude of the federal judiciary to the situation of teachers in government-operated schools was made evident in *Keyishian v. Board of Regents of New York* (1967) In *Keyishian* the Court overturned the same New York "loyalty oath" law that it had sustained fifteen years earlier in *Adler v. Board of Education.* The law excluded anyone from public employment who advocated the overthrow of the government by force or violence. Pursuant to the law, the Board of Regents of the state university system had required university employees to certify that they were not members of the Communist party or, if they were, that they had communicated the fact to the president of the university. Keyishian and three other faculty members refused to certify themselves and challenged the constitutionality of the law and its application.

In *Adler,* the Court had turned back such a challenge and declared:

A teacher works in a sensitive area in a classroom. There he shapes the attitude of young minds toward the society in which they live. In this, the state has a vital concern. It must preserve the integrity of the schools. That the school authorities have the right and the duty to screen the officials, teachers, and employees as to their fitness to maintain the integrity of the schools as a part of ordered society cannot be doubted.

But in *Keyishian*, the Court decided that the New York law was unconstitutional. Declared the Court:

> There can be no doubt of the legitimacy of New York's interest in protecting its education system from subversion. But "even though the governmental purpose be legitimate and substantial, that purpose cannot be pursued by means that broadly stifle fundamental personal liberties when the end can be more narrowly achieved." *Shelton v. Tucker*.... "The vigilant protection of constitutional freedoms is nowhere more vital than in the community of American schools." *Shelton v. Tucker.*

In *Adler*, the Court had said that teachers "may work for the school system upon the reasonable terms laid down by the proper authorities of New York. If they do not choose to work on such terms, they are at liberty to retain their beliefs and association and go elsewhere." But throughout the *Keyishian* opinion, the Court cited numerous cases that it had decided in the area of the First Amendment since 1952. What had happened between 1952 and 1967 was that the reach of the First Amendment had been dramatically extended by the Court.

In the 1968 case of *Pickering v. Board of Education*, the *Shelton* and *Keyishian* rationales for freedom of association for teachers were applied by the Supreme Court to freedom of speech for teachers. A county board of education in Illinois had dismissed a teacher, after a public hearing, for publishing a letter in a newspaper criticizing the board's performance in the area of school finance. The board found that numerous statements in the letter were false and that the publication of the statements unjustifiably impugned the board and the school administration.

The Supreme Court found that the teacher's right to free speech prevented his dismissal:

> To the extent that the Illinois Supreme Court's opinion may be read to suggest that teachers may constitutionally be compelled to relinquish the First Amendment rights they would otherwise enjoy as citizens to comment on matters of public interest in connection with the operation of the public schools in which they work, it proceeds on a premise that has been unequivocally rejected in numerous prior decisions of this Court.... *Shelton v. Tucker.... Keyishian v. Board of Regents....* "The theory that public employment which may be denied altogether may be subjected to any conditions, regardless of how unreasonable, has been uniformly rejected." *Keyishian v. Board of Regents....* the threat of dismissal from public employment is nonetheless a potent means of inhibiting speech.

In *Tinker v. Des Moines* (1969), the rights established in *Shelton* and *Keyishian* were extended to students:

> First Amendment rights, applied in light of the special characteristics of the school environment, are available to teachers and students. It can hardly be ar-

gued that either students or teachers shed their constitutional rights to freedom of speech or expression at the schoolhouse gate.

The case stemmed from the deliberate defiance of a school system's rule prohibiting the wearing of armbands—in this instance protesting the Vietnam War. "Our problem," the Court said, "lies in the area where students in the exercise of First Amendment rights collide with rules of the school authorities." Wearing of armbands was akin to "pure speech" and implicated "direct, primary First Amendment rights." The students' expression of their political views by wearing armbands had caused no disorder or disturbance in the schools, had not interfered with schools' work, and had not intruded upon the rights of other students. Furthermore, the mere fear of a disturbance was not reason enough to justify this curtailment of speech, the Court decided, because "our Constitution says we must take this risk." With this ruling, the Court established a new presumption in American education. "In the absence of a specific showing of constitutionally valid reasons to regulate their speech, students are entitled to freedom of expression of their views."

In a scorching dissent, Justice Black, a lifelong First Amendment advocate, asserted that the Court had launched a "new revolutionary era of permissiveness in this country fostered by the judiciary" by arrogating to itself "rather than to the State's elected officials charged with running the schools, the decision as to which school disciplinary regulations are 'reasonable'." Although he did not explicitly deny that students have free speech rights, Black may have argued so in effect, writing: "Nor are public school students sent to the schools at public expense to broadcast political or any other views to educate and inform the public . . . taxpayers send children to school on the premise that at their age they need to learn, not teach."

With its decision, the Court reversed what had been the unquestioned social agreement that school authorities were to be obeyed always and that only in the rarest and most extraordinary cases, where a student had been seriously wronged, could a redress of grievances be pursued. Now, with regard to speech in schools, the reasons for student obedience must be demonstrable beforehand.

Implications

The issue of the *Brown* case was student assignment; in *Everson* and its progeny, the Supreme Court was intervening to prevent religion from influencing education. In both areas, the Court rearranged traditional ways of doing things in American education. However, when it applied the constitutional principles of freedom of speech and freedom of association to education, the Court added to the educational enterprise. To the business of teaching and learning were added "direct, primary First Amendment rights" of teachers and students, that is to say, personal liberties, independent of educational purposes but applied to education, enforceable in a court of law.

Schools have a purpose other than that for which they were established, the Supreme Court has said. This purpose is often called "academic freedom," and as the Supreme Court has outlined, it is protected by courts even when not desired by those who founded, and continue to fund, the public schools. For students, it means that they have a legally enforceable right to do other things than learn at school. And for teachers, it means that they have a legally enforceable right to be employed at schools, regardless of whether the school authorities want them there, and a legally enforceable right to say things other than what the school hired them to say. These rights, especially with the powerful presumptions that they carry with them, have fundamentally altered the school board-teacher and teacher-student relationships.

The Bakke *Decision: Mixed Signals from the Court*

William R. Hazard, a teacher, school administrator, and lawyer, has been a professor in and the associate dean of the School of Education at Northwestern University in Evanston, Illinois. He is the author of *Education and the Law: Cases and Materials on Public Schools* (Free Press, 1978).

The following selection represents one of Hazard's important contributions to the understanding of American constitutional law as it relates to the conduct of schooling in the United States. In "The *Bakke* Decision: Mixed Signals from the Court," *Phi Delta Kappan* (September 1978), Hazard looks at the issues of equity and due process raised in the case of *Regents of the University of California v. Allan Bakke* (1978). The case, in which Bakke sued the University of California, Davis, because he was denied admission to its medical school even though he had ranked higher than some minority applicants who were admitted, achieved national attention and concern. The case involved a test of affirmative action policies to guarantee equal treatment of persons seeking either employment or admission to educational programs, based on legislation passed by Congress in 1974 in its efforts to enforce the Civil Rights Act of 1964. Many persons in the United States at the time viewed this case as a constitutional test of affirmative action programs. The United States Supreme Court ruled that Bakke had been wrongfully denied admission to medical school, but it *also* ruled that affirmative action programming is both constitutional and necessary to ameliorate past circumstances of discrimination against cultural minorities and women. The Court then detailed what constitutes a just, equitable affirmative action program and gave its reasons why some types of affirmative action programs are unconstitutional while others are not.

Key Concept: special admissions programs and affirmative action

*T*he long-awaited decision in the *Bakke* case was announced by the U.S. Supreme Court on June 28.[1] In a sharply divided Court, Justice Lewis F. Powell, speaking for two majorities, affirmed the opinion of the California Supreme Court insofar as it ordered Allan Bakke's admission to the University of California Medical School at Davis and invalidated the special admissions program,[2] but reversed the state court insofar as it barred the Medical School's consideration of race as a factor in future admissions decisions. Justices William J. Brennan, Byron R. White, Thurgood Marshall, and Harry A. Blackmun joined in the opinion to the extent that it permits the use of race as a factor in admissions to the Medical School; Justices John Paul Stevens, Potter Stewart, William H. Rehnquist, and Chief Justice Warren E. Burger joined to the extent that the special admissions program was invalidated and ordered Bakke's admission to the Medical School. Thus Justice Powell, in a key swing-vote role, led the evenly divided Court on the three fundamental questions presented in this case:

1. Is the special admissions program at Davis Medical School constitutionally adequate? (No, it is not and is therefore invalidated.)
2. Was Bakke wrongfully denied admission to the Medical School? (Yes, he was.)
3. May race be considered in admissions decisions? (Yes, it may.)

The public attention surrounding the *Bakke* case since its inception in 1974 makes a recounting of the basic facts useful. Briefly, the case arose after Allan Bakke, twice denied admission to the Davis Medical School (1973 and 1974), sued the regents of the University of California in the state court, challenging the special program of the Medical School that is designed to assure the admission of students from certain minority groups. Under this program, 16 of the 100 first-year "slots" in the Medical School were reserved for applicant members of a "minority group" (blacks, Chicanos, Asians, American Indians). Special admissions applicants, rated for admission by a separate committee, a majority of whom were members of minority groups, were not ranked against the candidates in the general admissions process. These special admissions applicants, after rating, were reviewed by the general admissions committee (which could reject special candidates for failure to meet course requirements or other specific deficiencies) until 16 selections had been made. Bakke, a white male, was rejected under the general admissions process in both 1973 and 1974. In both years, special applicants were admitted with significantly lower rating scores than his.

Bakke's suit, filed in the Superior Court of California, alleged that the special admissions program denied him admission on the basis of his race in violation of the equal protection clause of the Fourteenth Amendment; Article 1, Section 21 of the California Constitution; and Section 601 of Title VI, Civil Rights Act of 1964, which title provides, essentially, that no person shall on the ground of race or color be excluded from participating in federally supported programs. He thus raised the unfortunately labeled "reverse discrimination" issue. The trial court, finding that the special admissions program operated as a racial quota, declared that the Medical School could not consider race in making admissions decisions and that the special program violated the federal and state constitutions and Title VI. The trial court did not order Bakke's admission, however, for lack of proof that, except for the special program, he would have been admitted to the Medical School. Bakke appealed that portion of the court's decision denying him admission, and the regents appealed both the portion invalidating the special admissions program and the order enjoining the university from considering race in the application process.

The Supreme Court of California, taking the case directly from the trial court, held that Bakke, in fact, was barred from the special admissions program because of his race and that the program rationale, as advanced by the Medical School, was insufficient to justify the racial classification central to the program. Without passing on the state constitutional or Title VI issues raised in the trial court, the California Supreme Court held that the equal protection clause of the Fourteenth Amendment requires that "no applicant may be rejected because of his race, in favor of another who is less qualified, as measured by standards applied without regard to race."[3] As to Bakke's appeal, the court held that, inasmuch as he had established that the university had discriminated against him on the basis of his race, the burden of proof thereupon shifted to the university to demonstrate that, even without the special admissions program, Bakke would not have been admitted. The university conceded its inability to carry that burden, and the state court thereupon amended its opinion to direct the trial court to order Bakke's admission to the Medical School.[4] The sharply divided, two-pronged decision of the U.S. Supreme Court in part reflects the passions and the strongly held conflicting views aroused by the *Bakke* case. A few words about the central issues may be instructive.

The nature and purpose of the Davis special admissions program reflect the commendable determination there, and undoubtedly at other colleges and universities across the country, to develop and promote affirmative action in expanding access to higher and professional education to heretofore excluded minority applicants. The minority applicants, rated on a number of factors, including academic record, science course grades, Medical College Admissions Test (MCAT) scores, letters of recommendation, extracurricular activities, and other biographical data, competed with non-minority applicants for the 84 "regular" admissions, but only with other minority applicants for the 16 "special" admissions. Bakke argued that his denial of consideration for one of the 16 "special" admissions was based solely on his race and thus violated his rights under the federal and state constitutions and Title VI of the Civil Rights Act of 1964. The High Court found that the special admissions program is a classification based on race and ethnic background. Such classifications are inherently suspect and, accordingly, require the most exacting judicial examination. The university urged the Court "to adopt for the first time a more restrictive view of the equal protection clause and hold that discrimination against members of the white 'majority' cannot be suspect if its purpose can be characterized as 'benign'."[5] In considering this interpretation, the Court argued that the criteria for membership in the "preferred" minorities are based on the shifting sands of political compromise and delineation of the threshold deserving such preferential judicial treatment is not the role of the judiciary. The minority view of the Court agreed that racial classifications called for strict judicial scrutiny but, in this instance, the university purpose of overcoming substantial, chronic minority underrepresentation in the medical profession was important enough to justify its remedial use of race in the special admissions program.

The Court distinguished Bakke's treatment from the preferential treatment approved in the areas of school desegregation, employment discrimination, and sex discrimination and, in this examination, concluded that the special admissions program denied an individual (Bakke) opportunities or benefits enjoyed by others solely because of his race, and thus it must be regarded as suspect. In reaching this conclusion, the Court noted:

> [T]he purpose of helping certain groups whom the faculty of the Davis Medical School perceived as victims of "societal discrimination" does not justify a classification that imposes disadvantages upon persons like [Bakke], who bear no responsibility for whatever harm the beneficiaries of the special admissions program are thought to have suffered. To hold otherwise would be to convert a remedy heretofore reserved for violations of legal rights into a privilege that all institutions throughout the nation could grant at their pleasure to whatever groups are perceived as victims of societal discrimination. That is a step we have never approved.

The Court examined sympathetically the university's claim of the desirability of, and need for, a heterogeneous student body, but concluded that the special admissions program, as conceived and operated at the Medical School, was not the only effective means to achieve this. Justice Powell's opinion discussed Harvard University's admissions program in some detail, noting that it treats each applicant as an individual and recognizes, on its face, each applicant's right to individualized consideration without regard to race. In summarizing the constitutional flaw in the Davis special admissions program, Justice Powell noted:

> It tells applicants who are not Negro, Asian, or Chicano that they are totally excluded from a specific percentage of the seats in an entering class. No matter how strong their qualifications, quantitative and extracurricular, including their own potential for contribution to educational diversity, they are never afforded the chance to compete with applicants from the preferred groups for the special admission seats. At the same time, the preferred applicants have the opportunity to compete for every seat in the class. The fatal flaw in [the Davis] preferential program is its disregard of individual rights as guaranteed by the Fourteenth Amendment.

The state of California, by choosing to apportion medical school admission on the basis of race, was thereupon obligated to demonstrate that the challenged classification was necessary to promote a substantial state interest. The university's failure to defend its selection process successfully resulted in the invalidation of its special admissions program. In enjoining the university from ever considering the race of any applicant in the admissions process, the California Supreme Court failed to recognize that the state has a substantial interest that may be served legitimately by appropriate consideration of race or national origin in admissions decisions. For this reason, a different majority of the Court reversed that part of the state court decision barring any race-conscious admissions programs in the future.

In the view of the minority opinion (that of Justices Brennan, White, Marshall, and Blackmun), Title VI bars only those uses of racial criteria that would violate the Fourteenth Amendment if used by a state or its agencies, but it does not bar preferential treatment of minorities to remedy past societal discrimination. The dissent proposed a two-pronged test to determine if racial classifications can be sustained or not. First, an important purpose must be shown, and, second, there must be no stigma cast on those bearing the brunt of the classification. After reviewing at length the legislative history of Title VI and recent decisions (*Lau* v. *Nichols*,[6] *Washington* v. *Davis*,[7] and others), the dissent concluded that the Davis Medical School's purpose of remedying the effects of past societal discrimination is of such importance as to justify the use of race-conscious admissions programs where, as here, there is ample evidence of the pervasive nature of minority underrepresentation in and impeded access to medical education. As to the special admissions program, according to the dissent, "There is no question that Davis's program is valid. . . ."

In the opinion of Justice Stevens (joined by Chief Justice Burger and Justices Stewart and Rehnquist), the question of whether race can ever be an issue in an admissions decision is not an issue in the case, and discussion of the issue is inappropriate. In their view, Title VI is the controlling point on which the judgment should turn, and the special admissions program violated Title VI by excluding Bakke from the Medical School because of his race.[8] In a limiting opinion, Justice Stevens concluded: "I concur in the Court's judgment insofar as it affirms the judgment of the Supreme Court of California. To the extent that it purports to do anything else, I respectfully dissent."

Justices White, Marshall, and Blackmun filed separate opinions.

Thus, in an unusual dual-majority opinion, the Court answered, though it hardly settled, the question raised by the rejection of Allan Bakke's application to the Davis Medical School. The special admissions program at Davis, designed to recruit 16 first-year students from four named minority groups, was declared invalid for its violation of the individual rights secured by the equal protection clause. Allan Bakke was ordered admitted to the freshman class at the Davis Medical School, and the door was left open to design and employ race-conscious programs of admission that properly consider individual rights protected by the Fourteenth Amendment.

What does the *Bakke* decision mean? What consequences follow from this obviously difficult and troublesome opinion? Does the opinion of the Court signal a retreat from the national commitment to social justice, equality of educational opportunity, and the majestic judicial resolve to remedy the ache of generations of racial discrimination? Given the emotional baggage loaded onto the issues in *Bakke*, initial reactions to the decision ran the gamut from sighs of relief to cries of moral outrage. One early commentator feared that the Court, by legitimizing the concept of "reverse discrimination," has "lent the weight of its moral authority to retrenchment rather than progress."[9] Others took the more cautious view that it's far too early to predict the decision's impact on affirmative action, minority educational access, and the like.[10]

Clearly, the split decision reflects both the terrible agony and the Solomonic judgments faced by the Supreme Court, and indeed the nation, in this matter. The significant gains in employment, access to educational opportunity, housing, and human spirit of the past two decades should not be jeopardized, at any level, by misreading or misapplying what the Court has decided in *Bakke.* Perhaps it is just as important to reflect on what the *Bakke* opinion does *not* say as on what it does say.

First, the High Court did not reach a definitive conclusion as to the individual's right of action under Title VI. On this point the Court stated:

> The question of respondent's right to bring an action under Title VI was neither argued nor decided in either of the courts below. . . . We therefore do not address this difficult issue . . . *we assume only for the purpose of this case that [Bakke] has a right of action under Title VI.* (Emphasis added)

This decision appears to set no standard for other cases involving the individual's right of action under alleged violations of Title VI. To conclude that *Bakke* confers such rights on individuals in future cases would seem to go beyond the clear statement of the Court.

The Supreme Court did not invalidate affirmative action programs in general or minority admissions programs in particular. By this opinion, the Court explicitly affirmed the notion that the university's efforts to achieve an ethnically diverse student body, and thus obtain the educational benefits that flow from such diversity, were proper and acceptable. Further, the Court recognized that the state (though not a medical school faculty) has a legitimate and substantial interest in dealing with the "disabling effects of identified discrimination." These two important reaffirmations, in conjunction with the Court's clear support for race-conscious remedies, leave the door fully open for affirmative action programs and, specifically, minority admissions programs. To argue that the Court's rejection of the Davis quota program for minority admissions is a breach of moral faith by the Court is patent nonsense. Those who argue that to remedy "societal discrimination" one may properly impose substantial burdens on otherwise innocent others may overlook the fact that the major civil rights cases of the past two decades have attempted to redress intolerable burdens so created. It makes no sense to claim that a nonminority victim should feel a lighter burden from such deprivation than does a minority victim. As the Court clearly stated, race can be considered properly in admissions decisions but not in disregard of constitutionally protected individual rights.

The interests of various organizations and groups supporting wider minority access to and participation in the mainstream of American economics, schooling, and other perpetually competitive benefits clearly are not served by the *Bakke* decision. Understandably, there is grave concern about this decision and the impact it may have on employment, schooling, career opportunities, and a range of critical societal benefits. Such concern should be tempered by the fact that this Court does not diminish the capacity of the Davis Medical

School or any other institution to open wider the door for qualified minority applicants. The Court discussed at length the design of an admissions program that will promote educational diversity; the elements and nature of an effective and constitutionally acceptable program are laid out with some degree of clarity. What the Court proscribes is an admissions program that discriminates on racial bases. If the state or state-supported institutions are committed to those programs, practices, and procedures that, to varying extents, remedy past racial, ethnic, economic, or gender discriminations, they will be limited more by their lack of imagination than by the *Bakke* decision. To hold that racial discrimination against purported "majority" group members (whoever they are, and membership seems to be increasingly elusive) is not permitted under the Constitution hardly should be viewed as an outrageous conclusion. The Court, in short, struck down the particular special admissions program before it, but it explicitly left the door open for universities and other institutions to establish race-conscious admissions programs in the future.

The immediate impact of *Bakke* is difficult to predict. It seems highly improbable that the Court will retreat from *Brown, Swann, Lau,* and the other monumental civil rights cases of the past quarter century. There is little evidence that our nation would tolerate turning back the clock to *Plessy* v. *Ferguson* and its despicable social progenies. Surely, that defect in the American social fabric has been removed for all time. The Court's invalidation of the remedy expressed in the Davis special admissions program does not, on its face, foreclose other constitutionally acceptable race-conscious remedies.

Undoubtedly the *Bakke* decision will stimulate widespread challenges to affirmative action programs of all kinds, including minority recruitment, preferential hiring practices, and admission to highly competitive educational programs. Given the likelihood of such challenges, it seems prudent for universities, particularly, to review carefully their minority admissions programs in light of the Court's rejection of "quota" or quota-comparable approaches. For the majority of academic programs, the reality of a buyers' market will likely influence colleges and universities to encourage minority admissions through flexible policies and variable inducements. I don't want to be unduly cynical, but it is true that institutional admissions policies tend to become remarkably flexible in the face of empty lecture halls.

In distinguishing *Bakke* from *Lau* v. *Nichols* and *United Jewish Organizations* v. *Carey* (wherein the Supreme Court approved racial classifications without strict scrutiny), the Court noted that in *Bakke* there has been no determination of discriminatory practice by the legislature or a responsible administrative agency to support the race-conscious remedy; this fact, in part, supported the Court's conclusion that a race-conscious remedy must fail under strict scrutiny. The minority opinion challenges the logic of the apparent need for judicial or legislative determination of past racial discrimination as a prerequisite to a race-conscious remedy:[11]

> Because the regents can exercise plenary legislative and administrative power, it elevates form over substance to insist that Davis could not use race-conscious

remedial programs until it had been adjudged in violation of the Constitution or an antidiscrimination statute. For if the equal protection clause required such a violation as a predicate, the regents could simply have promulgated a regulation prohibiting disparate treatment, not justified by the need to admit only qualified students, and could have declared Davis to have been in violation of such a regulation on the basis of the exclusionary effect of the admissions policy applied during the first two years of its operation.

This issue, admittedly minor in the opinion, is troublesome nonetheless. One may wonder if the outcome might have been different if the regents (presumably a "legislative" body in this instance) had preceded their approval of the Davis admissions program by a finding of past racial discrimination in Medical School admissions.

The signals from the two majority opinions are, indeed, mixed. It will take considerable time and explanatory cases to reveal the full impact of *Bakke* on higher education admission policies and other race-conscious affirmative action programs. One indication of the future for affirmative action probably will come in the Court's handling of pending appeals on existing affirmative action programs in a wide range of industries. The Court's recent refusal to reconsider the AT&T consent agreement may signal that *Bakke* is, indeed, a narrowly confined ruling.

This appears to be a time, not for cries of alarm, but for recommitment to social justice in all aspects of our universities and our communities.

NOTES

1. *Regents of the University of California, Petitioner* v. *Allan Bakke.* (See *U.S. Law Week*, vol. 46, June 27, 1978, p. 4896.)
2. 18 Cal. 3d 34, 553 P. 2d 1152 (1976).
3. Ibid. 55, 553 P. 2d, p. 1166.
4. 18 Cal. 3d., p. 64, 553 P. 2d, p. 1172.
5. *U.S. Law Week*, vol. 46, June 27, 1978, p. 4903.
6. 414 U.S. 563 (1974).
7. 426 U.S. 229 (1976).
8. The language of Section 601 states, "No person in the United States shall, on the ground of race, color, or national origin, be excluded from participation in, be denied the benefits of, or be subjected to discrimination under any program or activity receiving federal financial assistance."
9. See, for example, Ralph Smith, "To Millions of Americans, the Bottom Line Is Bakke Won," *Chicago Sun-Times*, July 2, 1978, Section 2, p. 1.
10. As representative of this more cautious, wait-and-see view of *Bakke*, see Philip Kurland, *Chicago Sun-Times*, July 2, 1978, Section 2, pp. 1, 2.
11. *U.S. Law Week*, vol. 46, June 27, 1978, pp. 4921, 4922.
12. Ibid., n. 42.

A Better Chance to Learn: Bilingual-Bicultural Education

In May 1975 the United States Commission on Civil Rights issued a thoroughly documented, in-depth statement on the history of the education of language minority students in the United States and on how the struggle of language minority students to achieve equality of educational opportunity is linked to the broader struggle for equality in the field of education. The commission specifically discussed the direct relationship between the United States Supreme Court decision in *Brown v. Board of Education of Topeka, Kansas* (1954) and various federal court decisions involving the educational rights of limited English proficiency (LEP) students. The commission's document was distributed to all public school districts that had or were putting into place either bilingual educational programs or English as a Second Language programs for language minority children. This document, which is excerpted in the following selection, clarifies how the Supreme Court decision in *Lau v. Nichols* (1975) is based on Fourteenth Amendment "equal protection of the laws" precedents, which had led the Court to declare in *Brown* that segregated schools are "inherently unequal." The historical precedents for bilingual educational programs in the United States are also reviewed in the document.

Key Concept: bilingual education

INTRODUCTION

No public institution has a greater or more direct impact on future opportunity than the school. Between the ages of 6 and 16, American children spend much of their time in school. Early educational success or failure dictates to a large extent a student's expectations for the future, including whether he or she will seek postsecondary education and thus have a wide range of economic options available following formal schooling. The importance of an equal opportunity to public education was underscored in the case of *Brown* v. *Board of Education* and was followed in the 1960's by civil rights activity to end segregated schools. Similarly, much of the effort to overcome discrimination against limited or non-English speaking persons in the 1970's has been focused on schools.

The term "language minority" is used in this report to refer to persons in the United States who speak a non-English native language and who belong to an identifiable minority group of generally low socioeconomic status. Such language minority groups—including Mexican Americans, Puerto Ricans, Native Americans, and Asian Americans—have been subject to discrimination and limited opportunity. The emphasis given attainment of an education places them at a further disadvantage, since the public school does not appear to have met the needs of language minority groups.

Not only have many language minority children been subject to segregated education, low teacher expectations, cultural incompatibility with dominant culture-oriented curricula, and the educational neglect experienced by minority children in general, many also face a unique and equally severe form of discrimination which results from lack of proficiency in the language of instruction. In January 1974, the Supreme Court affirmed in *Lau* v. *Nichols* that school districts are compelled under Title VI of the Civil Rights Act of 1964 to provide children who speak little or no English with special language programs which will give them an equal opportunity to an education. The form such assistance should take is the subject of debate among educators, concerned language minority parents, and others.

There is little disagreement that learning English is essential to economic and social mobility in this monolingual English speaking society. The main controversy surrounds the issue of how language minority children can be taught English in a manner so that they do not fall so far behind in subject matter instruction that they cannot recover. Questions also have been raised concerning what methods are best for teaching English to language minority students; whether the learning of English alone will equalize educational opportunity and what role, if any, should be played by the native language and culture in the educational process.

Bilingual bicultural education is instruction using the native language and culture as a basis for learning subjects until second language skills have been developed sufficiently; it is the most widely discussed of approaches to providing language minority children with an equal educational opportunity. On the one hand, it has been hailed as a sound educational approach that overcomes the incompatibility between language minority students and the monolingual English public school. On the other, it has been criticized as failing to provide language minority students with sufficient English skills and as fostering ethnic separateness.

In this report, the Commission examines the extent to which bilingual bicultural education is an effective educational approach for increasing the opportunity of language minority students. In undertaking this study, the Commission assessed the educational principles behind bilingual bicultural education but did not analyze findings from existing bilingual bicultural programs, since few reliable evaluation data are available.

Because of the Commission's civil rights jurisdiction, this report concentrates primarily on bilingual bicultural education as a means for overcoming a denial of equal educational opportunity. However, another valuable objective of bilingual bicultural education is the enrichment of the education of children of all socioeconomic levels and racial/ethnic groups through learning two languages and two cultures. . . .

THE NEED TODAY

Although the height of immigration has long since passed, a large proportion of Americans still have a native language that is other than English. According to the 1970 census, 33.2 million Americans, or roughly 16 percent of the population, speak a language other than English as a native tongue. Spanish, German, and Italian speakers are the most numerous, in that order. Spanish is the only one of the three which has experienced substantial growth in the number of speakers since 1940, largely owing to increased immigration from Latin America.

Although persons of Mexican origin are native to the Southwest, the number of Spanish speaking persons in this country has grown noticeably since 1920. In the 1920's two factors contributed to a major influx of Mexican immigrants: a socially disruptive revolution in Mexico and the agricultural development of the Southwest United States and the subsequent need for labor. Between 1920 and 1973, 1,480,887 or more than 60 percent of all Mexican immigrants came to the United States.

Similarly, since 1920, Puerto Ricans have migrated in greater numbers, stimulated by the crowded living and bad economic conditions of Puerto Rico and the need in urban areas for low-paid, unskilled workers. The Puerto Rican migration swelled from 7,000 in 1920 to 852,061 in 1970.

Between 1920 and 1973, 215,778 Central Americans and 487,925 South Americans immigrated to this country. By 1973, Spanish origin persons numbered 9,072,602 nationwide and constituted the second largest minority group in the United States at roughly 4.4 percent of the total American population.

Immigration continues to be a major source for increasing the size of American language minority communities. Asian groups, for example, have experienced rapid increases in size since restrictive legislation barring or limiting their entry was repealed. In the less than 10 years since 1965, when all immigration quotas were liberalized, 654,736 or more than one-third of all Asian immigrants since 1820 have entered the United States. In 1973 more Asians immigrated than any other group. Other language minority groups, including Italians, Greeks, French Canadians, and Portuguese, have been part of a steady stream of language minorities coming to this country.

The 1970 census estimates that 31 percent of the 760,572 Native Americans counted speak a Native American tongue as their first language. Unlike the other groups, the survival of Native American languages is primarily the result of their continued use by existing groups and geographic isolation, rather than of replenishment through immigration.

Although precise data are not available on the numbers of limited or non-English speaking children currently in school, at the present time, the U.S. Office of Education estimates that at least 5 million need special language programs. The Census Bureau reports that 4.5 million Spanish speaking children under 20 years of age speak Spanish at home. An estimated 259,830 Asian American children speak little or no English, and some 56,493 Native American children speak a Native American language as a first language.

Unlike earlier non-English speaking children in this country, these children face an increasingly technical, skills-oriented society. There has been a shift in jobs from manual labor to skilled occupations. Although there is no direct correlation between years of schooling and ability to perform many jobs, educational level has become one frequently employed means of differentiating job applicants from one another.

Educators have known for many years that language minority children have difficulty succeeding in English monolingual schools. As early as 1930 it was documented that, in Texas, overageness and dropout rates were higher for Mexican American children than for either black or white students, and that most Mexican American children never progressed beyond third grade. In addition, while approximately 95 percent of Anglo children were enrolled in schools, only 50 percent of Mexican American children were. The causes were considered at the time to include lack of English language knowledge, low socioeconomic status, and inaccurate measuring instruments.

Although some scattered attempts were made to improve the education of Mexican American children from 1920–1940, no large scale effort was undertaken to alter the effects of education on them. A number of questions were raised about the education of non-English speaking children, including whether children would suffer less language handicap in school if first instruction in reading were in their native language. In the 1940's one researcher called for action to be taken by the Texas Department of Education, teacher training institutions, and schools to better meet the needs of Spanish speaking students. In 1946, the First Regional Conference on the Education of Spanish-speaking People in the Southwest was held in Austin, Texas. Recommendations included an end to segregated schools for Spanish speaking children, improved teacher training, and more efficiency in teaching English.

That public education continued to neglect the needs of language minority students for another 20 years is evident in the fact that recommendations of the 1964 Orange County Conference on the Education of Spanish Speaking Children and Youth were almost identical to those developed 18 years before. Nearly three decades after the First Regional Conference on the Education of Spanish-speaking People compiled information on the difficulties experienced by Mexican American students, the U.S. Commission on Civil Rights conducted a five-year Mexican American education study. It revealed that problems of segregation, teacher training, and language difficulty are still severe for Mexican American students in the five Southwestern States. In addition, the Commission's State Advisory Committees have examined the problems of Puerto Ricans, Native Americans, and Asian Americans. All of these studies document the continuing failure of public schools to provide language minority children with a meaningful education.

Compared with the median number of 12.0 school years completed for whites, the median is 8.1 for Mexican Americans, 8.6 for Puerto Ricans, 9.8 for Native Americans, and 12.4 for Asian Americans. The Commission's Mexican American Education Study shows that 40 percent of Mexican Americans who enter first grade never complete high school. As of 1972, the drop out rate for Puerto Ricans in New York City from 10th grade to graduation was 57 percent. In New England, 25 percent of the Spanish speaking student population had been retained in grade for at least 3 years; 50 percent, for at least 2 years. Only 12 percent were found to be in the correct grade for their age group. The dropout rate for Native Americans in the Southwest between grades 9 and 12 is 30.6 percent. For Navajos, the largest Native American tribe, the median educational level achieved is fifth grade.

Academic achievement scores recorded for language minority groups in the 1966 Coleman report show that they lag significantly behind majority group Americans. By the 12th grade the Mexican American student is 4.1 years behind the national norm in math achievement; 3.5, in verbal ability; and 3.3, in reading. The Puerto Rican student is 4.8 years behind the national norm in math; 3.6, in verbal ability; and 3.2, in reading. The Asian American student is 0.9 years behind the norm in math; 1.6, in verbal ability; and 1.6, in reading. Studies indicate that the longer language minority students stay in school the further they fall behind their classmates in grade level achievements. On tests of general information—including humanities, social sciences, and natural sciences—the median 12th grade score is 43.3 for Mexican Americans, 41.7 for Puerto Ricans, 44.7 for Native Americans, and 49.0 for Asian Americans as compared to a median score of 52.2 for whites.

In the 1960's there was a growing recognition that language minority children needed some manner of special assistance if they were to have an opportunity to succeed in school. Where efforts were made to provide such assistance, they usually took the form of supplemental English language development, or what is commonly known as the English as a Second Language (ESL) approach. In 1968, the Bilingual Education Act provided funds to support a few bilingual programs, which were to use the children's native language and culture for instruction while they were learning English. Since 1971, Massachusetts, Texas, Illinois, and New Jersey have enacted mandatory bilingual education laws.

The first expression of Executive policy in the area of equal educational opportunity for language minority students came in 1970 when the Department of Health, Education, and Welfare (HEW) issued its May 25 memorandum, which required federally-funded school districts to provide assistance for language minority children. The memorandum indicated that failure to provide such assistance, where needed, would be considered a violation of Title VI of the Civil Rights Act of 1964.

In *Lau* v. *Nichols*, the Supreme Court affirmed that interpretation of Title VI's scope, stating:

> Under these state-imposed standards there is no equality of treatment merely by providing students with the same facilities, textbooks, teachers, and curriculum;

for students who do not understand English are effectively foreclosed from any meaningful education.

Basic English skills are at the very core of what these public schools teach. Imposition of a requirement that, before a child can effectively participate in the educational program, he must already have acquired those basic skills is to make a mockery of public education. We know that those who do not understand English are certain to find their classroom experiences wholly incomprehensible and in no way meaningful.

. . . It seems obvious that the Chinese-speaking minority receives less benefits than the English-speaking majority from respondents' school system which denies them a meaningful opportunity to participate in the educational program. . . .

Both HEW and the Supreme Court declined to prescribe for school districts the type of assistance program which would provide language minority children with equal benefits in the attainment of an education, leaving the ultimate decision to the local districts themselves. Many school districts are faced with determining what constitutes that equality of educational opportunity. If we assume that the goal of public education is to provide basic skills and knowledge needed for participation in American society, then equal educational opportunity means that all students should have the same chance to acquire those skills and knowledge. In considering ESL and bilingual bicultural education—the two major approaches to meeting the needs of language minority children—it is important, therefore, to examine their overall potential for providing such an education.

CONCLUSION

The Commission's basic conclusion is that bilingual bicultural education is the program of instruction which currently offers the best vehicle for large numbers of language minority students who experience language difficulty in our schools.

Many language minority children, including Mexican Americans, Puerto Ricans, Native Americans, and Asian Americans, face two obstacles in attaining an education. Not only may they be the target of discrimination because they belong to identifiable minority groups, they also may not understand English well enough to keep up with their English speaking counterparts.

Under *Lau* v. *Nichols*, the Supreme Court has held that school districts receiving Federal funds cannot discriminate against children of limited or non-English speaking ability by denying them the language training they need for meaningful participation in the educational process. In this report, the Commission has examined whether the bilingual bicultural education approach is an effective means of providing that opportunity. Primary emphasis was placed on the educational principles which support the use of the native language in educating children, in nurturing positive self concept, and in developing proficiency in English. However, consideration was also given the effect on successful learning of the attitudes toward language minority groups in this country.

PART FIVE

Testing and Assessment of Learning

CHAPTER 12 Behaviorist Objectives

12.1 BENJAMIN S. BLOOM ET AL.

The Nature and Development of the Taxonomy

Benjamin S. Bloom (b. 1913) was a pioneer in the development of the categorization of educational objectives. During his long career at the University of Chicago, he conducted ongoing research on mastery learning with children and young adults. His work became the basis for behavioral objectives in instruction. Bloom has published a number of works on learning, including *Every Kid Can: Learning for Mastery* (College/University Press, 1973) and *Handbook on Formative and Summative Evaluation of Student Learning* (McGraw-Hill, 1971), coedited with J. Thomas Hastings and George F. Madaus. Bloom's work on mastery learning as well as his taxonomy of educational objectives in the cognitive domain have had enormous impact on the testing and measurement of school learning in the United States.

Bloom worked with a committee composed of members of the American Educational Research Association to produce *Taxonomy of Educational Objectives, Handbook I: Cognitive Domain* (David McKay, 1956). This became the conceptual basis for the development of behavioral objectives in American curriculum and instruction in the 1970s and 1980s. Although this taxonomy was first published in 1956, its use in the development of instructional objectives really did not begin to achieve widespread acceptance by American educators until the late 1960s. The following selection, which is from *Taxonomy of Educational Objectives, Handbook I,* introduces the reader to the overall structure of the taxonomy in the cognitive domain.

Key Concept: cognitive objectives of instruction and evaluation

THE TAXONOMY AS A CLASSIFICATION DEVICE

The major purpose in constructing a taxonomy of educational objectives is to facilitate communication. In our original consideration of the project we conceived of it as a method of improving the exchange of ideas and materials among test workers, as well as other persons concerned with educational research and curriculum development. For instance, the use of the taxonomy as an aid in developing a precise definition and classification of such vaguely defined terms as "thinking" and "problem solving" would enable a group of schools to discern the similarities and differences among the goals of their different instructional programs. They could compare and exchange tests and other evaluative devices intended to determine the effectiveness of these programs. They could, therefore, begin to understand more completely the relation between the learning experiences provided by these various programs and the changes which take place in their students.

Set at this level, the task of producing a taxonomy, that is, a classification of educational outcomes, is quite analogous to the development of a plan for classifying books in a library. Or, put more abstractly, it is like establishing symbols for designating classes of objects where the members of a class have something in common. In a library these symbols might be the words "fiction" and "nonfiction" and would apply to classes of books having something in common. If the problem is essentially one of finding new symbols for the classes, any set of symbols, numbers, nonsense syllables, or words could be used. Thus, we could have used the symbols "F" and "NF" for fiction and nonfiction. Further, since the symbols selected are not intended to convey that one class is of a higher order than another or that there is any particular relationship between the classes, they can be selected in very arbitrary fashion. The labels "fiction" and "nonfiction" do not imply that the one class of book is better, more abstract, or more complex than the other kind.

Of course, such a classification procedure cannot be a private fantasy since it is of value only if used by the workers who wish to communicate with each other. Thus, the classifications "fiction" and "nonfiction" are of value only if librarians use them. Acceptance of such classifications by potential users is likely to be facilitated if the class names are terms which are reasonably familiar to them and if these terms are given precise and usable definitions. Thus, one might expect more ready acceptance of a library classification scheme if he took such a term as "fiction," which is already in use, and defined it so that any competent librarian would easily be able to determine which books fit the classification.

In summary then, the major task in setting up any kind of taxonomy is that of selecting appropriate symbols, giving them precise and usable definitions, and securing the consensus of the group which is to use them. Similarly, developing a classification of educational objectives requires the selection of an appropriate list of symbols to represent all the major types of educational outcomes. Next, there is the task of defining these symbols with sufficient precision to permit and facilitate communication about these phenomena among teachers, administrators, curriculum workers, testers, educational research workers, and others who are likely to use the taxonomy. Finally, there is the task of trying the classification and securing the consensus of the educational workers who wish to use the taxonomy.

WHAT IS TO BE CLASSIFIED

Before one can build a classification scheme, it must be clear what it is that is to be classified. This is not much of a problem when one is classifying books. But descriptions of curricula are set up on such different bases as descriptions of teacher behavior, descriptions of instructional methods, and descriptions of intended pupil behaviors. As achievement testers and educational research workers, the major phenomena with which we are concerned are the changes produced in individuals as a result of educational experiences. Such changes may be represented by the global statements of the educational objectives of an educational unit, or they may be represented by the actual description of the student behaviors which are regarded as appropriate or relevant to the objectives. Objectives may also be inferred from the tasks, problems, and observations used to test or evaluate the presence of these behaviors.

We are of the opinion that although the objectives and test materials and techniques may be specified in an almost unlimited number of ways, the student behaviors involved in these objectives can be represented by a relatively small number of classes. Therefore, the taxonomy is designed to be a classification of the student behaviors which represent the intended outcomes of the educational process. It is assumed that essentially the same classes of behavior may be observed in the usual range of subject-matter content, at different levels of education (elementary, high school, college), and in different schools. Thus, a single set of classifications should be applicable in all these instances.

It should be noted that we are not attempting to classify the instructional methods used by teachers, the ways in which teachers relate themselves to students, or the different kinds of instructional materials they use. We are not attempting to classify the particular subject matter or content. What we are classifying is the *intended behavior* of students—the ways in which individuals are to act, think, or feel as the result of participating in some unit of instruction. (Only such of these intended behaviors as are related to mental acts or thinking are included in the part of the taxonomy developed in this Handbook.)

It is recognized that the *actual behaviors* of the students after they have completed the unit of instruction may differ in degree as well as in kind from the *intended behaviors* specified by the objectives. That is, the effects of instruction may be such that the students do not learn a given skill to the desired level of perfection; or, for that matter, they may not develop the intended skill to any degree. This is a matter of grading or evaluating the goodness of the performance. The emphasis in the Handbook is on obtaining evidence on the extent to which desired and intended behaviors have been learned by the student. It is outside the scope of the task we set ourselves to properly treat the matter of determining the appropriate value to be placed on the different degrees of achievement of the objectives of instruction.

It should also be noted that the intended behaviors specified by educational objectives do not include many of the behaviors which psychologists are interested in classifying and studying. One reason is that the intended behaviors represent the social goals imposed upon youngsters by their society or culture. Thus, the intended or desired behaviors included in educational objectives usually do not include undesirable or abnormal behaviors which are socially disapproved. Similarly, certain natural or unsocialized behaviors which might be of interest to psychologists may fall outside the categories of the taxonomy.

Our present studies of the affective area have indicated that the selective nature of intended behaviors will be even more apparent there than in the cognitive domain. The fact that we include objectives which specify social and emotional adjustment as a part of the affective domain points up this fact.

GUIDING PRINCIPLES

Since the determination of classes and their titles is in some ways arbitrary, there could be an almost infinite number of ways of dividing and naming the domains of educational outcomes. To guide us in our selection of a single classification system and to make the product more readily understood and used, we established certain guiding principles. First, since the taxonomy is to be used in regard to existing educational units and programs, we are of the opinion that the major distinctions between classes should reflect, in large part, the distinctions teachers make among student behaviors. These distinctions are revealed in the ways teachers state educational objectives. They are also found in their curricular plans, their instructional material, and their instructional methods. To the extent it was possible, the subdivisions of the taxonomy are intended to recognize these distinctions.

A second principle is that the taxonomy should be logically developed and internally consistent. Thus, each term should be defined and used in a consistent way throughout the taxonomy. In addition, each category should permit logical subdivisions which can be clearly defined and further subdivided to the extent that appears necessary and useful.

A third principle is that the taxonomy should be consistent with our present understanding of psychological phenomena. Those distinctions which are psychologically untenable, even though regularly made by teachers, would be avoided. Further, distinctions which seem psychologically important, even though not frequently made in educational objectives, would be favorably considered for inclusion. Perhaps it should be reiterated that, since the taxonomy deals only with educationally intended behavior, it falls considerably short of being a classification scheme for all psychological phenomena.

A fourth principle is that the classification should be a purely descriptive scheme in which every type of educational goal can be represented in a relatively neutral fashion. Thus, the Dewey decimal classification system for libraries describes all the classes of books. It does not indicate the value or quality of one class as compared with another, nor does it specify the number and kind of books any particular library should possess. Similarly, to avoid partiality to one view of education as opposed to another, we have attempted to make the taxonomy neutral by avoiding terms which implicitly convey value judgments and by making the taxonomy as inclusive as possible. This means that the kinds of behavioral changes emphasized by *any* institution, educational unit, or educational philosophy can be represented in the classification. Another way of saying this is that any objective which describes an intended behavior should be classifiable in this system. On the other hand, the taxonomy will probably include a greater variety of behaviors than those emphasized by any one school, course, or educational philosophy. Thus, one course might have objectives classifiable in four of the categories, another in only three of the categories, and so on.

In one sense, however, the taxonomy is not completely neutral. This stems from the already-noted fact that it is a classification of intended behaviors. It cannot be used to classify educational plans which are made in such a way that either the student behaviors cannot be specified or only a single (unanalyzed) term or phrase such as "understanding," or "desirable citizen," is used to describe the outcomes. Only those educational programs which can be specified in terms of intended student behaviors can be classified.

DEVELOPING THE TAXONOMY

Keeping in mind the aforementioned principles, we began work by gathering a large list of educational objectives from our own institutions and the literature. We determined which part of the objective stated the behavior intended and which stated the content or object of the behavior. We then attempted to find divisions or groups into which the behaviors could be placed. We initially limited ourselves to those objectives commonly referred to as knowledge, intellectual abilities, and intellectual skills. (This area, which we named the cognitive domain, may also be described as including the behaviors: remembering; reasoning; problem solving; concept formation; and, to a limited extent, creative thinking.) We proceeded to divide the cognitive objectives into subdivisions from the simplest behavior to the most complex. We then attempted to find ways of defining these subdivisions in such a way that all of us working with the material could communicate with each other about the specific objectives as well as the testing procedures to be included.

We have not succeeded in finding a method of classification which would permit complete and sharp distinctions among behaviors. . . . There are two basic views. First, we were again made aware of what any teacher knows—two boys may appear to be doing the same thing; but if we analyze the situation, we find they are not. For example, two students solve an algebra problem. One student may be solving it from memory, having had the identical problem in class previously. The other student has never met the problem before and must reason out the solution by applying general principles. We can only distinguish between their behaviors as we analyze the relation between the problem and each student's background of experience. This then introduces a new aspect of the classification problem, namely, the experiential backgrounds of the students to whom the objective is to apply. . . . [T]his may be a very important factor in using the taxonomy to classify test exercises.

A second difficulty in classification results from the fact that the more complex behaviors include the simpler behaviors. If we view statements of educational objectives as intended behaviors which the student shall display at the end of some period of education, we can then view the process of one of change. As teachers we intend the learning experiences to change the student's behavior from a simpler type to another more complex one which in some ways at least will include the first type.

One may take the Gestalt point of view that the complex behavior is more than the sum of the simpler behaviors, or one may view the complex behavior as being completely analyzable into simpler components. But either way, so long as the simpler behaviors may be viewed as components of the more complex behaviors, we can view the educational process as one of building on the simpler behavior. Thus, a particular behavior which is classified in one way at a given time may develop and become integrated with other behaviors to form a more complex behavior which is classified in a different way. In order to find a single place for each type of behavior, the taxonomy must be organized from simple to complex classes of behavior. Furthermore, for consistency in classification, a rule of procedure may be adopted such that a particular behavior is placed in the most complex class which is appropriate and relevant.

But, having specified that the classes shall be arranged from simple to complex, we have exceeded the simple classification scheme which called primarily for a series of categories without order or rank. The next section addresses itself to this problem.

THE PROBLEM OF A HIERARCHY—CLASSIFICATION VERSUS TAXONOMY

We have so far used the terms "classification" and "taxonomy" more or less interchangeably. It is necessary, however, that we examine the relationship between these terms because, strictly speaking, they are not interchangeable. Taxonomies, particularly Aristotelian taxonomies, have certain structural rules which exceed in complexity the rules of a classification system. While a classification scheme may have many arbitrary elements, a taxonomy scheme may not. A taxonomy must be so constructed that the order of the terms must correspond to some "real" order among the phenomena represented by the terms. A classification scheme may be validated by reference to the criteria of communicability, usefulness, and suggestiveness; while a taxonomy must be validated by demonstrating its consistency with the theoretical views in research findings of the field it attempts to order.

As educators and specialists in research, we are interested in a long-term inquiry into the nature of the phenomena with which we deal, and no simple set of terms and definitions by itself really is a satisfactory tool in making this inquiry. We need a method of ordering phenomena such that the method of ordering reveals significant relationships among the phenomena. This is the basic problem of a taxonomy—to order phenomena in ways which will reveal some of their essential properties as well as the interrelationships among them. Members of the taxonomy group spent considerable time in attempting to find a psychological theory which would provide a sound basis for ordering the categories of the taxonomy. We reviewed theories of personality and learning but were unable to find a single view which, in our opinion, accounted for the varieties of behaviors represented in the educational objectives we attempted to classify. We were reluctantly forced to agree with Hilgard[1] that each theory of learning accounts for some phenomena very well but is less adequate in accounting for others. What is needed is a larger synthetic theory of learning than at present seems to be available. We are of the opinion that our method of ordering educational outcomes will make it possible to define the range of phenomena for which such a theory must account. The taxonomy also uses an order consistent with research findings and it should provide some clues as to the nature of the theory which may be developed. This is an extremely complex problem; and although it has probably not been solved completely satisfactorily, it is the opinion of the writers that we have made some progress toward a solution.

As the taxonomy is now organized, it contains six major classes:

1.00 Knowledge
2.00 Comprehension
3.00 Application
4.00 Analysis
5.00 Synthesis
6.00 Evaluation

The classes of Bloom's taxonomy are defined in an appendix in the original source. The following are abbreviated definitions of the six classes:

1.00 Knowledge: *the recall of specifics and universals, the recall of methods and processes, or the recall of a pattern, structure, or setting.*

2.00 Comprehension: *the lowest level of understanding, in which the individual has a basic understanding or apprehension such that he or she knows what is being commu-*

nicated and can make use of the material or idea being communicated without necessarily relating it to other material or seeing its fullest implications.

3.00 Application: *the use of abstractions in particular and concrete situations; abstractions may be in the form of general ideas, rules of procedures, generalized methods, or technical principles, ideas, and theories that must be remembered and applied.*

4.00 Analysis: *the breakdown of a communication into its constituent elements or parts such that the relative hierarchy of ideas is made clear or the relations between the ideas expressed are made explicit.*

5.00 Synthesis: *the putting together of elements and parts so as to form a whole; this involves the process of working with pieces, parts, elements, etc., and arranging and combining them in such a way as to constitute a pattern or structure that was not clearly there before.*

6.00 Evaluation: *judgments about the value of material and methods for given purposes; quantitative and qualitative judgments about the extent to which material and methods satisfy criteria, which could be provided for the student or determined by the student; and the use of a standard of appraisal.*

Although it is possible to conceive of these major classes in several different arrangements, the present one appears to us to represent something of the hierarchical order of the different classes of objectives. As we have defined them, the objectives in one class are likely to make use of and be built on the behaviors found in the preceding classes in this list. . . .

Our attempt to arrange educational behaviors from simple to complex was based on the idea that a particular simple behavior may become integrated with other equally simple behaviors to form a more complex behavior. Thus our classifications may be said to be in the form where behaviors of type A form one class, behaviors of type AB form another class, while behaviors of type ABC form still another class. If this is the real order from simple to complex, it should be related to an order of difficulty such that problems requiring behavior A alone should be answered correctly more frequently than problems requiring AB. We have studied a large number of problems occurring in our comprehensive examinations and have found some evidence to support this hypothesis. Thus, problems requiring knowledge of specific facts are generally answered correctly more frequently than problems requiring a knowledge of the universals and abstractions in a field. Problems requiring knowledge of principles and concepts are correctly answered more frequently than problems requiring both knowledge of the principle and some ability to apply it in new situations. Problems requiring analysis and synthesis are more difficult than problems requiring comprehension. Scatter plots of the performances of individuals on one test composed of items at a simple level in the taxonomy against their performances on another test composed of items at a more complex level in the taxonomy show that it is more common to find that individuals have low scores on complex problems and high scores on the less complex problems than the reverse. Our evidence on this is not entirely satisfactory, but there is an unmistakable trend pointing toward a hierarchy of classes of behavior which is in accordance with our present tentative classification of these behaviors.

While we have been primarily concerned with the cognitive domain, we have done some thinking about the classification versus taxonomy problem as it applies to all the domains. The arrangement of behaviors from simple to complex and the differentiation of behaviors into three domains—the cognitive, the psychomotor, and the affective—were made primarily from an educational viewpoint. That is, these are the distinctions which teachers make in the development of curriculum and teaching procedures. We as educational testers also make similar distinctions. As we examine the classification system so far developed, however, we note an additional dimension not usually considered in educational and teaching procedures. One of the major threads running through all the taxonomy appears to be a scale of consciousness or awareness. Thus, the behaviors in the cognitive domain are largely characterized by a rather high degree of consciousness on the part of the individual exhibiting the behavior, while the behaviors in the affective domain are much more frequently exhibited with a low level of awareness on the part of the individual. Further, in the cognitive domain especially, it appears that as the behaviors become more complex, the individual is more aware of their existence. We are of the opinion that this applies to the other domains as well. Clearly there is no precise scale of consciousness which may be used to test these speculations. However, some of our research on the thought processes involved in problem solving[2] indicates that students are able to give more complete reports of their attack on a problem as the problem becomes more complex, that is, as the problem is classified in the more complex classes of intellectual abilities and skills.

If the level of consciousness can be demonstrated to be an important dimension in the classification of behavior, it would pose a great range of problems and point to a whole new set of relationships which would be of interest to researchers in the field of educational psychology. One might hope that it would provide a basis for explaining why behaviors which are initially displayed with a high level of consciousness become, after some time and repetition, automatic or are accompanied by a low level of consciousness. Perhaps this would provide a partial basis for explaining why some learning, especially of the affective behaviors, is so difficult. Perhaps it will also help to explain the extraordinary retention of some learning—especially of the psychomotor skills.

NOTES

1. Hilgard, E. R., *Theories of Learning* (Century Psychology Series), New York: Appleton-Century-Crofts, 1948.
2. Bloom, B. S., and Broder, Lois, *Problem-solving processes of college students* (A Supplementary Educational Monograph), Chicago: University of Chicago Press, Summer, 1950.

12.2 DAVID R. KRATHWOHL, BENJAMIN S. BLOOM, AND BERTRAM B. MASIA

Affective Domain

David R. Krathwohl, in collaboration with Benjamin S. Bloom and Bertram B. Masia, developed a classification scheme for educational objectives in the affective (emotional) domain. In the following selection from *Taxonomy of Educational Objectives, Handbook II: Affective Domain* (David McKay, 1964), which presents a section from the book's very important fourth chapter, Krathwohl, Bloom, and Masia discuss the relationship between the cognitive and the affective domains of human behavior and how these interrelationships impact on the task of preparing or evaluating affective behavior. The authors emphasize that the cognitive and affective domains are linked, not autonomous (independent) dimensions of behavior.

Krathwohl, currently a professor emeritus at Syracuse University in Syracuse, New York, was teaching at Michigan State University when *Taxonomy of Educational Objectives, Handbook II* was published. Bloom and Masia both held academic appointments at the University of Chicago at that time.

Key Concept: affective educational objectives

Internalization as It Appears in the Taxonomy Structure

The process of internalization can be described by summarizing the continuum at successive levels as they appear in the *Affective Domain Taxonomy*. The process begins when the attention of the student is captured by some phenomenon, characteristic, or value. As he pays attention to the phenomenon, characteristic, or value, he differentiates it from the others present in the perceptual field. With differentiation comes a seeking out of the phenomenon as he gradually attaches emotional significance to it and comes to value it. As the process unfolds he relates this phenomenon to other phenomena to which he responds that also have value. This responding is sufficiently frequent so that he comes to react regularly, almost automatically, to it and to other things like it. Finally the values are interrelated in a structure or view of the world, which he brings as a "set" to new problems.

Even from this abstract description it can be seen that the internalization process represents a continuous modification of behavior from the individual's being aware of a phenomenon to a pervasive outlook on life that influences all his actions.

While this description of the process seemed reasonably satisfactory, if a hierarchical structure was to be provided and more adequate description of the process developed, it was clear that the continuum needed to be divided into steps or stages. In so far as possible, when this was done, the breaking points between steps were located where there appeared to be some kind of transition, such as the addition of a new component or kind of activity. Since the boundaries of the categories are completely arbitrary and can be defended only on pragmatic grounds, it is possible that later work may suggest that other breaking points would be more satisfactory. The divisions between major categories have proved quite useful in the analysis of objectives. We feel more sure of the major divisions than of the subcategories, some of which appear to be easier to delineate than others.

The steps in the process and their description . . . are reviewed here to acquaint the reader with them and to show the parallel between the description of internalization which has been developed and the steps and levels into which it has been arbitrarily divided.

We begin with the individuals being aware of the stimuli which initiate the affective behavior and which form the context in which the affective behavior occurs. Thus, the lowest category is 1.0 *Receiving*. It is subdivided into three categories. At the 1.1 *Awareness* level, the individual merely has his attention attracted to the stimuli (e.g., he develops some consciousness of the use of shading to portray depth and lighting in a picture).[1] The second subcategory, 1.2 *Willingness to receive*, describes the state in which he has differentiated the stimuli from others and is willing to give it his attention (e.g., he develops a tolerance for bizarre uses of shading in modern art). At 1.3 *Controlled or selected attention* the student looks for the stimuli (e.g., he is on the alert for instances where shading has been used both to create a sense of three-dimensional depth and to indicate the lighting of the picture; or he looks for picturesque words in reading).

At the next level, 2.0 *Responding*, the individual is perceived as responding regularly to the affective stimuli. At the lowest level of responding, 2.1 *Acquiescence in responding*, he is merely complying with expectations (e.g., at the request of his teacher, he hangs reproductions of famous paintings in his dormitory room; he is obedient to traffic rules). At the next higher level, 2.2 *Willingness to respond*, he responds increasingly to an inner compulsion (e.g., voluntarily looks for instances of good art where shading, perspective, color, and design have been well used, or has an interest in social problems broader than those of the local community). At 2.3 *Satisfaction in response* he responds emotionally as well (e.g., works with clay, especially in making pottery for personal pleasure). Up to this point he has differentiated the affective stimuli; he has begun to seek them out and to attach emotional significance and value to them.

As the process unfolds, the next levels of 3.0 *Valuing* describe increasing internalization, as the person's behavior is sufficiently consistent that he comes to hold a value: 3.1 *Acceptance of a value* (e.g., continuing desire to develop the ability to write effectively and hold it more strongly), 3.2 *Preference for a value* (e.g., seeks out examples of good art for enjoyment of them to the level where he behaves so as to further this impression actively), and 3.3 *Commitment* (e.g., faith in the power of reason and the method of experimentation).

As the learner successively internalizes values he encounters situations for which more than one value is relevant. This necessitates organizing the values into a system, 4.0 *Organization*. And since a prerequisite to interrelating values is their conceptualization in a form which permits organization, this level is divided in two: 4.1 *Conceptualization of a value* (e.g., desires to evaluate works of art which are appreciated, or to find out and crystallize the basic assumptions which underlie codes of ethics) and 4.2 *Organization of a value system* (e.g., acceptance of the place of art in one's life as one of dominant value, or weighs alternative social policies and practices against the standards of public welfare).

Finally, the internalization and the organization processes reach a point where the individual responds very consistently to value-laden situations with an interrelated set of values, a structure, a view of the world. The *Taxonomy* category that describes this behavior is 5.0 *Characterization by a value or value complex*, and it includes the categories 5.1 *Generalized set* (e.g., views all problems in terms of their aesthetic aspects, or readiness to revise judgments and to change behavior in the light of evidence) and 5.2 *Characterization* (e.g., develops a consistent philosophy of life).

Stripped of their definitions, the category and subcategory titles appear in sequence as follows:

1.0 Receiving (attending)

    1.1 Awareness

    1.2 Willingness to receive

    1.3 Controlled or selected attention

2.0 Responding

    2.1 Acquiescence in responding

    2.2 Willingness to respond

    2.3 Satisfaction in response

3.0 Valuing

    3.1 Acceptance of a value

    3.2 Preference for a value

    3.3 Commitment (conviction)

4.0 Organization

    4.1 Conceptualization of a value

    4.2 Organization of a value system

5.0 Characterization by a value or value complex

    5.1 Generalized set

    5.2 Characterization

Relation of the Affective-Domain Structure to Common Affective Terms

. . . [T]he analysis of such commonly used terms as interest, attitude, appreciation, and value showed each of them to have a wide range of meanings. When we examined the range of meanings for any one term and compared this range to the *Taxonomy* structure we found that each term generally took on meanings over a section of the internalization continuum. Figure 1 illustrates this.

FIGURE 1 *The Range of Meaning Typical of Commonly Used Affective Terms Measured Against the Taxonomy Continuum*

David R. Krathwohl et al.

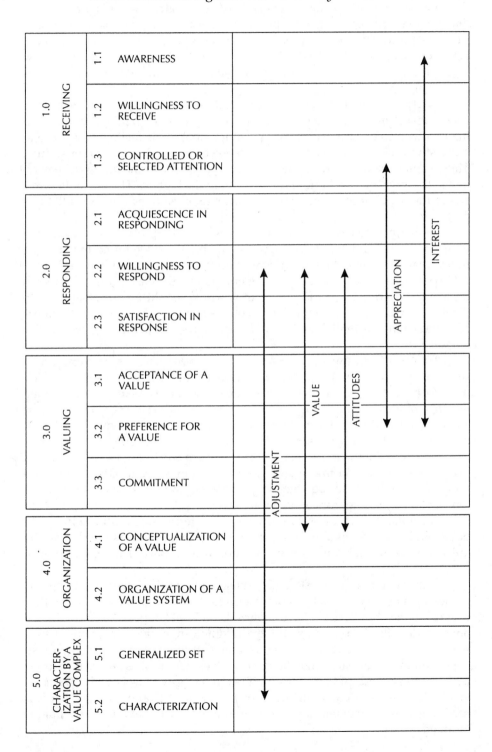

Thus, objectives were found where interpretation of the term "interest" ranged all the way from the student's being aware that a phenomenon exists to the behavior of avidly seeking a phenomenon. This is shown in Figure 1 by the line marked "Interest" extending from the *Taxonomy* category of 1.1 *Awareness* to 3.2 *Preference for a value.* Apparently the term "interest" typically describes behavior that would be classified at the lower levels of the *Taxonomy.* Rarely would it be interpreted as describing a behavior we would describe as *Commitment* or higher.

Interpretation of the term "appreciation" as it appears in objectives shows that it may refer to such simple behavior as the person's being willing to attend to certain aspects of a phenomenon, to his feeling a response to some stimulus, or to his showing a preference for certain behavior or stimuli. Thus, appreciation would not be interpreted typically as including the behaviors at the lowest levels of the *Taxonomy* nor at the highest. The line in Figure 1 shows the segment of the continuum which appears to include the bulk of its range of meanings.[2]

Similarly when we examined the range of interpretations given to the terms "attitude" and "value" in educational objectives, we found they ranged from situations where the student was expected to display a particular behavior, especially with a certain amount of emotion (enthusiasm, warmth, or even disgust, if appropriate), to situations in which he might go out of his way to display the value or to communicate to others about it. Thus the lines in Figure 1 for these terms extend from 2.2 *Willingness to respond* to 4.1 *Conceptualization of a value.*

The term "adjustment" appeared to take on a range of meanings, from a simple display of appropriate behavior in social interaction to the interrelation of one aspect of self to another—one's outlook on life. Thus, the line indicating its range of meanings extends from 2.2 *Willingness to respond* through 5.2 *Characterization.* It has the widest potential range of meanings of any of the terms, extending nearly across the entire range of taxonomic categories.

Several points with respect to this figure are worth noting. All the terms overlap one another in meaning in the middle range of the *Taxonomy* continuum. No specificity can be gained by replacing one term by another in this range, and possibilities for confusion are great.

A corollary of this observation is that no term (e.g., attitude) uniquely describes its entire segment of the continuum. Every term is overlapped by at least one other term for a major portion of that part of the continuum it describes.

Only the terms "interest" and "adjustment," at the lower and upper extremes, are not overlapped by another term for a portion of the continuum they include. In the objectives we have analyzed, "interest" appears to be used more often to describe behavior toward the middle range of the continuum than where it might be used with unique meaning, at the lowest extreme. "Adjustment," on the other hand, most frequently does refer in these objectives to the more complex kinds of behavior described in the upper levels of the *Taxonomy* to which it alone extends. In this respect, despite the range over which it is used, in its most frequent application it is intended to have a nearly unique meaning.

Finally, the figure indicates the increase in precision which it is hoped that the use of the affective continuum can achieve if its terms replace those in common use. For instance, the behavior involved in an "interest" objective could be given increased specificity if the objective were defined by placing it in one of the eight *Taxonomy* categories typically embraced by the term "interest." . . .

THE RELATION OF THE AFFECTIVE TO THE COGNITIVE DOMAIN

There has been much research on and logical analysis of the relation of cognitive to affective behavior, particularly the attainment of affective goals by cognitive means. We hope that the development of the *Affective Domain Taxonomy* will stimulate further research and thought on the relation between it and the cognitive domain. . . .

The Fundamental Unity of the Organism

The fact that we attempt to analyze the affective area separately from the cognitive is not intended to suggest that there is a fundamental separation. There is none. As Scheerer puts it, " . . . behavior may be conceptualized as being embedded in a cognitive-emotional-motivational matrix in which no true separation is possible. No matter how we slice behavior, the ingredients of motivation-emotion-cognition are present in one order or another" (Scheerer, 1954, p. 123). . . .

Thus James, a forerunner of modern psychology, admits a fundamental unity of affective and cognitive behavior but proceeds to a fragmenting analysis showing how one is involved in the other. That this kind of reasoning continues is indicated by Rokeach, a contemporary psychologist who, also realizing the unity, shows how the one domain is involved in the other. This is what we, too, have done in developing the *Taxonomy*. Our problem has been (recognizing the arbitrariness of our conceptualization) to gain a perspective of our task essential to the formulating of a useful framework.

The Arbitrariness of Classification Schemes

Every classification scheme is an abstraction which arbitrarily makes divisions among phenomena solely for the convenience of the user, more particularly to emphasize some special characteristic of the phenomena of importance to the user. Some of these divisions seem "natural," since they correspond to differences which are readily perceived in the phenomena categorized. In other instances, the differences may be much more difficult to perceive and thus seem more arbitrary. One may find both "natural" and quite arbitrary classifications within the same framework, depending upon the nature of the phenomenon to be classified and what is important to the person using the framework. To the biochemist, the dichotomy between the physical and the biological sciences is extremely arbitrary, and there is nothing "natural" about it, though this division may be highly useful and "natural" to the administrators of a large university.

The arbitrariness of the *Taxonomy* structure is at once apparent in, among other things,[3] its division of the realm of educational goals into three domains: cognitive, affective, and psychomotor. These seem to be "natural" divisions, since teachers and educators have more or less traditionally divided their objectives into these categories, either explicitly or implicitly. It is hoped that the divisions within each of the domains will also seem "natural," once the reader is familiar with them. We have tried to make the breaks between categories at what appeared to be the "natural" places without attempting to force a correspondence between domains. Whether this permits the most useful and meaningful analysis remains for the user to judge. . . . The increasing use of the *Taxonomy's* already published portion encourages us to believe that this kind of analysis has proved useful and meaningful and that this second portion may prove to be of worth as well.

With full recognition of the arbitrariness of the *Taxonomy's* division between cognitive and affective behavior, we may find it helpful to examine the way teachers' statements of objectives split cognitive from affective behavior, and then how the cognitive domain is related to the affective in terms of the particular categories used in this taxonomic analysis.

The Affective Component of Cognitive Objectives

The "garden variety" of objectives concentrates on specifying behavior in only one domain at a time. No doubt this results from the customarily analytic approaches to building curricula. Only occasionally do we find a statement like "The student should learn to analyze a good argument with pleasure." Such a statement suggests not only the cognitive behavior but also the affective aspect that accompanies it. In spite of the lack of explicit formulation, however, nearly all cognitive objectives have an affective component if we search for it. Most instructors hope that their students will develop a continuing interest in the subject matter taught. They hope that their students will have learned certain attitudes toward the phenomena dealt with or toward the way in which problems are approached. But they leave these goals unspecified. This means that many of the objectives which are classified in the cognitive domain have an implicit but unspecified affective component that could be concurrently classified in the affective domain. Where such an attitude or interest objective refers, as it most often does, to the content of the course as a whole or at least to a sizable segment of it, it may be most convenient to specify it as a separate objective. Many such affective objectives—the interest objective, for example—become the affective components of all or most of the cognitive objectives in the course. The affective domain is useful in emphasizing the fact that affective components exist and in analyzing their nature. Perhaps by its very existence it will encourage greater development of affective components of cognitive objectives.

It is possible that a different affective objective accompanies every cognitive objective in a course.[4] Were this a common situation, the present form of the *Taxonomy* would be unwieldy, for it would require a dual categorization of each objective. While the present state of the art of curriculum development suggests that the latter concern is by no means immediate, this is not a possibility to be discarded.

The relation of cognitive to affective objectives as conceived by teachers is mirrored in the relations of the taxonomies of the two domains. We turn next to this matter.

Relations Between the Taxonomy Categories of the Two Domains

When one looks for relations between the subcategories of the two domains one finds that they clearly overlap. This overlap is implicit in the following descriptions of roughly parallel steps in the two continua. The terms set in italic are used as heads of divisions in the *Taxonomy* of the cognitive or affective domains. Their category numbers are given in parentheses.

1. The cognitive continuum begins with the student's recall and recognition of *Knowledge* (1.0),

1. The affective continuum begins with the student's merely *Receiving* (1.0) stimuli and passively attending to it. It extends through his more actively attending to it,

2. it extends through his *Comprehension* (2.0) of the knowledge,

2. his *Responding* (2.0) to stimuli on request, willingly responding to these stimuli, and taking satisfaction in this responding,

3. his skill in *Application* (3.0) of the knowledge that he comprehends,

3. his *Valuing* (3.0) the phenomenon or activity so that he voluntarily responds and seeks out ways to respond,

4. his skill in *Analysis* (4.0) of situations involving this knowledge, his skill in *Synthesis* (5.0) of this knowledge into new organizations,

4. his *Conceptualization* (4.1) of each value responded to,

5. his skill in *Evaluation* (6.0) in that area of knowledge to judge the value of material and methods for given purposes.

5. his *Organization* (4.2) of these values into systems and finally organizing the value complex into a single whole, a *Characterization* (5.0) of the individual.

The most apparent places at which the affective domain meets the cognitive domain in this description are at steps 1, 4, and 5. Setting the two domains parallel, as we have done to facilitate the examination of the relationship, suggests a much closer level-to-level correspondence than actually exists, however. Let us examine this correspondence, taking steps 1, 4, and 5, and 2 and 3 in that order.

STEP 1.   The first point of close parallelism between the domains is at step 1, where "receiving" a phenomenon, or attending to it to some extent, corresponds to having "knowledge" of the phenomenon. But the emphasis in 1.0 *Receiving* is different from that in 1.0 *Knowledge* in that we are less concerned with memory and retrieval on demand. There is a relation, however, for certainly attending to a phenomenon is prerequisite to knowing about it. Further, only as one is willing to attend to a phenomenon will he learn about it.

On first glance, one might assume that "receiving" would always refer to awareness of certain information, and thus its parallel in the cognitive domain would always be the *Knowledge* category (e.g., the simple awareness of the way perspective is portrayed in a painting). While frequently true, this is not necessarily the case. Thus, *Receiving* includes the objective "Listens to music with some discrimination as to its mood and meaning and with some recognition of the contributions of various musical elements and instruments to the total effect." This certainly involves 2.0 *Comprehension*, the second category of the cognitive continuum, and probably 3.0 *Application* and 4.0 *Analysis*, the third and fourth levels of it. On looking over the objectives in the lowest levels of the affective domain, however, this is about as high a level in the cognitive continuum as one finds implied by the cognitive concomitants of these affective objectives.

But whatever the behavior specified in the lowest level in the affective domain, it is almost a certainty that one could interpret the objective so that, except for the fact that it is a building stone for more complex affective objectives, the objective might be restated so as to be classified in the cognitive domain. Some of our critics have argued that we should have begun the affective domain with 2.0 *Responding*, because of the heavily cognitive nature of this bottom category. But the fact that this behavior is a necessary first step to building objectives higher in the affective-domain hierarchy is the reason—an important one—for its being included as the bottom rung in the affective domain. Further, the emphasis in "receiving" is different from that of "knowledge," stressing, as is proper for an affective category, the volitional aspects of the knowing act.

STEPS 4 AND 5.   A second point of apparent close contact between the affective and cognitive domains is the correspondence in the upper levels of the two continua at steps 4 and 5. Here the behavior described by the affective domain is at least in part cognitive, as the student conceptualizes a value to which he has been responding, and this value is in turn integrated and organized into a system of values which comes eventually to characterize the individual. Such objectives would appear to require, at the very least, the ability to 2.0 *Comprehend*, for the student must translate his behavior into a set of verbal terms describing the value involved. In some instances this might call for the student to 4.0 *Analyze* the common value element from a series of activities or situations in which he has been involved and to 5.0 *Synthesize* this commonality into a value which encompasses all of them. The ability to organize and interrelate values into systems must certainly call for the ability to 4.0 *Analyze*, as it is described in the cognitive domain, and the development of new value complexes also most likely involves the ability to 5.0 *Synthesize*. Further, the ability to balance values against one another, which is implied by the very highest affective categories, implies capability for 6.0 *Evaluation* as it is defined in the cognitive domain. For example, "Judges problems and issues in terms of situations, issues, purposes, and consequences involved rather than in terms of fixed, dogmatic precepts or emotionally wishful thinking" (Part II, p. 184).

It is possible, however, that in everyday behavior much of this balancing of values is at a semiconscious intuitive level rather than at the rational, objective, conscious, level implied by 6.0 *Evaluation* in the cognitive domain. Such semiconscious behavior is described in the affective domain by category 5.1 *Generalized Set*, where the behavior is so internalized that it is displayed almost automatically, without conscious consideration. On the surface, this makes the affective domain appear to extend further than the cognitive in the sense that it describes a behavior so deeply internalized that it is automatic. No such behavior appears in the cognitive continuum.

But one could argue that some cognitive evaluation behavior ought also to be that well learned. Indeed, one may question whether such regularity of behavior is not implicit in most cognitive and affective objects at all *Taxonomy* levels. In general, in both the cognitive and affective domains the regularity of behavior is measured, not in terms of the *Taxonomy* level of behavior, but as such regularity affects the test score. Given a test which includes a variety of situations in which the observed behavior should be displayed if learned or internalized, the regularity with which it is displayed across these situations is reflected in the person's score. At the top level of the affective domain we happen to have specified a level of behavior which is so well learned, so deeply internalized, that it is automatic.

In this sense, at the 5.1 *Generalized Set* level we have described a kind of behavior which can be attained only with complete regularity, and the level of performance required in scoring is implicit in the behavior description. (This is the only category in the *Taxonomy* which so specifies the score performance for achievement of that level.) It was included because affective objectives were found which described this regularity of the behavior. Certain affective objectives have made explicit a complete regularity and automaticity of response which may also be implied in many cognitive objectives. Thus a discrepancy wherein the affective domain appears to extend beyond the cognitive domain can be reconciled on careful examination. The overlap between the two domains at this level appears to be real.

STEPS 2 AND 3. In the middle portions of the affective continuum the individual begins to respond to the stimuli, at first on request (2.1 *Acquiescence in responding*), then increasingly on his own volition to the point where he is actively seeking instances in which he may respond (3.3 *Commitment*). These are not unrelated to the cognitive domain, but the nature of the relation is much less easily specified. The range of cognitive behavior corresponding to this portion of the affective continuum appears to cover a wide portion of the cognitive domain. But in all the affective behavior the cognitive element is present and implied. For example, in the lowest level of this portion, in the subcategory 2.1 *Acquiescence in responding*, we find the objective "Willingness to comply with health regulations." This objective implies that at least there is comprehension of these regulations and the ability to apply them to new situations; both of these are cognitive behaviors. At the highest level of this middle range of the continuum, in the subcategory 3.3 *Commitment*, we find the objective "Devotion to those ideas and ideals which are the foundation of democracy." This objective in turn implies cognitive behaviors such as the ability to analyze situations in order to determine how the ideas and ideals apply in a given situation.

It can be noted that throughout this analysis of the five steps there is some tendency for the cognitive counterpart of a low-level objective to come from the lower levels of the affective continuum and for objectives at the upper level of the affective continuum to have upper-level cognitive counterparts.

From the analysis above it appears that at all levels of the affective domain, affective objectives have a cognitive component, and one can find affective components for cognitive objectives. But lest this relationship appear more obvious than it really is, it should be noted that the examples of objectives in the preceding discussion were chosen so as to make the relation clear. We could have chosen affective-domain objectives for which the cognitive component is much more obscure; for instance, "Enjoyment of worship" or "Responds emotionally to a work of art." While we could recognize a cognitive component in such objectives, we should clearly be less certain to secure agreement among educators about the most appropriate cognitive behavior to accompany the affective behavior. Though undoubtedly there is some cognitive component in every affective objective, its nature is much more easily seen in some instances than in others.

Other Relationships Between the Cognitive and Affective Domains . . .

Cognitive Objectives as Means to Affective Goals   The fact that our learning research and theories focus largely on cognitive behavior is an indication that we feel we know better how to handle the cognitive domain. Moving from the cognitive domain to the affective thus tends to be the preferred orientation. Attitudes, and even feelings, for example, tend to be defined in cognitive terms. James, in the quotation cited earlier in this chapter, defined feeling as a kind of knowing. Asch (1952) stated that an "attitude contains a more or less coherent ordering of data . . . an organization of experience and data with reference to an object" (p. 580). Rhine (1958) surveyed the definitions of attitudes by outstanding psychologists and concluded that the common element is the essence of what is generally meant by a concept. He therefore defined an attitude as a concept with an evaluative component and proceeded to explain attitude formation in the cognitive terms usually reserved for concept formation. As he pointed out, this approach could make attitudes more amenable to laboratory scrutiny, one indication of why this approach to the affective domain is preferred.

Rokeach, as already noted, saw a basic congruence between the cognitive and affective systems. He stated further, " . . . although our approach to belief systems, including esthetic ones, is a purely cognitive one . . . if the assumption is correct that every emotion has its cognitive counterpart, then we should be able to reach down into the complexities of man's emotional life via a study of his cognitive processes. . . . If we know something about the way a person relates himself to the world of ideas we may also be able to say in what way he relates himself to the world of people and to authority" (Rokeach, 1960, p. 8).

Similarly, Rosenberg (1956) examined attitudes in terms of cognitive structure. Noting the relations between cognitive and affective components, he argued that a tendency to respond to an object with positive or negative affect is "accompanied by a cognitive structure made up of beliefs about the potentialities of that object for attaining or blocking the realization of valued states" (p. 367). He further argued that both the direction of the affect—whether it is positive or negative with reference to the object—and the strength of the affect are correlated with the content of the associated cognitive structure. Here again we see the affective component made a function of cognitive components which are more easily dealt with, thus permitting manipulation of the affective by the cognitive.

Festinger (1957) and Heider (1958), among others, have propounded so-called "balance theories" which provide another approach to the study of affective changes as a result of cognitive behavior. Festinger, in his theory of cognitive dissonance, described the motivating effect of disharmonious or dissonant states in cognition. He defined cognition so broadly as to include affectively tinged states such as opinions and beliefs as well as cognitive states of knowledge. Thus his theory easily bridges the cognitive-affective distinction and cannot be seen as one which manipulates cognitive behavior (in its usual sense) alone. But Festinger did describe the effects of changes in knowledge on affective behavior, and this represents one kind of approach to affective behavior through cognition.

The careful observer of the classroom can see that the wise teacher as well as the psychological theorist uses cognitive behavior and the achievement of cognitive goals to attain affective goals. In many instances she does so more intuitively than consciously. In fact, a large part of what we call "good teaching" is the teachers' ability to attain affective objectives through challenging the students' fixed beliefs and getting them to discuss issues.

In some instances teachers use cognitive behavior not just as a means to affective behavior but as a kind of prerequisite. Thus appreciation objectives are often approached cognitively by having the student analyze a work of art so that he will come to understand the way in which certain effects are produced—the nuances of shading to produce depth, color to produce emotional tone, etc. Such analysis on a cognitive level, when mastered, may be seen as learning necessary for "truly" appreciating a work of art.

In other instances teachers use cognitive behavior and cognitive goals as a means to multiple affective ends. This occurs especially in areas where the problem of indoctrination arises. Cognitive behavior may be used to indoctrinate points of view and to build attitudes and values. Indeed, we do this shamelessly in the aesthetic fields, where we want our students to learn to recognize "good" poetry, painting, architecture, sculpture, music, and so on. But in most areas of the curriculum we have a horror of indoctrinating the student with any but our most basic core values (we cannot always agree on the nature of these core values, the court cases on religion in the schools are an example). In most instances where indoctrination is avoided, we seek to have the student take his own position with respect to the issue. Thus a discussion may result in the development of a variety of "correct" positions and attitudes with respect to the area of concern, rather than in a single type of behavioral outcome as when a cognitive objective has been achieved. This also occurs where there are conflicts in values within our own culture. For example, the problems of honesty vs. dishonesty vs. "white lies," or of competition vs. cooperation, usually result in a variety of acceptable solutions, each a function of the situation in which such a conflict arises.

There are some instances where the cognitive route to affective achievement has resulted in learning just the opposite of that intended. Thus the infamous example of the careful and detailed study of "good" English classics, which was intended to imbue us with a love of deathless prose, has in many instances alienated us from it instead. Emphasis on very high mastery of one domain may in some instances be gained at the expense of the other.

Similarly, . . . emphasis on one domain may tend to drive out the other. New courses often start with a careful analysis of both cognitive and affective objectives. But we feel more comfortable in teaching for cognitive than for affective objectives. Our drive for subject-matter mastery and the ever-increasing amount of knowledge available gives us more and more subject matter to cover. Further, our preference for approaching affective achievement through the attainment of cognitive objectives tends to focus attention on these cognitive goals as ends in themselves without our determining whether they are actually serving as means to an affective end. Over time the emphasis in most courses tends more and more to concentrate on the cognitive objectives at the expense of the affective ones. This erosion may be inevitable, but it could be lessened or stopped if we were conscious of its action. One of the major uses of *Handbook I: Cognitive Domain* has been to provide a basis for showing the current overwhelming emphasis on knowledge objectives at the expense of the development of skills and abilities in using that knowledge. Similarly, the development of *Handbook II: Affective Domain* should help to highlight the current emphasis on cognitive objectives at the expense of the affective.

Affective Objectives as Means to Cognitive Goals   From the previous discussion it seems clear that the cognitive approach to affective objectives is a frequently traveled route. What about the reverse? One of the main kinds of affective-domain objectives which are sought as means to cognitive ends is the development of interest or motivation. As viewed from the cognitive pole, the student may be treated as an analytic machine, a "computer" that solves problems. In contrast, viewed from the affective pole, we take greater cognizance of the motivation, drives, and emotions that are the factors bringing about achievement of cognitive behavior.

Obviously motivation is critical to learning and thus is one of the major ways in which the affective domain is used as a means to the cognitive. The large number of interest objectives indicates the importance of this aspect of the learning situation. The influence of hedonic tone on memory and learning is also important: children are more likely to learn and remember material for which they have a positive feeling. Note for instance the prevalence of girls who dislike mathematics and so cannot learn it, as well as boys who dislike school in general and do poorly. Though these "likes" may be produced by role expectancies, it is the internalized preferences which produce the effect.

Where educational objectives are involved we are almost always concerned with positive affect, with leading rather than driving the student into learning. But there are some school situations where negative affect is used to prevent certain behaviors from occurring and to facilitate cognitive learning. Such is the use of negative affect (fear of punishment, for instance) rather than the attempt to attain affective objectives as means to cognitive ends. In some instances social pressure may be exerted to change a student's position or viewpoint. We recognized that occasionally the school will have affective goals of this kind when we provided category 2.1 *Acquiescence in responding* but noted that this was a rarely used category.

Both the theoretical and experimental literature suggest that this is not an easy route to cognitive change. Both Kelman's (1958) model and Jahoda (1956) point to the likelihood that persons may outwardly comply under such situations but inwardly remain unchanged. Festinger's (1957) theory of cognitive dissonance posits that severe external threat or pressure represents a justification to the individual for engaging in behavior contrary to his beliefs, so that there is less need to reduce the dissonance caused by his engaging in this behavior under the threat conditions. Where the threat is mild, there is less justification for engaging in the behavior, and we can thus expect more change in private opinion to reduce the dissonance. Experimentation by Festinger and Carlsmith (1959) backs up this theoretical prediction. It appears that certain threatening school climates could actually defeat teachers' attempts to bring about both cognitive and affective learning.

But, as already noted, more often our motivation results from positive affect. Increasingly this is taking the form of building upon the method of self-discovery as a means of fostering interest in learning material. In thus enhancing curiosity and exploratory activity we may be building upon a basic drive. White (1959), giving careful consideration to previous literature on motivation and to recent experimentation on curiosity and the attractiveness of novel stimuli, posits a drive for competency, a need for a feeling of efficacy. He suggests that curiosity, exploratory behavior, manipulation, and general activity bring man in contact with his environment and make him more competent to deal with it. White's competency drive underlies these and similar activities. Few of us have recognized that with discovery-type objectives we may have been building on a basic drive.

Discovery-type material, such as that going into the University of Illinois School Mathematics Program, uses the affective effects of self-discovery as a means of simultaneously achieving the goals of mastery of the material and developing interest in it. This corresponds to what Bruner (1960) points to as an important goal in our new curricula. He suggests that we must increase "the inherent interest of the materials taught, giving the student a sense of discovery, translating what we say into thought forms appropriate to the child and so on. What this amounts to is developing in the child an interest in what he is learning and with it an appropriate set of attitudes and values about intellectual activities in general" (p. 73). This suggestion, that we build in a set of attitudes toward learning and the value of learning, represents another of the all-encompassing goals of most curricula. It is another common way in which attainment of the affective goal is a means to the facilitation of cognitive learning.

Simultaneous Achievement of Cognitive and Affective Goals   In some instances it is impossible to tell whether the affective goal is being used as a means to a cognitive goal or vice versa. It is a chicken and egg proposition. Perhaps it is fairest to say they are both being sought simultaneously. . . .

In some instances the joint seeking of affective and cognitive goals results in curricula which use one domain as the means to the other on a closely-knit alternating basis. Thus a cognitive skill is built and then used in rewarding situations so that affective interest in the task is built up to permit the next cognitive task to be achieved, and so on. Perhaps it is analogous to a man scaling a wall using two step ladders side by side, each with rungs too wide apart to be conveniently reached in a single step. One ladder represents the cognitive behaviors and objectives, the other the affective. The ladders are so constructed that the rungs of one ladder fall between the rungs of the other. The attainment of some complex goal is made possible by alternately climbing a rung on one ladder, which brings the next rung of the other ladder within reach. Thus alternating between affective and cognitive domains, one may seek a cognitive goal using the attainment of a cognitive goal to raise interest (an affective goal). This permits achievement of a higher cognitive goal, and so on. . . .

Summary

This really only scratches the surface of what is undoubtedly a very complex relationship between the cognitive and affective domains. We still have much to learn about it. But the fact should be clear that the two domains are tightly intertwined. Each affective behavior has a cognitive-behavior counterpart of some kind and vice versa. An objective in one domain has a counterpart in the opposite domain, though often we do not take cognizance of it. There is some correlation between the *Taxonomy* levels of an affective objective and its cognitive counterpart. Each domain is sometimes used as a means to the other, though the more common route is from the cognitive to the affective. Theory statements exist which permit us to express one in terms of the other and vice versa.

Our split between the affective and cognitive domains is for analytical purposes and is quite arbitrary. Hopefully the analysis of the two domains will have heuristic value so that we may better understand the nature of each as well as the relationship of one to the other.

NOTES

1. This same objective is successively modified to carry it through many of the levels of the continuum.

2. Appreciation is sometimes interpreted to mean that the student can describe that aspect of a phenomenon (e.g., a dance) that he appreciates. In this respect the line should extend to 4.1 *Conceptualization of a value.* Yet, rarely does an appreciation objective connote a commitment to a value.

David R. Krathwohl et al.

3. We could, for example, cite as arbitrary the insistence that educational goals are most meaningfully stated as student behaviors rather than teacher activities. But this aspect is less relevant to the chapter topic.

4. This is not to imply that the full range from 1.1 to 5.2 of affective behaviors would apply to every cognitive objective, however. This matter is explored further in the next section.

CHAPTER 13 The Critical Response to the Behaviorist Challenge

13.1 CLARENCE J. KARIER

Testing for Order and Control in the Corporate Liberal State

Clarence J. Karier, a distinguished historian of American education, has taught at the University of Rochester in New York and at the University of Illinois. Professor Karier was one of the early revisionist historians of education, and his work has contributed to the development of an ongoing critical response to the uses of behaviorist measurement techniques in American schools. His work also contributed to the critical pedagogical dialogue that Paulo Freire and several other critical and liberation pedagogical theorists developed in the early 1970s, both in the United States and around the world. Karier is a coeditor, with Paul C. Violas and Joel Spring, of *Roots of Crisis: American Education in the Twentieth Century* (Rand McNally, 1973).

Karier's article "Testing for Order and Control in the Corporate Liberal State," from which the following selection has been excerpted, was originally published in the Philosophy of Education Society's journal *Educational Theory* (Spring 1972). The essay developed out of the critical response to the uses of intelligence testing and national standardized achievement testing in the United States in the late 1960s and early 1970s.

The excerpt that follows deals with the history of psychological testing in the United States. Karier's discussion of the uses of psychological testing brought to light serious issues concerning the misuses of such testing in the past.

Key Concept: intelligence testing

BACKGROUND TO TESTING

Historians generally mark the beginning of the testing movement with the mass testing of 1.7 million men for classification in the armed forces during World War I. The roots of the American testing movement, however, are deeply imbedded in the American progressive temper, which combined a belief in progress, certain racial attitudes, and faith in the scientific expert working through state authority to ameliorate and control the evolutionary progress of the race.

A key leader of the eugenics movement in America was Charles Benedict Davenport who, having studied Galton and Pearson, sought to persuade the new Carnegie Institution of Washington to support a biological experiment station with himself as director. In 1904, he became director of such a station at Cold Spring Harbor on Long Island. As his interest in experiments in animal breeding began to wane, Davenport used his position as secretary of the Committee on Eugenics of the American Breeders Association to solicit aid for the study of human heredity. Supported by donations from Mrs. E. H. Harriman, Davenport founded the Eugenics Record Office in 1910. Eight years later the Carnegie Institution of Washington assumed control of it. The endeavors of the Record Office were facilitated by the work of various committees. The Committee on Inheritance of Mental Traits included among its members Robert M. Yerkes and Edward L. Thorndike. The Committee on Heredity of Deafmutism included Alexander Graham Bell. H. H. Laughlin was on the Committee on Sterilization, and the Committee on the Heredity of the Feeble Minded included, among others, Henry Herbert Goddard.

Race Betterment

These committees took the lead in identifying persons who carried defective germ-plasm and disseminating the propaganda that became necessary to pass sterilization laws. It was Laughlin's Committee to Study and Report on the Best Practical Means of Cutting off the Defective Germ-Plasm in the American Population, for example, that reported that "society must look upon germ-plasm as belonging to society and not solely to the individual who carries it."[1] Laughlin found that approximately 10 percent of the American population

288

Chapter 13
The Critical
Response to the
Behaviorist
Challenge

carried bad seed, and he wished to sterilize the group. He defined these people as "feebleminded, insane, criminalistic (including the delinquent and wayward), epileptic, inebriate, diseased, blind, deaf, deformed and dependent (including orphans, ne'er-do-wells, the homeless, tramps and paupers)."[2] Social character, from murder to prostitution, was associated with intelligence and the nature of one's germ-plasm. Indiana passed the first sterilization law in 1907, followed in quick succession by fifteen other states. In Wisconsin, such progressives as Edward A. Ross and Charles R. Van Hise, president of the University of Wisconsin, took strong public stands supporting sterilization laws. Fully twenty years ahead of other nations, America pioneered in the sterilization of mental and social defectives.

Between 1907 and 1928, twenty-one states practiced eugenic sterilization involving over 8,500 people. California under the influence of the Human Betterment Foundation, which counted Lewis M. Terman and David Starr Jordan as its leading members, accounted for 6,200 sterilizations. California's sterilization law was based on concepts of race purity as well as those having to do with criminology. Persons "morally and sexually depraved" could be sterilized. Throughout the sterilization movement in America ran a *Zeitgeist* reflecting the temper of pious reformers calling for clean living, temperance, and fresh-air schools as well as for sterilization. The use of sterilization for punishment reached the point where laws were introduced calling for sterilization for chicken stealing and car theft, as well as for prostitution.[3]

Henry Herbert Goddard, fresh from G. Stanley Hall's seminars at Clark University, translated the Binet-Simon scale in 1908 and used the test to identify feebleminded at the training school at Vineland, New Jersey. Various scales and tests freely used and patterned after the original scale were later proven to lack reliability to the extent that, according to some testers, upwards of half the population was feebleminded. From the Binet scale, Goddard went on to publish *The Kallikak Family*, which showed the family history of Martin Kallikak as having both a good and a bad side. The bad side, which began with Martin's involvement with a feebleminded girl, contributed such "social pests" as "paupers, criminals, prostitutes and drunkards." Goddard's next book *Feeble-mindedness: Its Causes and Consequences*, gave further "scientific" support to the notion that feeblemindedness and moral character were related.

Interestingly enough, the American liberal tradition from Jefferson on usually assumed a positive relationship between "talent and virtue." So it is not surprising to find people assuming that a person low in talent will also lack virtue, a relationship assumed in most sterilization laws. Society would rid itself of not only the genetic defective but, more importantly, the socially undesirable. Laughlin, Goddard, Terman, and Thorndike all made similar assumptions. Terman argued that the feebleminded were incapable of moral judgments and, therefore, could be viewed only as potential criminals. He said:

> All feebleminded are at least potential criminals. That every feebleminded woman is a potential prostitute would hardly be disputed by anyone. Moral judgements, like business judgement, social judgement or any other kind of higher thought process, is a function of intelligence.[4]

The same thinking that guided Terman to find a lower morality among people of lesser intelligence had its mirror image in the work of Edward L. Thorndike, who found a higher morality among those with greater intelligence. Thorndike was convinced that "To him that hath a superior intellect is given also on the average a superior character."[5] Both Thorndike and his pupils continued to advocate the sterilization solution to moral behavior problems and the improvement of intelligence. By 1940, in his last major work, he concluded that

> By selective breeding supported by a suitable environment we can have a world in which all men will equal the top ten per cent of present men. One sure service of the *able* and *good* is to beget and rear offspring. One sure service (about the only one) which the inferior and vicious can perform is to prevent their genes from survival.[6]

The association of inferiority with viciousness and intelligence with goodness continued to appear in the psychology textbooks. Henry E. Garrett, who was a former student and colleague of Thorndike and who won a "reputation for eminence,"[7] continued to project the story of Martin Kallikak in terms of goods and bads in his textbook on *General Psychology* as late as 1961. Just in case someone might miss the point, the children of the feebleminded tavern girl were pictured with horns, while the offspring of the "worthy Quakeress" wife were described as the "highest types of human beings" and portrayed as solid Puritan types.[8]

This view of the Kallikaks was no accident. As chairman of Columbia's department of psychology for sixteen years and as past president of the American Psychological Association as well as a former member of the National Research Council, Garrett sympathized with Thorndike's views on the place of the "inferior and vicious" in American life. By 1966, as a professor emeritus from Columbia, in the midst of the civil rights movement, he produced a series of pamphlets that proclaimed what he believed to be the implications of sixty years of testing in America. Published by the Patrick Henry Press, over 500,000 copies of his pamphlets were distributed free of charge to American teachers. In *How Classroom Desegregation Will Work*, *Children Black and White*, and especially in *Breeding Down*, Garrett justified American racism on "scientific" grounds. Returning to Davenport and the Eugenics Record Office as well as to Terman's work and others, Garrett argued:

> You can no more mix the two races and maintain the standards of White civilization than you can add 80 (the average I.Q. of Negroes) and 100 (average I.Q. of Whites), divide by two and get 100. What you would get would be a race of 90s, and it is that 10 per cent differential that spells the difference between a spire and a mud hut; 10 per cent—or less—is the margin of civilization's "profit"; it is the difference between a cultured society and savagery.
>
> Therefore, it follows, if miscegenation would be bad for White people, it would be bad for Negroes as well. For, if leadership is destroyed, all is destroyed.[9]

Going on to point out that the black man is at least two hundred thousand years behind the white, he asserted that intermarriage, as well as desegregation, would destroy the genetic lead the white man had achieved through "hard won strug-

290

*Chapter 13
The Critical
Response to the
Behaviorist
Challenge*

gle" and "fortitudinous evolution." The state, he argued, " . . . can and should prohibit miscegenation, just as they ban marriage of the feeble-minded, the insane and various undesirables. Just as they outlaw incest."[10]

"Scientific" Justification

The style and content of Garrett's arguments were but echoes of similar ones developed earlier by Davenport, Laughlin, Terman, Brigham, Yerkes, and Thorndike. C. C. Brigham, for example, praised the superior Nordic draftees of World War I and worried about the inferior germ-plasm of the Alpine, Mediterranean, and Negro races in *A Study of American Intelligence.*[11] What disturbed Brigham, and the U.S. Congress as well, was, of course, the fact that 70 percent of the total immigration in the early 1920s was coming from Mediterranean racial stock. H. H. Laughlin of the Carnegie Foundation of Washington provided the scientific evidence on this problem to the Congress in his report, "An Analysis of America's Melting Pot." Using information from the army tests and from his Eugenics Record Office dealing with the insane and feebleminded, Laughlin built his case—the numbers of southern Europeans appearing as wards of the state proved that those immigrants were of inferior racial stock.[12]

Supported by the Commonwealth Fund, Lewis M. Terman reported similar evidence from his study. Addressing the National Education Association at Oakland, California, on July 2, 1923, he expressed concern about the fecundity of the superior races. As he put it:

> The racial stocks most prolific of gifted children are those from northern and western Europe, and the Jewish. The least prolific are the Mediterranean races, the Mexicans and the Negroes. The fecundity of the family stocks from which our gifted children come appears to be definitely on the wane. . . . It has been figured that if the present differential birth rate continues, 1,000 Harvard graduates will at the end of 200 years have but 50 descendants, while in the same period 1,000 South Italians will have multiplied to 100,000.[13]

This kind of hard "scientific" data derived from the testing and eugenics movements entered the dialogue that led to the restrictive immigration quota of 1924, which clearly discriminated against southern Europeans.

America had moved definitely toward a more restrictive immigration policy after World War I. While small manufacturers, represented by the National Association of Manufacturers and the Chamber of Commerce, tended to favor a sliding-door policy that would open and close according to the labor needs of small manufacturers, most larger manufacturers and labor unions, represented by the National Civic Federation, favored restrictive immigration. The motivation, one suspects, was best stated by Bostonian Edward A. Filene, a pioneer in employee management, when he said:

> Employers do not need an increased labor supply, since increased use of labor saving machinery and elimination of waste in production and distribution will

for many years reduce costs more rapidly than wages increase, and so prevent undue domination of labor.[14]

The Carnegie money that Laughlin used in his campaign for greater restrictions ultimately became money well spent in the interest of the larger manufacturer. Generally, though, the rhetoric of the times and the testers was, perhaps, best symbolized by President Coolidge, who proclaimed, "America must be kept American."

RISE OF THE MERITOCRACY

Nativism, racism, elitism, and social-class bias, so much a part of the testing and the eugenics movement in America, were in a broader sense part of the *Zeitgeist* that was America. This was the land of the Ku Klux Klan, the Red Scare, the Sacco-Vanzetti and Scopes trials. It was also the land where the corporate liberal state took firm root, fostering the development of a kind of meritocracy that even Plato could not have envisioned. Just as Plato ascribed certain virtues to certain occupational classes, so Lewis Terman assigned numbers standing for virtue to certain occupational classes. Terman clearly saw America as the land of opportunity, where the best excelled and where the inferior found themselves on the lower rungs of the occupational order. Designing the Stanford-Binet intelligence test, Terman developed questions that were based on presumed progressive difficulty in performing tasks he believed necessary for achievement in ascending the hierarchical occupational structure. He then proceeded to find that, according to the results of his tests, the intelligence of different occupational classes fit his ascending hierarchy. Little wonder the intelligence quotient reflected social-class bias! It was *based* on the social-class order. Terman believed that, for the most part, people were at a certain level because of heredity and not social environment:

> Preliminary investigations indicate that an I.Q. below 70 rarely permits anything better than unskilled labor; that the range from 70 to 80 is preeminently that of semi-skilled labor, from 80 to 100 that of the skilled or ordinary clerical labor, from 100 to 110 or 115 that of the semi-professional pursuits; and that above all these are the grades of intelligence which permit one to enter the professions or the larger fields of business. Intelligence tests can tell us whether a child's native brightness corresponds more nearly to the median of (1) the professional classes, (2) those in the semi-professional pursuits, (3) ordinary skilled workers, (4) semi-skilled workers, or (5) unskilled laborers. This information will be of great value in planning the education of a particular child and also in planning the differentiated curriculum here recommended.[15]

Plato had three classes, Terman had five. Both maintained the "myth of the metal." And both advocated a differentiated curriculum to meet the needs of the individuals involved. Terman so completely accepted the assumption of the social-class meritocracy and the tests that were based on that meritocracy that he never seemed to even wonder why, in his own study of the gifted, "The

292

*Chapter 13
The Critical
Response to the
Behaviorist
Challenge*

professional and semi-professional classes together account for more than 80 percent. The unskilled labor classes furnish but a paltry 1 percent or 2 percent."[16]

Social class was not the only problem with the tests. Whether one reads Terman's Stanford-Binet or his Group Test of Mental Ability or the Stanford Achievement Tests, the army tests, or the National Intelligence Tests,[17] certain characteristics emerge. They all reflect the euphemisms, the homilies, and the morals that were, indeed, the stock and trade of *Poor Richard's Almanac*, Noah Webster's *Blue-back Speller,* and *McGuffey's Readers.* The child who grew up in a home and attended a school where these books were in common usage had a distinct advantage over the newly arrived immigrant child. At a time when over half the children in American schools were either immigrants or children of immigrants, the testing movement represented massive discrimination.

In 1922, Walter Lippmann, in a series of six articles for *The New Republic*, questioned whether intelligence is fixed by heredity and whether the tests actually measured intelligence.[18] Although Lippmann seemed to have the better of the argument, Terman fell back to the high ground of the condescending professional expert who saw little need to debate proven "scientific" principles.[19]

Conscious of the social implications of their work, Goddard, Terman, and Thorndike viewed themselves as great benefactors of society. Concern for social order and rule by the intelligent elite was ever present in their writings. Goddard put it bluntly when he argued: "The disturbing fear is that the masses—the seventy or even eighty-six million—will take matters into their own hands."[20] The "four million" of "superior intelligence" must direct them. The definition of democracy had changed. It no longer meant rule by the people. It meant rule by the intelligent. As Thorndike put it, "The argument for democracy is not that it gives power to men without distinction, but that it gives greater freedom for ability and character to attain power."[21] Meritocracy had replaced democracy.

Luckily, mankind's wealth, power, ability, and character were all positively correlated. This, indeed, was not only Plato's ideal, but also the testers' view of the meritocracy they in fact were fashioning. Reflective late in life, Thorndike said:

> It is the great good fortune of mankind that there is a substantial positive correlation between intelligence and morality, including good will toward one's fellows. Consequently, our superiors in ability are on the average our benefactors, and it is often safer to trust our interests to them than to ourselves. No group of men can be expected to act one hundred per cent in the interest of mankind, but this group of the ablest men will come nearest to the ideal.[22]

To be sure, there have been and still are inequities between men of intelligence and of wealth, Thorndike argued, but through the "beneficence of such men as Carnegie and Rockefeller," this discrepancy had been somewhat overcome.[23]

Although Thorndike was directly involved in army classification testing during World War I and the creation of the National Intelligence Test after the war—all of which skyrocketed the testing movement in American schools—perhaps he influenced American schools most profoundly through his work in organizing the curriculum. His name appears on approximately 50 books and

450 monographs and articles, including the much used Thorndike *Dictionary.* He wrote many textbooks, tests, achievement scales, and teacher's manuals. In short, he told teachers what to teach and how to teach and, finally, how to evaluate what they had done. Much of his work was, indeed, made possible through the beneficence of Carnegie. The Carnegie Foundation from 1922 to 1938 had made grants supporting his work totaling approximately $325,000.[24] It was men like Thorndike, Terman, and Goddard, supported by corporate wealth,[25] who successfully persuaded teachers, administrators, and school boards to classify and standardize the school's curriculum with a differentiated track system based on ability and values of the corporate liberal society. The structure of that society was based, then, on an assumed meritocracy, a meritocracy of white middle-class, management-oriented professionals.

Tests discriminated against members of the lower class—southern Europeans and blacks—indirectly by what they seemed to leave out, but more directly by what they included. For example: on a Stanford-Binet (1960 revision), a six-year-old child is asked the question, "Which is prettier?"[26] He must select the Nordic Anglo-Saxon type to be correct. If, however, the child happens to be Mexican-American or of southern European descent, has looked at himself in a mirror, and has a reasonably healthy respect for himself, he will pick the wrong answer. Worse off yet is the child who recognizes what a "repressive society" calls the "right" answer and has been socialized enough to sacrifice himself for a higher score. The same holds true for the black six-year-old. Neither blacks nor southern Europeans were beautiful according to the authors of the Stanford-Binet, but then, there was no beauty in these people when Goddard, Laughlin, Terman, Thorndike, and Garrett called for the sterilization of the "socially inadequate," the discriminatory closing of immigration, the tracking organization of the American school or, for that matter, when they defined these peoples' place in the meritocracy.[27]

Tests, then, discriminated in content against particular groups in the very questions that were used as well as in the questions that were not used with respect to particular minority experiences. While some educational psychologists sought to eliminate bias from the content of the tests, as well as introduce a broader cultural basis for them, others sought the impossible: a culturally free I.Q. test. Still other educational psychologists, hard pressed to define intelligence, fell back on the assertion that intelligence was simply that which the tests measured. Although many gave up their concern about intelligence, others argued that the various intelligence tests were achievement tests that could also be good predictors of success within both the corporate society and the bureaucratic school system serving that society. At this point, the testers ended up where Terman started.

NOTES

1. Quoted in Mark H. Haller, *Eugenics: Hereditarian Attitudes in American Thought* (New Brunswick, N.J.: Rutgers University Press, 1963), p. 133.
2. Ibid.

294

Chapter 13
The Critical
Response to the
Behaviorist
Challenge

3. On March 4, 1971, a bill was introduced into the Illinois legislature that required sterilization of a mother who had two or more children while on welfare roles before that mother could draw further support. The argument, however, is no longer based on racial purity or punishment, but rather more on the economic burden to society. The federal government also carries on voluntary sterilization programs for the poor. By the spring of 1972, the Office of Economic Opportunity was deeply involved in trying to persuade the poor people of Appalachia to submit to sterilization. See *New York Times,* May 28, 1972, p. 40.

   While the constitutionality of pauper sterilization might be questionable, the right of the state to sterilize for eugenic purposes was settled in *Buck v. Bell,* when Justice Holmes argued: "The principle that sustains compulsory vaccination is broad enough to cover the cutting of the Fallopian tubes . . . three generations of imbeciles is enough" (quoted in Haller, *Eugenics,* p. 129).

4. L. M. Terman, *The Measurement of Intelligence* (Boston: Houghton Mifflin, 1916), p. 11.

5. Edward L. Thorndike, "Intelligence and Its Uses," *Harper's,* January 1920, p. 233.

6. Edward L. Thorndike, *Human Nature and the Social Order* (New York: Macmillan, 1940), p. 957 (emphasis added).

7. Geraldine Jonich, *The Sane Positivist* (Middletown, Conn.: Wesleyan University Press, 1968), p. 443.

8. For much of the research in this essay I am indebted to the research assistance of Russell Marks, University of Illinois. See also Russell Marks, "Testing for Social Control" (Paper delivered at the A.E.R.A. meetings, New York City, February 4–7, 1971).

9. Henry E. Garrett, *Breeding Down* (Richmond: Patrick Henry Press, n.d.), p. 10.

10. Ibid., p. 17.

11. C. C. Brigham, *A Study of American Intelligence* (Princeton, N.J.: Princeton University Press, 1923), pp. 159, 207, 210. It should be noted that during the thirties, however, Brigham went to considerable effort to refute his former work.

12. See House Committee on Immigration and Naturalization, *Europe as an Emigrant-Exporting Continent and the United States as an Immigrant-Receiving Nation,* by H. H. Laughlin, 68th Congress, 1st sess., Mar. 8, 1924, p. 1311.

13. Lewis M. Terman, "The Conservation of Talent," *School and Society* 19(Mar. 29, 1924):363.

14. Quoted by Robert DeC. Ward, "Our New Immigration Policy," *Foreign Affairs* 3(September 1924):104.

15. Lewis M. Terman, *Intelligence Tests and School Reorganization* (New York: World Book Co., 1923) pp. 27–28.

16. Terman, "Conservation of Talent," p. 363.

17. The National Intelligence Test, interestingly enough, was standardized on army officers and used in the schools after World War I.

18. See Walter Lippmann, "A Future for the Tests," *New Republic,* Nov. 29, 1922. See also "The Mental Age of Americans," *New Republic,* Oct. 25, 1922; "The Mystery of the 'A' Men," *New Republic,* Nov. 1, 1922; "The Reality of Intelligence Tests," *New Republic,* Nov. 8, 1922; "The Abuse of Tests," *New Republic,* Nov. 15, 1922; "Tests of Hereditary Intelligence," *New Republic,* Nov. 22, 1922.

19. See Lewis M. Terman, "The Great Conspiracy," *New Republic,* Dec. 27, 1922, p. 117.

20. H. H. Goddard, *Human Efficiency and Levels of Intelligence* (Princeton, N.J.: Princeton University Press, 1920), p. 97.

21. Thorndike, "Intelligence and Its Uses," p. 235.

22. Edward L. Thorndike, "How May We Improve the Selection, Training and Life-Work of Leaders?" in *Addresses Delivered Before the Fifth Conference on Educational Policies* (New York: Teachers College, Columbia University Press, 1939), p. 32.

23. Ibid., p. 31.

24. U.S. House of Representatives, *Special Committee to Investigate Tax Exempt Foundations, Summary of Activities,* June 9, 1954, p. 20.

25. It should be noted here that up to 1954 the Carnegie Foundation alone had invested approximately $6.5 million in testing. Ibid., p. 78.

26. It should be noted here that this is the latest revision of the Stanford-Binet Intelligence Test. For calling my attention to the racial bias on this Stanford-Binet Test, I am indebted to Lamont Wyche.

27. Of this group, only Terman wavered from the original position. When he wrote his autobiography in 1932 he had stated as his belief that "the major differences between children of high and low I.Q. and the major differences in the intelligence test-scores of certain races, such as Negroes and whites, will never be fully accounted for on the environmental hypothesis." By 1951 he had penciled in around that statement, "I am less sure of this now"; in 1955 another note said, "I'm still less sure." See Ernest R. Hilgard, "Lewis Madison Terman," *American Journal of Psychology* 70(September 1957):472–479.

Black Genes— White Environment

J. McVicker Hunt has contributed much to the clarification of the history of intelligence and achievement testing. Even more broadly, his essays have helped to clarify the evolution of the field of educational psychology in general. Hunt's career as a psychologist and as a historian of psychology has helped many persons to better comprehend the issues involved in the "nature versus nurture," or "heredity versus environment" debates in the social sciences and education. He has been an adviser to the National Laboratory on Early Childhood Education at the University of Illinois, and he was the chair of the White House Task Force on the Role of the Federal Government in Early Childhood Development and Education.

The paper from which the following selection has been excerpted was originally presented to the Midwestern Psychological Association Meeting in May 1967. An extended version of it was published in *Trans-action* in June 1969. In the following selection, Hunt discusses common fallacies in the early debate regarding both the nature of intelligence and the uses of intelligence testing. He discusses the relationship between human development in general and human intelligence in particular. Hunt relates this to how children learn, and he identifies the problems of making predictive generalizations from intelligence testing of children.

Key Concept: intelligence testing and human development

What determines human intelligence? What determines the competence of people? Is it fixed and immutable at a child's birth? Or does it change with time and circumstance? If it does, then what circumstances will best foster its maximum growth?

These questions once agitated only a small group of scholars and scientists. No longer. Today they have acquired urgent social and political significance. The fates of vast programs and many a career may hinge on the conclusions of the most recondite social-psychological study. A scholarly paper, a thicket of statistical tables, becomes an object of burning interest for journalists, politicians, and others concerned to find "the" answer to why the children of the poor don't seem to learn as much in school as their own children do.

I had thought, though, that at least in the years since World War II we had learned something about most of these matters. I had thought we had learned that it was no longer tenable to conceive of intelligence tests as indicators of fixed capacity or innate potential in children. I had thought we had learned that it was quite wrong to think we could predict an adult's intellectual competence from his score on a test taken as a child without specifying the circumstances he would encounter in the interim.

In fact our political and educational leaders do seem to have gotten this message. The circumstances that affect a child's experiences in the course of growing up *are* believed to play an important role in affecting intelligence and the motivation for achievement and competence. This notion has been used in formulating solutions to the crisis of the cities created by the heavy migration of the poor from the South. Only a little imagination and goodwill has been needed to infer that the children of lower socioeconomic backgrounds, once very widely considered to be innately stupid and lazy, may instead be viewed as children who have been cheated of that equality of opportunity which our forefathers considered to be the birthright of all.

Unfortunately, however, these changing conceptions of intelligence and growth appear to have reached the leaders even before they have been fully appreciated among those of us trained in the psychological sciences. I say "unfortunately" because the newer conceptions may have led to excessive hopes among politicians and the administrators of our educational systems. Too many of them have a tendency to confuse the perfectly justifiable expectation that there can be significant improvement in the competence of the children of the poor with the basic scientific know-how required to carry out, or even to plan, the broad educational programs needed to do the job. What I am worried about is that the confusion and excessive hopes may have created an "oversell" that will now be followed by an "overkill" of support for the efforts to develop and deploy effective educational programs. One has only to recall the recent vicissitudes of the Head Start program.

Moreover, the possibility of an overkill is made all the more dangerous by the revival of interest and belief in the notion that races differ in inherited potential for competence. People so persuaded are far from extinct. We all witnessed the great flurry of attention given by the national press to Arthur Jensen's recent paper on the relative immutability of the I.Q. Although one cannot with certainty rule out the possibility of racial differences in potential for competence, the whole issue is of very little import so long as the great majority of black, Puerto Rican, and Indian children grow up in poverty with extremely limited opportunities to acquire the language and number abilities and the motivation that underlie full participation in our society.

But I am no less fearful that the failure of some of our most expensive and publicized efforts to improve dramatically the learning potential of poor children may lead to an unjustified discouragement on the part not only of politicians but of the public that must pay for these efforts. I am afraid that our ignorance of how to proceed effectively may now deprive us, for an indefinite period, of the opportunity to do what I am confident ultimately can be done to meet these challenges. What we need is the opportunity to innovate and evaluate, to fail, to correct our misinterpretations and our failures, and gradually to

298

*Chapter 13
The Critical
Response to the
Behaviorist
Challenge*

develop programs of educational technology, beginning even at birth, that *are* effective in fostering development.

It is these concerns that have prompted me to review here the evidence for the crucial importance of life's circumstances for the development of the cognitive skills and the attitudes that comprise competence.

INTELLIGENCE TEST SCORES NOT INDICATORS OF CAPACITY OR POTENTIAL

It should have been obvious from the beginning that scores on tests of intelligence could not possibly serve as indicators of hereditary capacity or potential. It is a truism to say that one's genetic endowment sets limits on intellectual potential and also that it greatly influences what happens when we encounter any given series of circumstances. As a scientific statement, however, this is basically meaningless, as Alfred Binet, the developer of the most widely used I.Q. test, recognized as early as 1909 when he struck out against

> " . . . some recent philosophers [who] appear to have given their moral support to this deplorable verdict that the intelligence of an individual is a fixed quantity . . . we must protest and act against this brutal pessimism . . . (for) a child's mind is like a field for which an expert farmer has advised a change in the methods of cultivation, with the result that in the place of a desert land, we now have a harvest. It is in this particular sense, the one which is significant, that we say that the intelligence of children may be increased. One increases that which constitutes the intelligence of a school child, namely the capacity to learn, to improve with instruction."

Although the complex tests of Binet and Theodore Simon remained preeminent in the intelligence-testing movement, the conceptual framework built up around their use was developed by the students of Francis Galton and G. Stanley Hall, rather than by Binet. This framework emphasized from the beginning the role of heredity as a fixer of intelligence and a pre-determinant of development in the interpretation of test scores.

Moreover, throughout more than the first four decades of this century, American textbooks on genetics tended to emphasize the work of Gregor Mendel on the hereditary transmission of traits and to neglect the work of Walter Johannsen on the crucial role of the interaction of the *genotype* (the constellation of genes received by an organism from its progenitors) with the environment in determining the *phenotype* (the observable characteristics of an organism).

To be sure, some of the early evidence did seem to confirm the notion of intelligence tests as indicators of adult capacity. For instance, the I.Q.s of groups of children showed great constancy (which was a consequence of the way the tests were constructed) and also considerable individual constancy once a child got into school. Moreover, efforts at training children directly on the intellectual functions tested turned out to have but short-lived effects. Furthermore, the I.Q.s of persons closely related to a child proved to be more similar than the I.Q.s of persons less closely related or unrelated.

Since World War II, however, evidence has been accumulated that is so out of keeping with the belief that the tests indicate fixed innate capacity or potential that the belief is no longer tenable.

Perhaps the most incontrovertible of this evidence is that of rising intelligence in the face of predicted deterioration. The prediction of deterioration came from combining two observations. First, it has been obvious since the 17th century that poor families have more children than families of the middle and upper classes. Second, many studies have shown that people from low socioeconomic background typically average about 20 points of I.Q. below people in the upper-middle class. In 1937, R. B. Cattell multiplied the number of people at each I.Q. level by the reproduction rate at that level and computed the new mean to estimate the I.Q. of the next generation. From this procedure, he estimated a drop of a little over three points a generation, or about one point a decade. This he characterized as a "galloping plunge toward intellectual bankruptcy."

But Cattell's dire prediction has been repeatedly contradicted by rising I.Q.s in those populations where the children of a given age have been tested and retested after intervals of a decade or more. Thirteen years after his own forecast, Cattell himself published a study comparing ten-year-old children living in the city of Leicester, England in 1949 with the ten-year-old children living in that same city in 1936. In the place of the predicted drop of something slightly more than one point in I.Q., Cattell actually found an increase of 1.28 points. Although small, this increase was highly significant from the statistical standpoint.

In other studies, the predicted drop in I.Q. has been proven wrong by gains substantially larger than these. S. Smith reported a growth of around 20 points between the scores of children in various Honolulu schools in 1924, and the scores of children in those same schools in 1938. Lester Wheeler reported a 10-point increase in the mean I.Q. of children from a single group of families in the ten-year period before and after the great changes brought about in that community by the Tennessee Valley Authority. When Frank Finch compared the I.Q.s of all students in a sample of high schools in the 1920's and again in those same high schools in the 1940's, he found the average gains ranging between 10 and 15 points. But perhaps the most dramatic evidence of an upward shift came when the test performances of soldiers in World War II were compared with those of World War I soldiers. Clearly, if the tests measure fixed intellectual capacity or innate potential, and if the majority of each new generation comes from parents in the lowest third in tested intelligence, something very, very strange is happening.

I.Q. TESTS ARE LIKE ACHIEVEMENT TESTS

It has long been customary to differentiate intelligence tests from achievement tests. Some differences do exist. All are differences in degree, however, rather than in kind.

300

*Chapter 13
The Critical
Response to the
Behaviorist
Challenge*

First, intelligence tests tend to tap a wider variety of experience, both in and out of school than do achievement tests. Most achievement tests are closely tied to specific courses of study. Intelligence tests are not. School experience still contributes, however, to performance on more broadly based tests of intelligence. Moreover, experiences in the home and in social groups contribute to performance on achievement tests. Second, achievement tests are aimed at relatively new learning, while intelligence tests depend typically on older learning.

Intelligence tests and achievement tests, then, are measures of current capacity depending directly upon previously acquired skills and information and motivation. Binet saw this at the turn of the century, but he had escaped the "advantages" of the tutelage of men with strong theoretical beliefs in intelligence fixed by heredity.

A CASE OF MISPLACED CONCRETENESS

Semantics can often have unfortunate consequences. The terms "dimension" and "scale" when applied to such matters as intelligence are a case in point. These terms were borrowed from measurement in the physical world where scales are instruments for measuring unvarying dimensions. When these terms are applied to the behavior of people, we tend also to apply notions of concreteness and constancy derived from the world of physical objects. Thus, calling intelligence a *dimension* of behavior and speaking of tests as *scales* tends to obscure reality. This becomes especially unfortunate when the semantics sap the motivation of teachers to change their approaches to promote increased development in children who resist their standard approaches and curricula.

DEVELOPMENT

Let me turn next to those propositions concerning development that I believe are no longer tenable and that I believe are highly unfortunate in their influence upon those working in programs of early childhood education.

Fallacy: The Rate of Development is Predetermined

I am confident that belief in a predetermined rate of human development is quite untenable. In the history of our thinking about psychological development, the constant I.Q. was the epitome of this notion. But it got support from the widely cited work of G. E. Coghill in the 1920's which related developmental sequences in the behavior of salamander larvae from head to tail and from trunk to limbs to microscopic histological evidences of neuromuscular maturation. Support also came from various other observations that I cannot take time to review here. Suffice it to say that maturation and learning were seen as two distinctly separate processes with maturation predetermined by heredity and learning controlled by the circumstances encountered.

Evidence contradicting the notion of a predetermined rate of development also appeared. Wendell Cruze reported that chicks allowed to peck for only 15 minutes a day failed to improve in the accuracy of their pecking. Moreover, the early longitudinal studies of intellectual development in children uncovered individual growth curves with changes in I.Q. as large as 60 points. Several students in the 1930's found increases in the I.Q.s of young children associated with nursery schooling.

At the time, however, the credibility of these observations of change in the rate of development was questioned by other observers who posited differing inherited patterns of growth or found methodological weaknesses in the studies. Differences of more than 20 points of I.Q. were found between identical twins reared apart under differing kinds of circumstances, but, because such instances were rare, they were considered to be merely examples of errors of measurement.

One of the most impressive of the early studies to cast doubt on the notion of a predetermined rate of development is that of Harold M. Skeels and Murlon H. Dye. This study was prompted by a "clinical surprise." Two residents of a state orphanage, one aged 13 months with a Kühlmann I.Q. of 46 and the other aged 16 months with an I.Q. of 35, were committed to an institution for the retarded. After six months there, where the mentally retarded women doted on them, these two children showed a remarkably rapid rate of development. Coupled with change from apathy to liveliness was an improvement of 31 points of I.Q. in one and 52 points in the other. After this, a group of 13 infants—ranging in age from 7 months to 30 months and in I.Q.s from 36 to 89, with a mean of 64—were transferred from the orphanage (but not committed) to these wards for moron women. After being there for periods ranging from 6 months for the seven-month-old child to 52 months for the 30-month-old child, every one of these infants showed a gain in I.Q. The minimum gain was 7 points; the maximum was 58 points, and all but four showed gains of over 20 points.

On the other hand, 12 other infants—ranging in age from 12 to 22 months and in I.Q. from 50 to 103, with a mean I.Q. of 87—were left in the orphanage. When these infants were retested after periods varying from 20 to 43 months, all but one of them showed decreases in I.Q. that ranged from eight to 45 points, and five of the decreases exceeded 35 points. These findings suggested strongly that the effects of these two institutional environments differed greatly, but the idea that children's I.Q.s had been improved by moving them from an orphanage to a school for the mentally retarded was merely ridiculed, and the ridicule deprived the findings of their highly suggestive import.

In the light of the evidence accumulated since World War II, this study of Skeels and Dye has acquired the status of a classic, and the notion of a predetermined rate of development has become almost incredible.

Fallacy: Maturation Is Independent of Circumstances

Locomotor development has long been considered to be predetermined, but in 1957 Wayne Dennis discovered an orphanage in Tehran where 60 per-

302

*Chapter 13
The Critical
Response to the
Behaviorist
Challenge*

cent of those infants in their second year were still not sitting up alone and where 84 percent of those in their fourth year were still not walking. When one considers that nearly all family-reared infants are sitting alone at eight months and nearly all such infants are walking alone by 20 months of age, it becomes clear that locomotor development cannot be independent of circumstances.

In the 1940's, the theorizing of Donald Hebb prompted investigators to rear animals under circumstances varying in complexity, especially in perceptual complexity. In the first such study, Hebb himself found the adult ability of rats reared as pets to be superior in solving maze problems to that of litter-mates reared in laboratory cages. Other investigators have found that dogs reared freely in complex environments are better as adults at learning mazes than their litter-mates reared in the monotony of laboratory cages.

The neuropsychological theorizing of Hebb and the theorizing of Holger Hydén, a Swedish biochemist, have prompted investigators to rear animals in the dark and in environments of various levels of complexity to determine the effects of such variations in rearing on both behavioral development and neuroanatomical maturation. Dark-reared chimpanzees, cats, rabbits, rats and mice have all shown deficiencies of both nerve cells and glial cells of their retinal ganglia when compared with animals or litter-mates reared in the light of laboratory cages. More recent investigations have extended these neuroanatomical deficiencies associated with dark-rearing to the appropriate nuclei of the thalamus and even to the striate area of the occipital lobe of the brain. These highly exciting finds indicate that even neuroanatomical maturation can no longer be considered to be independent of the circumstances in which animals develop.

Fallacy: Longitudinal Prediction Is Possible

Despite such an accumulation of evidence as I have indicated (and there is much more), the belief in a constant I.Q. has given us the habit of thinking of the validity of tests in longitudinal terms. We have used and still use the scores based on the performances of children on tests administered at one age to predict what their school or test performances will be at later ages.

Yet, if even neuroanatomic maturation can be influenced by circumstances, and if psychological development is as plastic as this evidence implies, *longitudinal prediction is impossible from test scores alone.* The plasticity that appears to exist in the rate at which human organisms develop renders longitudinal prediction basically impossible unless one specifies the circumstances under which this development is to take place. In fact, trying to predict what a person's I.Q. will be at 20 on the basis of his I.Q. at age one or two is like trying to predict how heavy a two-week-old calf will be when he is a two-year old without knowing whether he will be reared in a dry pasture, in an irrigated pasture, or in a feed lot.

To be sure, longitudinal prediction improves with age. This results from the fact that test-retest validities involve part-whole relationships. Thus, if one is predicting I.Q. at 20, the older the child is at the time of the initial test, the larger becomes the predictor part of the criterion *whole.* Moreover, in actual situations, individuals tend to remain within sets of social, economic, and educational circumstances that are relatively stable. Thus, a very large share of whatever constancy individual I.Q.s have had can be attributed to a combination of the increasingly congruent part-whole relationship and with the sameness of circumstances.

Belief in a predetermined rate of development and in the possibility of predicting performance over time has had very unfortunate consequences for educational practice. When children fail to learn and are found to have low scores on intelligence tests, teachers are prompt to feel that "these children are doing as well as can be expected." Such an attitude dampens any inclination teachers may have to alter their approach to such children. Consequence? The tutelage that the child encounters remains essentially stable, and the child continues in his rut of failure.

An important corollary of the finding that the rate of development depends upon the circumstances encountered is a needed change in the conception of "readiness." The notion that children are ready for certain kinds of experiences and not for others has validity. On the other hand, the notion that this "readiness" is a matter of predetermined maturation, as distinct from learning or past encounters with circumstances, is basically wrong and potentially damaging. What is involved is what I have been calling "the problem of the match." If encountering a given set of circumstances is to induce psychological development in the child, these circumstances must have an appropriate relationship to the information and skills already accumulated by the child. This is no easy matter. Ordinarily, the best indicators of an appropriate match are to be found, I now believe, in emotional behavior. They are evidences of interest and of mild surprise. If the circumstances are too simple and too familiar, the child will fail to develop and he is likely to withdraw into boredom. If the circumstances demand too much of a child, he will withdraw in fear or explode in anger. So long as the child can withdraw from the circumstances without facing punishment, loss of love, fear of disapproval, or what-not, I believe it is impossible to over-stimulate him. The challenge in such a conception of "readiness" as that involved in the "problem of the match" is basically the problem of preparing the environment to foster development. We are a long way from solid knowledge of how to do this, but I believe we do have some sensible suggestions about how to proceed.

DEVELOPMENTAL ORDER AND PREDETERMINISM

One more point about development and its implications. Order has always been obvious in behavioral development. In locomotor development, for instance, it is obvious that the infant is at first rooted to a given spot, that he learns to wheel and twist even before he sits up, that he sits up alone before he can creep, that he creeps or scoots before he stands, that he stands before he cruises, that he cruises while holding on to things before he toddles, that he toddles before he walks, and that he walks before he runs. Arnold Gesell and his collaborators at Yale devoted their total normative enterprise to describing the

304

*Chapter 13
The Critical
Response to the
Behaviorist
Challenge*

order in the various domains of behavioral development that take place with advancing age. Jean Piaget and his collaborators have also been concerned with describing the order in intelligence and in the construction of such aspects of reality as object permanence, as constancy of quantity, of shape, and of color, and causality, space, and time. Ina Uzgiris and I have been using these orderly landmarks in development as a basis for our ordinal scales of psychological development in infancy. In short, order in development is an obvious fact.

Although Gesell gave occasional lip service to the interaction between child and environment in behavioral development, all but one of his various principles of growth (that of "individuating maturation") described predetermined processes. Moreover, in 1954 Gesell explicitly said that "the so-called environment, whether internal or external, does not generate the progressions of development. Environmental factors support, inflect, and specify; but they do not engender the basic forms and sequences of ontogenesis."

Similarly, Mary Shirley saw evidence of Coghill's head-to-tail principle when she wrote that "motor control begins headward and travels toward the feet beginning with the eye muscle and progressing through stages in which the head and neck muscles are mastered, arms, and upper trunk come under control . . . the baby at last achieves mastery of his whole body. . . ."

Yet such an interpretation is not a necessary implication of the observed fact of orderliness in development. While Piaget, like Gesell, has found order in psychological development, he, unlike Gesell, has emphasized the role of interaction. According to Piaget, development occurs in the course of adaptive interaction between the child and the environment. This interaction involves two complimentary and invariant processes: *assimilation* and *accommodation*. Piaget conceives these processes as basically common to the physiological as well as the psychological domain. Assimilation occurs whenever an organism utilizes something from the environment and incorporates it into its own structures. Accommodation, the complement of assimilation, operates whenever encounters with the environment evoke a change in the existing structure of the central processes that mediate the interpretation of events and control action. Thus, accommodation is another term for adaptive learning.

Although I cannot here go into Piaget's ideas, they have definitely influenced my own thinking about learning. Attempting to understand them has opened my own eyes to the fact that circumstances influence development in ways quite other than those within the traditional rubrics under which we have studied learning.

IMPLICATIONS

Learning in Poverty

As I have already noted, the factors controlling the development of competence in early childhood are no longer purely an academic topic. These factors have acquired both social and political significance from the fact that our advancing technology is rapidly decreasing the economic opportunities for those without linguistic and mathematical abilities, the motivation to solve problems, and the inclination to carry social responsibility, and from the fact that a large number of black people, coming from a background of poverty and limited opportunity, lack these skills and motives. In the light of these challenges, what are the implications of the foregoing argument?

The intellectual capacity that underlies competence in substantial part is not fixed. In this connection, various lines of evidence suggest strongly that being reared in conditions of poverty and cultural deprivation deprives a child of opportunities to learn. The children in poor families have typically encountered many fewer kinds of objects than children of the middle class. As infants, the children of poverty often have inadequate diets and they live in crowded circumstances which expose them to a continuous vocal racket to which they become habituated. This habituation may account for the inadequacies in hearing other people speak that was found by Cynthia Deutsch and by Deutsch and Brown. Too often, the verbal interaction of children of the poor with their elders is limited to commands to stop whatever the child is doing without explanations as to why. Seldom are these children invited to note what is going on around them or to formulate their observations in their own language. These children are especially unlikely to learn the syntactical rules of the standard language. Seldom is their ingenuity rewarded except when they learn to avoid the punishment that comes when they get caught at something arbitrarily prohibited. In such circumstances, the low test scores repeatedly observed in the children of poverty are to be expected.

With respect to motivation, moreover, the children of poverty, black or white, have little opportunity to learn to take initiative, to give up present satisfactions for larger satisfactions in the future, or to take pride in problem-solving achievement. Seldom have the poor acquired such motives. Thus, their response to their children's demands are dictated largely by their own immediate impulses and needs, not the children's. To these parents, a good child is typically a quiet child who does not bother them.

Regarding conduct, finally, these children of the poor are exposed to circumstances and standards that are hardly those prescribed by the demands of the dominant society. The models of behavior for these children often make them unfit for adaptation to either schools or marketplace. So long as a large percentage of black people are reared in poverty under these conditions of childrearing it is not tenable to attribute to race the existing deficiency in competence as measured by intelligence tests.

From such evidence as has been accumulating on the matter of class differences in child-rearing, it is becoming clearer and clearer that the accident of being born in poverty serves to deprive children of that equality of opportunity which our founding fathers considered to be the right of all Americans.

On Standardized Testing

Vito Perrone is the director of Programs in Teacher Education and the chair of the Teaching, Curriculum and Learning Environments Program in the Graduate School of Education at Harvard University. He is also a senior fellow at the Carnegie Foundation for the Advancement of Teaching. He has had a long career in teacher education, and in the 1970s he helped to get the British methods of teaching in informal, "open classroom" schools adopted in American teacher education programs.

The following selection is from a position paper prepared by Professor Perrone for the Association for Childhood Education International. In it, Perrone explores the controversy surrounding the uses of standardized tests in schools. He finds that there has been much misunderstanding regarding what can be tested accurately and how test results should be interpreted. He argues against using existing standardized tests with children in the preschool years and in the early school grades. Perrone believes that attempts to achieve standardized behavioral test performance norms with young children have had deleterious effects for the children. He further believes that the frequency with which standardized tests are given to children in the middle grades and to secondary school students should be reduced.

Key Concept: standardized testing

Given the power of standardized testing in society, it comes as a surprise to many that the history of this form of testing is so short. Produced in 1909, the *Thorndike Handwriting Scale* was, for example, the first popular standardized achievement test used in the public schools.[1] A wide variety of achievement and aptitude tests quickly followed.

By the 1930s, a majority of schools in the United States and Canada engaged in some form of standardized testing, but the scope was exceedingly small by today's standards. Few people who completed high school before 1950, for example, took more than three standardized tests in their *entire* school careers.[2] The results were hardly ever discussed, parents didn't receive the scores and school-wide results were not grist for local newspapers. By contrast to this earlier period, those who complete high school in 1991 will have taken, on average, from 18 to 21 standardized tests; many will have taken more, the majority of them in the K–5 years.[3] And test scores will not only fill newspapers, but also become part of the sales-pitch of real estate brokers, especially if test scores are high in a particular district. To understand the overall magnitude of the shift, it should be noted that since 1950 the volume of testing has grown at the annual rate of 10–20 percent (Haney & Madaus, 1989).

While the tests are problematic at all ages and levels of schooling, they are particularly questionable for children in the primary grades. These are years when children's growth is most uneven, in large measure idosyncratic; the skills needed for success in school are in their most fluid acquisitional stages. Implications of failure in these years can be especially devastating.

SOME HARD QUESTIONS ABOUT STANDARDIZED TESTING

Acknowledging that standardized tests overwhelm much of classroom practice, Harvard psychologist Sheldon White suggests that we are contending with "an affair in which magic, science, and myth are intermixed" (1975). He is offering, of course, an understatement! How many of us actually believe that an individual's intelligence, achievement and competence can be represented adequately by any of the standardized tests that fill our schools? Or that *one* distribution curve—whatever the metric—is capable of classifying all children? Or that a particular score on a test can provide a genuinely defensible demarcation between those who should be promoted to the next grade level and those who should be retained? Between those who should be provided enrichment and those needing remediation? Such assumptions defy almost everything we have come to understand about children's growth, as well as their responses to particular educational encounters. Teachers and parents know this. When they have a chance to step back and reflect on their children, few will accept that any test score can define any child.

Even if one fails to take note of the implicit assumptions of the tests—essentially that children's knowledge and competence *can be measured* by the number of correct answers they supply—an examination of the test items and the composition of the tests (something those in schools need to do more often) ought to cause some measure of pause, if not enormous concern.[4] Are the questions clear? Do they address the particular educational concerns of teachers of young children or of parents? Do the tests as a whole provide useful information about individual children? About a class? Do they help children in their learning? Do they support children's intentions as learners? Do they provide *essential* information to children's parents? In our experience with teachers and parents, we have encountered few who can provide an affirmative response to *any* of these questions. That teachers and parents can offer so little positive response surely suggests problems with the tests and the emphasis given to them.

In contrast, however, almost all teachers respond affirmatively to the following questions: Do you feel any pressure to teach to the tests? If the tests were not given or used for the evaluation of individual children, teachers and schools, would you use fewer skill sheets, workbooks and other simple-re-

308

*Chapter 13
The Critical
Response to the
Behaviorist
Challenge*

sponse pedagogical materials? Would you use a broader range of instructional materials, giving more attention to integrated learning? Would expectations for *all* children enlarge? Would you devote more attention to active, inquiry-oriented programs in mathematics and science? Would you give more time to the arts? Would the curriculum be more powerful, more generative? Do you feel that you can assess children's learning in more appropriate ways than the use of standardized achievement tests?

Used for major educational decisions, as they are in many settings, the various tests clearly limit educational possibilities for children. We need to understand this well, for the pressure to use more tests for more purposes continues to mount.

The Tests and Their Uses

While many of the *prekindergarten* tests are of the paper-pencil variety, most have a more individual, performance-oriented quality. For measuring physical development, children are asked to skip or stand on one foot for 20 seconds; on the cognitive level, they are asked, for example, to retell a story in its proper sequence. With regard to social and environmental experience, they are asked to count to 10, recognize colors and shapes, manipulate a crayon or pencil, and follow directions. The results of these "screening" activities are often the basis for cautioning parents to "wait another year before starting your child in kindergarten." They are also used as a means of "early identification" of individuals who, as the preschool screeners say, might be expected to have difficulty in school and might need special assistance (essentially an early process of labeling). Although scant evidence exists that such early screening is beneficial for either children or schools, it has, nonetheless, become almost universal.

In kindergarten, children typically receive their first paper-pencil test, which ostensibly gauges "reading readiness." Those who score in the bottom quartile are encouraged, in some settings required, to spend another year in kindergarten; or they are placed in a K–1 transitional setting that often leads to later retention. The underlying rationale is that children benefit from the knowledge teachers gain from this kind of testing. But teachers gain little if any important knowledge from such tests. With so little evidence that reading readiness scores correlate with reading success, their use is unwarranted. It is a scandal to retain children on the basis of such tests (Shepard, 1987).

Beginning in grade 1 and continuing through the elementary grades, children in most schools complete at a minimum (and many children take even more) an annual achievement test battery such as the Metropolitan Reading Test, Metropolitan Achievement Test, California Test of Basic Skills, Stanford Achievement Test or Iowa Test of Basic Skills. In a small minority of districts (particularly those serving middle class, mostly white populations), the tests are rather benign. They are, as the administrators say, the sources for "staying in-touch with overall achievement levels." If scores go down significantly, that fact would likely prompt discussion in these districts, but changes in scores tend not to be dramatic enough to raise too much concern.

Given the pressures of the past two decades, however, the tests in the majority of school districts have expanded in their purposes. For example, how well individual children score determines whether they will be placed in a gifted and talented program or become eligible for special tutoring. The results of annual achievement testing also determine eligibility for a variety of enrichment programs, special classes, foreign language instruction, and the like. The tests also determine a student's academic level. They become a basis for early tracking and then ongoing tracking, reflecting the belief that homogeneous achievement groups facilitate more efficient and effective teaching and learning. That such grouping on the basis of a test leads mostly to inequity has not been sufficiently considered. And in recent years, test results have been used increasingly to determine whether a child should advance from one grade to another. This represents a new dimension (Meisels, 1989; National Association for the Education of Young Children, 1988).

What Testing Means for Children and Teachers

All in all, increased testing results in increased pressure on teachers and children. In a school guided by developmental concerns, teachers place much less emphasis on the tests. If, however, tests play a significant role in grade advancement, or the tests are the primary basis for the school's so-called accountability, teachers feel compelled to spend considerable time preparing children to take the tests. In such settings, the tests become the school curriculum.

Preparation usually begins many weeks before the actual testing. During this period, two to three hours a day are often devoted to practice tests and related exercises, all alien to the ongoing instruction and the usual student response patterns. The teachers readily acknowledge that the questions comprising the practice exercises, similar to those on the real test, are "trivial and unimportant." Moreover, the possible responses contain words that children likely have never seen and certainly don't use. The practice time is wasted time, yet some teachers believe it is important to waste the time: *they are preparing students for the test.*

By the time the three days of real testing is completed—after children have been admonished to "get a lot of sleep," "remember that this test is very important," "take all your books off your desks," "leave your calculators at home," "keep your eyes down on your own papers" and "ask no one for help"—weeks, sometimes months, will have passed. Time for real books will have been sacrificed for time spent reading isolated paragraphs and then answering several multiple-choice questions. Rather than posing problems for which math might be used, in the process coming to a natural and deeper understanding of math concepts, time will have been spent on reviewing skills such as addition, subtraction, multiplication, fractions, division—all in isolation. Little time will have been given to science and social studies, other than the concentration on factual information that isn't particularly useful or generative of ongoing interest. Time is a valuable commodity; it should not be wasted in this manner.

310

Chapter 13
The Critical
Response to the
Behaviorist
Challenge

When it's over, the frustration of teachers in these schools will be high. They will feel that their own intentions have been undermined. They will not have had an opportunity to look carefully at the tests—to see what individual children did with various questions, to inquire why children selected particular responses as a way of getting closer to their logic, to get some sense of patterns in various sections of the test, or to determine how closely *any* of the questions got to their purposes. In the world of standardized testing, such issues are not viewed as particularly important. And the scores, when they come back several months later, will be of little use. Yet, because of their seeming authenticity, the scores will stand for how well each class and the school as a whole performed for the year. The scores may also affect the opportunities afforded individual students. This is all travesty! The substance and integrity of education are missing.

An educator's principal purpose is to enhance the growth of *every* child. When children are labeled "unready" or "slow learners" because of standardized test results, their educational opportunities generally become narrow, uninteresting and unchallenging. One-dimensional tasks such as those found in skill sheets, workbooks and drills figure prominently in their education. Who are the ones who tend most often to be labeled? A high proportion of children from lower socioeconomic populations, including large numbers of minorities, are represented in special education and lower-level tracks.[5] This ought to give us serious pause! Our commitment to democratic practice and equality of educational opportunity forces us to speak out strongly against any process that consistently produces such results.

Reasons for caution in the use of tests include the possible loss of children's self-esteem, the distortion of curriculum, teaching and learning, and the lowering of expectations. Other concerns relate to the tests themselves. For example, tests used in grades 1 and 2 are different from those used in grades 3–6. The early tests are picture and vocabulary dependent, while the later ones place greater stress on content. Consequently, high scores in early testing may not carry over to later testing. Because tests include diverse subject areas, they may or may not relate directly to what children have been taught or evoke from particular children any intrinsic interest. In addition, the multiple-choice format of standardized tests confuses many children who are not accustomed to sharing their understandings in that manner. Moreover, for a host of reasons having little to do with their reading ability, children who read very well may select "wrong" answers from among the limited choices available.

Peculiarities of testing abound. Children who have been routinely encouraged to be cooperative learners are forbidden to talk while testing. Children who have been taught to work problems out slowly are told speed is essential. Children who have come to understand that *they* must construct answers to problems, that many answers are possible, are confronted with someone else's answers and told that only one answer is possible. The message is clear: "Don't take your time—guess if necessary and forget what you have been learning day in and day out." Such conditions cause many children undue anxiety, even if the ultimate consequences of test-taking are not devastating. And we have only touched the surface.

Educators of young children have long believed that children learn in many different ways, demonstrating in the process that they have multiple patterns of growth and achievement. This belief has given direction to programs with diversified aims and goals. In these programs, children are respected, regardless of racial background or socioeconomic class. Their interests become basic starting points for learning. Such developmental programs tend to support more formal instruction in reading, for example, only when children are ready and not simply because they are 6 years of age.

Because teachers in such settings commit themselves to increasing successful learning experiences and improving children's self-esteem, many learning options are made available. The clock then tends not to determine to such a large degree when children begin and end learning activities. Peer interaction and communication are encouraged. Creative and expressive forms of communication that develop feeling—the most personal of human possessions—become integral, rather than peripheral, to a child's life in these classrooms. (Too often a teacher does little with the creative and expressive arts because they don't relate particularly well to the normative testing programs. They are not basic enough!)

Static expectations for the children, rooted in an array of basal materials and common curricula, do not reflect the diversity that actually exists in primary schools. Yet, standardized tests are rooted in standard curricular materials (basal textbooks, syllabuses, state or provincial guidelines) that have predetermined expectations all children must meet. To actually develop a responsive, developmental classroom environment is to risk lower scores on standardized tests. Teachers and children do not need this kind of external pressure.

Evaluation Consonant With Purpose

The need is to engage in assessment that is not only related to the best practice, but also rooted directly in the instructional process itself. While many possible entry points to such assessment exist, we share first the way a group of elementary teachers in New York City responded to a new city-wide science test for use in grades 3 and 5. We believe the example is instructive for other assessment areas, as well as other grade levels.

This group of teachers argued that *the* test (not science assessment itself) was inappropriate for use in their classrooms. It 1) covered too much ground too superficially and didn't get close enough to what children actually knew and understood; 2) didn't honor their slower, more intense, meaning-making, hands-on, observational and experience-oriented approaches to science; and 3) was a distraction at a time when serious science inquiry was becoming well-established. Working with a research psychologist at the Educational Testing Service, the teachers developed a science assessment that used the district's objectives and the questions asked on the city-wide test, but made the basic

312

*Chapter 13
The Critical
Response to the
Behaviorist
Challenge*

questions open-ended. They wanted to demonstrate the larger possibilities in an open-ended, less restricted assessment format.

In the document they prepared as part of their oppositional process, the teachers wrote that:

> ... the multiple-choice format ... allows no room for pupils to construct or generate answers based upon their knowledge and thought. ... Further, tests which consist solely of questions for which there is only one correct response constitute an inappropriate assessment or model for science education. We are concerned that testing in this form will undercut science as a process, the investigative, experimental components of our science program which entail observation, experiment, and field work. (Chittenden, 1986)

Their critique is worthy of more attention.

The city-wide test asked, "Which of the following trees can be found growing along the streets of our city? a) Redwood, b) Palm, c) Rubber, d) Maple." While not suggesting that the question was important, the teachers asked in their alternative test, "Name some trees that grow along the streets of New York." The 30 3rd-grade children who took the alternative test named 73 different species of trees (including the "Central Park tree"). For instructional purposes, teachers gained entry points they hadn't thought about.

Rather than ask, as the city-wide test did, "Which of the following planets is the largest? a) Venus, b) Mars, c) Pluto, d) Jupiter," the test prepared by the teachers asked students to draw a picture of the solar system. The drawings were enormously revealing. The teachers and the ETS researcher didn't argue that the questions they asked were wonderful, fully generative, connected to many of the issues they believed were critical. They did conclude, however, that their open-ended process provided information more useful to their ongoing instruction and got closer to children's understandings than the multiple-choice, city-wide test.

Assessment for purposes that go beyond the school—and that is what most current accountability efforts are about—need not, of course, have an *individual*, every-student basis. More open-ended, performance-oriented processes that typically take more time and demand more materials, for example, would likely be seen as more feasible if sampling were to be used. Sampling could also involve teachers in schools much more directly, making assessment more than a process "owned and operated" by some distant bureaucracy.

Centrality of the Teacher in Classroom-Based Assessment

Work in the area of writing represents the most serious break yet in the power of standardized testing. Those concerned about writing in the schools argue convincingly that writing cannot be assessed validly outside the instructional process itself and that writing to a real audience is central. Further, they assert that writing at its best is *situated*—in this sense, not easily standardized in current psychometric or technological terms.

Understanding children's writing cannot begin with one task, a single piece of work, or with writing that has not been completed within the norms of powerful classroom practice. Such writing isn't likely to bring forth students' best and most committed efforts. That understanding alone has changed the assessment landscape enormously. Teachers who encourage active writing programs make clear that serious writing takes thought and time, is close to personal experience or interest and connects to an individual's way of interpreting the world. Children write what they *know* and *feel* about their world—understandings that extend to all curricular areas, including social studies, science, math and the arts.

Teachers recognize that children have *much more* to talk and write about in settings where the ongoing school experience of the students is rich: teachers read a great deal to children, giving emphasis to authorship and personal style; books are plentiful; active learning is promoted; the world is permitted to intrude, to blow through the classroom. In this sense, writing is not something apart; rather, it has a context and that context is important to understanding the writing. Most writing assessment efforts that have existed, including those of NAEP (National Assessment of Educational Progress), provide little knowledge of contextual issues.

Experience has also shown that the best person to judge students' writing, who can monitor their progress as writers, is the teacher closest to them. That shouldn't surprise anyone. The classroom teacher knows, for example, the questions a particular child has been raising about various aspects of classroom learning. When reading a piece of writing, the teacher can refer to previous writing efforts, a book the child is currently reading, genres of authors the child is most inclined toward at the moment, a painting just completed, a trip recently taken, the new baby sister, the spring flooding across the community's many glacial lakebeds, the special meadow colors, the classroom's human mosaic. Thoughtfully responding to the surrounding context, which is never really separate from the text, the teacher can better interpret the writing.

It is that teacher, deeply involved with the child as writer, who knows the next question to raise, when to push and when not to, who can judge the meaning and quality of a piece of that child's writing. This outlook governs our perspective about evaluation issues as a whole.

The foregoing becomes clear when reading children's work in the various publications of the Teachers and Writers Collaborative (see Landrum, 1971; Murphy, 1974) or the accounts prepared by Don Graves and Lucy Calkins And we have seen similar creative and energetic writing in large numbers of elementary schools where active writing programs have been established.

As we read the wonderful writing, knowing that each of the pieces was completed over time—not at one sitting, not without conversation, not without several tries, not without some peer response and early teacher response—we wonder what would have been produced had these writers been forced to write on April 1 at 10:00 a.m., knowing they had 30 minutes and the readers would be persons far away. Actually, we don't wonder too much. We have seen the writing and it isn't the same. And we talk with enough teachers to know that they don't believe what students produce on those days represents any-

314

*Chapter 13
The Critical
Response to the
Behaviorist
Challenge*

thing approximating their best work. Many of the students, often the most skilled writers, leave much of the writing assessment page blank.

Teachers who honor children's work as the genuine product of thought, capable of evoking thought, can certainly describe their students' writing. They are authentic readers. And they have been convincing in their view that any talk of assessment is doomed intellectually if it doesn't acknowledge the importance of being close to the student writer and the surrounding context.

So where does this lead us regarding an assessment program? Having acknowledged the centrality of the classroom setting, the classroom teacher and work over time, we are convinced the principal direction is rooted in carefully organized and considered classroom documentation. Classroom teachers can, for example, systematically preserve copies of drafts of students' writings as well as finished pieces. Two to three pieces a month would provide a reasonable collection. Reviewing them periodically can inform a teacher's ongoing efforts to assist particular students, an important purpose of documentation. At year's end, the accumulation—organized chronologically—can be subjected to a careful review, with some of the following questions serving as a framework: Over time what are the salient features, dominant motifs? How much invention? What about complexity? Choice of topics? Discourse frameworks? Connections to ongoing academic and social strengths? Diversity of word use? Voice? Use of conventions?

This review often provides a perspective missed in the course of addressing work that stands alone. Such a portfolio is almost always enormously revealing to parents, bringing the kind of overview, or large picture, that parents often miss as they interact with their children about the school experience.

Classroom-based review addresses concerns about the ongoing support of individual students and informs further instructional practice. It also serves as a way for a teacher to describe children's growth as writers over the course of a year, as well as inform their subsequent teacher more fully. In addition, students learn to bring careful self-examination and more solid interpretation to their own efforts as writers. Such an opportunity should not be missed.

For purposes of a larger school-wide review, randomly selected students from each classroom in a school might be asked to choose five or six pieces of their writing to be read by groups of teachers in the school as a whole—providing the readers with a context of the individual works. At the level of the school, using such samples as a base—knowing that they were written within the instructional program itself and not apart from it in a forced, unsituated exercise—provides readers with more confidence about describing, for example, the writing of 4th-graders in a particular school. And they should be able to do it with good authority.

Further, as "a community of readers of writing," the teachers involved in this school-wide review can actually enlarge *their* understandings of writing, in the process becoming better teachers and facilitators of writing. If the evaluation effort doesn't produce these kinds of results, it is quite clearly a failed and faulty exercise. . . .

This Association for Childhood Education International position paper decries the continuing potency of standardized testing in primary school programs. Stressing the inappropriateness of standardized testing, it argues that teachers and parents should oppose using test results to make any important judgment about a child. And it sets forth unequivocally the belief that *all* testing of young children in preschool and grades K–2 and the practice of testing every child in the later elementary years should cease. To continue such testing in the face of so much evidence of its deleterious effects, its opposition to most of what we know about the developmental needs of young children, is the height of irresponsibility. We know, for example, that testing:

- Results in increased pressure on children, setting too many of them up for devastating failure and, consequently, lowered self-esteem.
- Does not provide useful information about individual children, yet often becomes the basis for decisions about children's entry into kindergarten, promotion and retention in the grades, and placement in special classes.
- Leads to harmful tracking and labeling of children.
- Compels teachers to spend precious time preparing children to take the tests, undermining their efforts to provide a developmentally sound program responsive to children's interests and needs.
- Limits educational possibilities for children, resulting in distortion of curriculum, teaching and learning, as well as lowered expectations.
- Fails to set the conditions for cooperative learning and problem-solving.

In emphasizing the critical need to seek more constructive directions for staying close to children's growth, this position paper also presents teachers and schools with a means of entering the assessment arena systematically and beneficially. The classroom setting and the teacher are acknowledged as central to an assessment program that, over time, is rooted in carefully organized and considered documentation. This kind of systematic, classroom-based review can inform not only a teacher's efforts to help individual children, but also ongoing instructional practice. Additionally, children learn to subject their work to careful self-examination and interpretation. Most important, authentic, performance-based assessment guarantees a greater understanding of the growth of individual children, which should reduce the need for any of the testing programs that currently exist.

NOTES

1. Alfred Binet began his work on "mental ability" tests in 1904. This work, which contributed to the development of achievement tests, resulted in the Stanford-Binet test (and the "IQ score") in 1916. While IQ testing became popular in many schools, particularly as a means of separating children from various special education programs, it has been reduced substantially in the past two decades because of court-imposed limitations. We begin this position paper with the premise that all IQ testing should end. Such testing serves *no* educational purpose. When we speak here of standardized testing, we are referring to the array of readiness and achievement tests that continue to be so dominating in the schools.
2. Students in New York state, who pursued regents' diplomas, were among those who would have taken more. There were also some school districts—generally in

316

*Chapter 13
The Critical
Response to the
Behaviorist
Challenge*

urban communities—that made more frequent use of tests for purposes of promotion and graduation. These were, however, exceptions.

3. The difference in numbers is matched by the magnitude of their meaning. The tests were used for many more purposes. They determined a good deal about the educational experiences made available to children and whether they would be promoted or retained; they also became a basis for evaluating classrooms, schools and teachers.

4. A large number of publications have provided thoughtful critiques of sample test items from a variety of popularly used standardized tests. See, among others: D. Meier, *Reading Failure and the Tests* (New York: Workshop Center for Open Education, 1973); D. Meier, H. Mack & A. Cook, *Reading Tests: Do They Hurt Your Child?* (New York: Community Resources Institute, 1973); B. Hoffman, *The Tyranny of Testing* (New York: Collier Books, 1964); *National Elementary Principal* (Mar./Apr. 1975 and Aug. 1975); *Standardized Tests and Our Children* (Cambridge: FairTest, 1990).

5. J. Mercer, *Labelling the Mentally Retarded* (Berkeley: University of California Press, 1972). See also P. Olson, "Power and the National Assessment of Education Progress," *National Elementary Principal* (July/Aug. 1975) for some of the cultural problems with tests as well as a review of some of the important related court cases. M. E. Leary, "Children Who Are Tested in an Alien Language: Mentally Retarded?" *New Republic* (May 23, 1970), pp. 17–19, discusses the *Diana et al. vs California State Board of Education* case regarding the placement of Mexican-American and Black children in special education classes on the basis of test scores. *Hobson vs Hanson,* Civil Action No. 82–66, U.S. District Court for Washington, DC, 1968, provides an excellent review of standardized tests and teaching. For readers interested in an excellent review of the serious problems of standardized testing and minorities, see R. Williams, Chairperson, "Position Paper of the American Personnel and Guidance Association Committee on Standardized Testing and Evaluation of Potential Among Minority Group Members," 1975; N. Medina & M. Neill, *Fallout from the Testing Explosion: How 100 Million Standardized Exams Undermine Equity and Excellence in America's Public Schools* (Cambridge: FairTest, 1988); and A. Hilliard, "Testing African-American Students," *Negro Educational Review*, 1987.

CHAPTER 14 The Cognitive Revolution in Learning

14.1 ANN L. BROWN ET AL.

Learning, Remembering, and Understanding

The selection that follows explores two foundational concepts in the cognitivist tradition in the psychology of learning and human development: metacognition and self-regulation. Metacognition deals with how we acquire strategies for learning, remembering, understanding, and problem solving. The concept of self-regulation is important in understanding how we learn to master strategies for achieving "executive" (self) control over those cognitive processes whereby we learn how to apply old and newly acquired knowledge to the problems that we encounter in life.

The following selection is an excerpt from chapter 2, "Learning, Remembering, and Understanding," of Paul H. Mussen, ed., *Handbook of Child Psychology, vol. 3: Cognitive Development,* 4th ed. (John Wiley, 1983). The chapter represents the efforts of Ann L. Brown and her colleagues to summarize the development of research on human learning, remembering, and understanding that had taken place since the 1960s. This source has had a very extensive impact on thought regarding human learning from a cognitive perspective. The authors of this selection are prominent cognitive researchers. The senior author, Brown, developed her ideas and understandings of metacognition so that she could inquire into how students can learn to become consciously aware of learning strategies they can use and practice to meet the challenges of school learning and to remember and use what they learn.

Brown grew up in England and studied psychology at the University of London. Although she was schooled in the behaviorist tradition, she began to study the cognitive approach to the psychology of learning and human development after moving to the United States in 1968. She did research on the teaching of reading and developed her pioneering insight into the concept of metacognition. She currently teaches and performs research on student learning in schools at the University of California, Berkeley. She has also held teaching positions at the University of Sussex in England and at the University of Illinois, and in 1994 she gave the Presidential Address before the annual meeting of the American Educational Research Association (AERA).

Key Concept: metacognition and self-regulation

A TETRAHEDRAL FRAMEWORK FOR EXPLORING PROBLEMS OF LEARNING

The majority of developmental memory research conducted in the late 1960s and throughout the 1970s led to the establishment of a fairly detailed picture of how the child becomes a school expert, that is, how the young learner acquires academic skills and comes to know how to learn deliberately. To illustrate the current state of our knowledge, we would like to introduce the diagram in Figure 1. At first glance this seems like a simple model, particularly in comparison with the elaborate flow diagrams favored by modern cognitive psychologists, who were imprinted on the computer in their formative years. Unfortunately, as is often the case in psychology, the simple model becomes more complex on closer examination, it does, however, provide a useful aid to help us remember the major factors that should be taken into account when considering any aspect of learning. We would like to stress that not only should we, the psychologists, consider the tetrahedral nature of the learning process but also that this is exactly what expert learners come to consider when they design their own plans for learning (Flavell & Wellman, 1977; also see *Metacognition, Executive Control . . .*).

There are a minimum of four factors that comprise the learner-in-context, and these factors interact in nontrivial ways. The four factors are: (1) the learner's activity, (2) the characteristics of the learner, (3) the nature of the materials to be learned, and (4) the criterial task. Because of the sheer weight of empirical evidence, we will give only a few illustrations of the types of factors that have been considered under each of these rubrics and then provide selected examples of the essentially interactive nature of the model.

Ann L. Brown
et al.

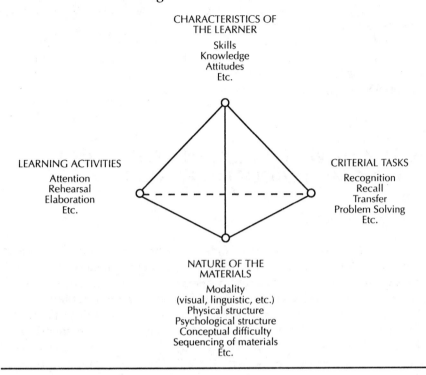

CHARACTERISTICS OF
THE LEARNER

Skills
Knowledge
Attitudes
Etc.

LEARNING ACTIVITIES

Attention
Rehearsal
Elaboration
Etc.

CRITERIAL TASKS

Recognition
Recall
Transfer
Problem Solving
Etc.

NATURE OF THE
MATERIALS

Modality
(visual, linguistic, etc.)
Physical structure
Psychological structure
Conceptual difficulty
Sequencing of materials
Etc.

Adapted from Jenkins, 1979, and Bransford, 1979.

Learning Activities

The activities that the learner engages in are a prime determinant of efficiency. Some systematic activities that learners use are referred to as strategies, although what is strategic and what is not has not been made particularly clear in the literature. . . .

Strategies are part of the knowledge base and, therefore, could be classified as a characteristic of the learner within the model. But the learner's activities are not necessarily synonymous with the strategies available in the knowledge base. Learners can access strategies or any other form of knowledge to help learning, but they need not. Having knowledge, of any kind, does not necessitate using it effectively. . . .

One of the most established facts is the active strategic nature of a great deal of learning in older children. During the 1960s and 1970s, developmental psychologists provided a rich picture of the development of strategies for learning and remembering as well as quite convincing evidence that efficient performance in a wide variety of tasks is in large part dependent on the appropriate activities the subject engages in, either on his own volition when trained to do so or even when tricked into doing so by means of a cunning incidental orienting task. As children mature, they gradually acquire a basic repertoire of strategies, first as isolated task-dependent actions, but gradually these may evolve into flexible, and to some extent generalizable, skills. With extensive use, strategic intervention may become so dominant that it takes on many of the characteristics of automatic and unconscious processing (Shiffrin & Schneider, 1977). Under instructions to remember, the mature learner employs a variety of acquisition and retrieval strategies that are not readily available to the developmentally less mature individual. . . .

METACOGNITION, EXECUTIVE CONTROL, SELF-REGULATION, AND OTHER EVEN MORE MYSTERIOUS MECHANISMS

What is Metacognition?

In this section, we will describe some of the historical roots and discuss the current status of the fashionable but complex concept of metacognition and other topics with which it shares a family resemblance. Various forms of meta-cognition have appeared in the literature and some of these instantiations are puzzling and mysterious. For example, Marshall and Morton (1978) refer to the mechanism that permits the detection and correction of errors in speech production as an EMMA—even more mysterious apparatus; it is a mechanism that could be an optional extra. We will argue that far from being an optional extra, the processes that have recently earned the title metacognitive are central to learning. . . .

Knowledge about cognition refers to the relatively stable, statable, often fallible, and late-developing information that human thinkers have about their own cognitive processes and those of others (Flavell & Wellman, 1977). This form of knowledge is relatively *stable.* One would expect that knowledge of pertinent facts about a domain, for example, memory (that it is fallible, that it is severely limited for short-term verbatim retention, etc.), would be a permanent part of one's naive theory on the topic. This form of knowledge is often *statable,* in that one can reflect on the cognitive processes involved and discuss them with others. Of course, this form of knowledge is often *fallible,* in that the child (or adult for that matter) can perfectly well know certain facts about cognition that are not true. Naive psychology is not always empirically supportable. Finally, this type of knowledge is usually assumed to be *late developing,* in that it requires that learners step back and consider their own cognitive processes as objects of thought and reflection (Flavell & Wellman, 1977).

The second cluster of activities dubbed metacognitive in the developmental literature consists of those used to regulate and oversee learning. These processes include *planning* activities prior to undertaking a problem (predicting outcomes, scheduling strategies, various forms of vicarious trial and error, etc.), *monitoring* activities during learning (testing, revising, rescheduling one's strategies for learning), and *checking* outcomes (evaluating the outcome of any strategic actions against criteria of efficiency and effectiveness). It has been assumed that these activities are not necessarily statable, somewhat unstable, and relatively age independent, that is, task and situation dependent (Brown, 1978, 1980, in press-a).

Although knowledge and regulation of cognition are incestuously related, the two forms of activity have quite different roots and quite different attendant problems. The tension generated by the use of the same term, metacognition, for the two types of behavior is well illustrated by the fact that even the leading proponents in the field tend to answer questions about the nature of metacognition with, "It depends." Is metacognition late developing? It depends on the type of knowledge or process to which one refers. Is metacognition conscious? It depends. . . .

Self-regulation

Any active learning process involves continuous adjustments and fine tuning of action by means of self-regulating processes and "other even more mysterious" mechanisms (Marshall & Morton, 1978). Psychologists interested in mechanisms of growth and change have traditionally been concerned with such self-regulating processes. Of course, substantial contributions are made by external agents. . . . But even without external pressure, human thinkers "play" with thinking (Gardner, 1978), that is, subject their own thought processes to examination and treat their own thinking as an object of thought. Similarly, learners regulate and refine their own actions, sometimes in response to feedback concerning errors, but often in the absence of such feedback. Indeed, even if the system with which one is experimenting is adequate, active learners will improve upon their original production (Karmiloff-Smith, 1979a, 1979b).

Recently, the term metacognition has been extended to encompass such regulatory functions as error detection and correction (Brown & DeLoache, 1978; Clark, in press), but the historical roots of such concepts can be found in most of the major developmental theories. . . .

Given space limitations, we will concentrate here primarily on relatively recent Genevan research on self-regulatory mechanisms in children's thinking and on the growing emphases in developmental psycholinguistics on error correction, systematization, and metalinguistic awareness.

PIAGET'S THEORY OF REGULATION. In the latter part of his career, the transformational period (Riegel, 1975), Piaget became more and more interested in mechanisms of learning and the influence of both conscious and unconscious regulatory functions in promoting conceptual change. Again, owing to space restrictions, we cannot begin to describe the complex theory of Piaget's latter years. . . . Briefly (and probably too simplistically), Piaget distinguished between three primary types of self-regulation: autonomous, active, and conscious.

Autonomous regulation is an inherent part of any knowing act; learners continually regulate their performance, fine tuning and modulating actions, however small the learner and however simple the action (Bruner, 1973; Koslowski & Bruner, 1972). *Active regulation* is more akin to trial and error, where the learner is engaged in constructing and testing theories-in-action (Karmiloff-Smith & Inhelder, 1974/1975). Under the guidance of a powerful theory-in-action, the learner tests a current theory via concrete actions that produce tangible results. Not until a much later stage can the learner mentally construct and reflect upon the hypothetical situations that would confirm or refute a current theory without the need for active regulation. *Conscious regulation* involves the mental formulation of hypotheses capable of being tested via imaginary counterexamples or confirmatory evidence.

Consciousness first emerges as the child becomes capable of reflecting upon her own actions in the presence of the actual event. At this initial stage, consciousness is tied to concrete action but does not direct it. The child's "reactions remain elementary, the subject is likely to distort conceptualizations of what he observes, instead of recording it without modification." Such distortion can be quite dramatic. For example, having witnessed an event that is contrary to a tenaciously held belief, the "subject contests the unexpected evidence of his own eyes and thinks that he sees what he predicted would happen" (Piaget, 1976, p. 340).

At the most mature level, which Piaget would prefer to restrict to the stage of formal operations, the entire thinking process can be carried out on the mental plane. The learner can consciously invent, test, modify, and generalize theories and discuss these operations with others. . . .

In brief, the developmental progression is from unconscious autonomous regulation to active regulation but in the absence of anything more than a "fleeting consciousness." The beginning of conscious reflection occurs when the child is capable of considering her actions and describing them to others, albeit sometimes erroneously. The mature level of reflected abstraction, however, is characterized by conscious processes that can be carried out exclusively on the mental plane. Mature learners can create imaginary worlds and theories to explain actions and reactions within them. Such theories can be confirmed or refuted by means of the further construction of mental tests, conflict trials, or thought experiments that extend the limits of generality of the theory. This is the essence of scientific reasoning and the end state for a Piagetian development progression of "child as scientist.". . .

METAPROCEDURAL REORGANIZATION AND SYSTEMATIZATION. Piaget's colleagues, Inhelder and Karmiloff-Smith, have introduced another concept relevant to this discussion of self-regulation, that of *metaprocedural reorganization* (Karmiloff-Smith, 1979a; Karmiloff-Smith & Inhelder, 1974/1975). The basic idea is that learning within a domain follows a predictable sequence that is characterized by internal pressure to systematize, consolidate, and generalize knowledge. The prototypical microgenetic sequence is that the child first works on developing an adequate partial theory for a salient aspect of the problem space; the partial theory is practiced and perfected until it is fully operational. Only when the partial theory is consolidated and functioning efficiently can the child step back and consider the system as a whole. Typically, the child will develop several juxtaposed theories adequate for various parts of the problem space, each theory operating in isolation from the other. Once the procedures are functioning well, the next stage of development is possible and the child "steps up" and reconsiders the problem-space metaprocedurally. Once children become aware of the discrepancies or contradictions resulting from the simultaneous existence of several different partial theories, they begin attempts to reconcile the differences and obviate contradictions resulting from the juxtaposition (Inhelder et al., 1974).

A concrete example might help to clarify this complicated theoretical notion. Karmiloff-Smith and Inhelder (1974/1975) asked 4- to 9-year-old children to balance rectangular wooden blocks on a narrow metal rod fixed to a larger piece of wood. Length blocks had their weight evenly distributed, and the correct solution was to balance the blocks at the geometric center. With weight blocks, the weight of each "side" varied either conspicuously (by gluing a large square block to one end of the base rectangular block) or inconspicuously (by inserting a hidden weight into a cavity on one end of the rectangular block).

At first, the children made the blocks balance by brute trial and error, using proprioceptive information to guide action. Behavior was purely directed at the goal of balancing. This ploy was obviously successful; the children balanced each block in turn. There was no attempt to examine the properties of the objects that led to balance and no attempt to subject each block to a test of a unified theory.

This early errorless, but unanalyzed, phase was supplanted by the emergence of strong theories-in-action. These theories were directed at uncovering the rules governing balance in the miniature world of these particular blocks. Unfortunately, they were incomplete rules that produced errors. A common early theory developed by the children was to concentrate exclusively on the geometric center and attempt to balance all blocks in this fashion. This works for unweighted blocks. When the theory did not result in balance, the blocks involved were discarded as exceptions ("impossible to balance").

After this theory was well established and working well for length blocks, the children became discomforted by the number of, and regularity of, the errors. A new juxtaposed theory was then developed for the conspicuous weight blocks. For these, the children compensated for the weight that was obviously added to one end and adjusted the point of balance accordingly. For a time, however, length and weight were considered independently. Length blocks were solved by the geometric center rule and conspicuous weight blocks were solved by the rule of estimate weight first and then compensate. Inconspicuous weight problems still generated errors; they looked identical to the unweighted blocks and were, therefore, subjected to the dominant geometric center rule. When they did not conform to the theory they were discarded as anomalies that were "impossible to balance." The children's verbal responses reflected these juxtaposed solutions, with exclusively length justifications given for unweighted blocks and weight justifications given for conspicuously weighted blocks.

Gradually and reluctantly, the children entered the period of metaprocedural reorganization, which was only possible when both their juxtaposed procedures were working smoothly. Now, the young theorists were made uncomfortable by the remaining exceptions to their own rules and began to seek a rule for them. In so doing, a metaprocedural reorganization was induced that resulted in a single rule for all blocks. The children abandoned the simple theories and reorganized the problem space so that a single unifying theory predominated. Now, the children paused before balancing any block and roughly assessed the point of balance. Verbal responses reflected their consideration of both length and weight, for example, "You have to be careful, sometimes it's just as heavy on each side and so the middle is right, and sometimes it's heavier on one side." *After* inferring the probable point of balance, and only then, did the child place the block on the bar.

There are three main points to note about this example: first, there is the finding of a developmental lull or even a seemingly retrogressive stage when errors predominate. Initially, the children made no errors; all blocks were balanced. But, during the quest for a comprehensive theory of balance, the children generated partially adequate procedures that resulted in errors. Only when the unifying theory was discovered did the children revert to perfect performance. If errors alone formed the data base, a U-shaped developmental growth curve would be apparent (Strauss & Stavey, in press). Actually, what was happening was that the children were analyzing the problem space to generate a theory that would incorporate all the blocks. In so doing, they made what looked like errors but what were often tests of the existing partial theory.

A second main point is that metaprocedural reorganization leading to a "stepping up" in theory complexity is only possible when the partially adequate, juxtaposed systems are well established (see also Siegler, 1981). It is essential that the child gain control of simple theories in her quest for a more complex and more adequate theory. Karmiloff-Smith and Inhelder refer to this as creative simplification:

> The construction of false theories or the over-generalization of limited ones are in effect productive processes. Overgeneralization, a sometimes derogatory term, can be looked upon as the *creative simplification* of a problem by ignoring some of the complicating factors (such as weight in our study). This is implicit in the young child's behavior but could be intentional in the scientist's. Overgeneralization is not just a means to simplify but also to unify; it is then not surprising that the child and the scientist often refuse counterexamples since they complicate the unification process. However, to be capable of unifying positive examples implies that one is equally capable of attempting to find a unifying principle to cover counterexamples ... [there is] a general tendency to construct a powerful, yet often inappropriate hypothesis which [learners] try to verify rather than refute. This temporarily blinds the [learner] to counterexamples which should actually suffice to have them reject their hypothesis immediately. (Karmiloff-Smith & Inhelder, 1974/1975, p. 209)

Progress comes only when the inadequate partial theory is well established and the learner is free to attempt to extend the theory to other phenomena. In this way, the theorists, be they children or scientists, are able to discover new properties that, in turn, make it possible for new theories to be constructed.

The third main point is that metaprocedural reorganization is not solely a response to external pressure or failure but rather occurs spontaneously when the child has developed well-functioning procedures that are incomplete but adequate for the task at hand. It is not failure that directs the change but success, success that the child wishes to extend throughout the system. . . .

LEVELS OF SELF-REGULATION.   In this brief and oversimplified synopsis of latter-day Genevan psychology and language-acquisition data, a central place in theoretical speculation is afforded to the concept of self-regulation; there is basic agreement that self-regulatory functions are integral to learning and are central mechanisms of growth and change. Similarly, in the emergent field of metacognition, the notion of self-regulatory mechanisms has a central place (Brown & DeLoache, 1978).

All agree that there are many degrees of self-regulation and that self-regulation is essential for any knowing act. It is important to note, however, that a sharp distinction is made in both theories of language acquisition and in Genevan psychology, a sharp distinction that has not been made as clearly in the metacognitive literature. The distinction is between conscious awareness and direction of thought versus self-correction and regulation that can proceed below this level.

Piaget (1976, 1978) distinguishes sharply between active regulation as part of any knowing act and conscious regulation and direction of thought, the keystone of formal operations. The first process is age independent, even the young learner succeeds in action by regulating, correcting, and refining his current theories. Some form of error correction must be part of any active learning attempt, even very young children are capable of regulating their activities by means of a systematic procedure of error detection and correction. For example, in a recent study, DeLoache, Sugarman, and Brown (1981) observed young children (24 to 42 months) as they attempted to assemble a set of nesting cups. Children in this age range did not differ in the likelihood of their attempting to correct a set of nonseriated cups. They did, however, differ in their strategies for correction.

The most primitive strategy, used frequently by children below 30 months, was brute force. When a large cup was placed on a smaller one, the children would press down hard on the nonfitting cup. Variants of brute pressure were twisting and banging, but the same principle held—the selected cup will fit if only one can press hard enough. Older children also used the brute-force approach, but only after an unsuccessful series of maneuvers; for them, it appeared to be a last resort.

A second strategy initiated by some of the younger subjects was that of trying an alternative. After placing two nonfitting cups together, the child removed the top cup and did one of two things. He either looked for an alternative base for the nonfitting cup or he tried an alternative top for the original base. Both ploys involve minimal restructuring and necessitate considering the relation between only two cups at any one time. The third characteristic ploy of children below 30 months was to respond to a cup that would not fit into a partially completed set of cups by dismantling the entire set and starting again.

Older children (30 to 42 months) faced with a nonfitting cup engaged in strategies that involved consideration of the entire set of relations in the stack. For example, one sophisticated strategy was insertion; the children took apart the stack at a point that enabled them to insert the new cup in its correct position. A second strategy, reversal, was also shown by older children. After placing two nonfitting cups together, the child would *immediately* reverse the relation between them (5/4 immediately switched to 4/5).

The rapidly executed reversal strategy was not shown by the younger group. Some young children would repeatedly assemble, for example, cups 4 to 1, starting with 4 as a base and then inserting 3, 2, and 1. Then, they encountered the largest cup, that is, 5 and attempted to insert it on top of the completed partial stack, pressing and twisting repeatedly. When brute force failed, they would dismantle the whole stack and start again. Similarly, having assembled 1, 2, 4, and 5 and then encountering 3, the younger children's only recourse was to begin again. . . .

The DeLoache et al. (1981) study of self-correction in young children is used as one example (see also Koslowski & Bruner, 1972) of the obvious fact that even very young children correct their errors while solving a problem. Of more interest is the demonstration that the child's error-correction strategies provide us with a window through which to view the child's theories-in-action. The very processes used to correct errors reflect the level of understanding the child has of the problem space. Similarly, developmental psycholinguists have argued that production errors are most informative, "the tongue slips into patterns" (Nooteboom, 1969). Such errors reveal a great deal about the organization of the semantic knowledge of the speaker (Bowerman, in press; Clark, in press). . . .

Beyond Cold Cognition

. . . Virtually everything we have discussed so far involves what many would call the "cold cognitive" aspect of learning (Zajonc, 1980). But there are other dimensions to learning that are extremely important; for example, people have feelings about particular learning tasks and about themselves as learners that can have pervasive effects on their performance (Bransford, 1979; Brown, 1978; Henker, Whalen, & Hinshaw, 1980; Holt, 1964). Some individuals may be convinced of their inability to learn mathematics for example (Tobias, 1978) or of their incapacity to solve certain types of problems. Some children actively resist learning because their peers think it inappropriate or demeaning (McDermott, 1974) or because of their own diagnosis of personal incompetency. A particularly sweeping self-diagnosis was given by Daniel, a learning disabled 10-year-old, who worked with the first author. Upon encountering his first laboratory task, Daniel volunteered this telling comment: "Is this a memory thing?" (it wasn't)—"Didn't they tell you I can't do this stuff?"—"Didn't they tell you I don't have a memory?" Given this devastating estimate of his own ability, it is not surprising that Daniel would be diagnosed as passive, even resistant in situations that he classified as tests of his nonexistent faculty. It would take many sessions of systematically mapping out the specific nature of his memory problem and providing feedback about just where the problem was acute but also where there were no problems at all before Daniel could derive a more realistic evaluation of his learning problem and, as a consequence, would be willing to attempt active learning strategies to overcome a recognized problem.

It is by no means difficult, therefore, to imagine ways that negative feelings about a task or about oneself can affect learning. Nor is it surprising that people tend to avoid situations that tap their areas of weakness, thus conspiring to provide themselves with less practice in areas where it is most needed. Teachers inadvertently conspire to help students do this by, for example, addressing questions to students capable of answering and passing by those that need help to save everyone embarrassment. For example, recent observations of reading groups (Au, 1980; McDermott, 1978) have shown that good and poor readers are not treated equally. Good readers are questioned about the meaning behind what they are reading, asked to evaluate and criticize material, and so on. By contrast, poor readers receive primarily drill in pronunciation and decoding. Rarely are they given practice in qualifying and evaluating their comprehension (Au, 1980). There is considerable evidence that teachers give less experience in this learning mode to those who, because of their lack of prior experience, need it most (Gumperz & Hernandez-Chavez, 1972).

A plausible emotional block to effective learning involves an inefficient use of limited attention because a significant amount of cognitive effort is being directed to self-defeating, anxiety-producing self-evaluation. If learners focus on thoughts, such as "I can't do this" or "I'm going to fail again," they will not be able to attend to the details of the actual problem. Such negative ideation (Meichenbaum, 1977) can have a paralyzing effect on learning (*Dweck, vol. IV, chap. 8*).

Another related block to learning includes a lack in the confidence necessary to debug one's own errors. Some learners may not be sufficiently secure to enable them to tolerate mistakes; hence, they may ignore any errors they make or forget about them as quickly as possible (Bransford, 1979; Holt, 1964). Others may refuse to take the risk of responding incorrectly and, hence, be deprived of valuable feedback. It seems clear that the cold cognitive aspects of learning are only part of a much larger system that influences development; indeed, the purely cognitive aspects may be less primary than we like to think they are.

Beyond Isolated Cognition

In this last section, we would like to stress that learning is not only a less purely cognitive activity than we often suppose but it is also a less individual activity than might be readily apparent from a consideration of learning studies. . . . Here we will discuss only one issue to illustrate the importance of social mediation in learning. We will concentrate on tutors as agents of change in cognitive development. . . .

Many of the activities employed by effective mediators are specifically focused on cold cognitive aspects of instruction, on particular concepts, factual knowledge, or strategies for example. But effective mediators do much more than impart cognitive lore. They encourage children, try to help them stay on task, express joy at the child's accomplishments, and so forth. Learning proceeds smoothly when child and mediator are in synchrony (Schaffer, 1977, 1979). But it is often very difficult to establish and maintain this synchrony; many of the moves made by effective mediators are designed to do just this.

To give one example, a side benefit of the zone-of-proximal-development testing procedures being developed (Brown & Ferrara, in press; Campione et al., in press) is that of increasing the child's feelings of competence. The procedure is such that if children fail to solve a problem unaided, they are given a set of increasingly explicit hints toward solution. The interactive and collaborative value of the adult/child relationship is such that the children believe that they are collaborating in the problem-solving process. Even when the adult provides such explicit clues that the answer is virtually given to the children, the prior collaboration leads the children to maintain faith in their own vital part in the learning solution. They seem to feel they have worked toward a solution that they eventually discover for themselves (Brown & Ferrara, in press). . . .

Mediators vary in how effectively they can establish the necessary empathy so that learning can occur. The present authors have had the opportunity to observe videotapes of Feuerstein (1980) working with academically less successful adolescents. Feuerstein is a gifted clinician, a cognitive therapist, if you will. He does a great deal of prompting to help children improve their approaches to various academic problems, but this is only part of his function; many of the moves that he makes are designed to alter the child's general reactions to the situation and the task. For example, one child faced with her first figural analogy problem said, in an extremely agitated and whiney voice: "I can't do that! I'm not used to that kind of problem." Feuerstein's response was: "Of course you can't do it—*yet*. Nobody can do things well until they have learned them. You can *learn* to do these problems, and I'm going to help you learn to do them." The girl did indeed learn to solve the problems (much to her amazement as well as that of her parents); furthermore, the session ended with the girl demanding to be given more problems when Feuerstein decided that it was time to stop. . . .

There is an ever-present conflict faced by mediators, a conflict between their humanitarian side and their cold cognitive side. Mediators hesitate to push too hard for fear of making learners anxious and unhappy (sometimes rebellious perhaps). But the failure to push at all may protect the child from learning something new. Effective learning environments are those where the humanitarian and cold cognitive side of mediators are not in direct conflict. Many of the moves made by successful mediators can be viewed as attempts to create and maintain a balance between these two dimensions. If the balance is not developed and maintained, effective mediation does not occur.

There are many things that mediators do intuitively that eventually need to become part of a comprehensive theory of learning. When working with less successful students who are anxious about being tested, an effective mediator may adapt the role of helper or benefactor rather than tester. There are other common ploys that enhance learning. For example, rather than emphasizing the student's ability (or inability) to remember information one can focus on the degree to which the material is easy or difficult. Students, then, focus on evaluating the material rather than themselves and are open to suggestions concerning methods of making difficult materials easier to learn. Similarly, the ability to detect errors in one's own work and then make revisions can be viewed as a positive achievement rather than a sign of failure.

One of the most important aspects of effective mediation may involve procedures that enable children to experience a sense of mastery, that let them see that they have some control over learning situations, and that systematic analysis can lead to successful performance. An important outcome of such mediation may be a more positive attitude toward the general task of learning and problem solving and toward one's self as a learner. These outcomes may be as important as number of problems solved successfully, although one would hope that they would be positively correlated. Successful mediation involves much more than the act of dispensing pearls of cognitive wisdom. Successful researchers in cognitive development implicitly know this, of course, and use the information to design effective experiments and training studies; but it is important to move this knowledge from the domain of lab lore to the domain of theory. If we do not, we may be ignoring some of the most important influences on development that exist. The emotional cannot be divorced from the cognitive nor the individual from the social.

Teaching Thinking and Problem Solving

John Bransford is a prominent cognitive psychologist whose many books and articles on cognitive learning have been well received within the academic community of cognitive psychologists. He has published research with Ann L. Brown, Barry Stein, and several other cognitive researchers, and he is the coauthor, with Stein, of *The Ideal Problem Solver: A Guide to Improving Thinking, Learning, and Creativity* (W. H. Freeman, 1984).

In the selection that follows, Bransford and his colleagues review some of the research on human thinking and problem solving that psychologists in the cognitive tradition have undertaken. The authors take the position that students need to be taught specific strategies for solving problems as well as specific knowledge bases, which students should be taught to consciously organize for problem-solving purposes. Bransford et al. discuss some of the major findings from two types of cognitive research on human learning: studies of individuals who are experts in particular areas of knowledge, and studies of the general and specific strategies used by persons to develop metacognitive skills. The authors provide an excellent overview of the concept of metacognition, and they agree with other major researchers in cognitive psychology that the idea of metacognition is central to the search for how human beings can be taught to be expert learners. Finally, Bransford et al. predict the direction of future research in this area of study.

Key Concept: teaching thinking and problem solving skills

*T*he topic of teaching thinking and problem solving is currently receiving a great deal of attention. One reason is that increasingly fast-paced changes in society make it necessary for people to think for themselves and to solve novel problems (Simon, 1980); another is that assessments of student achievement suggest that today's students may be failing to develop effective thinking and problem-solving skills (e.g., National Assessment of Educational Progress, 1983).

Books such as Mann's (1979) history of cognitive process training remind us that the goal of teaching thinking and problem solving is not unique to the 1980s. Attempts to achieve this goal have been espoused for centuries and have stimulated a variety of suggestions for increasing thinking. Many have focused on the need to develop "mental discipline" by subjecting students to the rigors of learning difficult subjects such as mathematics and Latin. Mann (1979) cited Plato's arguments: "Arithmetic stirs up him who is by nature sleepy and dull, and makes him quick to learn, retentive, and shrewd. He makes progress quite beyond his natural powers" (p. 125). Similar ideas were espoused by Sir Francis Bacon, who favored the study of mathematics as a remedy to students' lack of attention (Mann, 1979, p. 13). In the 1800s, many educators argued that the study of Latin would develop the mental discipline necessary to learn in any domain.

Research conducted during the 1940s and 1950s (e.g., Dunker, 1945; Katona, 1940; Wertheimer, 1959), and especially during the 1970s and 1980s, goes considerably beyond a general emphasis on "mental discipline" as the active ingredient underlying effective thinking and problem solving. Our goal in this article is to discuss some of the relevant research and to consider its implications for the issue of teaching thinking and problem solving. Our major emphasis is on the need for both (a) general problem solving strategies and (b) specific knowledge that is organized in ways that are appropriate for individual needs. . . .

The Concept of Metacognition

. . . [R]esearchers who have studied differences in approaches to learning have tried to work with materials that require knowledge that is potentially available to participants. The goal of the research has been to assess the degree to which people spontaneously utilize knowledge previously acquired. Results . . . have led to a number of researchers to argue that people's ability to use what they know—to access task-relevant information—is an important hallmark of intelligence (e.g., A. Brown & Campione, 1981; Butterfield & Belmont, 1977; Sternberg, 1980, 1984). This concern with the utilization of previously acquired knowledge has led to an emphasis on the concept of executive or metacognitive processes (e.g., A. Brown, 1977; A. Brown & DeLoache, 1978; Flavell, 1979; Flavell & Wellman, 1977; Scardamalia & Bereiter, 1985).

An important methodological tool for exploring the role of metacognition has been the training study (A. Brown et al., 1983). Researchers have provided individuals with different types of learning opportunities and assessed the effects on mastery tasks and transfer tasks. In a discussion of this literature, A. Brown, Campione, and Day (1981) noted that different types of teaching environments have strong effects on transfer. Many of the training studies that have resulted in failures of transfer involved what A. Brown and her colleagues called *blind training*. Individuals were taught to use strategies but were not helped to understand why they were useful and when they might be used.

A. Brown and her colleagues differentiated blind training from informed training and from informed training plus self-control. In informed training, students are helped to understand when and why to use various strategies. The informed plus self-control training adds the opportunity to practice strategies and monitor their effects.

Experiments conducted by other investigators also provide evidence that an emphasis on executive or metacognitive processes can result in improvements in thinking and problem solving. Data from several studies illustrate how such training can increase learning (e.g., Paris, Cross, & Lipson, in press; Paris & Jacobs, in press; Wong 1980, 1982; Wong & Sawatsky, 1984). Similarly, work by Lodico, Ghatala, Levin, Pressley, and Bell (in press) illustrates how executive training can help children learn to select and evaluate new strategies. Furthermore, work in the areas of writing (Bereiter & Scardamalia, 1985; Flower & Hayes, 1980) and mathematical problem solving (Schoenfeld, 1982, 1983, 1985) provides evidence for the importance of a metacognitive or executive approach to teaching. An exciting implication of these studies is that it may be possible to help people improve their abilities to think and learn in a wide variety of domains. Researchers have also studied the types of early social environments that facilitate the development of the types of skills that enable children to learn in formal educational settings. Heath's (1983) work is particularly relevant here.

RELATIONSHIPS BETWEEN EXECUTIVE PROCESSES AND SPECIFIC KNOWLEDGE

. . . [I]n most studies, relationships between training in executive processes and in specific knowledge are confounded. For example, although research illustrating the advantages of "informed" training on transfer emphasizes the effects on metacognitive processes (e.g., A. Brown et al., 1983), it seems clear that this type of training also affects the nature and organization of the knowledge acquired by learners. The acts of (a) informing them about uses of strategies and (b) allowing them to practice and evaluate the effects, help students "conditionalize" their knowledge. . . . [S]uch knowledge organizations increase the probability that relevant information will be accessed when needed. By placing more emphasis on the systematic development of well-organized knowledge in addition to executive processes, it may be possible to increase considerably the speed with which people can become able to think effectively in a variety of knowledge-rich domains (see also N. Stein, in press).

Take the example of deciding whether to buy a soft-top jeep. Recently, one of the authors bought one after weighing the pleasure of open-air summer rides against the inconveniences of drafty winter rides and having to raise the top manually. Three days later, when the radio was stolen, the oversight of not considering the soft-top jeep's vulnerability to theft became apparent.

There are several ways to think about the preceding shortcomings in thinking about the jeep. At one level we can fault the individual's attempts to systematically search memory in order to access relevant categories for evaluation. Our decision maker may have been too impulsive and hence prematurely ended his memory search. On the other hand, something needs to guide one's search of memory. . . . The ability to search selectively should be affected by the organization or representation of knowledge. For example, the knowledge representation of a person who has owned a soft-top jeep that was broken into will have information such as "easily accessible to burglars" linked directly to jeep. Because of this organization of the knowledge base, failures to assess such information should be much less likely to occur.

Metacognition and Teaching

Research on both metacognitive, or control, processes and domain-specific knowledge has important implications for teaching thinking and problem solving. Consider first the emphasis on metacognition. Analyses of a number of existing programs for teaching thinking and problem solving suggest that they vary with respect to their emphasis on metacognitive or executive processes (e.g., see Chipman, Segal, & Glaser, 1985; Segal, Chipman, & Glaser, 1985; Tuma & Reif, 1980). Programs such as Instrumental Enrichment (Feuerstein et al., 1980), Philosophy for Children (Lipman, 1985), Analytic Reasoning (Lochhead, 1985), Intelligence Applied (Sternberg, 1986), Patterns of Problem Solving (Rubenstein, 1975, 1980), and Guided Design (e.g., Wales & Stager, 1977) place a heavy emphasis on the importance of helping students analyze their current problem-solving processes and learn about themselves as learners. Similarly, researchers in the area of science education have emphasized the importance of helping students develop a conceptual and practical understanding of scientific reasoning and inquiry skills rather than merely memorize scientific facts (e.g., Aarons, 1984a, 1984b; Lawson, 1985; Renner & Lawson, 1973). In contrast, many descriptions of attempts to teach thinking by programming computers in *Logo* (e.g., Papert, 1980, 1985) place little explicit emphasis on the need to systematically help students reflect on their approaches to programming and to think about these activities as instances of more general problem-solving strategies. Some researchers argue that this lack of explicit focus on metacognitive processes may be a major reason why evidence of general effects of *Logo* programming on thinking ability have proved to be so difficult to find (e.g., Bransford, Stein, Delclos, & Littlefield, 1986; Delclos, Littlefield, & Bransford, 1985; Pea & Kurland, 1984).

An especially promising aspect of metacognitive approaches to teaching is that they can be used to transform basic fact- and skill-oriented activities into lessons involving thinking. For example, Hasselbring, Goin, and Bransford (1985) discussed work with math-delayed fifth and sixth graders who were working on arcade-like software designed to give them practice at basic addition problems such as 7 + 8. The arcade program awarded points for speed and accuracy. All the students wanted to increase their scores. However, most had little idea of how to "debug" their current approaches to the game. For example, the vast majority paid little attention to the fact that they often counted on their fingers and hence could not significantly increase their speed until they moved from productive to reproductive strategies (Greeno, 1978). Furthermore, students knew the answers to some problems (e.g., 5 + 5) and hence needed to memorize answers to only a subset of the problems. Nevertheless, they did not spontaneously attempt to identify the set of problems that would be most beneficial for them to practice at home. With specific guidance from the teacher, the students were prompted to view the arcade game as a problem-solving situation, and they were helped to debug their current approaches to the problem of increasing their scores. Without the teaching, it is doubtful that the students would have taken a "higher order thinking" approach to the development of "lower order" skills (for additional discussion of the role of teaching in the development of problem-solving abilities, see Collins & Stevens, 1982; Feuerstein et al., 1980; Vygotsky, 1978; Wertsch, 1979; Wood, 1980).

Systematic Approaches to Knowledge Acquisition

Programs that emphasize metacognitive or executive processes do not necessarily attempt to develop well-organized knowledge structures that can function as tools for problem solving. For example, Feuerstein et al.'s (1980) Instrumental Enrichment program is purposely designed to involve problem situations that do not presuppose a great deal of content knowledge. The use of these types of problems can be very important, especially for building confidence among students who have had a number of failure experiences in academic settings (for example, see Covington, 1985; Dweck & Elliott, 1983). However, Feuerstein et al. also emphasized the need to "bridge" from the Instrumental Enrichment exercises to specific areas such as mathematics, reading, and so forth (for example, see Bransford, Stein, Arbitman-Smith, & Vye, 1985). Nevertheless, it can often be difficult for teachers to bridge to other areas—especially if these are being taught by different teachers. Because of this, one can often find evidence for positive effects of Instrumental Enrichment in the context of everyday tasks such as planning a field trip yet see much less evidence in the context of achievement tests—tests that generally presuppose the availability of rich knowledge domains (for example, Arbitman-Smith, Haywood, & Bransford, 1985).

Programs such as Philosophy for Children (e.g., Lipman, 1985) and Guided Design (Wales & Stager, 1977) provide prototypes for teaching thinking in the context of domains such as science, art, engineering, and so forth. There certainly seems to be room for more approaches such as these. In mathematics, for example, evidence suggests that children often make a variety of systematic errors because they rather blindly learn procedures rather than understand how the information being presented simplifies the solution to important, real-world problems (e.g., J. Brown & Burton, 1978; Clement, 1982; Resnick, in press; Sleeman, 1983; Soloway, Lochhead, & Clement, 1982). Similarly, students learning science are often asked to memorize information about density, displacement, and so forth yet are not helped to understand its value for interpreting everyday situations and for solving problems. They therefore acquire facts rather than conceptual tools (e.g., Bransford, in press; Bransford, Sherwood, & Sturdevant, in press; di Sessa, 1982; Lochhead & Clement, 1979; Perkins, in press).

Theories of access should provide an important framework for helping students learn to think and solve problems. For example, it seems clear that instruction that emphasizes memory for a variety of facts and definitions (a large number of introductory courses fit this definition) will *seem* effective if we simply test students on this information. However, data reviewed in the present article suggest that this information will generally remain inert even though it is relevant for various problems.

DIRECTIONS FOR FUTURE RESEARCH

Overall, it seems clear that research on thinking and problem solving is thriving and is producing information that has important implications for teaching. The results of this research also suggest some issues that seem particularly fruitful to explore.

One set of issues centers around the concept of gaining access to previously acquired knowledge. We noted earlier that different ways of presenting information had powerful effects on the degree to which relevant knowledge was accessed when it was needed. Experimental paradigms such as those used by Gick and Holyoak (1980, 1983) can provide important information about access. Work on the architecture of cognition and on the role of different knowledge representations (e.g., J. Anderson, 1983; Simon, 1980) should provide the basis for well-articulated theories about conditions under which access occurs.

An emphasis on access also highlights the role of perceptual learning and pattern recognition. Simon (1980) noted this by pointing out the importance of helping problem solvers learn to differentiate problem types and the relation of different problem types to solutions. The research illustrating more sophisticated performance of learners and problem solvers in familiar compared to unfamiliar domains also supports the idea that perceptual learning may play an important role in problem solving. The Gibsons (e.g., Gibson, 1969, 1982; Gibson & Gibson, 1955) emphasized that perceptual learning involves differentiating the features and dimensions in situations where there is variation and learning the significance of those variations to the problem at hand. Many teaching activities fail to educate students' attention to the relevant features that are critical to solving different problems and problem types, and research is needed to determine how to educate attention. Teaching often involves telling learners the relevant information and asking them to combine it in some way to arrive at a problem situation. For example, students may be asked to solve word problems in arithmetic for which they are poor at differentiating parts of the problem situation that are numerically relevant from those that are irrelevant to its solution (Littlefield & Rieser, 1985).

Teaching without a systematic emphasis on perceptual learning can account for access failures that lead to poor generalization of learning. For example, clinical psychology students often learn to diagnose psychological syndromes by reading case descriptions. However, many case descriptions suggest situations (e.g., the client is "anxious" and somewhat "hostile") that represent outputs of an expert's pattern-recognition process. Therefore, students who can correctly diagnose clinical syndromes from verbally stated symptoms in the classroom may fail to transfer that diagnostic skill to actual interview situations where the symptoms are not stated so clearly. Recent advances in interactive videotape and videodisc technology make available rapid access and review of video (e.g., Bransford, Sherwood, & Hasselbring, 1985). This technology can be used to study how perceptual experiences within specific domains can be arranged to supplement traditional instruction and facilitate transfer to new domains.

In addition to research on access and perceptual learning, we expect to see more work that combines an emphasis on general metacognitive and domain-specific knowledge. For example, consider the exciting work of Palincsar and Brown (1984) on the use of reciprocal teaching to increase reading comprehension. This type of instruction might produce even more powerful effects if it were carried out in a semantically rich problem-solving context that enabled children to see how the information in each of their stories or passages could be used to solve problems in this context. Similarly, global problem-solving contexts might be used to provide more continuity to each child's day so that mathematics, reading, writing, and other subjects are all seen as relevant to the same contextual domain (e.g., Bransford, Sherwood, & Hasselbring, 1985).

Finally, we expect to see more research on the nature of cognitive development. We noted earlier that knowledge-base alternatives to stage theories are beginning to flourish. These new alternatives have important implications for educational practice. For example, they focus on the need to assess children's initial conceptions of concepts and principles so that misconceptions can be corrected (e.g., Carey, 1985), and they provide important information about ways in which tasks might be made manageable to children at different developmental levels (e.g., Gelman & Baillargeon, 1983). Furthermore, research on both micro- and macrodevelopment should help us understand the kinds of "natural learning conditions" that facilitate problem solving. For example, whereas many courses in thinking are taught in terms of piecemeal, workbook-like tasks, it is not clear that these types of experiences result in the types of knowledge representations that support understanding, access, and transfer (e.g., Lipman, 1985; Palincsar & Brown, 1984; N. Stein, in press). Research on this issue should be especially helpful to educators who want to help students learn to think and learn.

The Mind's Journey from Novice to Expert

In the selection that follows, John T. Bruer provides an excellent summary account of what the cognitive revolution in psychology has been about. He discusses the origins of the cognitive approach to studying human thinking and then focuses on how "novice" (new or unskilled) learners become "expert" learners. Bruer discusses several key ideas of cognitive psychology and refers to some of the most influential examples of cognitive research on thinking, understanding, and problem-solving strategies. He notes that the objective of cognitive educators is to teach for improved understanding (as well as memory) of the subject matter being taught. Bruer explores the "journey" from novice to expert learner in various areas of knowledge.

Bruer (b. 1949) is the president of the James S. McDonnell Foundation in St. Louis, Missouri. He is the author of *Schools for Thought: A Science of Learning in the Classroom* (MIT Press, 1993), from which the following selection has been adapted, and he is a coeditor, with Harriet Zuckerman and Jonathan R. Cole, of *The Outer Circle: Women in the Scientific Community* (W. W. Norton, 1991).

Key Concept: cognitive science and education

*I*n 1956, a group of psychologists, linguists, and computer scientists met at the Massachusetts Institute of Technology for a symposium on information science (Gardner 1985). This three-day meeting was the beginning of the cognitive revolution in psychology, a revolution that eventually replaced behaviorist psychology with a science of the mind. In essence, the revolutionaries claimed that human minds and computers are sufficiently similar that a single theory—the theory of computation—could guide research in both psychology and computer science. "The basic point of view inhabiting our work," wrote two of the participants, "has been that the programmed computer and human problem solver are both species belonging to the genus IPS" (Newell and Simon

1972, p. 870). Both are species of the genus *information-processing system;* both are devices that process symbols.

That scientific revolution became a movement, and eventually a discipline, called cognitive science. Cognitive scientists study how our minds work—how we think, remember, and learn. Their studies have profound implications for restructuring schools and improving learning environments. Cognitive science—the science of mind—can give us an applied science of learning and instruction. Teaching methods based on this research—methods that result in some sixth-graders' having a better understanding of Newtonian physics than most high school students, or that, as recounted above, help remedial students raise their reading comprehension scores four grade levels after 20 days of instruction—are the educational equivalents of polio vaccine and penicillin. Yet few outside the educational research community are aware of these breakthroughs or understand the research that makes them possible.

Certainly cognitive science, or even educational research in general, isn't the sole answer to all our educational problems. Yet it has to be part of any attempt to improve educational practice and to restructure our schools. The science of mind can guide educational practice in much the same way that biology guides medical practice. There is more to medicine than biology, but basic medical science drives progress and helps doctors make decisions that promote their patients' physical well-being. Similarly, there is more to education than cognition, but cognitive science can drive progress and help teachers make decisions that promote their students' educational well-being.

In the years following the MIT symposium, cognitive scientists worked to exploit the similarities between thinking and information processing. Allen Newell and Herbert Simon developed the first working artificial intelligence computer program, called the Logic Theorist. It could prove logical theorems using methods a human expert might use. Besides logic, Newell and Simon studied problem solving in other areas, ranging from tic-tac-toe to arithmetic puzzles to chess. Problem solving in each of these areas depends on learning facts, skills, and strategies that are unique to the area. As cognitive scientists say, expertise in each area requires mastery of a distinct knowledge *domain.* Cognitive research began to have relevance for education as scientists gradually started to study knowledge domains that are included in school instruction—math, science, reading, and writing.

In their 1972 book *Human Problem Solving,* Newell and Simon summarized the results of this early research program and established a theoretical outlook and research methods that would guide much of the work that now has educational significance. Newell and Simon argued that if we want to understand learning in a domain, we have to start with a detailed analysis of how people solve problems in that domain. The first step is to try to discover the mental processes, or programs, that individuals use to solve a problem. To do this, cognitive scientists give a person a problem and observe everything the subject does and says while attempting a solution. Newell and Simon prompted their subjects to "think aloud"—to say everything that passed through their minds as they worked on the problems. Cognitive psychologists call these "think-aloud" data *protocols.* Analysis of the protocols allows cognitive scientists to form hypotheses about what program an individual uses to solve a problem. Cognitive scientists can test their hypotheses by writing computer programs based on their hypotheses to simulate the subject's problem-solving performance. If the scientists' analysis is correct, the computer simulation should perform the same way the human did on the problem. If the simulation fails, the scientists revise their hypotheses accordingly and try again. After studying and simulating performances from a variety of subjects, Newell and Simon could trace individual differences in problem-solving performance to specific differences in the mental programs the subjects used.

To be sure they could find clear-cut differences among individual programs, Newell and Simon initially compared the problem-solving performances of experts and novices—which were almost certain to be different—in a variety of domains. In such studies (now a mainstay of the discipline), cognitive scientists consider any individual who is highly skilled or knowledgeable in a given domain to be an "expert" in that domain. The domains can be ordinary and commonplace; they don't have to be arcane and esoteric. In the cognitive scientists' sense of the word, there are experts at tic-tac-toe, third-grade arithmetic, and high school physics. Comparing experts with novices makes it possible to specify how experts and novices differ in understanding, storing, recalling, and manipulating knowledge during problem solving.

Of course Newell and Simon knew that experts in a domain would be better at solving problems in that domain than novices, but it was not always obvious how experts and novices actually differed in their problem-solving behavior. In one early expert-novice study, Simon and Chase (1973) looked at chess players. One thing we do when playing chess is to choose our next move by trying to anticipate what our opponent's countermove might be, how we might respond to that move, how the opponent might counter, and so on. That is, we try to plan several moves ahead. One might think that experts and novices differ in how far ahead they plan: a novice might look ahead two or three moves, an expert ten or twelve. Surprisingly, Simon and Chase found that experts and novices both look ahead only two or three moves. The difference is that experts consider and choose from among vastly superior moves. When expert chess players look at a board, they see configurations and familiar patterns of pieces; they see "chunks" of relevant information. Novices, in contrast, see individual pieces. The experts' more effective, more information-rich chunks allow them to see superior possible moves and choose the best of these. Chunking, rather than planning farther ahead, accounts for the experts' superiority. Experts process more and better information about the next few moves than novices.

Newell and Simon's emphasis on problem-solving performance and expert-novice differences was a first step toward a new understanding of learning. In short, learning is the process by which novices become experts. As one learns chess, math, or physics, one's problem-solving performance in the domain improves as the programs one uses to solve problems improve. If we know what programs a person first uses to solve problems in a domain, and if we can compare them with the programs the person eventually constructs, we have a measure and a description of what the person learned. We can study learning by tracing changes in the mental processes students use as they progress from novice to higher levels of proficiency. If we have detailed knowledge of these processes, such as the computer simulations give us, we can know not only that learning has occurred but also *how* it has occurred.

Other investigators joined in the program that Newell and Simon had outlined, and the research developed and expanded along two dimensions.

First, the kinds of problems and tasks the scientists studied became more complex. To play games and solve puzzles, even in logic and chess, one has to know a few rules, but one doesn't need much factual knowledge about the world. As cognitive scientists honed their methods on puzzle problems and accumulated insights into how people solve them, they became more ambitious and began applying their methods to more knowledge-rich domains. They started to study problem solving in physics, mathematics, and medical diagnosis. They began to study language skills, such as reading and writing, and how students use these skills to acquire more knowledge. Extending their research into these domains made it applicable to understanding expert and novice performance in school subjects.

Second, the research evolved from merely comparing novices against experts to studying the process by which novices *become* experts. Psychologists began to develop intermediate models of problem-solving performance in a variety of domains. The intermediate models describe how domain expertise *develops* over time and with experience. If learning is the process by which novices become experts, a sequence of intermediate models in a domain traces the learning process in that domain. The intermediate models describe the stages through which students progress in school.

By the mid 1970s, cognitive scientists were studying school tasks over a range of competencies—from novice to expert, from pre-school through college. In many subject areas, our knowledge of students' cognitive processes is now sufficiently detailed that we can begin to describe their performance at every level of competence, from novice to expert. We can describe the normal trajectory of learning in these subject areas. If we understand the mental processes that underlie expert performance in school subjects, we can ask and answer other questions that are important for education. How do students acquire these processes? Do certain instructional methods help students acquire these processes more quickly or more easily? Can we help students learn better? Answers to these questions can guide educational practice and school reform. For example, research in science learning shows that novices—and all beginning students are novices—hold naive theories about how the physical world works. These theories so influence how the students interpret school instruction that the instruction is often ineffective. Curricula based on cognitive research that build from and correct these naive theories can overcome this problem. . . .

WHAT DOES EXPERTISE CONSIST OF?

Imagine that a small, peaceful country is being threatened by a large, belligerent neighbor. The small country is unprepared historically, temperamentally, and militarily to defend itself; however, it has among its citizens the world's reigning chess champion. The prime minister decides that his country's only chance is to outwit its aggressive neighbor. Reasoning that the chess champion is a formidable strategic thinker and a deft tactician—a highly intelligent, highly skilled problem solver—the prime minister asks him to assume responsibility for defending the country. Can the chess champion save his country from invasion?

This scenario is not a plot from a Franz Lehar operetta, but a thought experiment devised by David Perkins and Gavriel Salomon (1989). As they point out, our predictions about the chess champion's performance as national security chief depend on what we believe intelligence and expertise are. If the goal of education is to develop our children into intelligent subject-matter experts, our predictions about the chess champion, based on what we believe about intelligence and expertise, have implications for what we should do in our schools.

Since the mid 1950s cognitive science has contributed to the formulation and evolution of theories of intelligence, and so to our understanding of what causes skilled cognitive performance and what should be taught in schools. In this section, we will review how our understanding of intelligence and expertise has evolved over the past two decades and see how these theories have influenced educational policy and practice.

Four theories will figure in this story.

The oldest theory maintains that a student builds up his or her intellect by mastering formal disciplines, such as Latin, Greek, logic, and maybe chess. These subjects build minds as barbells build muscles. On this theory the chess champion might succeed in the national security field. If this theory is correct, these formal disciplines should figure centrally in school instruction.

At the turn of the twentieth century, when Edward Thorndike did his work, this was the prevailing view. Thorndike, however, noted that no one had presented scientific evidence to support this view. Thorndike reasoned that if learning Latin strengthens general mental functioning, then students who had learned Latin should be able to learn other subjects more quickly. He found no evidence of this. Having learned one formal discipline did not result in more efficient learning in other domains. Mental "strength" in one domain didn't transfer to mental strength in others. Thorndike's results contributed to the demise of this ancient theory of intelligence and to a decline in the teaching of formal disciplines as mental calisthenics.

In the early years of the cognitive revolution, it appeared that general skills and reasoning abilities might be at the heart of human intelligence and skilled performance. If this is so, again the chess champion might succeed, and schools should teach these general thinking and problem-solving skills—maybe even in separate critical-thinking and study-skills classes.

But by the mid 1970s, cognitive research suggested that general domain-independent skills couldn't adequately account for human expertise. Research shows that either the teaching of traditional study skills has no impact on learning or else the skills fail to transfer from the learning context to other situations. Either way, teaching these general skills is not the path to expertise and enhanced academic performance.

A wide variety of books and commercially available courses attempt to teach general cognitive and thinking skills. (For reviews and evaluations see

Nickerson et al. 1985, Segal et al. 1985, and Chipman et al. 1985.) Analysis and evaluation of these programs again fail to support the belief that the teaching of general skills enhances students' overall performance.

Most of these programs teach general skills in stand-alone courses, separate from subject-matter instruction. The assumption is that students would find it too difficult to learn how to think and to learn subject content simultaneously. Like the early artificial intelligence and cognitive science that inspire them, the courses contain many formal problems, logical puzzles, and games. The assumption is that the general methods that work on these problems will work on problems in all subject domains.

A few of these programs, such as the Productive Thinking Program (Covington 1985) and Instrumental Enrichment (Feuerstein et al. 1985), have undergone extensive evaluation. The evaluations consistently report that students improve on problems like those contained in the course materials but show only limited improvement on novel problems or problems unlike those in the materials (Mansfield et al. 1978; Savell et al. 1986). The programs provide extensive practice on the specific kinds of problems that their designers want children to master. Children do improve on those problems, but this is different from developing *general* cognitive skills. After reviewing the effectiveness of several thinking-skills programs, one group of psychologists concluded that "there is no strong evidence that students in any of these thinking-skills programs improved in tasks that were dissimilar to those already explicitly practiced" (Bransford et al. 1985, p. 202). Students in the programs don't become more intelligent generally; the general problem-solving and thinking skills they learn do not transfer to novel problems. Rather, the programs help students become experts in the domain of puzzle problems.

Researchers then began to think that the key to intelligence in a domain was extensive experience with and knowledge about that domain.

One of the most influential experiments supporting this theory was William Chase and Herb Simon's (1973) study of novice and expert chess players, which followed on earlier work by A.D. De Groot (1965). Chase and Simon showed positions from *actual* chess games to subjects for 5 to 10 seconds and asked the subjects to reproduce the positions from memory. Each position contained 25 chess pieces. Expert players could accurately place 90 percent of the pieces, novices only 20 percent. Chase and Simon then had the subjects repeat the experiment, but this time the "positions" consisted of 25 pieces placed randomly on the board. These were generally not positions that would occur in an actual game. The experts were no better than the novices at reproducing the random positions: both experts and novices could place only five or six pieces correctly.

Other researchers replicated the Chase-Simon experiment in a variety of domains, using children, college students, and adults. The results were always the same: Experts had better memories for items in their area of expertise, but not for items in general. This shows, first, that mastering a mentally demanding game does not improve mental strength in general. The improved memory performance is domain specific. Chess isn't analogous to a barbell for the mind. Second, it shows that if memory *strategies* account for the expert's improved memory capacity, the strategies aren't general strategies applicable across all problem-solving domains. Chess experts have better memories for genuine chess positions, but not for random patterns of chess pieces or for strings of words or digits. Thus, experts aren't using some general memory strategy that transfers from chess positions to random patterns of pieces or to digit strings.

From long experience at the game, chess experts have developed an extensive knowledge base of perceptual patterns, or chunks. Cognitive scientists estimate that chess experts learn about 50,000 chunks, and that it takes about 10 years to learn them. Chunking explains the difference between novice and expert performance. When doing this task, novices see the chessboard in terms of individual pieces. They can store only the positions of five or six pieces in their short-term, or working, memory—numbers close to what research has shown our working memory spans to be. Experts see "chunks," or patterns, of several pieces. If each chunk contains four or five pieces and if the expert can hold five such chunks in working memory, then the expert can reproduce accurately the positions of 20 to 25 individual pieces. Chase and Simon even found that when experts reproduced the positions on the board, they did it in chunks. They rapidly placed four or five pieces, then paused before reproducing the next chunk.

Expertise, these studies suggest, depends on highly organized, domain-specific knowledge that can arise only after extensive experience and practice in the domain. Strategies can help us process knowledge, but first we have to have the knowledge to process. This suggested that our chess expert might be doomed to failure, and that schools should teach the knowledge, skills, and representations needed to solve problems within specific domains.

In the early 1980s researchers turned their attention to other apparent features of expert performance. They noticed that there were intelligent novices—people who learned new fields and solved novel problems more expertly than most, regardless of how much domain-specific knowledge they possessed. Among other things, intelligent novices seemed to control and monitor their thought processes. This suggested that there was more to expert performance than just domain-specific knowledge and skills.

Cognitive scientists called this new element of expert performance *metacognition*—the ability to think about thinking, to be consciously aware of oneself as a problem solver, and to monitor and control one's mental processing.

As part of an experiment to see which metacognitive skills might be most helpful when learning something new, John Bransford, an expert cognitive psychologist, tried to learn physics from a textbook with the help of an expert physicist. He kept a diary of his learning experiences and recorded the skills and strategies most useful to him (Brown et al. 1983). Among the things he listed were (1) awareness of the difference between understanding and memorizing material and knowledge of which mental strategies to use in each case; (2) ability to recognize which parts of the text were difficult, which dictated where to start reading and how much time to spend; (3) awareness of the need to take problems and examples from the text, order them randomly, and then try to solve them; (4) knowing when he didn't understand, so he could seek help from the expert; and (5) knowing when the expert's explanations solved his immediate learning problem. These are all metacognitive skills; they all involve awareness and control of the learning problem that Bransford was trying to solve. Bransford might have learned these skills originally in one domain (cognitive psychology), but he could apply them as a novice when trying to learn a second domain (physics).

This self-experiment led Bransford and his colleagues to examine in a more controlled way the differences between expert and less-skilled learners. They found that the behavior of intelligent novices contrasted markedly with that of the less skilled. Intelligent novices used many of the same strategies Bransford had used to learn physics. Less-skilled learners used few, if any, of them. The less-skilled did not always appreciate the difference between memorization and comprehension and seemed to be unaware that different learning strategies should be used in each case (Bransford et al. 1986; Bransford and Stein 1984). These students were less likely to notice whether texts were easy or difficult, and thus were less able to adjust their strategies and their study time accordingly (Bransford et al. 1982). Less-able learners were unlikely to use self-tests and self-questioning as sources of feedback to correct misconceptions and inappropriate learning strategies (Brown et al. 1983; Stein et al. 1982).

The importance of metacognition for education is that a child is, in effect, a universal novice, constantly confronted with novel learning tasks. In such a situation it would be most beneficial to be an intelligent novice. What is encouraging is that the research also shows that it is possible to teach children metacognitive skills and when to use them. If we can do this, we will be able to help children become intelligent novices; we will be able to teach them how to learn.

We are just beginning to see what this new understanding of expertise and intelligence might mean for educational practice. The most important implication of the theory is that how we teach is as important as what we teach. Domain-specific knowledge and skills are essential to expertise; however, school instruction must also be metacognitively aware, informed, and explicit. . . .

In a section of the original article, not included here, Bruer describes a cognitive science approach to teaching taken by Jim Minstrell, a physics teacher at Mercer Island High School in Seattle, Washington. Minstrell's approach—which involves identifying students' intuitions about physics, changing their misconceptions, and building upon their correct perceptions—has resulted in greater student understanding of course material than traditional teaching methods.

Does It Work? Why?

In 1986 Minstrell initiated a collaboration with Earl Hunt, a cognitive psychologist at the University of Washington, to assess and refine his classroom method. Hunt, a "basic" cognitive scientist who has developed an interest in an applied science of learning, describes himself as the "wet blanket" of the project. "I'm the professional skeptic who must be convinced that it is the cognitive approach and not just Minstrell that accounts for the effects," he says.

A comparison of students' scores on pretests and posttests makes it clear that Minstrell's method works. The students learn physics. But why does it work?

One concern is whether the method's success depends entirely on Jim Minstrell's pedagogical talents. This was the first issue Hunt and Minstrell investigated. Could someone other than Minstrell use the method successfully?

Minstrell trained Virginia Stimpson and Dorothy Simpson, two math teachers at Mercer Island High who had never taught physics, to use his method. At Mercer Island, as at most high schools, which students end up in which physics sections is due more to scheduling than to student choice or teacher selection. Thus, students of varying abilities are likely to end up in each section. This allowed Minstrell and Hunt to make reliable comparisons between the performances of Minstrell's students and the performances of Stimpson's and Simpson's. Gini's and Dottie's students did at least as well as Jim's, so the effect (at least at Mercer Island High) is not due to Minstrell himself.

Is Minstrell's method better than other instructional methods currently in use? Minstrell himself has shown at Mercer Island High that his method is superior to traditional methods. His students have fewer misconceptions at course's end than do students taught traditionally. For example, on the pretest 3 percent of Minstrell's students showed correct understanding of both Newton's First and Second Laws. When he used the traditional methods and curriculum, Minstrell observed that after instruction 36 percent understood the First Law and 62 percent the Second Law. When he used his cognitive approach, 95 percent of the students ended up with a correct understanding of the First Law and 81 percent with a correct understanding of the Second Law (Minstrell 1984).

Minstrell and Hunt compared Mercer Island students with students at a neighboring, comparable high school that Hunt calls "Twin Peaks." The physics instructor there also uses a conceptual, non-quantitative approach in his course. Performance on standardized math tests is the best predictor of high school physics performance. On this measure, Mercer Island and Twin Peaks students were not significantly different. So, in physics one would expect similar outcomes at the two schools. However, on the same final exam in mechanics, taken after 3 months of studying that topic, the Mercer Island students scored about 20 percent higher than the Twin Peaks students across the entire range of math scores. "This is an important result," skeptic Hunt emphasizes, "because it shows that the method does not selectively appeal to brighter students as measured by math achievement."

For good measure, Minstrell and Hunt also compared Mercer Island students with students in a "nationally known experimental, physics teaching, research and development program." The Mercer Island students consistently outperformed the other experimental group on all topics tested. Hunt adds: "We regard these data as particularly important because the questions we used in this comparison were developed by the other experimental group."

These results have allayed some of Hunt's initial skepticism, but Hunt and Minstrell realize that much remains to be done. The success of Minstrell's theory-based curriculum vindicates the cognitive approach, but for Hunt success raises further theoretical questions. He has begun a research program back in his laboratory to refine the theory underlying Minstrell's method. Why are benchmark lessons so important? How does transfer occur? How do students develop deep representations and make appropriate generalizations? Minstrell's classroom is a good laboratory, but a teacher who is responsible for seeing that his students learn physics is limited in the experiments he can conduct. No doubt, in a few years results from Hunt's basic research will feed back into Minstrell's applied research at Mercer Island High.

The next challenge for Minstrell and Hunt will be to test the method elsewhere. What will happen when teachers who are not under the innovators' direct supervision try to use the method? Instructional materials, including videotapes of benchmark lessons for each unit, will soon be ready for dissemination. The next step will be to assemble an implementation network and conduct applied research in a variety of classroom situations.

Teaching for Understanding

Jim Minstrell's students end up with a better understanding of physics, in part, because they learn more expert-like representations and concepts, as well as how to reason with them. There is a price to pay for this deeper understanding. As Earl Hunt points out, "From a traditional perspective one might argue that Minstrell's classes fail, because often students don't get through the standard curriculum. Last year, they did not complete electricity, and atomic physics and waves were barely mentioned." Hunt thinks that changes in curricular time and course coverage will be crucial in making science instruction more effective. Hunt is quick to add that in other countries curricula sometimes allow two to three years to teach what we cram into one.

The applied work of Minstrell and others shows that we can teach in such a way as to make a significant impact on students' scientific understanding. All who have attempted to teach for understanding, though, emphasize that doing so takes time. Minstrell spends over a week developing Newton's laws, not one or two days as in most traditional courses. Reflecting on his classroom experiences, Minstrell (1989, p. 147) advises: "We must provide the time students need for mental restructuring. Hurrying on to the next lesson or the next topic does not allow for sufficient reflection on the implications of the present lesson."

Results from cognitive research indicate that if we want more students to understand science, the instruction should start early in school, and that throughout the curriculum instruction should build on students' correct intuitions and prior understanding. We should try to teach experts' conceptual understandings, not just formulas and equations, and along with this content we should teach students how to reason scientifically. Better science instruction along these lines may require a "less is more" (or at least a "longer is better") approach to the science curriculum.

CONCLUSION

Learning is the process whereby novices become more expert. Teaching is the profession dedicated to helping students learn, helping them become more expert. Cognitive research has matured to where it can now tell us what is involved in the mental journey from novice to expert not just in reading and physics, but across a variety of school subject domains. The research can now describe these journeys in sufficient detail—recall Siegler's exacting, fine-grained analysis of learning the balance scale—that it can serve as a map and guide for improved learning and teaching. We have at our disposal the basis for an applied science of learning that can inform the design of new materials, teaching methods and curricula. These are the tools students and teachers must have, if, as a nation, we are serious about becoming more productive and helping all students develop their intelligence as fully as possible.

Developing these tools and restructuring our schools to use them won't be easy. We will have to start in the classroom, where teachers interact with students. We will need teachers who can create and maintain learning environments where students have the smoothest possible journey from novice to expert and where they can learn to become intelligent novices. To do this, we will have to rethink, or at least re-evaluate, much of our received wisdom about educational policy, classroom practices, national standards, and teacher training.

Admittedly, there is much we still don't know about how our minds work, how children best learn, and how to design better schools. On the other hand, we already know a great deal that we can apply to improve our schools and our children's futures.

PART SIX

Society, Culture, and Education

CHAPTER 15 Social Change

15.1 JOHN DEWEY

Education and Social Change

The journal *The Social Frontier* was a very important publishing forum for the ideas of progressive-liberal scholars in American education from 1934 to 1944. During its brief history, *The Social Frontier* published many important essays by William Heard Kilpatrick, Goodwin Watson, Harold Rugg, and many other prominent liberal scholars in the fields of teacher education and social foundations of education. John Dewey was a regular contributor to this journal. Dewey's view was that schools have an important role in forging any society's future.

In the following selection, from "Education and Social Change," *The Social Frontier* (May 1937), Dewey uses one of his favorite rhetorical techniques: He gives the reader three clearly different arguments; he then phrases two of them so as to lead the reader to support the one he prefers. Dewey delivers in this essay a stirring defense of democracy as well as of freedom of information and communication in schools as a way to better prepare students for social change.

Dewey (1859–1952) was a professor of philosophy at Columbia University. His many publications include *Democracy and Education: An Introduction to the Philosophy of Education* (Macmillan, 1916) and *How We Think: A Restatement of the Relation of Reflective Thinking to the Educative Process* (D. C. Heath, 1933).

Key Concept: schools and social change

351

*U*pon certain aspects of my theme there is nothing new to be said. Attention has been continually called of late to the fact that society is in process of change, and that the schools tend to lag behind. We are all familiar with the pleas that are urged to bring education in the schools into closer relation with the forces that are producing social change and with the needs that arise from these changes. Probably no question has received so much attention in educational discussion during the last few years as the problem of integration of the schools with social life. Upon these general matters, I could hardly do more than reiterate what has often been said.

Nevertheless, there is as yet little consensus of opinion as to what the schools can do in relation to the forces of social change and how they should do it. There are those who assert in effect that the schools must simply reflect social changes that have already occurred, as best they may. Some would go so far as to make the work of schools virtually parasitic. Others hold that the schools should take an active part in *directing* social change, and share in the construction of a new social order. Even among the latter there is, however, marked difference of attitude. Some think the schools should assume this directive role by means of indoctrination; others oppose this method. Even if there were more unity of thought than exists, there would still be the practical problem of overcoming institutional inertia so as to realize in fact an agreed-upon program.

There is, accordingly, no need to justify further discussion of the problem of the relation of education to social change. I shall do what I can, then, to indicate the factors that seem to me to enter into the problem, together with some of the reasons that prove that the schools do have a role—and an important one—in *production* of social change.

SCHOOLS REFLECT THE SOCIAL ORDER

One factor inherent in the situation is that schools *do* follow and reflect the social "order" that exists. I do not make this statement as a grudging admission, nor yet in order to argue that they should *not* do so. I make it rather as a statement of a *conditioning* factor which supports the conclusion that the schools thereby do take part in the determination of a future social order; and that, accordingly, the problem is not whether the schools *should* participate in the production of a future society (since they do so anyway) but whether they should do it blindly and irresponsibly or with the maximum possible of courageous intelligence and responsibility.

The grounds that lead me to make this statement are as follows: The existing state of society, which the schools reflect, is not something fixed and uniform. The idea that such is the case is a self-imposed hallucination. Social conditions are not only in process of change, but the changes going on are in different directions, so different as to produce social confusion and conflict. There is no single and clear-cut pattern that pervades and holds together in a unified way the social conditions and forces that operate. It would be easy to cite highly respectable authorities who have stated, as matter of historic fact and not on account of some doctrinal conclusion to be drawn, that social conditions in all that affects the relations of human beings to one another have changed more in the last one hundred and fifty years than in all previous time, and that the process of change is still going on. It requires a good deal of either ignorance or intellectual naiveté to suppose that these changes have all been tending to one coherent social outcome. The plaint of the conservative about the imperiling of old and time-tried values and truths, and the efforts of reactionaries to stem the tide of changes that occur, are sufficient evidence, if evidence be needed to the contrary.

Of course the schools have mirrored the social changes that take place. The efforts of Horace Mann and others a century ago to establish a public, free, common school system were a reflection primarily of the social conditions that followed the war by the colonies for political independence and the establishment of republican institutions. The evidential force of this outstanding instance would be confirmed in detail if we went through the list of changes that have taken place in (1) the kind of schools that have been established, (2) the new courses that have been introduced, (3) the shifts in subject-matter that have occurred, and (4) the changes in methods of instruction and discipline that have occurred in intervening years. The notion that the educational system has been static is too absurd for notice; it has been and still is in a state of flux.

The fact that it is possible to argue about the desirability of many of the changes that have occurred, and to give valid reasons for deploring aspects of the flux, is not relevant to the main point. For the stronger the arguments brought forth on these points, and the greater the amount of evidence produced to show that the educational system is in a state of disorder and confusion, the greater is the proof that the schools have responded to, and have reflected, social conditions which are themselves in a state of confusion and conflict.

INCONSISTENT CONSERVATISM

Do those who hold the idea that the schools should not attempt to give direction to social change accept complacently the confusion that exists, because the schools *have* followed in the track of one social change after another? They certainly do not, although the logic of their position demands it. For the most part they are severe critics of the existing state of education. They are as a rule opposed to the studies called modern and the methods called progressive. They tend to favor return to older types of studies and to strenuous "disciplinary" methods. What does this attitude mean? Does it not show that its advocates in reality adopt the position that the schools can do something to affect positively and constructively social conditions? For they hold in effect that the school should discriminate with respect to the social forces that play upon it; that instead of accepting the latter *in toto,* education should select and organize in a given direction. The adherents of this view can hardly believe that the effect of selection and organization will stop at the doors of school rooms. They must expect some ordering and healing influence to be exerted sooner or later upon the structure and movement of life outside. What they are really doing when they deny directive social effect to education is to express their opposition to some of the directions social change is actually taking, and their choice of other social forces as those with which education should throw in its lot so as to promote as far as may be their victory in the strife of forces. They are conservatives in education because they are socially conservative and vice-versa.

ALTERNATIVE COURSES

This is as it should be in the interest of clearness and consistency of thought and action. If these conservatives in education were more aware of what is involved in their position, and franker in stating its implications, they would help bring out the real issue. It is not whether the schools shall or shall not influence the course of future social life, but in what direction they shall do so and how. In some fashion or other, the schools will influence social life anyway. But they can exercise such influence in different ways and to different ends, and the important thing is to become conscious of these different ways and ends, so that an intelligent choice may be made, and so that if opposed choices are made, the further conflict may at least be carried on with understanding of what is at stake, and not in the dark.

There are three possible directions of choice. Educators may act so as to perpetuate the present confusion and possibly increase it. That will be the result of drift, and under present conditions to drift is in the end to make a choice. Or they may select the newer scientific, technological, and cultural forces that are producing change in the old order; may estimate the direction in which they are moving and their outcome if they are given freer play, and see what can be done to make the schools their ally. Or, educators may become intelligently conservative and strive to make the schools a force in maintaining the old order intact against the impact of new forces.

If the second course is chosen—as of course I believe it should be—the problem will be other than merely that of accelerating the rate of the change that is going on. The problem will be to develop the insight and understanding that will enable the youth who go forth from the schools to take part in the great work of construction and organization that will have to be done, and to equip them with the attitudes and habits of action that will make their understanding and insight practically effective.

DRIFT OR INTELLIGENT CHOICE?

There is much that can be said for an intelligent conservatism. I do not know anything that can be said for perpetuation of a wavering, uncertain, confused condition of social life and education. Nevertheless, the easiest thing is to refrain from fundamental thinking and let things go on drifting. Upon the basis of any other policy than drift—which after all is a policy, though a blind one—every special issue and problem, whether that of selection and organization of subject-matter of study, or methods of teaching, of school buildings and equipment, of school administration, is a special phase of the inclusive and fundamental problem: What movement of social forces, economic, political, religious, cultural, shall the school take to be controlling in its aims and methods, and with which forces shall the school align itself?

Failure to discuss educational problems from this point of view but intensifies the existing confusion. Apart from this background, and outside of this perspective, educational questions have to be settled *ad hoc* and are speedily unsettled. What is suggested does not mean that the schools shall throw themselves into the political and economic arena and take sides with some party there. I am not talking about parties; I am talking about social forces and their movement. In spite of absolute claims that are made for this party or that, it is altogether probable that existing parties and sects themselves suffer from existing confusions and conflicts, so that the understanding, the ideas, and attitudes that control their policies, need re-education and re-orientation. I know that there are some who think that the implications of what I have said point to abstinence and futility; that they negate the stand first taken. But I am surprised when educators adopt this position, for it shows a profound lack of faith in their own calling. It assumes that education as education has nothing or next to nothing to contribute; that formation of understanding and disposition counts for nothing; that only immediate overt action counts and that it can count equally whether or not it has been modified by education.

NEUTRALITY AIDS REACTION

Before leaving this aspect of the subject, I wish to recur to the utopian nature of the idea that the schools can be completely neutral. This idea sets up an end incapable of accomplishment. So far as it is acted upon, it has a definite social effect, but that effect is, as I have said, perpetuation of disorder and increase of blind because unintelligent conflict. Practically, moreover, the weight of such action falls upon the reactionary side. Perhaps the most effective way of re-inforcing reaction under the name of neutrality, consists in keeping the oncoming generation ignorant of the conditions in which they live and the issues they have to face. This effect is the more pronounced because it is subtle and indirect; because neither teachers nor those taught are aware of what they are doing and what is being done to them. Clarity can develop only in the extent to which there is frank acknowledgment of the basic issue: Where shall the social emphasis of school life and work fall, and what are the educational policies which correspond to this emphasis?

REVOLUTIONARY RADICALS BELIEVE EDUCATION IMPOTENT

So far I have spoken of those who assert, in terms of the views of a conservative group, the doctrine of complete impotence of education. But it is an old story that politics makes strange bedfellows. There is another group which holds the schools are completely impotent; that they so necessarily reflect the dominant economic and political regime, that they are committed, root and branch, to its support. This conclusion is based upon the belief that the organization of a given society is fixed by the control exercised by a particular economic class, so that the school, like every other social institution, is of necessity the subservient tool of a dominant class. This viewpoint takes literally the doctrine that the school can only reflect the existing social order. Hence the conclusion in effect that it is a waste of energy and time to bother with the schools. The only way, according to advocates of this theory, to change education in any important respect is first to overthrow the existing class-order of society and transfer power to another class. Then the needed change in education will follow automatically and will be genuine and thorough-going.

This point of view serves to call attention to another factor in the general issue being discussed. I shall not here take up in detail the basic premise of this school of social thought, namely the doctrine of domination of social organization by a single rather solidly-unified class; a domination so complete and pervasive that it can be thrown off only by the violent revolutionary action of another distinct unified class. It will be gathered, however, from what has been said that I believe the existing situation is so composite and so marked by conflicting criss-cross tendencies that this premise represents an exaggeration of actual conditions so extreme as to be a caricature. Yet I do recognize that so far as any general characterization of the situation can be made, it is on the basis of a conflict of older and newer forces—forces cultural, religious, scientific, philosophic, economic, and political.

But suppose it is admitted for the sake of argument that a social revolution is going on, and that it will culminate in a transfer of power effected by violent action. The notion that schools are completely impotent under existing conditions then has disastrous consequences. The schools, according to the theory, are engaged in shaping as far as in them lies a mentality, a type of belief, desire, and purpose that is consonant with the present class-capitalist system. It is evident that if such be the case, any revolution that is brought about is going to be badly compromised and even undermined. It will carry with it the seeds, the vital seeds, of counter-revolutions. There is no basis whatever, save doctrinaire absolutism, for the belief that a complete economic change will produce of itself the mental, moral, and cultural changes that are necessary for its enduring success. The fact is practically recognized by the school of thought under discussion in that part of their doctrine which asserts that no genuine revolution can occur until the old system has passed away in everything but external political power, while within its shell a new economic system has grown to maturity. What is ignored is that the new system cannot grow to maturity without an accompanying widespread change of habits of belief, desire, and purpose.

It is unrealistic, in my opinion, to suppose that the schools can be a *main* agency in producing the intellectual and moral changes, the changes in attitudes and disposition of thought and purpose, which are necessary for the creation of a new social order. Any such view ignores the constant operation of powerful forces outside the school which shape mind and character. It ignores the fact that school education is but one educational agency out of many, and at the best is in some respects a minor educational force. Nevertheless, while the school is not a sufficient condition, it is a necessary condition of forming the understanding and the dispositions that are required to maintain a genuinely changed social order. No social change is more than external unless it is attended by and rooted in the attitudes of those who bring it about and of those who are affected by it. In a genuine sense, social change is accidental unless it has also a psychological and moral foundation. For it is then at the mercy of currents that veer and shift. The utmost that can be meant by those who hold that schools are impotent is that education in the form of *systematic indoctrination* can only come about when some government is sufficiently established to make schools undertake the task of single-minded inculcation in a single direction.

The discussion has thus reached the point in which it is advisable to say a few words about indoctrination. The word is not free from ambiguity. One definition of the dictionary makes it a synonym for teaching. In order that there may be a definite point to consider, I shall take indoctrination to mean the systematic use of every possible means to impress upon the minds of pupils a particular set of political and economic views to the exclusion of every other. This meaning is suggested by the word "inculcation," whose original signification was "to stamp in with the heel." This signification is too physical to be carried over literally. But the idea of stamping in is involved, and upon occasion does include physical measures. I shall discuss this view only as far as to state, in the first place, that indoctrination so conceived is something very different from education, for the latter involves, as I understand it, the active participation of students in reaching conclusions and forming attributes. Even in the case of something as settled and agreed upon as the multiplication table, I should say if it is taught educatively, and not as a form of animal training, the active participation, the interest, reflection, and understanding of those taught are necessary.

The upholders of indoctrination rest their adherence to the theory in part upon the fact that there is a great deal of indoctrination now going on in the schools, especially with reference to narrow nationalism under the name of patriotism, and with reference to the dominant economic regime. These facts unfortunately *are* facts. But they do not prove that the right course is to seize upon the method of indoctrination and reverse its objective.

DEMOCRACY AS A FRAME OF REFERENCE

A much stronger argument is that unless education has some frame of reference it is bound to be aimless, lacking a unified objective. The necessity for a frame of reference must be admitted. There exists in this country such a unified frame. It is called democracy. I do not claim for a moment that the significance of democracy as a mode of life is so settled that there can be no disagreement as to its significance. The moment we leave glittering generalities and come to concrete details, there is great divergence. I certainly do not mean either that our political institutions as they have come to be, our parties, legislatures, laws, and courts constitute a model upon which a clear idea of democracy can be based. But there is a tradition and an idea which we can put in opposition to the very much that is undemocratic in our institutions. The idea and ideal involve at least the necessity of personal and voluntary participation in reaching decisions and executing them—in so far it is the contrary of the idea of indoctrination. And I, for one, am profoundly sceptical of the notion that because we now have a rather poor embodiment of democracy we can ultimately produce a genuine democracy by sweeping away what we have left of one.

The positive point, however, is that the democratic ideal, in its human significance, provides us with a frame of reference. The frame is not filled in, either in society at large or in its significance for education. I am not implying that it is so clear and definite that we can look at it as a traveler can look at a map and tell where to go from hour to hour. Rather the point I would make is that the *problem* of education in its relation to direction of social change is all one with the *problem* of finding out what democracy means in its total range of concrete applications; economic, domestic, international, religious, cultural, economic, *and* political.

I cannot wish for anything better to happen for, and in, our schools than that this problem should become the chief theme for consideration until we have attained clarity concerning the concrete significance of democracy—which like everything concrete means its application in living action, individual and collective. The trouble, at least one great trouble, is that we have taken democracy for granted; we have thought and acted as if our forefathers had founded it once for all. We have forgotten that it has to be enacted anew in every generation, in every year and day, in the living relations of person to person in all social forms and institutions. Forgetting this, we have allowed our economic and hence our political institutions to drift away from democracy; we have been negligent even in creating a school that should be the constant nurse of democracy.

I conclude by saying that there is at least one thing in which the idea of democracy is not dim, however far short we have come from striving to make it reality. Our public school system was founded in the name of equality of opportunity for all, independent of birth, economic status, race, creed, or color. The school cannot by itself alone create or embody this idea. But the least it can do is to create individuals who understand the concrete meaning of the idea with their minds, who cherish it warmly in their hearts, and who are equipped to battle in its behalf in their actions.

Democracy also means voluntary choice, based on an intelligence that is the outcome of free association and communication with others. It means a way of living together in which mutual and free consultation rule instead of force, and in which cooperation instead of brutal competition is the law of life; a social order in which all the forces that make for friendship, beauty, and knowledge are cherished in order that each individual may become what he, and he alone, is capable of becoming. These things at least give a point of departure for the filling in of the democratic idea and aim as a frame of reference. If a sufficient number of educators devote themselves to striving courageously and with full sincerity to find the answers to the concrete questions which the idea and the aim put to us, I believe that the question of the relation of the schools to direction of social change will cease to be a question, and will become a moving answer in action.

John Dewey

Conflicting Theories of Education

I. L. Kandel (1881–1965), a professor of education, is considered the father of the study of comparative and international education in the United States. He founded the Center for International Studies of Education at Teachers College, Columbia University, in the 1930s and edited more than 20 of the yearbooks on world education published by the center. He published lengthy studies on the educational systems in Germany, France, and several other nations as well as on issues in American education. He wrote one of the first textbooks on comparative education and one of the first critiques of the Nazi educational program in Germany, *The Making of Nazis* (Teachers College Press, 1935).

Kandel saw a threat to democratic nation states in the 1930s. What he had to say about it is as relevant for our time as it was for his. The selection that follows is from *Conflicting Theories of Education* (Macmillan, 1938). In it, Kandel discusses the role of education in defense of freedom of thought, and he addresses the issue of education and social change. He argues that educational processes do not take place in a social or cultural vacuum; schools are institutions created by societies to achieve certain specific purposes. He maintains that students should be taught to understand the world in which they live. Here he discusses teachers' responsibilities in dealing with social controversies. He says that there is no choice but to bring conflicting social issues into the classroom.

Key Concept: education and social change

*E*ducation does not . . . take place in a vacuum. The school is an agency established by society to achieve certain ends. These ends will differ according to the form of each society. Totalitarian states have adopted fixed patterns into which the individual is to be molded. Democracies will fail if they attempt to adopt a type of education which ignores any values but those chosen by each individual to suit the needs of the moment. The mystical, irrational notion that freedom is synonymous with the right to follow inner drives ignores both the history and the meaning of freedom.

I. L. Kandel

That freedom is a conquest has been as true of the progress of humanity as it is of the growth of the individual. The whole history of humanity has been—despite aberrations in recent years—the history of the emancipation from external controls and, at the same time, of the ways in which man has learned to control himself. This history has been one of the emancipation of man from servitude to fears—fears of nature, slavery, political tyranny, and external controls and coercion over life. Man's struggle for personal freedom, freedom of movement, freedom of thought and expression, freedom of worship, justice, tolerance, and equality of opportunity has been painfully slow and is not yet ended. But in emerging successfully from the struggle, man did so by learning that he must accept certain limitations on his freedom, by recognizing his responsibility and duty to others. It was only as man learned to appreciate the moral consequence of his actions that he became free.

What has been true of the history of civilization applies equally to the education of the individual—freedom is not an inherent right (totalitarian states have proved how easily it may be lost) but a privilege to be won. And it is in confusing freedom with noninterference and in failing to stress social and moral obligations adequately that those who have most loudly urged freedom in education have erred. The slogan of self-expression, for example, failed to recognize that the true self can be realized only in and through a social milieu. Hence, the fundamental issue is the extent to which such realization of the self can be free and yet result in a personality enriched through and by a consciousness of social values. Here again the answer will be found in the principle that freedom is a right which, like all other rights, must be won, and that all rights imply a corresponding responsibility in their use, no matter what the field of activity may be.

A free society cannot divest itself of the obligation of handing on to new generations those common traditions, loyalties, and interests which make community life possible, but it can and should avoid that claim to omniscience and infallibility which must in the long run spell stagnation and failure to permit adaptation to changing conditions. If this is accepted, then the only thing that a free society should indoctrinate is faith in freedom and in free inquiry. But the essence of freedom and free inquiry is the recognition of responsibility. Not until the concept of responsibility is incorporated in the discussion of education in a free society, can education be expected to make its rightful contribution to a troubled world. For such a discussion Santayana's description of English liberty may well furnish the text, for in it may be found the answer of a free society to the criticisms of the totalitarian: "It moves by a series of checks, mutual concessions, and limited satisfactions; it counts on chivalry, sportsmanship, brotherly love, and on that rarest and least lucrative of virtues, fair-mindedness; it is a broad-based, stupid, blind adventure, groping towards an unknown goal."

And this, in essence, is the definition of liberal education, which has unfortunately acquired a connotation in terms of familiarity with certain subjects. But a liberal education implies more than a knowledge of classical or modern languages, science and mathematics. It implies breadth of interests, knowledge and information, standards of taste and appreciation, and the possession of certain moral and social qualities. It should result in tolerance and open-mindedness, in ability to meet new situations because one has knowledge and insight, and in readiness to co-operate because of a refined sense of responsibility. All these are social values, values which make the existence of a free society possible and which cannot be acquired incidentally as and when the pupil feels the need of them.

. . . And if a free society is to accept the challenge and meet the charges of totalitarianism it will be only as it realizes that there must be common agreement, common social faith, and common values as a foundation for that freedom upon which it is based. It is upon these common elements, consciously and deliberately recognized and defined, that education can build a free personality. To set up the child as an idol and to worship his inner drives, urges, and impulses is to encourage chaos; to set up the ideal of a free personality implies a vision of social purposes which alone can give meaning to education and save the rising generation from immersion in the destructive element which sees no values in the past, no meaning in the present, and no hope in the future. In this task of defining the meaning of freedom in education the English-speaking peoples can find a field of common endeavor—England with her reverence for traditional values and deliberate and cautious acceptance of change, the United States with her buoyant optimism and preference for change at the cost of traditions, and the Dominions rooted in British traditions but with the vigor and vision of youthful pioneers. Democratic institutions may safely be entrusted to them, but only as these nations become conscious of the significance of these institutions for humanity and the part to be played by education in their preservation. . . .

EDUCATION AND SOCIAL CHANGE

The general social and cultural unrest which can be traced back to the beginnings of the modern scientific movement and the consequent technological changes, an unrest which has grown in intensity since the War, has had its repercussions on educational thought. This has, indeed, been the history of education, for education has been most vigorous and vital in periods of great social changes, as, for example, in Athens, during the Renaissance and the Reformation, at the time of the early scientific movement of the seventeenth century, and at the beginning of the nineteenth century following the Industrial Revolution and the consolidation of nation-states. The period through which the world is passing in the present era is probably one of those nodal periods in which old ideas and ideals, standards and loyalties, are being questioned and modified, if not revolutionized. Science is remaking the world and bringing an economic upheaval in its train; political institutions are being questioned or overturned; a war of ideas is going on in every field that concerns human relationships. The conflicts are more profound and more widespread than those which have always existed between the older and younger generations.

I. L. Kandel

Under these conditions unrest in education is inevitable, but in the discussions on education and social change it is not clear whether a formula is being sought whereby the rising generation shall be acquainted with the social changes going on about it or whether it is proposed that the school itself should be made an instrument for the reconstruction of society. These alternatives can be answered only in the light of the purposes for which society establishes schools.

The earliest and most persistent reason for the establishment of schools as formal agencies of education is the desire on the part of a group, society, or state to conserve and transmit its culture and heritage to the younger generation and to equip this generation with those habits, skills, knowledges, and ideals that will enable it to take its place in a society and contribute to the stability and perpetuation of that society. This purpose is based on faith in the possibilities of formal education during the formative and plastic period of childhood and adolescence. This is the principle in Plato's statement that the effectual functioning of the state depends upon the proper training of the young, and in Aristotle's insistence that the stability of systems of government has its basis in the adaptation of education to the form of government.

Education does not proceed in a vacuum; its character is determined by the group culture, and schools are institutions created by society to attain certain specific ends. These ends began to be defined when the national states at the beginning of the nineteenth century undertook to establish systems of education to initiate their future citizens into the national culture. Stability was to be secured by instructing the pupils in the schools in a common language, common history, common government and political ideals, common economic and social ideas and ideals, and common objects of social allegiance in order that there might emerge a common group, or national, self-consciousness. If the younger generation is to enter into meaningful partnership in and responsibility for its heritage the first function of the school is to initiate it into its common culture. Society is, in fact, prior to the individual, and the school is an agency for promoting stability and adapting the individual to the environment in which he lives. Without entering into other considerations which justify the transmission of the social heritage or the experiences of the race as a basis for understanding the present, it will be generally agreed that the function here described has received wide acceptance from the days of Plato down to modern times.

If, however, the school stops with the performance of this function, then a society either stagnates, as was the case in China, or its progress is determined by the will of the few who lead the rest, trained through the school to habits of duty, discipline, quiescent obedience, and uncritical acceptance of authority. The method of such a school is that of direct indoctrination and education becomes indistinguishable from propaganda. This was already the trend in authoritarian states of the last century; it is the principle definitely accepted in the totalitarian states of the present, in which education is directed by and to a common ideology. The social changes wrought by revolutions have produced patterns which know no compromise and are not open to question or criticism. Education has become adjustment to a fixed and unchanging environment, and national culture is something that is colored by a particular ideology and controlled by organizations created to prevent changes in it.

The situation is different in those countries in which culture is accepted as the spontaneous expression of individuals and the free interplay among individuals or groups. It is at this point that education and social change begin to be clothed with meaning and to challenge traditional practices. The procedure in the past was to impart a body of content, knowledge, and information representing selections from the group culture designed primarily to "train the mind." It tended to become stereotyped and formal and rarely came to grips with the present. The school was a cloistered institution which eschewed any contact with the environment into which the pupil was soon to pass. It must be remembered, however, that even this type of procedure did not ignore the changing environment and was not designed to maintain a static society, but it was conducted with the conviction that a mind trained by "academic" or "scholastic" material would have no difficulty in dealing with the realities of life. Nor was the procedure in the education of the masses differentiated from the procedure in the education of the potential leaders.

These practices were not accepted without protest. Since the days of Seneca educators have urged that education must be for life and not for the school, but it was not until the beginning of the present century that widespread efforts began to be made to bring school and society together. A better understanding of the process of child growth, a new interpretation of the concept of interest, a clearer realization of the meaning of democracy and the part to be played by the individual in it, and the rapid changes in the culture, due in the main to the progress of science—all these forces and many others contributed to the spread of the theory that if education is a social process, it must contribute to an understanding of the society which it serves. The influence of John Dewey's philosophy in bringing about the change of outlook not only in the United States but in other parts of the world is too well known to need further discussion. The vast body of educational literature which has grown up in the United States in the past three decades speaks eloquently of this influence. The educational trend in Germany during the period of the short-lived Republic was rooted in *Bodenständigkeit*, the relation of education to the environment. In England the latest edition of the *Handbook of Suggestions for Teachers* is inspired by the same principle, as is illustrated by a statement in the general introduction that "we feel more deeply the need of relating what is taught in the schools to what is happening in the world outside."

The new theory of education, in insisting that the work of the school must be related to the environment in which and for which its pupils are being educated, contains in its definition the suggestion that discussions of social change are implicit in the curriculum. It means that pupils should be taught to understand the world in which they live. Up to this point the problem is fairly simple. Difficulties arise, however, when it is suggested that change is the characteristic note of the present world—and change not merely in its material but in its ideational aspects. To what extent should or can the school concern itself with political and economic conflicts, with changes in the attitudes to authority, or with the general atmosphere that questions all traditions?

Changes in the material world are facts; political and economic theories are matters of opinion. If the teacher is an agent of the state, to what extent is he free to introduce controversial issues into the classroom? It is not necessary here to state that the issues should be relevant to the stage of development and the maturity of the pupils concerned and to the subject of instruction. But if the function of education is to develop an understanding of the problems of the environment in which the learner lives, the opportunity of discussing controversial issues in the school cannot be ignored. Indeed, one may argue that it is essential to train the pupil in recognizing the importance of accurate knowledge before reaching an opinion.

If the doors of the school are to be closed to the discussion of controversial issues, it might well be asked what the alternative would be; in a period of change the schools would be guilty of turning pupils out into the world ignorant of the problems that will confront them. There is, in fact, no choice but to bring those elements of conflict into the classroom. To adopt an ostrichlike attitude and ignore the existence of such issues, to deny the right to mention even the existence of what may be regarded as subversive ideas, is to follow the old practice of ignoring the existence of sex. Carried to its logical conclusion, such a policy could be used to justify the suppression of a free press and of freedom of opinion, and the arrest of anyone suspected of "harboring dangerous thoughts."

Any reference to the introduction of controversial issues in politics and economics arouses the fear that pupils will be exposed to the bias of the teachers. It may be true that no teacher can successfully conduct a discussion of controversial issues without the pupils' detecting his bias. Nevertheless, pupils pass through the hands of a large number of teachers during their school careers; to suspect that all teachers have the same bias has no justification in fact; nor are teachers the only educational influences that play upon the growing youth. The choice is whether the rising generation is to receive its political and economic education through informal agencies or through methods that are truly educative; whether the young are to be enlightened and trained through the scientific study of facts or whether they are to be exposed to deliberate propaganda without the support of accurate information on both sides of an issue. If the relationship between school and society or education and the environment means anything, then the schools must, at the appropriate stage, impart the realities of society. And if that society is in process of change, then all that the school can do is to place the pupils in possession of full knowledge of the facts in the issues involved and to give them that training which will enable them to make up their own minds on the basis of that knowledge.

The emphasis in this argument is on training in methods of thinking through issues that are real. There is some truth in the objection that solutions cannot be given to contemporary controversial issues; this objection is, however, not a valid argument for their exclusion from the schools. Neither the issues nor the solutions are likely to be the same when pupils now in school take their places in life as adult citizens; the detailed facts of an issue and the knowledge requisite to its solution will inevitably be different, but unless some training is given in the schools in the patterns of thinking with which a problem is to be approached, the intellectual equipment necessary to recognize even the existence of problems will have been withheld. If democracy depends for its survival upon the intelligence and understanding of the ordinary man, it is the function of the school to equip him in advance with the necessary knowledge and powers of clear thinking to discharge his duties as a citizen.

It is only in this sense that education and social change can be discussed. Education must go beyond its task of imparting a knowledge and appreciation of the common interests, or what Dewey has called the objects of that social allegiance which makes common social understanding and consciousness of group membership possible. It must help men and women to think for themselves, unless they are to succumb to the will of an authority which claims omniscience and infallibility.

There has, however, been injected into discussions of education and social change the suggestion that schools should, in a period of change, educate for a new social order, and that teachers should ally themselves with some political group and use their classrooms to propagate certain doctrines. Schools and teachers should, in other words, participate more directly and vitally in projecting particular ideas or patterns of social change and in their execution. The whole history of education emphasizes the impossibility of this idea, for society establishes schools to provide a firm basis for itself and to sustain the common interest. Schools are a part of the environment which they serve; they are not autonomous or insulated against the social forces and influences around them; nor can teachers on the basis of a guess as to the active forces of the day help to build a new social order. Society changes first and schools follow.

It is, however, becoming increasingly important that teachers should be more alive than they have been in the past and better informed about the environment in and for which they are educating their pupils. Only in this way can they give meaning to the subjects for which they are responsible, for subjects, if they are to have any significance, must be saturated with social meaning. To attempt to instill ready-made ideas on controversial issues or to influence pupils to accept one doctrine rather than another is to adopt the methods of totalitarian states and to confuse education with propaganda.

In a democracy the only acceptable aim in bringing the school and society more closely together is to develop the knowledge and understanding that make for enlightened citizenship. But the acquisition of knowledge, facts, and information about the environment in all those aspects that concern the conduct of the citizen is not the sole end of education; such an acquisition must be made the vehicle for training in scientific methods of thinking and for cultivating free and disciplined minds. To educate for a new social order is to close the minds of the pupils, for, in a society in transition, no one can have a final answer concerning the issues that are involved. True education would help to put the pupils in a position to appreciate the urgent necessity of acquiring knowledge, to discriminate between facts and prejudices, to weigh and judge evidence, to reach conclusions warranted by the information secured, and to recognize the issues involved in a period of social transition or crisis. If this end is to be achieved, if the aim of education is to develop free and enlightened citizens, then the teachers who are to be entrusted with carrying out this aim must themselves be enlightened and free. The problem, like all other problems in education, becomes one of teacher preparation and of the status of teachers. In the words of a former president of the English Board of Education, "The standards of the teaching profession itself are the only sure protection" against the abuse of the teachers' positions in discussing educational and social change.

The problem of education and social change solves itself if education is defined as the process of bringing pupils to an understanding of the environment in and for which they are being educated. That environment is a constantly expanding one; to concentrate on change alone is to deal only with the immediate present and to avoid the development of an understanding of the rich heritage which the environment carries with it. But understanding must lead to conduct, and if democracy is to survive, the schools must cultivate in their pupils ideals of freedom, tolerance, and open-mindedness, a critical attitude and intellectual sensitiveness based on ascertained facts and knowledge, a spirit of inquiry and insight, and those emotional qualities in addition which make for a sense of responsibility and cooperation. For democracy, in the words of Santayana, is a blind, groping adventure which implies openmindedness and sensitiveness to the need of flexibility and adaptation of social institutions. These are the qualities which education can cultivate as the basis of social change. . . .

EDUCATION AND THE CHALLENGE TO DEMOCRACY

In the war of ideas which is raging between totalitarianism and democracy the special responsibility which falls on education in a democracy is too frequently ignored. This is in part due to failure to recognize the challenge to democratic ideals; it is due also to the basic difference between the two groups of ideas—totalitarianism because it is built on a set body of doctrines dominated by acceptance of the supremacy of the state has by far the simpler task in education, while democracy as an ideal is a way of life based on the freedom and responsibility of the individual. The democratic state depends upon the collective will of the individuals who make it up and exists to guarantee the rights of individuals and to maintain justice between them; though too frequently the free citizen of a democracy is more conscious of his rights than he is of his duties. The totalitarian state insists upon the co-ordination of all individuals so that all think and behave like all other individuals, and how they may think and behave is determined by a dictator or a party. The essence of democracy is that each individual thinks for himself and behaves as his conscience dictates, provided that he does not encroach on the right of others to do the same. In the one case the individual must be "in the right line"; in the other the individual has a right to his own opinions.

The totalitarian state has recognized more clearly than the democratic the axiom already enunciated by Plato and Aristotle that education and the form of government are closely interdependent, that education, in other words, is an instrument of social control employed to perpetuate society and to advance social progress. Whether education is defined as a process of molding all individuals to the same pattern or of promoting progress through the enlightenment of all individuals depends upon the nature of the state and its form of government. Here is to be found the explanation of the interest shown in the provision of education by the nation states in the nineteenth century as well as the insistence of George Washington on the enlightenment of public opinion through "institutions for the general diffusion of knowledge."

Education and the Social Crisis: A Proposed Program

William Heard Kilpatrick (1871–1965), one of the principal founders of progressive, experience-based education, was deeply concerned about what roles teachers should play with regard to social reform and reconstruction. Kilpatrick taught in the Mercer public schools and at Mercer University in Macon, Georgia, and he was a professor of philosophy of education in the Teachers College at Columbia University in New York. He published several books, including *Education for a Changing Civilization* (1926).

In 1932 Kilpatrick gave the biennial, national Kappa Delta Pi lecture and then extended it for publication that year. The selection that follows is from that publication. In it, Professor Kilpatrick discusses the social crisis that faced American society in the depth of the great economic depression of the 1930s. He examines the issues of partisanship, indoctrination, and open-mindedness, as well as the roles of teachers and whether or not they should discuss their personal views in the classroom. Kilpatrick, who opposed the use of indoctrinational teaching methods, asserts that teachers should share their social ideas with students but that they should not exclude or inhibit the students' development of their own ideas about social institutions and beliefs. He further argues that it is inevitable that teachers will develop social opinions of their own and that the issue for teachers is how they should deal with their own beliefs in working with students.

Key Concept: the role of teachers

EDUCATION AND INDOCTRINATION

This problem of indoctrination is so complex and those who discuss it so easily get lost in the maze of definitions that we must pick our way here with care.

Originally education as an intentional process was precisely limited to handing down unimpaired the tribal customs, such customs, that is, as might suffer if they were not given special consideration. The presupposition to this educational practice was that neither elders nor youth might properly question what was thus handed down. Learn meant that the youth should accept and acquire what was authoritatively set before them. Teach meant the process of setting out the official tribal doctrines and customs and requiring the youth to learn them. Docility was the chief virtue of youth, as fidelity to tribal ways was that of the elders.

After letters came and philosophic doctrine was formulated in Greece, the schools, which had already become literary, now became formal, with, however, the same presuppositions underlying. Knowledge was not to be questioned, though it might be understood so as to be better learned. In any event it must be accepted. Learn still meant faithful acquisition. Teach still meant supervising and enforcing the process. With the coming of Christianity and orthodoxy, these presuppositions were even sharpened and made more rigid. In other respects knowledge and learning and docility kept their old definitions. Docility became even more surely a virtue.

With the Reformation orthodoxy became plural, but the presuppositions otherwise remained. Schools now became strictly partisan, with indoctrination their conscious policy. The aim was to fix our doctrine in our young—and in any others we could get access to—so that when they became old they would not depart from it. This was the education brought to America.

With the coming of American independence, the necessity of respecting many religious faiths and the general Deistic outlook among the leaders united to bring about the American doctrine of the separation of church and state. When state public schools became prevalent religious teaching was (nominally) excluded, and the ideal arose of impartiality before sectarian and partisan differences; so that in professed theory the public school avoids indoctrination along any partisan line. Fairness has seemed to demand it.

Meanwhile another line of influence was developing within the social life of the people. Science and invention brought on industrialization. Changes within our institutional life became more numerous and immigration more divergent from the original stock. Two opposed reactions then arose, one to question tradition and criticize institutional life in the wish to facilitate changes along better lines, the other to fear and oppose change and cultural diversity and to seek accordingly to unify the nation on a crystallized American tradition.

Whereupon it became evident that the public school had never ceased to "indoctrinate," even in the matter of sectarian and partisan differences. The rule against indoctrination held only where old stock America was locally divided. Otherwise a different rule prevailed. By a sort of tacit agreement there has been presupposed in the opening exercises of our public schools, in the songs, holidays, text-books, and teaching emphases the united old stock outlook—the Protestant, Nordic, American democratic-republican, *laissez-faire*, capitalistic way of looking at things. The Bible (King James version) is often, if not commonly, read (certain states require it). Protestant Christian songs may be sung. Nordic superiority is assumed, any questioning of the perfection of our political and social institutions is taboo, socialism and communism may be denounced but hardly otherwise discussed. Programs are made on this basis, text-books are so written, teaching is so conducted. After the World War this hitherto more or less unconscious inculcation of the favored position became a more conscious policy. The Ku Klux, the American Legion, the D.A.R., the National Security League, and the like, virtually joined hands to establish in our schools a conscious and compulsory system of indoctrination in what they proclaim to be the only true American tradition.

Against this obscurantist position another has meanwhile been at work, especially among the better educated. This claims to represent more truly the better American tradition as propounded by Franklin, Adams, Jefferson, Madison and Washington in favor of free speech and conscious study, but even more to represent the necessity of open study if in these shifting times we are to direct our policies in the light of intelligence. This position, admitting differences due to age, would encourage the frank investigation on the part of teachers, pupils and students of our social and political history and institutional life, believing that only from such open-minded study and investigation can the best education be got.

The proponents of this latter position are particularly impressed with the historic fact that most, if not all, of present-day approved institutions had at their inception to fight for a chance to live as against the opposition of the then *status quo* outlook. They think the like opposition is at work now. They freely admit that many worthless and even hurtful proposals are from time to time offered for acceptance, but they still hold that the open-minded discussion of any and all proposals on their merits seems the only reliable means by which to select the better from the worse. From this point of view that kind of education is to be sought which best makes for the habit and disposition of open-minded criticism with reliable skill in the process. Moreover—those of this position go on still further to assert—intelligent citizenship is impossible without such open study and criticism of institutional life, for intelligent action is impossible apart from an all-round knowledge of weaknesses as well as strengths. This position, accordingly, favors this open-minded study and rejects indoctrination (in the bad sense). The latter it defines as any kind of education which sets out so to teach anything that later on it cannot or will not be questioned on its merits even if reasonable cause so to do should appear. Or, from another angle, indoctrination is any kind of education which does not intend so to teach as to make the learner a better independent judge of the matter under consideration. Thus has the "liberal" position hitherto opposed indoctrination.

More recently, however, a new line of thought has been presented. Some who wish to see adopted a thorough-going scheme of social planning have questioned the adequacy of the foregoing discussion of "indoctrination." These ask whether or not merely to be born and grow up in a given group does not inevitably indoctrinate one in the habits, customs and outlooks of that group and whether this is not good rather than evil, whether to fail so to indoctrinate would not leave the young without culture at all—than which no worse state could well be imagined. These go on further to ask whether, therefore, the most important of all problems is not as to the kind of culture which will be imposed upon the young, and whether, accordingly, education should not assume the task of helping to devise a better culture and teaching this openly and intentionally to the young. These ask, more specifically, whether or not there does not now go on in this country, partly unconsciously but partly intentionally, an actual indoctrination in outworn and now hurtful institutional forms and theories, particularly in the matter of the economic system, and whether it is not necessary for the educational profession, as of right and duty the protagonist of the best possible culture and civilization, to take effectual steps to supplant this hurtful indoctrination with a better. And they ask, still further, whether our ideal citizen is the impartial student of each new proposal that comes along. Is not the ideal citizen, on the contrary, rather, one who feels values and has convictions so that he is ready to give himself to them, to work and fight for them if necessary? And amid such times as these, when selfishness sits entrenched in tradition, can men of insight rest in such scholarly impartiality? Must they not—teachers as well as others—so burn with conviction and zeal that they will seek in season and out to tear down the selfish tradition and build instead the needed tradition of supreme allegiance to the common good? . . .

THE TEACHER AND HIS CONVICTIONS

That our schools now help to indoctrinate our pupils in outworn and now hurtful social and institutional beliefs and attitudes appears to be quite true. That a better school should work against this indoctrination and should besides take positive steps to help bring a better day is one of the underlying theses of this book. But the writer finds himself still unwilling to have our schools embark on any policy of partisan indoctrination, even in behalf of a course dear to himself. The reasons for this reluctance lie along two main lines; first, such indoctrination fails of giving the children what seems to be the highest available type of education; second, such a partisan indoctrination means that I approve a public policy for the schools when I and my party are in control but which I am unwilling to have put into operation when rival doctrines are in control.

If, then, I am teaching young people, I shall feel it my supreme duty to them that they shall grow in such fashion that they become more and more significantly sensitive to life about them, both its deficiencies and its possibilities, how to correct the former and how to better attain the latter, believing that if they will so grow they will at one and the same time be both happier as individual persons and more effectually coöperative with others who are working for better things.

What shall I in connection do about my own convictions? Shall I use them in teaching these young people or shall I teach quite independently of what I think? If I really have convictions that matter to me I cannot possible teach independently of them. They are an essential part of me. Does this mean that I shall set up my convictions as formulations which my pupils should accept and so "teach" them? It does not. That would not be education. I must know that there are difficulties here and I must guard against the dangers involved. I must use the best knowledge I have in helping my pupils to survey the field and to weigh the arguments. But I must be careful that my superior knowledge does not keep them from searching and thinking and concluding for themselves. Probably I must at some stage tell openly what I think, but I must so tell it and so couple other possibilities with it that my pupils are not unduly influenced to accept my position on any basis of authority. Otherwise, I am not making them independent and capable in thinking, or, more exactly, I am keeping them from really thinking and so from growing as they should.

If I teach in this manner, what hope have I that my pupils will think "as they should"? My hope is in the working of intelligent study. My pupils may not conclude what I have concluded. I am not properly working for that. What I should wish is that they shall so think while I am helping them that they shall better think then and even better also later. As for concluding what I think, I may be wrong, I may myself think differently later. As I should not wish to tie my later thinking to my present conclusions, so I should not wish to tie their thinking to my present conclusions. I must wish them to grow even as I wish for myself to grow, and this even to the point of improving over what I now think.

I shall, accordingly, use my present best knowledge to help map out the field of study. In so doing I must avoid the extremes, on the one hand, of too broad a field so as to weary my pupils and waste their endeavors, and, on the other hand, of too narrow a field lest their vision be limited to a view that sees only the selected evidence that precisely supports my conclusion and they have no fair chance to study and judge for themselves. Also, I must help them to see as alternatives, the chief rivals to my conclusions. And similarly all through, what I have judged best at each stage and point must be the basis for mapping an area on both sides of my own thought process, neither too broad nor too narrow. For my pupils must study fairly and conclude accordingly, else I am not helping them the best possible.

This way of utilizing my best knowledge, yet so as not to indoctrinate my pupils, gives me my just defense when others would charge me with using my school access to foster in partisan fashion my own position. I have not "taught" my position. I have made my pupils study not so much it as an area. My position will be considered as one of the possible hypotheses, but always in comparison with other positions. I may even present the argument that influenced my own decision, but in such fashion that through it all my pupils have been helped to learn to think and decide for themselves. This, and not that they reach my decision, has been my aim. That I shall not entirely succeed in maintaining my intended fairness is but probable, but I must make the effort.

Some may ask whether this care to keep the teacher's conviction from affecting unduly the thought processes of the pupils may not deprive them of possibly the best part of an education, namely vision and zeal, vision of a worthy cause and zeal to pursue it. That there is danger need not be denied, but is it not fairer to charge the possible loss here rather to the attitude within the community than to the teacher? It is this which makes it a partisan matter. Because the parents feel as they do, the teacher cannot speak freely. His long-run effectual influence demands that he make manifest his fairness on the partisan question, even at some loss elsewhere. Even so he can present his position with its vision as one hypothesis for consideration, so that, even at the worst, there need be no total loss. Of course, if the parents were united in sharing the teacher's conviction, or if they were indifferent, he could work more effectually on the vision and zeal, though even then he should have to guard the pupils' thinking lest his position interfere there. The teacher's task in the face of partisan opposition is simply the common situation involving contradictory values. Do what he will, he cannot get all. He must act for the largest whole as best he can see it.

CHAPTER 16 Culture and Education

16.1 JOEL SPRING

Education as a Form of Social Control

Joel Spring is a professor of education at the State University of New York College at Old Westbury. He has also taught at Case Western Reserve University in Cleveland, Ohio, and at the University of Cincinnati. Spring has published several important books in which he has tried to document the uses of schooling as a means of social control in society, including *The American School: 1642–1990,* 2d ed. (Longman, 1990) and *The Sorting Machine Revisited: National Educational Policy Since 1945* (Longman, 1989).

In the following selection, from Clarence J. Karier, Paul C. Violas, and Joel Spring, eds., *Roots of Crisis: American Education in the Twentieth Century* (Rand McNally, 1973), Spring discusses how schools are used by dominant social groups whose values the schools represent to maintain social control. An insightful treatment of the idea of schooling and the social uses of schooling, Spring's analysis of the social foundations of education shares the perspective of theorists in critical and liberation pedagogy.

Key Concept: schooling and social control

*B*y the beginning of the twentieth century, industrialization and urbanization had severely eroded the influence of family, church, and community on individual behavior. As the power of these institutions waned, the school became increasingly important as a primary instrument for social control. It became *the* agency charged with the responsibility of maintaining social order and cohesion and of instilling individuals with codes of conduct and social values that would insure the stability of existing social relationships. Although a preserving institution, the school was viewed as a form of internal control—and therefore more in the "democratic" tradition than such external forms as law, government, and police.

American sociologist Edward A. Ross, in a series of articles published in the *American Journal of Sociology* between 1896 and 1898, was the first to state explicitly the ideology of social control. The articles were later gathered together as a book under the title *Social Control* and attracted a wide audience among both sociologists and educators. In his study of social control mechanisms, Ross referred to education as an inexpensive form of police. In what was to become a traditional way of defining the concept, Ross divided social control into external and internal forms, stressing that future societies would probably rely more on internal or psychic than on external forms of social manipulation. Traditionally, Ross argued, internal forms of control had centered on the family, the church, and the community. The family and church had worked on the child to inculcate moral values and social responsibility to insure social stability and cohesion. The small community had provided the individual with a social context in which he saw his own interests as inseparable from those of others. In terms of social psychology, Ross believed, the individual developed within a small community a social self that was shared by other members of that same community.

SOCIAL CONTROL

Ross, writing from the perspective of the 1890s, when industrialization and urbanization were rapidly taking hold in America, arrived at the conclusion that it was precisely these institutions—the family, the church, and the community—that were disintegrating under the forces of modernity. To replace these deteriorating institutions Ross suggested new forms of control, such as mass media, propaganda, and education. Reliance on education as a new means of control, Ross argued, was in fact exactly what was becoming a characteristic of American society. More and more the school was taking the place of the church and the family. "The ebb of religion is only half a fact," Ross wrote. "The other half is the high tide of education. While the priest is leaving the civil service, the schoolmaster is coming in. As the state shakes itself loose from the church, it reaches out for the school."[1] In an extremely perceptive statement Ross saw quite clearly the parallel between the decline of the church and the rise of the school. "Step by step," he said, "with disestablishment of religion proceeds the establishment of education; so that today the moneys, public or private, set apart for schools and universities far surpass the medieval endowments of abbeys and sees."[2]

The advantages Ross saw in using the school as a central agency of control centered on his faith in the malleability of youth. In a startling and revealing statement, he argued that civilization was reaching an understanding of the effectiveness of education for social control. "To collect little plastic lumps of human dough from private households and shape them on the social kneadingboard," he wrote, "exhibits a faith in the power of suggestion which few peoples ever attain."[3] Ross emphasized the process of schooling over curriculum content as the key to preparing the individual for society. And the advantage of the school over the home as a means of control lay in the fact that a public official was substituted for the parent. "Copy the child will, and the advantage of giving him his teacher instead of his father to imitate, is that the former is a picked person, while the latter is not." In school the child learned "the habit of obedience to an external law which is given by a good school discipline." The teacher, in Ross's terms, also represented a subtle form of authority that heightened the effectiveness of the school as an instrument of social control. He believed that "the position of the teacher gives him prestige, and the lad will take from him suggestions that the adult will accept only from rare and splendid personalities."[4]

The ideology of social control also found its place in the early university departments of urban sociology. Among the first and probably the most important was the University of Chicago Department of Urban Sociology founded by Robert Park. From here poured forth a flood of projects that influenced the whole course of urban studies in the United States. Park defined the breakdown of the neighborhood and family as the major problem of modern urban living. Deterioration of these social controls was causing social disorganization that could be halted only through the establishment of new institutional forms of control. To Park, for example, art museums and spectator sports represented means of calming the restlessness of the urban man. "It is at this point that sport, play, and art function," Park noted. "They permit the individual to purge himself by means of symbolic expression of these wild and suppressed impulses."[5] For Park the school was to have a central role in replacing the role of the neighborhood and family. Writing in the 1920s, Park concluded that indeed the school was already replacing family and neighborhood controls. "The school," he stated, " . . . has taken over some of the functions of the family. It is around the public school and its solicitude for the moral and physical welfare of the children that something like a new neighborhood and community spirit tends to get itself organized."[6]

The schools in the early part of the twentieth century were in fact expanding their responsibilities to act as effective instruments of control. It became common to say that the school was responsible for the whole child, which meant it had responsibility for all the child's activities. This led naturally to the idea that the school should expand its custodial functions beyond the classroom to include the child's entire social life. Play, dancing, and hobbies were to fall under the umbrella of schooling. The playground movement of the late nineteenth and early twentieth centuries had as its goal the ending of juvenile crime within the city. A Committee on Small Parks in New York City report in the 1890s claimed: "Crime in our large cities is to a great extent simply a question of athletics."[7] It seemed logical to the developers of playgrounds that the place to establish small parks was next to schoolhouses and that teachers be utilized to supervise play activities.

The role of the school expanded not only in terms of activities but also in terms of the amount of the child's time the institution occupied. This meant not only an expanded school day and year but also the institution of a summer session. Arguments given for summer schools show clearly how schooling was coming to be viewed more and more as an instrument of social control. The School Committee of Cambridge, Massachusetts, became in 1872 the first to ask for a summer school. The committee report for that year stated that summer was "a time of idleness, often of crime, with many who are left to roam the streets, with no friendly hand to guide them, save that of the police." Fifteen years later, the Cambridge superintendent wrote: "the value of these [summer] schools consists not so much in what shall be learned during the few weeks they are in session, as in the fact that no boy or girl shall be left with unoccupied time. Idleness is an opportunity for evil-doing. . . . These schools will cost money. Reform schools also cost money."[8]

THE SORTING PROCESS

Maintaining social order represents only one aspect of social control ideology. The second role of the school as an instrument of social control consists of differentiating pupils so that their educational training prepares them for a particular social slot. Within this context, social efficiency results from the efficient allocation of human resources for the industrial needs of society. While a differentiated curriculum and vocational guidance have been important means to achieve this goal, a more important development historically was the writing of group intelligence tests for the "scientific" differentiation of students. Studying the development of group intelligence tests lends insight into what this aspect of the sorting process meant with respect to social control and schooling.

Everyone acquainted with psychology knows that there is no adequate definition of intelligence. In fact, the question of what is intelligence has been widely debated in the twentieth century. In the absence of definition, intelligence tests have been validated by correlating their results with other factors, such as social success and other tests. The selection of outside criteria for validating the tests introduces value judgments. As will be explained in more detail later, the criteria used to judge the results of the first major group I.Q. test was the ability to be a good soldier. Immediate questions about the nature of the selective process arise, of course, when these same tests are used by the schools.

The World War I army Alpha and Beta were the first major group intelligence tests developed and administered, and they became a model for the construction of future testing programs. After the armistice in 1918, the government flooded the market with unused Alpha and Beta test booklets, which educators immediately utilized. Guy M. Whipple, a leading psychologist of the time, reported in 1922 that the army Alpha test was most widely used in colleges because it was the first group test constructed by a team of well-known psychologists that had been tried on large numbers of men in the army, and because "the test blanks were procurable for several months after the armistice at prices far below what other tests could be produced."[9]

The committee of psychologists that developed the army tests first met at Henry Herbert Goddard's Vineland Institute in New Jersey on May 28, 1917. Working with amazing speed the group completed its work by June 10 and after trying the tests in army camps, sent a copy of the examiner's guide to the printer on July 7. It was appropriate that the Vineland Institute was the site for this history-making event that still has a great influence on school organization. Goddard, director of Vineland, was primarily responsible for the translation and the introduction of French psychologist Alfred Binet's writings and tests into the United States. Binet had constructed intelligence tests as a vehicle for separating mentally retarded children from normal children at the behest of a commission organized by the French Minister of Public Instruction to establish standards for placing children in special schools.

From these intelligence tests Americans drew many of their ideas on test construction. Underlying the Binet test was a definition of intelligence both vague and relative. On the one hand Binet defined native intelligence as "judgment, otherwise called good sense, practical sense, initiative, the faculty of adapting one's self to circumstances."[10] On the other hand, Binet stated that intelligence was relative to the social situation of an individual. Thus "an attorney's son who is reduced by his intelligence to the condition of a menial employee is a moron . . . likewise a peasant, normal in ordinary surroundings of the fields, may be considered a moron in the city."[11] Confronted with the fact that his measurement of native intelligence varied with social class, Binet reflected the values implied in the test. While admitting that important differences in language ability between social classes might effect test results, he stated that social-class differences added validity to his test. "That this difference exists one might suspect," he wrote, "because our personal investigations, as well as those of many others, have demonstrated that children of the poorer class are shorter, weigh less, have smaller heads and slighter muscular force, than a child of the upper class; they less often reach the high school; they are more often behind in their studies."[12]

The army Alpha and Beta were developed with an equally vague definition of intelligence and depended for their validity on correlation with factors in army life. The team of army testers examined over one million men during the course of the war, evaluating results in terms of the test's ability to select good soldiers. For instance, in one army camp officers were asked to rate their men according to "practical soldier value." Comparing these ratings to soldiers' test scores, examiners found a high correlation between an officer's rating and the results of the Alpha and Beta tests. Validating the tests with officer's ratings in other army camps, examiners placed the coefficient of correlation between 0.50 and 0.70. The head of the army psychological team concluded: "The results suggest that intelligence is likely to prove the most important single factor in determining a man's value to the military service."[13]

What "practical soldier value" means in army life is the ability to follow orders and function within a rigidly disciplined and highly organized institutional structure. Instructions for the group examination for the Alpha test provide ample evidence that this was the meaning of intelligence that the test sought to measure, and the instructions were used almost word for word in subsequent examination booklets. For years after World War I, students taking tests were subjected to the same type of instructions given soldiers during the war. The instructions began: "When everything is ready E. [examiner] proceeds as follows: 'Attention! The purpose of this examination is to see how well you can remember, think and carry out what you are told to do.... The aim is to help find out what you are best fitted to do in the Army.... Now in the Army a man often has to listen to commands and carry them out exactly. I am going to give you some commands to see how well you can carry them out.' " In the schools these words might be translated into, "Part of being a good student is your ability to follow directions." Anyone who has taken such a test will recognize the instructions, "When I call 'Attention,' stop instantly whatever you are doing and hold your pencil up—so. Don't put your pencil down to the paper until I say 'Go! . . . Listen carefully to what I say. Do just what you are told to do. As soon as you are through, pencils up. Remember, wait for the word 'Go'."[14]

The army and the school are, of course, similar organizations. In a school, the superintendent sits as commander of the armies, the principal acts as field commander, the teachers as lesser officers, and below this command is a vast number of pupils. Orders flow from above and pupils, like soldiers, receive privileges but lack rights. Both organizations handle large numbers of recruits, which requires discipline and obedience to instructions. Soldiers must loyally obey commands and students must have faith that the directions they receive are in their best interests. Army test correlations with teacher ratings were very close to that of "practical soldier value." Reported correlations were between 0.67 and 0.82. Interestingly, correlations with officer ratings and teacher ratings were both higher than the 0.50 and 0.60 correlations with school marks.[15] If one assumes officer and teacher ratings depend more on character evaluation than marks, one could conclude that the group intelligence test might be more of a test of social character than of something called native intelligence.

Looked at within the context of social-control ideology, group I.Q. tests provided the mechanism for selectivity within the school. After World War I, the head of the army psychology team wrote, "Before the war mental engineering was a dream; today it exists, and its effective development is amply assured."[16] The dream of most psychologists, following their war experience, was to apply the selective procedures of I.Q. tests in all areas of society. After the war, Henry Herbert Goddard was willing to admit, "We do not know what intelligence is and it is doubtful if we even know what knowledge is." Even so, Goddard still insisted that "the efficiency of the human group is not so much a question of the absolute numbers of persons of high and low intelligence as it is whether each grade of intelligence is assigned a part, in the whole organization, that is within its capacity."[17] Selective differentiation in the school was to prepare students for selected social roles in society. The army model fit not only the school but also modern corporate structures dependent on a highly organized and stratified bureaucracy.

Quite obviously I.Q. tests, with their high degree of correlation with "practical soldier value," did much more than differentiate individuals on the basis of something called native intelligence. Implied in the whole testing movement was judgment about individual character. Good performance on the tests was enshrined as having more social value than traditional yardsticks used to measure the worth of a man. At times in the history of Western man, qualities such as humility, honor, justice, and compassion have been considered standards by which men judged a person's social worth. Among test makers the new standard became test ability. Some test constructers, such as Edward L. Thorndike, went so far as to suggest that ability to do well on tests gave evidence of justice and compassion. From this point of view, those who were "intelligent" were also good. Thorndike tried to make his intelligence tests difficult and long so they would show not only an individual's intelligence but also "his ability to stick to a long and, at the end, somewhat distasteful task." A report received from one institution of higher learning using the Thorndike test in the early 1920s stated "that two or three students fainted under the three-hour strain, and the faculty became indignant at this alleged imposition of hardship."[18]

On the other hand, I.Q. tests discriminate against certain personality types. Tests such as Alpha and Beta that correlated with army life, and others that correlated with ability in school, discriminated against those who could not or would not function well in a highly organized institutional structure. Because the tests were validated in terms of an individual's success within such institutions, they became not so much a test of something called native intelligence but rather one of ability to perform well in organized institutions. If one assumes—and this assumption has not been proven or disproven—that engineers represent a more organizationally directed type of personality than doctors, one result of Alpha test lends support to the assumption. Army psychologists during World War I had difficulty explaining the fact that engineering officers scored one grade higher on the test than medical officers. The head of the army psychology team admitted, "There is no obvious reason for assuming that the military duties of the engineer demand higher intelligence or more mental alertness than do those of the medical officer."[19] Army psychologists tried to handle this result by arguing that there was an uneven distribution of intelligence among the various branches of the service. They might have missed the point that medical men might have less "practical soldier" value than engineers, which after all was what the group intelligence tests were supposed to measure.

The quest for social control turned the school into a custodial institution designed to maintain the social order. It also led to differentiating and selecting students for social roles on the basis of tests validated primarily on success at institutional manipulation. All this placed extreme power in an institution that on the surface maintains the image of being benign and interested in helping the individual. The student, told it is for his own good, finds himself molded not in terms of personal needs but in terms of defined social needs and roles.

The school has truly become an inexpensive form of police, one whose very authority is supported by the argument that it is a place that helps the individual, and that an individual's interests cannot be separated from social needs.

Testing as an important part of the social control mechanism fragments the individual personality by placing emphasis only on certain individual characteristics. Whether one sees I.Q. test as determining some quantity called native intelligence, or ability to conform and survive in an institution, the result is the same. Honor, justice, compassion, humility, and goodwill all fall by the wayside when this selective mechanism is applied in the school. The student learns to place the greatest importance on that quality of intelligence that best meets the needs of society, which generally means the needs of industry and the corporate structure. In the end, the loss of other qualities creates not only incompletely developed individuals, but also a society directed intelligently, but not necessarily humanely.

NOTES

1. Edward A. Ross, *Social Control* (New York: Macmillan, 1906), p. 175.
2. Ibid., p. 175.
3. Ibid., p. 168.
4. Ibid., pp. 164–165.
5. Robert E. Park, Ernest W. Burgess, and Roderick D. McKenzie, *The City* (Chicago: University of Chicago Press, 1967), p. 43.
6. Ibid., p. 24.
7. Sadie American, "The Movement for Small Playgrounds," *American Journal of Sociology* 4(1898):176.
8. Sadie American, "The Movement for Vacation Schools," *American Journal of Sociology* 4(1898):291–296.
9. Guy M. Whipple, "Intelligence Tests in College and Universities," *National Society for the Study of Education Year Book* 21(1922):254.
10. Alfred Binet and T. Simon, *The Development of Intelligence in Children* (Baltimore: Williams & Wilkins, 1916), pp. 42–43.
11. Ibid., pp. 266–267.
12. Ibid., p. 318.
13. Clarence S. Yoakum and Robert M. Yerkes, eds., *Army Mental Tests* (New York: Henry Holt, 1920), pp. 20–32.
14. Ibid., pp. 53–55.
15. Ibid., p. 20.
16. Ibid., p. 197.
17. Henry Herbert Goddard, *Human Efficiency and Levels of Intelligence* (Princeton: Princeton University Press, 1920), p. 35.
18. See Whipple, "Intelligence Tests," pp. 259–260.
19. Yoakum and Yerkes, *Army Mental Tests*, p. 36.

Savage Inequalities: Children in America's Schools

Jonathan Kozol first came to national attention in 1967 with the publication of *Death at an Early Age,* which documents his experiences as a substitute teacher in a Boston elementary school. Since then, Kozol has written seven more books that examine the social context of education. He has traveled all over the United States observing schools and the conditions of the lives of children and their parents. He has conducted an in-depth study of the educational system in revolutionary Cuba, and he has studied the lives of teachers, parents, and students who confront savagely complex circumstances. He has frequently testified before congressional committees and lectured to groups of educators.

The following selection is from *Savage Inequalities: Children in America's Schools* (Crown Publishers, 1991). In *Savage Inequalities,* Kozol argues that America's schools are even more segregated than they were in 1954. He bases his conclusions on two years of observation in public schools and on conversations with parents, educators, and students. Many of the anecdotes from his interviews and observations are poignant reminders of how much needs to be done in the area of public education in the United States.

Key Concept: life in urban public schools

*I*t was a long time since I'd been with children in the public schools.

I had begun to teach in 1964 in Boston in a segregated school so crowded and so poor that it could not provide my fourth grade children with a classroom. We shared an auditorium with another fourth grade and the choir and a group that was rehearsing, starting in October, for a Christmas play that, somehow, never was produced. In the spring I was shifted to another fourth grade that had had a string of substitutes all year. The 35 children in the class hadn't had a permanent teacher since they entered kindergarten. That year, I was their thirteenth teacher.

The results were seen in the first tests I gave. In April, most were reading at the second grade level. Their math ability was at the first grade level.

In an effort to resuscitate their interest, I began to read them poetry I liked. They were drawn especially to poems of Robert Frost and Langston Hughes. One of the most embittered children in the class began to cry when she first heard the words of Langston Hughes.

What happens to a dream deferred?
Does it dry up
like a raisin in the sun?

She went home and memorized the lines.

The next day, I was fired. There was, it turned out, a list of "fourth grade poems" that teachers were obliged to follow but which, like most first-year teachers, I had never seen. According to school officials, Robert Frost and Langston Hughes were "too advanced" for children of this age. Hughes, moreover, was regarded as "inflammatory."

I was soon recruited to teach in a suburban system west of Boston. The shock of going from one of the poorest schools to one of the wealthiest cannot be overstated. I now had 21 children in a cheerful building with a principal who welcomed innovation.

After teaching for several years, I became involved with other interests—the health and education of farmworkers in New Mexico and Arizona, the problems of adult illiterates in several states, the lives of homeless families in New York. It wasn't until 1988, when I returned to Massachusetts after a long stay in New York City, that I realized how far I'd been drawn away from my original concerns. I found that I missed being with schoolchildren, and I felt a longing to spend time in public schools again. So, in the fall of 1988, I set off on another journey.

During the next two years I visited schools and spoke with children in approximately 30 neighborhoods from Illinois to Washington, D.C., and from New York to San Antonio. Wherever possible, I also met with children in their homes. There was no special logic in the choice of cities that I visited. I went where I was welcomed or knew teachers or school principals or ministers of churches.

What startled me most—although it puzzles me that I was not prepared for this—was the remarkable degree of racial segregation that persisted almost everywhere. Like most Americans, I knew that segregation was still common in the public schools, but I did not know how much it had intensified. The Supreme Court decision in *Brown v. Board of Education* 37 years ago, in which the court had found that segregated education was unconstitutional because it was "inherently unequal," did not seem to have changed very much for children in the schools I saw, not, at least, outside of the Deep South. Most of the urban schools I visited were 95 to 99 percent nonwhite. In no school that I saw anywhere in the United States were nonwhite children in large numbers truly intermingled with white children.

Moreover, in most cities, influential people that I met showed little inclination to address this matter and were sometimes even puzzled when I brought it up. Many people seemed to view the segregation issue as "a past injustice" that had been sufficiently addressed. Others took it as an unresolved injustice that no longer held sufficient national attention to be worth contesting. In all cases, I was given the distinct impression that my inquiries about this matter were not welcome.

None of the national reports I saw made even passing references to inequality or segregation. Low reading scores, high dropout rates, poor motivation—symptomatic matters—seemed to dominate discussion. In three cities—Baltimore, Milwaukee and Detroit—separate schools or separate classes for black males had been proposed. Other cities—Washington, D.C., New York and Philadelphia among them—were considering the same approach. Black parents or black school officials sometimes seemed to favor this idea. Booker T. Washington was cited with increasing frequency, Du Bois never, and Martin Luther King only with cautious selectivity. He was treated as an icon, but his vision of a nation in which black and white kids went to school together seemed to be effaced almost entirely. Dutiful references to "The Dream" were often seen in school brochures and on wall posters during February, when "Black History" was celebrated in the public schools, but the content of the dream was treated as a closed box that could not be opened without ruining the celebration.

For anyone who came of age during the years from 1954 to 1968, these revelations could not fail to be disheartening. What seems unmistakable, but, oddly enough, is rarely said in public settings nowadays, is that the nation, for all practice and intent, has turned its back upon the moral implications, if not yet the legal ramifications, of the *Brown* decision. The struggle being waged today, where there is any struggle being waged at all, is closer to the one that was addressed in 1896 in *Plessy v. Ferguson,* in which the court accepted segregated institutions for black people, stipulating only that they must be equal to those open to white people. The dual society, at least in public education, seems in general to be unquestioned.

To the extent that school reforms such as "restructuring" are advocated for the inner cities, few of these reforms have reached the schools that I have seen. In each of the larger cities there is usually one school or one subdistrict which is highly publicized as an example of "restructured" education; but the changes rarely reach beyond this one example. Even in those schools where some "restructuring" has taken place, the fact of racial segregation has been, and continues to be, largely uncontested. In many cities, what is termed "restructuring" struck me as very little more than moving around the same old furniture within the house of poverty. The perceived objective was a more "efficient" ghetto school or one with greater "input" from the ghetto parents or more "choices" for the ghetto children. The fact of ghetto education as a permanent American reality appeared to be accepted.

Liberal critics of the Reagan era sometimes note that social policy in the United States, to the extent that it concerns black children and poor children, has been turned back several decades. But this assertion, which is accurate as a description of some setbacks in the areas of housing, health and welfare, is not adequate to speak about the present-day reality in public education. In public schooling, social policy has been turned back almost one hundred years.

These, then, are a few of the impressions that remained with me after revisiting the public schools from which I had been absent for a quarter-century. My deepest impression, however, was less theoretical and more immediate. It was simply the impression that these urban schools were, by and large, extraordinarily unhappy places. With few exceptions, they reminded me of "garrisons" or "outposts" in a foreign nation. Housing projects, bleak and tall, surrounded by perimeter walls lined with barbed wire, often stood adjacent to the schools I visited. The schools were surrounded frequently by signs that indicated DRUG-FREE ZONE. Their doors were guarded. Police sometimes patrolled the halls. The windows of the schools were often covered with steel grates. Taxi drivers flatly refused to take me to some of these schools and would deposit me a dozen blocks away, in border areas beyond which they refused to go. I'd walk the last half-mile on my own. Once, in the Bronx, a woman stopped her car, told me I should not be walking there, insisted I get in, and drove me to the school. I was dismayed to walk or ride for blocks and blocks through neighborhoods where every face was black, where there were simply *no white people anywhere.*

In Boston, the press referred to areas like these as "death zones"—a specific reference to the rate of infant death in ghetto neighborhoods—but the feeling of the "death zone" often seemed to permeate the schools themselves. Looking around some of these inner-city schools, where filth and disrepair were worse than anything I'd seen in 1964, I often wondered why we would agree to let our children go to school in places where no politician, school board president, or business CEO would dream of working. Children seemed to wrestle with these kinds of questions too. Some of their observations were, indeed, so trenchant that a teacher sometimes would step back and raise her eyebrows and then nod to me across the children's heads, as if to say, "Well, there it is! They know what's going on around them, don't they?"

It occurred to me that we had not been listening much to children in these recent years of "summit conferences" on education, of severe reports and ominous prescriptions. The voices of children, frankly, had been missing from the whole discussion.

This seems especially unfortunate because the children often are more interesting and perceptive than the grown-ups are about the day-to-day realities of life in school. For this reason, I decided, early in my journey, to attempt to listen very carefully to children and, whenever possible, to let their voices and their judgments and their longings find a place within this book—and maybe, too, within the nation's dialogue about their destinies. I hope that, in this effort, I have done them justice.

East St. Louis—which the local press refers to as "an inner city without an outer city"—has some of the sickest children in America. Of 66 cities in Illinois, East St. Louis ranks first in fetal death, first in premature birth, and third in infant death. Among the negative factors listed by the city's health director are the sewage running in the streets, air that has been fouled by the local plants, the high lead levels noted in the soil, poverty, lack of education, crime, dilapidated housing, insufficient health care, unemployment. Hospital care is deficient too. There is no place to have a baby in East St. Louis. The maternity ward at the city's Catholic hospital, a 100-year-old structure, was shut down some years ago. The only other hospital in town was forced by lack of funds to close in 1990. The closest obstetrics service open to the women here is seven miles away. The infant death rate is still rising.

As in New York City's poorest neighborhoods, dental problems also plague the children here. Although dental problems don't command the instant fears associated with low birth weight, fetal death or cholera, they do have the consequence of wearing down the stamina of children and defeating their ambitions. Bleeding gums, impacted teeth and rotting teeth are routine matters for the children I have interviewed in the South Bronx. Children get used to feeling constant pain. They go to sleep with it. They go to school with it. Sometimes their teachers are alarmed and try to get them to a clinic. But it's all so slow and heavily encumbered with red tape and waiting lists and missing, lost or canceled welfare cards, that dental care is often long delayed. Children live for months with pain that grown-ups would find unendurable. The gradual attrition of accepted pain erodes their energy and aspiration. I have seen children in New York with teeth that look like brownish, broken sticks. I have also seen teen-agers who were missing half their teeth. But, to me, most shocking is to see a child with an abscess that has been inflamed for weeks and that he has simply lived with and accepts as part of the routine of life. Many teachers in the urban schools have seen this. It is almost commonplace.

Compounding these problems is the poor nutrition of the children here— average daily food expenditure in East St. Louis is $2.40 for one child—and the underimmunization of young children. Of every 100 children recently surveyed in East St. Louis, 55 were incompletely immunized for polio, diphtheria, measles and whooping cough. In this context, health officials look with all the more uneasiness at those lagoons of sewage outside public housing. . . .

A 16-year-old student in the South Bronx tells me that he went to English class for two months in the fall of 1989 before the school supplied him with a textbook. He spent the entire year without a science text. "My mother offered to help me with my science, which was hard for me," he says, "but I could not bring home a book."

In May of 1990 he is facing final exams, but, because the school requires students to pass in their textbooks one week prior to the end of the semester, he is forced to study without math and English texts.

He wants to go to college and he knows that math and English are important, but he's feeling overwhelmed, especially in math. He asked his teacher if he could come in for extra help, but she informed him that she didn't have the time. He asked if he could come to school an hour early, when she might have time to help him, but security precautions at the school made this impossible.

Sitting in his kitchen, I attempt to help him with his math and English. In math, according to a practice test he has been given, he is asked to solve the following equation: "$2x - 2 = 14$. What is x?" He finds this baffling. In English, he is told he'll have to know the parts of speech. In the sentence "Jack walks to the store," he is unable to identify the verb.

He is in a dark mood, worried about this and other problems. His mother has recently been diagnosed as having cancer. We leave the apartment and walk downstairs to the street. He's a full-grown young man, tall and quiet and strong-looking; but out on the street, when it is time to say good-bye, his eyes fill up with tears.

In the fall of the year, he phones me at my home. "There are 42 students in my science class, 40 in my English class—45 in my home room. When all the kids show up, five of us have to stand in back."

A first-year English teacher at another high school in the Bronx calls me two nights later: "I've got five classes—42 in each! We have no textbooks yet. I'm using my old textbook from the seventh grade. They're doing construction all around me so the noise is quite amazing. They're actually *drilling* in the hall outside my room. I have more kids than desks in all five classes.

"A student came in today whom I had never seen. I said, 'We'll have to wait and see if someone doesn't come so you can have a chair.' She looked at me and said, 'I'm leaving.' "

The other teachers tell her that the problem will resolve itself. "Half the students will be gone by Christmastime, they say. It's awful when you realize that the school is *counting* on the failure of one half my class. If they didn't count on it, perhaps it wouldn't happen. If I *began* with 20 students in a class, I'd have lots more time to spend with each of them. I'd have a chance to track them down, go to their homes, see them on the weekends.... I don't understand why people in New York permit this."

One of the students in her class, she says, wrote this two-line poem for Martin Luther King:

*He tried to help the white and black.
Now that he's dead he can't do jack.*

Another student wrote these lines:

*America the beautiful,
Who are you beautiful for?*

"Frequently," says a teacher at another crowded high school in New York, "a student may be in the wrong class for a term and never know it." With only one counselor to 700 students system-wide in New York City, there is little help available to those who feel confused. It is not surprising, says the teacher, "that many find the experience so cold, impersonal and disheartening that they decide to stay home by the sad warmth of the TV set." ...

I stopped in Cincinnati on the way home so that I could visit in a school to which I'd been invited by some friends. It was, I thought, a truly dreadful school and, although I met a number of good teachers there, the place left me disheartened. The children were poor, but with a kind of poverty I'd never seen before. Most were not minority children but the children of poor Appalachian whites who'd settled in this part of Cincinnati years before and led their lives in virtual isolation from the city that surrounded them.

The neighborhood in which they lived is known as Lower Price Hill. Farther up the hill, there is a middle-income neighborhood and, at the top, an upper-income area—the three communities being located at successive levels of the same steep rise. The bottom of the hill, which stands beside the banks of the Ohio River, is the poorest area. The middle of the hill is occupied by working families that are somewhat better off. At the top of the hill there is a luxury development, which has a splendid view of Cincinnati, and a gourmet restaurant. The division of neighborhoods along this hill, with an apportionment of different scales of economics, domicile and social station to each level, reminded me of a painting by Giotto: a medieval setting in which peasants, burghers, lords and ladies lead their separate lives within a single frame.

To get to the neighborhood you have to drive from the center of the city through the West Side, which is mainly black, and then along a stretch of railroad tracks, until you come to the Ohio River. Lower Price Hill is on the north side of the river.

Some indication of the poverty within the neighborhood may be derived from demographics. Only 27 percent of adults in the area have finished high school. Welfare dependence is common, but, because the people here identify the welfare system with black people, many will not turn to welfare and rely on menial jobs; better-paying jobs are quite beyond their reach because of their low education levels.

The neighborhood is industrial, although some of the plants are boarded up. Most of the factories (metal-treatment plants and paint and chemical manufacturers) are still in operation and the smoke and chemical pollutants from these installations cloud the air close to the river. Prostitutes stand in a ragged line along the street as I approach the school. Many of the wood-frame houses are in disrepair. Graffiti . . . decorates the wall of an abandoned building near the corner of Hatmaker Street and State.

The wilted-looking kids who live here, says Bob Moore, an organizer who has worked with parents in the neighborhood for several years, have "by far the lowest skills in math and reading in the city." There is some concern, he says, about "developmental retardation" as a consequence perhaps of their continual exposure to the chemical pollutants, but this, he says, is only speculation. "That these kids are damaged is quite clear. We don't know exactly why."

Oyler Elementary School, unlike so many of the schools I've seen in poor black neighborhoods, is not so much intense and crowded as it is depleted, bleak and bare. The eyes of the children, many of whom have white-blond hair and almost all of whom seem rather pale and gaunt, appear depleted too. During several hours in the school I rarely saw a child with a good big smile.

Bleakness was the order of the day in fifth grade science. The children were studying plant biology when I came in, but not with lab equipment. There was none. There was a single sink that may have worked but was not being used, a couple of test tubes locked up in a cupboard, and a skeleton also locked behind glass windows. The nearly total blankness of the walls was interrupted only by a fire safety poster. The window shades were badly torn. The only textbook I could find (*Mathematics in Our World*) had been published by Addison-Wesley in 1973. A chart of "The Elements" on the wall behind the teacher listed no elements discovered in the past four decades.

"A lot of these kids have behavior problems," the science teacher said. He spoke of kids with little initiative whose "study habits," he said, "are poor." Much of what they learn, he said, "is gotten from the streets." Asked if more supplies, a cheerier classroom or a better lab would make a difference, he replied that he was "not sure money is the answer."

The class was studying a worksheet. He asked a question: "What is photosynthesis?"

After a long wait, someone answered: "Light."

"This is the least academic group I have," he told me after they were gone.

Children who attend this school, according to a school official, have the second-highest dropout rate in Cincinnati. Of young people age 16 to 21 in this community, 59.6 percent are high school dropouts. Some 85 percent of Oyler's students are below the national median in reading. The school spends $3,180 for each pupil.

The remedial reading program, funded by a federal grant, has only one instructor. "I see 45 children in a day," she says. "Only first and second graders—and, if I can fit them in, a few third graders. I have a waiting list of third grade children. We don't have sufficient funds to help the older kids at all."

There are four computers in the school, which holds almost 600 children.

The younger children seem to have a bit more fire than those in the science class. In a second grade class, I meet a boy with deep brown eyes and long blond hair who talks very fast and has some strong opinions: "I hate this school. I hate my teacher. I like the principal but she does not like me." In the morning, he says, he likes to watch his father shave his beard.

"My mother and father sleep in the bedroom," he goes on. "I sleep in the living room. I have a dog named Joe. I have a bird who takes her bath with me. I can count to 140. My mother says that I do numbers in my sleep."

Three girls in the class tell me their names: Brandy, Jessica, Miranda. They are dressed poorly and are much too thin, but they are friendly and seem glad to have a visitor in class and even act a little silly for my benefit.

Before I leave, I spend part of an hour in a class of industrial arts. The teacher is superb, a painter and an artisan, who obviously likes children. But the class is reserved for upper-level kids and, by the time they get here, many are worn down and seem to lack the spark of merriment that Jessica and Brandy and their classmates had. It does seem a pity that the best instruction in the school should be essentially vocational, not academic.

Next year, I'm told, the children of this school will enter a cross-busing program that will mix them with the children of the black schools on the West Side. Middle-class white neighborhoods, like Rose Lawn for example, will not be included in the busing plan. Nor will very wealthy neighborhoods, like Hyde Park, be included.

I ask a teacher why Hyde Park, where friends of mine reside, won't be included in desegregation.

"That," he tells me, "is a question you don't want to ask in Cincinnati."

Cincinnati, like Chicago, has a two-tier system. Among the city's magnet and selective schools are some remarkable institutions—such as Walnut Hills, a famous high school that my hosts compared to "a *de facto* private school" within the public system. It is not known if a child from Lower Price Hill has ever been admitted there. Few of these children, in any case, would have the preparation to compete effectively on the exams that they would have to take in order to get in. Long before they leave this school, most of their academic options are foreclosed.

From the top of the hill, which I returned to visit the next day, you can see across the city, which looks beautiful from here. You also have a good view of the river. The horizon is so wide and open, and so different from the narrow view of life to be surmised from the mean streets around the school—one wonders what might happen to the spirits of these children if they had the chance to breathe this air and stretch their arms and see so far. Might they feel the power or the longing to become inheritors of some of this remarkable vast nation?

Standing here by the Ohio River, watching it drift west into the edge of the horizon, picturing it as it flows onward to the place three hundred miles from here where it will pour into the Mississippi, one is struck by the sheer beauty of this country, of its goodness and unrealized goodness, of the limitless potential that it holds to render life rewarding and the spirit clean. Surely there is enough for everyone within this country. It is a tragedy that these good things are not more widely shared. All our children ought to be allowed a stake in the enormous richness of America. Whether they were born to poor white Appalachians or to wealthy Texans, to poor black people in the Bronx or to rich people in Manhasset or Winnetka, they are all quite wonderful and innocent when they are small. We soil them needlessly.

Acknowledgments

2.1   From John Dewey, *Democracy and Education: An Introduction to the Philosophy of Education* (Macmillan, 1916). Notes omitted.

2.2   From William Heard Kilpatrick, "The Project Method," *Teachers College Record*, vol. 19, no. 4 (September 1918).

3.1   From Henry A. Giroux, "Culture, Power and Transformation in the Work of Paulo Freire: Toward a Politics of Education," in Henry A Giroux, *Teachers as Intellectuals: Toward a Critical Pedagogy of Learning* (Bergin & Garvey, 1988). Copyright © 1988 by Bergin & Garvey Publishers, Inc. Reprinted by permission of Greenwood Publishing Group, Inc., Westport, CT.

4.1   From Katherine Camp Mayhew and Anna Camp Edwards, *The Dewey School: The Laboratory School of the University of Chicago, 1896–1903* (D. Appleton-Century, 1936). Notes omitted.

4.2   From Harold Rugg and Ann Shumaker, *The Child-Centered School: An Appraisal of the New Education* (World Book Company, 1928). Copyright © 1928 by Harcourt Brace & Company. Reprinted by permission. Some notes omitted.

4.3   From Boyd Henry Bode, *How We Learn* (D. C. Heath, 1940).

5.1   From Hilda Taba, *Curriculum Development: Theory and Practice* (Harcourt, Brace & World, 1962), under the general editorship of Willard B. Spalding. Copyright © 1962 by Harcourt Brace & Company. Copyright renewed 1990 by Margaret A. Spalding. Reprinted by permission of the publisher. Notes and references omitted.

5.2   From Harry S. Broudy, B. Othanel Smith, and Joe R. Burnett, *Democracy and Excellence in American Secondary Education: A Study in Curriculum Theory* (Rand McNally, 1964). Copyright © 1964 by Harry S. Broudy. Reprinted by permission.

6.1   From Michael W. Apple, *Ideology and Curriculum* (Routledge & Kegan Paul, 1979). Copyright © 1979 by Routledge & Kegan Paul. Reprinted by permission.

6.2   From Israel Scheffler, *The Language of Education* (Charles C. Thomas, 1960). Copyright © 1960 by Charles C. Thomas, Publisher, Springfield, IL. Reprinted by permission.

7.1   From Booker T. Washington during the Atlanta Exposition, Atlanta, Georgia, September 18, 1895.

7.2   From W. E. B. Du Bois, *The Negro Problem* (1903).

7.3   From James Baldwin, "A Talk to Teachers," *Saturday Review* (December 21, 1963). Copyright © 1963 by S. R. Publications, Ltd. Reprinted by permission.

7.4   From Meyer Weinberg, *A Chance to Learn: The History of Race and Education in the United States* (Cambridge University Press, 1977). Copyright © 1977 by Cambridge University Press. Reprinted by permission. Notes omitted.

8.1   From Paulo Freire and Donaldo Macedo, *Literacy: Reading the Word and the World* (Bergin & Garvey, 1987). Copyright © 1987 by Paulo Freire and Donaldo Macedo. Reprinted by permission of Greenwood Publishing Group, Inc., Westport, CT. Some notes omitted.

8.2   From Benjamin R. Barber, *An Aristocracy of Everyone: The Politics of Education and the Future of America* (Oxford University Press, 1992). Copyright © 1992 by Ballantine Books, a division of Random House, Inc. Reprinted by permission. Notes omitted.

9.1   From Elizabeth Cady Stanton, *Eighty Years and More (1815–1897): Reminiscences of Elizabeth Cady Stanton* (T. Fisher Unwin, 1898).

9.2 From American Association of University Women, *How Schools Shortchange Girls: A Study of Major Findings on Girls and Education* (American Association of University Women, 1992). Copyright © 1992 by The American Association of University Women Educational Foundation, 1111 16th Street, NW, Washington, DC 20036, (202) 785-7700. Reprinted by permission. Notes omitted.

9.3 From bell hooks, *Teaching to Transgress: Education as the Practice of Freedom* (Routledge, 1994). Copyright © 1994 by Gloria Watkins. Reprinted by permission.

10.1 From *Brown v. Board of Education of Topeka, Kansas,* 347 U.S. 483 (1954).

10.2 From Marian Wright Edelman, "Twenty Years After 'Brown': Where Are We Now?" *New York University Education Quarterly,* vol. 4 (Summer 1974). Copyright © 1974 by Marian Wright Edelman. Reprinted by permission.

10.3 From Thomas Black and Frank Aquila, "A Dream Realized: *Brown v. Board of Education of Topeka,*" in Frank D. Aquila, ed., *Race Equity in Education: The History of School Desegregation 1849–1979* (Indiana University School of Education, 1979).

10.4 From Biloine Whiting Young and Grace Billings Bress, "A New Educational Decision: Is Detroit the End of the School Bus Line?" *Phi Delta Kappan* (April 1975). Copyright © 1975 by *Phi Delta Kappan.* Reprinted by permission.

11.1 From Thomas R. Ascik, "The Courts and Education," *The World and I* (March 1986). Copyright © 1986 by The Heritage Foundation. Reprinted by permission. Notes omitted.

11.2 From William R. Hazard, "The *Bakke* Decision: Mixed Signals from the Court," *Phi Delta Kappan* (September 1978). Copyright © 1978 by *Phi Delta Kappan.* Reprinted by permission.

11.3 From United States Commission on Civil Rights, *A Better Chance to Learn: Bilingual-Bicultural Education* (Clearinghouse Publication 51, May 1975). Notes omitted.

12.1 From Benjamin S. Bloom, Max D. Engelhart, Edward J. Furst, Walker H. Hill, and David R. Krathwohl, *Taxonomy of Educational Objectives, Handbook I: Cognitive Domain* (David McKay, 1956). Copyright © 1956 and renewed 1984 by Longman Publishers USA. Reprinted by permission.

12.2 From David R. Krathwohl, Benjamin S. Bloom, and Bertram B. Masia, *Taxonomy of Educational Objectives, Handbook II: Affective Domain* (David McKay, 1964). Copyright © 1964 by Longman Publishers USA. Reprinted by permission. Some notes omitted.

13.1 From Clarence J. Karier, "Testing for Order and Control in the Corporate Liberal State," *Educational Theory,* vol. 22 (Spring 1972). Copyright © 1972 by the Board of Trustees of the University of Illinois and the editor of *Educational Theory.* Reprinted by permission.

13.2 From J. McVicker Hunt, "Black Genes--White Environment," *Trans-action: Social Science and Modern Society,* vol. 6 (June 1969). Copyright © 1969 by Transaction Publishers, Inc. Reprinted by permission.

13.3 From Vito Perrone, "On Standardized Testing," *Childhood Education,* vol. 67, no. 3 (Spring 1991). Copyright © 1991 by The Association for Childhood Education International, 11501 Georgia Avenue, Suite 315, Wheaton, MD. Reprinted by permission. References omitted.

14.1 From Ann L. Brown, John D. Bransford, Roberta A. Ferrara, and Joseph C. Campione, "Learning, Remembering, and Understanding," in Paul H. Mussen, ed., *Handbook of Child Psychology, vol. 3: Cognitive Development,* 4th ed. (John Wiley, 1983). Copyright © 1946, 1954, 1970, and 1983 by John Wiley & Sons, Inc. Reprinted by permission. Notes and references omitted.

14.2   From John Bransford, Robert Sherwood, Nancy Vye, and John Rieser, "Teaching Thinking and Problem Solving," *American Psychologist*, vol. 41, no. 10 (October 1986). Copyright © 1986 by The American Psychological Association. Reprinted by permission. References omitted.

14.3   From John T. Bruer, "The Mind's Journey from Novice to Expert," *American Educator* (Summer 1993). Copyright © 1993 by MIT Press. Reprinted by permission. References omitted.

15.1   From John Dewey, "Education and Social Change," *The Social Frontier: A Journal of Educational Criticism and Reconstruction*, vol. 3, no. 26 (May 1937). Copyright © 1937 by The Center for Dewey Studies, Southern Illinois University, Carbondale, IL. Reprinted by permission.

15.2   From I. L. Kandel, *Conflicting Theories of Education* (Macmillan, 1938).

15.3   From William Heard Kilpatrick, *Education and the Social Crisis: A Proposed Program* (Liveright, 1932). Copyright © 1932 by William Heard Kilpatrick, renewed 1959 by Marion Kilpatrick. Reprinted by permission of Liveright Publishing Corporation.

16.1   From Joel Spring, "Education as a Form of Social Control," in Clarence J. Karier, Paul C. Violas, and Joel Spring, eds., *Roots of Crisis: American Education in the Twentieth Century* (Rand McNally, 1973). Copyright © 1973 by Clarence J. Karier, Paul C. Violas, and Joel Spring. Reprinted by permission.

16.2   From Jonathan Kozol, *Savage Inequalities: Children in America's Schools* (Crown Publishers, 1991). Copyright © 1991 by Jonathan Kozol. Reprinted by permission of Crown Publishers, Inc.

Index

SOURCES

Sources: Notable Selections in Education brings together over 40 selections of enduring intellectual value—classic articles, book excerpts, and research studies—that have shaped the study of education and our contemporary understanding of it. *Sources* provides the opportunity for readers to encounter many of the greatest thinkers in educational studies at first hand. The book includes carefully edited selections from the works of the most distinguished educational observers, past and present, from John Dewey and Robert M. Hutchins to Jonathan Kozol, Ann L. Brown, and Marian Wright Edelman.

The selections are organized topically around major areas of study within education: foundations of education; curriculum and instruction; schools in a multicultural society; the American constitutional tradition and education; testing and assessment of learning; and society, culture, and education. Each topical section offers a diverse range of readings, all of which are high quality and lively. Each selection is preceded by a headnote that establishes the relevance of the selection and provides biographical information on the author.

Students of education will appreciate the broad range of coverage, the logic of the organization, and the accessibility of the material within this volume.

DPG

The Dushkin Publishing Group, Inc.

Sluice Dock, Guilford, CT 06437

ISBN: 1-56134-332-3

ISBN 1-56134-332-3

9 781561 343324

DATE DUE

MAY 1 1 2005			
MAY 2 4 REC'D			
GAYLORD			PRINTED IN U.S.A.